Neocolonialism and Built Heritage

Architectural relics of nineteenth- and twentieth-century colonialism dot cityscapes throughout our globalizing world, just as built traces of colonialism remain embedded within the urban fabric of many European capitals.

Neocolonialism and Built Heritage addresses the sustained presence and influence of historic built environments and processes inherited from colonialism within the contemporary lives of cities in Africa, Asia, and Europe. Novel in their focused consideration of ways in which these built environments reinforce neocolonialist connections among former colonies and colonizers, states and international organizations, the volume's case studies engage highly relevant issues such as historic preservation, heritage management, tourism, toponymy, and cultural imperialism.

Interrogating the life of the past in the present, authors challenge readers to consider the roles played by a diversity of historic built environments in the ongoing asymmetrical balance of power and unequal distribution of capital around the globe. They present buildings' maintenance, management, reuse, and (re)interpretation, and in so doing they raise important questions, the ramifications of which transcend the specifics of the individual sites and architectural histories they present.

Daniel E. Coslett earned a Ph.D. in the history and theory of built environments from the University of Washington's College of Built Environments, as well as an M.A. in the subject from Cornell University. His research addresses colonial and postcolonial North Africa, focusing on intersections of architectural design, urban planning, archaeology, and historic preservation, as well as heritage management and tourism development. At Western Washington University and the University of Washington he teaches subjects including historic preservation, architectural analysis, as well as modern and colonial architectural history. He is also an assistant editor at the *International Journal of Islamic Architecture*.

THE ARCHI*TEXT* SERIES

Edited by Thomas A. Markus and Anthony D. King

Architectural discourse has traditionally represented buildings as art objects or technical objects. Yet buildings are also social objects in that they are invested with social meaning and shape social relations. Recognizing these assumptions, the Archi*text* series aims to bring together recent debates in social and cultural theory and the study and practice of architecture and urban design. Critical, comparative and interdisciplinary, the books in the series, by theorizing architecture, bring the space of the built environment centrally into the social sciences and humanities, as well as bringing the theoretical insights of the latter into the discourses of architecture and urban design. Particular attention is paid to issues of gender, race, sexuality and the body, to questions of identity and place, to the cultural politics of representation and language, and to the global and postcolonial contexts in which these are addressed.

Edited by Daniel E. Coslett

Neocolonialism and Built Heritage

Echoes of Empire
in Africa, Asia, and Europe

Routledge
Taylor & Francis Group

LONDON AND NEW YORK

First published 2020
by Routledge
2 Park Square, Milton Park, Abingdon, Oxon OX14 4RN

and by Routledge
52 Vanderbilt Avenue, New York, NY 10017

*Routledge is an imprint of the Taylor & Francis Group, an
informa business*

British Library Cataloguing-in-Publication Data
A catalogue record for this book is available from the British Library

Library of Congress Cataloging-in-Publication Data
Names: Coslett, Daniel E., editor.
Title: Neocolonialism and built heritage : echoes of empire in Africa,
    Asia, and Europe / edited by Daniel E. Coslett.
Description: New York : Routledge, 2019. | Includes bibliographical
    references and index.
Identifiers: LCCN 2019007868| ISBN 9781138368378
    (hb : alk. paper) | ISBN 9781138368385 (pb : alk. paper) |
    ISBN 9780429429286 (ebook)
Subjects: LCSH: Imperialism and architecture. | Architecture and
    history. | Architecture and society.
Classification: LCC NA2543.I47 N46 2019 | DDC 720.1/03—dc23
LC record available at https://lccn.loc.gov/2019007868

ISBN: 978-1-138-36837-8 (hbk)
ISBN: 978-1-138-36838-5 (pbk)
ISBN: 978-0-429-42928-6 (ebk)

Typeset in Frutiger
by Servis Filmsetting Ltd, Stockport, Cheshire

MIX
Paper from
responsible sources
FSC
www.fsc.org FSC™ C013985

Printed in the United Kingdom
by Henry Ling Limited

Contents

Figures

Contributors

Robert Aldrich is a Professor of European history at the University of Sydney. He received his M.A. and Ph.D. from Brandeis University. Aldrich has authored many works on European colonialism, including *Vestiges of the Colonial Empire in France: Monuments, Museums and Colonial Memories* (2005), *Cultural Encounters and Homoeroticism in Sri Lanka: Sex and Serendipity* (2017), and *Banished Potentates: Dethroning and Exiling Indigenous Monarchs under British and French Colonial Rule, 1815–1955* (2018). He co-edited *The Routledge History of Western Empires* (2014), *Crowns and Colonies: European Monarchies and Overseas Empires* (2016) and *Royals on Tour: Politics, Pageantry and Colonialism* (2018).

Luce Beeckmans is a post-doctoral research FWO-fellow affiliated with Ghent University, University of Leuven, and Antwerp University. In 2005 she graduated as an engineer-architect from Ghent and worked in the office of Stéphane Beel Architects. In 2013 she obtained a Ph.D. from the University of Groningen with an award-winning dissertation on urban (planning) history in Africa. She has a keen interest in the circulation of spatial knowledge between Europe and Africa, both within the framework of colonization and development cooperation, and is currently investigating spatial manifestations of African diaspora in European mid-sized cities. Beeckmans has published widely and co-curated exhibitions on these topics.

Trésor Lumfuankenda Bungiena graduated as an architect in 2011 from the Institut Supérieur d'Architecture et d'Urbanisme (ISAU) in Kinshasa, DR Congo. He currently teaches at the Faculty of Architecture and Planning in the Université Kongo, Mbanza Ngungu. From 2015 through 2018 he presided over a committee within the Association of Congolese Architects, dealing with educational affairs and internships. Currently he is a Ph.D. candidate at the Free University of Brussels and Ghent University, investigating the role of architecture in policies related to the management and renovation of health care infrastructures in Kinshasa between 1975 and 2015.

Aidan Carter is an Italian language teacher and researcher. He currently teaches in the Italian studies program at La Trobe University and works as a Research Assistant at Swinburne University of Technology. He graduated with Bachelor of Arts (Honours) in Italian studies from the University of Melbourne in 2017 specializing in sociolinguistics and repressive language policies during Fascism in the Trentino-Alto Adige region. Carter's research interests also include: corpus-assisted language learning, L2 pedagogy, modern Italian literature, the contemporary Italian detective novel, and modern Italian history with a particular focus on the Fascist period.

Daniel E. Coslett earned a Ph.D. in the history and theory of built environments from the University of Washington's College of Built Environments, as well as an M.A. in the subject from Cornell University. His research addresses colonial and postcolonial North Africa, focusing on intersections of architectural design, urban planning, archaeology, and historic preservation, as well as heritage management and tourism development. At Western Washington University and the University of Washington he teaches subjects including historic preservation, architectural analysis, as well as modern and colonial architectural history. He is also an assistant editor at the *International Journal of Islamic Architecture*.

Nancy Demerdash-Fatemi is an Assistant Professor in the Department of Art and Art History at Albion College. She holds an S.M.Arch.S. degree from the Aga Khan Program for Islamic Architecture at the Massachusetts Institute of Technology, and a Ph.D. in Art & Archaeology from Princeton University. Her doctoral research and forthcoming book project focus on postwar reconstruction and development in Tunisia against the political backdrop of decolonization. She serves as an assistant editor at the *International Journal of Islamic Architecture* and publishes widely on modern and contemporary art and architecture of the Middle East and North Africa.

Simon De Nys-Ketels is a Ph.D. candidate in the Department of Architecture and Urban Planning at Ghent University, where he graduated in 2012 as an engineer-architect with a thesis on the urban development of the Kenya-neighborhood in Lubumbashi, DR Congo, based on archival research as well as fieldwork. In 2014, he participated in a heritage listing project in Nawalgarh, India, and worked one year as a research fellow at Antwerp University, exploring the relationship between social economy, architecture and urbanism (2015). In his Ph.D. work he focuses on the architecture and urban planning of colonial and postcolonial hospital infrastructure in Congo.

Kristien Geenen is a doctor of Social and Cultural Anthropology, and defended her Ph.D. dissertation — "On the pursuit of pleasure in a war-weary secondary city, Butembo, DRC" — in 2012 at the University of Leuven. In 2015–16, Geenen was a postdoctoral researcher with an interdisciplinary research project on hospital infrastructure in DR Congo at Ghent University. Geenen has longstanding fieldwork experience in urban DR Congo, exploring the use of public place by street gangs and the empowerment practices of single women. She has published widely and, as a trained photographer, also curated several Congo-related exhibitions.

Ralph Ghoche is an Assistant Professor of architecture at Barnard College, Columbia University. He holds professional and post-professional degrees in architecture from McGill University and a Ph.D. in the history and theory of architecture from Columbia University. His research is centered on French colonial architecture in Algeria during the nineteenth century, with a particular focus on the architectural, urban, and territorial interventions of the Catholic Church in Algiers. Ghoche has also written widely on French architecture and its relationship to theories of ornament, archaeology, and aesthetics in the nineteenth century, which is the subject of his forthcoming book to be published by McGill-Queen's University Press.

Stephanie Malia Hom writes and lectures on modern Italy and the Mediterranean, Italian literature and culture, colonialism and imperialism, and tourism studies. For her research, Hom has been awarded fellowships from the American Council of Learned Societies, American Academy in Rome, American School of Classical Studies in Athens, Harvard University, and the Stanford Humanities Center. She is the author of *Empire's Mobius Strip: Historical Echoes in Italy's Crisis of Migration and Detention*, *The Beautiful Country: Tourism and the Impossible State of Destination Italy*, and co-editor with Ruth Ben-Ghiat of *Italian Mobilities*. She works and lives in Northern California with her family.

Suzie Kim is an Assistant Professor of art history at the University of Mary Washington. She received her Ph.D. in Japanese and Korean modern art history from the University of Maryland, College Park, in 2015 and has held internships and fellowships in the Japanese art curatorial department at the Freer Gallery of Art and the Arthur M. Sackler Gallery, Smithsonian Institution, Washington, DC Her research investigates Constructivism as the primary source for a multifaceted cultural phenomenon in Japan and Korea since the 1920s. Her wider areas of expertise include postcolonial theory, colonial architecture in Korea, and cross-cultural interactions between European and East Asian avant-garde movements.

Justin Kollar is a researcher, planner, and urban designer at Sasaki where his research and professional experience in architecture and urban planning bring a social and economic perspective to the design of the built environment across multiple scales. His work is situated at the intersection of territorial studies,

administrative landscapes, infrastructural ecologies, real estate, and urban processes in cities in North America as well as across Central, Southeast and East Asia.
Kollar graduated from the Harvard University Graduate School of Design in 2017
and teaches at the Boston Architecture College.

Johan Lagae is Full Professor at Ghent University teaching twentieth-century
architectural history with a particular focus on the non-European context.
He obtained his Ph.D. in 2002 with a dissertation on twentieth-century colonial architecture in the former Belgian Congo. His current research interests
are colonial and postcolonial architecture in central Africa, African urban history, colonial photography, and colonial built heritage. He was co-chair of the
COST-action entitled "European Architecture beyond Europe" and is co-founder
and editorial board member of *ABE Journal*. He has published widely and is
active as a curator, having contributed to several acclaimed, Congo/Africa-
related exhibitions.

Flavia Marcello is an Associate Professor at Swinburne University of Technology.
She is an architectural historian and design teacher and a world expert on the
architecture and urban planning of Rome, in particular of the Italian Fascist period.
Marcello's areas of research have recently expanded to include: the political use
of Classicism, political manifestations in monuments and public space, and the
legacy of Fascism in contemporary society. She teaches in the areas of design,
history and theory with a particular focus on the inter-relationship between art
and architecture.

Vikramāditya Prakāsh is an architect, and an architectural historian and theo-
rist. He works on issues of modernism, postcoloniality, global history, and fashion
and architecture. His published books include *Chandigarh's Le Corbusier: The
Struggle for Modernity in Postcolonial India*, *A Global History of Architecture*
(with Francis D.K. Ching and Mark Jarzombek, and translated into five languages), *Colonial Modernities: Building, Dwelling and Architecture in British India
and Ceylon* (edited with Peter Scriver), *The Architecture of Shivdatt Sharma* and
Chandigarh: An Architectural Guide. *One Continuous Line: Art, Architecture and
Urbanism of Aditya Prakash* will be released by Mapin Publishing, India, in July
2019. Prakash is a Professor of architecture at the University of Washington in
Seattle, USA.

Valentina Rozas-Krause is a Ph.D. candidate in architectural history at the
University of California, Berkeley. She is an architect with a Master's Degree in
Urban Planning from the Pontificia Universidad Católica de Chile. In 2014, she
published the book *Ni tan Elefante: Ni tan Blanco* on the architectural, urban,
and political history of Chile's National Stadium. In 2011 she was awarded first
place in the public competition to design a public park surrounding the National
Stadium, in collaboration with Teodoro Fernández Architects. Rozas-Krause

designed *Memorial Patio 29* (2010), in Santiago with an interdisciplinary team. Between 2011 and 2014 she taught at the Universidad Diego Portales School of Architecture.

Mira Rai Waits is an Assistant Professor of art history and visual culture at Appalachian State University. Her research has addressed the development of fingerprinting in colonial India, the architectural history of British colonial Indian prisons, and the role remunerative prison labor played in the production of colonial Indian penology. She is currently working on a book project that explores the spatial and visual culture history of colonial Indian prisons.

Acknowledgements

This volume emerged from a 2018 Society of Architectural Historians (US) panel organized by the editor and entitled "The Colonial Past in the Neo-colonial Present." Many thanks are owed to paper presenters, as well as to the attendees who contributed constructive feedback during the productive session. Thanks as well go to the helpful peer reviewers whose insights strengthened many of the present chapters. Finally, the editor would also like to express his sincere gratitude to the generous colleagues who have offered kind suggestions and moral support at various stages of putting this volume together, chief among them Mohammad Gharipour and Vikramāditya Prakāsh.

Abbreviations and acronyms

ADER	Agence de Développement et de Réhabilitation (Morocco)
AfD	Alternative für Deutschland (Alternative for Germany party) (Germany)
AOI	Africa Orientale Italiana (Italian East Africa)
CHA	Cultural Heritage Association (South Korea)
DPP	Democratic Progressive Party (Taiwan)
DRC	Democratic Republic of the Congo (also DR Congo)
E42	Esposizione universale (Universal Exposition) of 1942 (Rome)
EIC	British East India Company
EUR	Esposizione universale Roma district (Rome)
FAO	United Nations Food and Agriculture Organization
GAHTC	Global Architectural History Teaching Collaborative
GDR	German Democratic Republic (East Germany)
GGB	Government-General Building of Chosŏn (South Korea)
ICOMOS	International Council on Monuments and Sites
INAA	National Institute of Archaeology and Art (Tunisia)
ISIS	So-called Islamic State
KMT	Kuomintang (Chinese Nationalist Party) (Taiwan)
NGO	Non-governmental organization
ONTT	National Office of Tunisian Tourism (Tunisia)
RAI	Radiotelevisione italiana (public broadcasting network) (Italy)
SED	Sozialistische Einheitspartei Deutschlands (Socialist Unity Party of Germany) (East Germany)
TSC	Taiwan Sugar Corporation
UK	United Kingdom
UN	United Nations
US	United States
UNESCO	United Nations Educational, Scientific and Cultural Organization
WWI	World War I
WWII	World War II

Introduction

1

The production and use of neocolonialist sites of memory

Daniel E. Coslett

Inherited monuments, architectures, and urban plans constitute the built "debris of imperial memory" that litters the globe.[1] These inescapable sites not only attest to historical colonial experiences, but also the powerful capacity of such sites to stir emotions and inspire meaning in today's history-conscious context. As the "first beacons of a globalized memory culture" they are in many cases tools actively involved in the making and ongoing renegotiation of identities in the postcolonial world.[2] Indeed, more than just *lieux de mémoire* (sites of memory) — to use Pierre Nora's influential term and concept — that index a society's past and its intentional creation of symbolic heritage, these relics of empire are to various degrees exploited by those negotiating new relationships with ex-colonies and other states.[3] In many cases extant colonial-era landmarks of memory are active contributors to neocolonialist processes, but in other contexts their sustained presence — also ultimately a choice — betrays a colonial amnesia that permits the avoidance of direct confrontation with darker histories. The sites thus possess accumulated agency that can be harnessed and wielded to reinforce longstanding or new power differentials, but also to obscure the potential reconciliation with the past arguably prerequisite for truly sovereign futures.

COLONIALISM (RE)VISITED

Empires have been the dominant political system for millennia. Those of ancient Rome and Ottoman Turkey each lasted for roughly six hundred years, and the Byzantine Empire twice that. In China, successive dynasties ruled for more than two thousand years. The British and French Empires of the eighteenth through twentieth centuries endured for far less time — about two hundred years and one hundred fifty, respectively — but covered far more territory. Indeed, in 1939 forty-two percent of the earth's surface was occupied by Western European, US, and Japanese powers, while thirty-two percent of the world's population lived under their control.[4] By far the largest, at its peak after WWI the British Empire

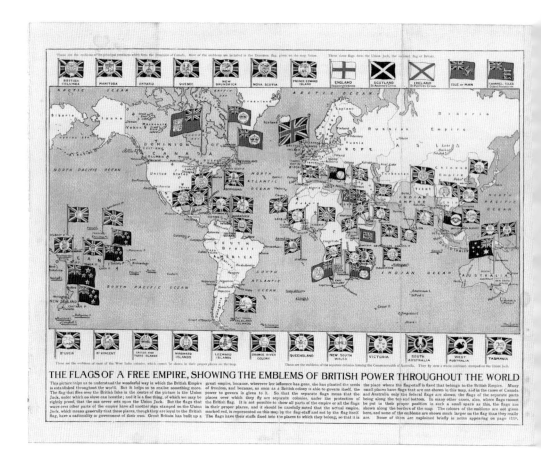

THE FLAGS OF A FREE EMPIRE, SHOWING THE EMBLEMS OF BRITISH POWER THROUGHOUT THE WORLD

alone ruled thirteen million square miles and a quarter of the world's population [Figure 1.1].[5] As their colonialist counterparts based elsewhere did, the British extracted resources and labor, profited from the sale of goods, amassed considerable power and influence, and pursued a so-called "civilizing mission" in an inherently violent, oppressive process. While the particulars of each modern empire differed in their respective contexts, empires' overall aims and effects were fairly similar. In the wake of the empires' formal dissolution during the 1950s and 1960s,[6] most colonizers left "fragmented societies and great disparities of economic condition" behind in their retreat.[7]. The Commonwealth of Nations and the International Organization of the Francophonie, "successor forms of empire," ensure the continued global relevance of the UK and France, and within the European Union (EU) these states enjoy substantial authority based on their colonial histories.[8] Not only do languages, institutions, socio-cultural norms — indeed entire ways of thinking and being — survive in many far-flung places as a result of long-entrenched colonialist systems, but extant colonial-era built environments also retain significance. As inherited relics of empire, their images, functions, and symbolic meanings in many ways still participate in and influence the lives of users and viewers, many of whom at this point may

Figure 1.1
The British Empire. Map 1910. Source: Arthur Mee, *The Children's' Encyclopaedia* vol. 2. (London: Educational Book Company, 1910) [Cornell University – PJ Mode Collection of Persuasive Cartography].

have never experienced the actual era of modern empires but nonetheless live in its shadow.

Cities and architecture were products and tools critical to the modern colonial system, and imperial administrators lavished considerable resources on the theorization, design, and construction of built environments deemed suitable for empire in their colonies. Around the globe colonizers erected monuments, adjusted and expanded existing cities, built adjacent to old ones, and elsewhere they started anew. Streets and sites were given names that brought colonialist conquerors and politicians, European toponyms, and other historic references into occupied cities. Tasked with accommodating the lives of colonizers and the colonized, but also with representing the power and "civilizing" authority of the respective metropoles, such architectures took on considerable meaning in addition to their actual functions.[9] The choice of style — imported, appropriated, or hybridized — mattered. So too did materials, whether recycled, luxurious, modern, or mass-produced. For example, the Roman Catholic cathedrals in French North Africa manifested much of this colonialist infatuation with imagery and materiality. Tunis' cathedral was designed to represent the rebirth of Christianity in the region. Its calculated appearance suggested continuity with early Christianity and Byzantium, and the use of stones from a restored Roman-era quarry emphasized historic precedent and the symbolic sacredness of construction materials [Figure 1.2].[10] In other contexts, many colonial projects were unprecedented in scale or otherwise noteworthy in their efficiency or structural sophistication. For example, the construction of New Delhi by the British in India during the early 1900s was lauded as the largest public works project undertaken in the modern world. The city's architecture was noteworthy and intended to be something totally new; it could "not be Indian, nor English, nor Roman, but it must be Imperial" according to architect Herbert Baker.[11] Architects in French-administered Casablanca — described as an urban laboratory critical to the rejuvenation of metropolitan France — developed new conceptions of spatial zoning and experimented successfully with new construction techniques and materials, emphasizing both efficiency and (relative) cultural sensitivity in their work [Figure 1.3].[12] Italian architects in Libya and the Horn of Africa took pride in their achievements, like their British, French, and Japanese counterparts elsewhere, viewing their architectures as expressions of their self-professed cultural supremacy and political power.[13] Colonialism thus generated substantial built environments that were integral to colonial identities and imagery. In many places they remain the most tangible vestiges of this inescapable past.

With the end of formal empires, some colonial-era structures and spaces were razed or radically altered to obscure the past and stake claims in sovereign, independent, futures [Figure 1.4]. Others were appropriated and reused with minimal modification for a diversity of reasons. Indeed, some liberated states used these buildings "as-is" because they sought no total disconnection with the past, while others were unable to afford or accomplish substantial modifications due to limited resources. Still others had more pressing concerns and simply

Figure 1.2
The Cathedral of St.
Vincent de Paul and
St. Olivia, Tunis, Tunisia
(Bonnet-Labranche,
1897). Photograph 201
Source: Daniel E. Coslet

chose not to prioritize such architectural projects [Figures 1.5 and 1.6]. On a more diffused level, throughout colonial cities many street names were changed at independence; nationalist heroes replaced colonizers and landmark dates of conquest became those of anti-colonial achievements [Figure 1.7].[14] Ultimately some extant colonial-era built environments have been critically changed with intent,

re 1.3
Central Post Office,
ablanca, Morocco
rien Laforgue, 1920).
tograph 2013.
rce: Daniel E. Coslett.

ure 1.4
e Liberation Monument,
giers, Algeria (M'Hamed
akhem, 1978)
corporates Paul-
aximilien Landowski and
arles Bigonet's 1928
onuments aux Morts
WI). Photograph 2017.
urce: Daniel E. Coslett.

while others have been maintained for convenience. Compellingly, some sites have been preserved and celebrated as didactic heritage, artistic assets, or valuable indices to modernity [Figure 1.8].[15] In countless cases — their current form notwithstanding — colonial-era sites contribute to urban identities and influence the lives of those that use and inhabit them.

While the socio-political and economic aftereffects of empire have been variously studied since the 1960s, and studies of memory have been popular in

Figure 1.5
The Presidential Palace
(ex-Government House,
Nicosia, Cyprus (Mauric
Webb, 1937). Photogra
2013. Source: Nicolas
Kantzilaris.

Figure 1.6
The Rashtrapati Bhavan
(ex-Viceroy's House),
New Delhi, India
(Edwin Lutyens, 1929).
Photograph 2014.
Source: Ronakshah1990
[Wikimedia Commons].

recent decades, the active roles played by historic built environments in the maintenance and promotion of postcolonial relationships have largely escaped scru-
tiny. Given that historical colonialism, like these spaces and structures, remains
in so many places unavoidable, this omission is unfortunate. Indeed, historic
structures of the colonial-era play roles in the lives of postcolonial states, individuals, and societies, not just as sites of memory passively present or subtly
influential, but often as actively engaged and exploited spaces that one might

re 1.7
rededication of Tunis'
nue Jules-Ferry as the
nue Habib Bourguiba,
oring Tunisia's
onalist leader and
president, on June 1,
6, the anniversary
is return from exile.
tograph 1956. Source:
on., "La Place de
dépendance et l'Avenue
rguiba," La Dépêche
isienne, June 2, 1956,
Note the sustained
of the colonial-era
isian-style green and
e enameled placard.

call "neocolonialist sites of memory."[16] In this form, the term recognizes the agency such sites wield as contributors to in developing processes of neocolonialism. Nora describes "sites of memory" as ambiguous, intentionally crafted products of our history-obsessed age, as "moments of history torn away from the movement of history, then returned; no longer quite life, not yet death, like

Figure 1.8
The Futurist Fiat Tagliero
service station, Asmara,
Eritrea (Giuseppe Pettazzi
1938). Photograph 2011
Source: Sailko [Wikimedia
Commons]. The Italian
colonial structure is an
iconic element of the
UNESCO World Heritage
Site that was designated
in 2017.

shells on the shore when the sea of living memory has receded."[17] Extending
the metaphor, as the borders of empires ebbed, colonial-era built environments
were left behind by the withdrawal of the imperial sea, thus strewn across the
postcolonial coast. These architectural sites of memory, however, are not just
passed over like innocuous shells abandoned by the surf. Rather, they stub toes
and scratch the feet of wandering beachcombers who may or may not see them
or take interest. Like the scattered seashells around which passersby tiptoe, inherited architectures impose themselves upon "the ever-changing terrain of imperial memory."[18]

SPEAKING OF COLONIAL, POST- AND NEO-

The terminology relating to empires, their formal end, and the contemporary state
of affairs existing between former colonies, ex-colonial powers, non-governmental organizations (NGOs), and others, remains contested. While the present volume uses the terms "colonial" and "imperial" interchangeably, some scholars opt
for one over the other, drawing distinctions between the nature of administrative
structures, the proximity of ruling classes, and the cultures affected.[19] Indeed, the
use of the latter may emphasize centralized administration within the metropole,
rather than the colony. Both terms, however, describe the rule of a nation by a
minority contingent of present outsiders (the colonizer) who have migrated to the
occupied territory. The meaning of empire is more generally accepted. Burbank
and Cooper capture the entity well in describing empires as "large political units,
expansionist or with a memory of power extended over space, polities that maintain distinction and hierarchy as they incorporate new people."[20] Whether more
colonial or imperial, the relationships addressed are essentially exploitational and
based on power imbalances, the ramifications of which were often rendered
starkly apparent in urban and architectural form.

The theoretical demise of empires and descriptions thereof remain relatively contentious issues, however. The customary use of the term "postcolonial" to describe the era following the formal end of empires during the 1950s and 1960s remains problematic, and the inadequacy of the term has been recognized. Some have indicated that it implies colonialism no longer exists, thus disregarding new, contemporary forms of colonialist dominance.[21] Others have adopted the term "neocolonial" in an effort to acknowledge technical or structural changes, but also continued forms of colonialism that may or may not conform to past formulae.[22] "The essence of neo-colonialism is that the State which is subject to it is, in theory, independent in all the outward trappings of international sovereignty," Kwame Nkrumah said in 1965, coining the term. "In reality its economic system and thus its political policy is directed from outside," he concluded.[23] Others have addressed neocolonialism through further analysis that recognizes the complex ways in which so many factors and processes contribute to the economics of new empire. For example, Michael Hardt and Antonio Negri, in their provocative and seminal work on the persistence of empire in the wake of colonialism's incomplete end, contend that today's "imperial control operates through three global and absolute means: the bomb, money, and ether."[24] Globalization reinforces power through military strength, capitalism, and the world marketplace, and the deterritorialized communication of, among other things, education and culture, they maintain.[25] "Soft power," that is knowledge, art, music, and other cultural elements, join traditional "hard power" means of control, including guns and laws. Architecture and built environments, as both functional features and meaningful ideas, are thus important components of "soft power" neocolonialist portfolios.

REALITIES AND APPEARANCES, BOOMS AND ECHOES OF NEOCOLONIALISM

Broadly speaking, contemporary neocolonialism can be seen in terms of structural realities, but also in appearances or images. That is to say, there exist situations in which states and organizations function in exploitative relationships that, because of imbalances in power, favor one participant over another. In other cases, the outward appearance of neocolonialism can suggest historical continuities that may or may not actually exist. All of these can be experienced as external relationships between sovereign states and/or between states and NGOs, or internally through the postcolonial continuation of historical colonialist policies or systems. The complexities of neocolonialism render neat categorization a difficult task, but attempting to do so reveals the meaningful ways in which neocolonialism can exist and ways in which it can be accommodated, challenged, or at the very least understood.

The most obvious type of neocolonialism — that experienced among two states or entities through an imbalanced relationship — is arguably the most predictable. In such cases former colonial masters can maintain their socio-cultural and economic dominance through trade deals, political manipulation, or other-wise. France as today's "gendarme of Africa" exemplifies this type of relation-ship.[26] In recent decades, however, one also finds states that were not necessarily participants in the modern (European) imperial system imposing themselves in regions that were once occupied by others. Indeed, both China and Russia are increasingly active in working to secure power, profits, and prestige in post-colonies. The former's investment in large infrastructure projects in Africa can be described as a form of neocolonialism designed to maximize Chinese influ-ence on the continent.[27] NGOs, such as the World Bank and the International Monetary Fund, have long since been criticized for the ways in which they manip-ulate dependent states through investments and loans while advancing Western and neoliberal agendas that may not suit all parties involved.[28] The products of these relationships can include tourism policy, strategically deployed devel-opment investments, conditional bailouts, and cultural policies, among other things. The promotion of Western heritage values, or what Laurajane Smith calls "authorized heritage discourse," globally through entities such as UNESCO rep-resents well a form of NGO-based neocolonialism with real ramifications in the built environment.[29]

Neocolonialism can arguably also be experienced domestically within a more closed system as well. When understood as continuity, neocolonialism can exist when postcolonial states perpetuate colonial-era policies and practices, whether out of necessity, convenience, or with the intent to control using familiar tools. Academic pedagogies,[30] state legal and penal systems, historic preservation prac-tices, and conceptions of national identity are all areas that can be affected by such domestic or internal neocolonialist activities. Within the realm of heritage management, for example, states can advance the image of colonialism through restorations and the commodification of built environments that date from, and appear to celebrate, historical colonialism.[31] Tourism is one major area wherein these issues collide, as "Empire, the globalization of capitalism, and tourism have been joined at the hip" throughout the modern era.[32] Indeed, the nostalgia that softens contemporary impressions of colonialism's brutal realities in many postcolonial metropolitan societies[33] can influence heritage policies in former colonies, particularly within the realm of tourism where colonial-era built envi-ronments can suggest continuity and attract visitors by exploiting long-standing Orientalist fantasies.[34]

Neocolonialsim can thus exist in very real, structural, or institutionalized forms, but it can also exist in appearances alone. It can boom and it can echo, reverberating across time and space through inherited colonial-era built envi-ronments. In some cases the presence of heritage structures invites investment and involvement from neocolonialist NGOs or former colonizing powers. In other cases these structures facilitate tourism and contribute to national iden-tities that may favour certain contemporary regimes. Still, in other cases the inherited spaces and structures may limit the sovereignty of postcolonial states, physically, psychologically, or symbolically. The present volume addresses the subject from a variety of perspectives and its authors define neocolonialism in different ways in their assessments of its built manifestations. The collected voices contained herein thus demonstrate the relevance of colonial-era spaces within the contemporary life of cities variously engaged in neocolonialist practices and open avenues to compelling new questions.[35] Ultimately the volume invites readers and scholars of other colonial-era contexts and sites to consider ways in which inherited built environments may contribute to developing neocolonial processes.

THE PRESENT VOLUME

The *Neocolonialism and Built Heritage* collection explores an expansive interpretation of contemporary neocolonialism. The collection of essays makes no attempt to conclusively settle debates or address *all* relevant questions regarding colonial-era built environments in today's postcolonial and globalizing contexts. Rather, the volume approaches these complex issues from a variety of angles using case studies in Africa and Asia — the chief domains of modern colonialism — and at sites within oft-overlooked European metropoles. Chapters are arranged around broad themes in an effort to highlight consistencies and linkages across geographies and time. Reflecting the different approaches one might take to neocolonialism conceptually, authors consider external relationships, that is to say relationships between ex-colonial masters and postcolonies, NGOs, and other entities, as well as internal or domestic ones. The resulting presentation thus incorporates a wide array of situations befitting the open interpretation of neocolonialism adopted here. As such, it offers ample material to fuel ongoing debates regarding the salience of the ever-present past.

Jean-Louis Cohen, in his studies of colonial-era architecture, considers the material to be "architecture in a colonial situation," rather than distinctively colonial or somehow separate from contemporary metropolitan architectural discourse and practice.[36] Similarly, authors of the present volume consider this inherited material now *in a postcolonial situation*, thus within the charged context of contemporary socio-political and economic environments wherein consciousness of the colonial past remains real and present. Further heeding suggestions made by Cohen, the authors consider broad "diachronic lines of continuity" so as to avoid limitations imposed by narrow focuses that can create historiographic and analytical "optical illusions."[37] Many of the volume's chapters thus begin with accounts of the colonial eras that generated the circumstances of today. Still further considering Cohen's call, contributors have been encouraged to incorporate the voices of the colonized where possible, but due to archival limitations, more often the voices of the postcolonial inheritors of colonial spaces and structures come into play.

A pioneer in the study of colonial architecture and urbanism, Anthony King reminds researchers that the study of colonial-era material necessitates knowledge of pre-colonial local, metropolitan, and colonized cultures.[38] By the same token, the study of postcolonial and contemporary spaces demands consideration of colonial, independence-era, and broader global trends, as is demonstrated by the chapters in *Neocolonialism and Built Heritage*. Inspired in part by the questions asked by King in his *Spaces of Global Cultures: Architecture, Urbanism, Identity* — "How persistent are postcolonial (imperial, or neo-imperial) forces in impacting urban space, not only in postcolonial and postimperial situations but in other cities elsewhere? And are these conceptual categories the most useful, valid, or appropriate to describe contemporary urban situations?"[39] — the volume directly explores neocolonialism through built environments. It asks very similar questions, but adds the inherited colonial-era site factor. Authors thus interrogate the contributions made by colonial-era built environments in the neocolonial processes now shaping postcolonial urban spaces.

As modern industrial and capitalist colonialism was at its core designed to benefit the metropoles, this volume begins with consideration of former European colonial powers. Paris, London, Rome, and other seats of imperial power have been largely overlooked in studies of colonial architecture and urbanism. For example, in the past, says G.A. Bremner in his valuable study of the postcolonial metropole:

> British imperial architecture was understood as something that resided outside the bounds of the modern British state, as if Britain's position at the centre of the largest territorial empire the world had ever known (both self-confessed and real) had no corresponding impact on the buildings and urban landscapes of Britain itself.[40]

Despite this historiographic deficiency, "[t]he colonial experience is part of the cultural DNA of both" France and the UK, and so too is it present within metropolitan built environments.[41] Indeed, given the immense wealth accumulated in London, Paris, Rome, Berlin, and elsewhere through the modern colonial system, and the substantial projects and spaces built there as a result, the conspicuous absence of these sites within discourses on colonial and postcolonial architecture remains noteworthy.[42] The present volume thus contributes to the expanding field by including three chapters on colonial spaces in postcolonial Europe. Together they demonstrate that the presence of colonial-era built environments in many cases reflects the avoidance of confrontation with the colonial past and neocolonialist behaviors. Robert Aldrich surveys the state of colonial-era built environments in contemporary Paris, and in so doing he sheds light on a longstanding ambivalence regarding imperial imagery and commemoration there. Rome is the focus of the subsequent chapter by Flavia Marcello and Aidan Carter. In it they present the Axum Obelisk — sent to Italy from Ethiopia in 1937 by the occupying Italian military — as an urban signpost whose shifting symbolism throughout the Fascist, post-Fascist, and contemporary eras recounts Italy's colonial legacy and, more broadly, the afterlife of the global colonialist project. Concluding Part I, Valentina Rozas-Krause introduces readers to a series of contemporary monuments to German colonialism on contested streets in Berlin, highlighting ways in which the country's ongoing reconciliation with dark periods of its past remains dominated by its attention to the Holocaust.

Part II of the present volume consists of three chapters that again engage the postcolonial metropoles, but do so in more direct communication with their former colonies. Rather than foregrounding the ambivalence or so-called "colonial amnesia"[43] observable in many places, these authors highlight connections. Ralph Ghoche considers recent controversy in France regarding the potential conversion of disused church buildings into mosques, recalling the colonial-era transformation of Algiers' Ketchaoua mosque into the city's Catholic cathedral during the colonial period. Turning readers' attention to Italian colonialism, Stephanie Malia Hom explores simulation in the service of empire through her case studies of the 1927–39 Tripoli Trade Fair and the Historical Museum Piana delle Orme, which today commemorates the Fascist-era reclamation of the Pontine Marshes south of Rome. Moving from European colonialism to the Asian context, Suzie Kim writes of the Government-General Building of Chosŏn built by Japanese colonizers in Seoul who sought to link the colony to both Japan and broad conceptions of modernity. The massive structure's demolition in 1995–96 physically removed it from the cityscape, but its legacy as a lost teaching tool for Korean architects ought not to be overlooked, Kim contends.

Inherited spaces that directly influence the contemporary function of present-day institutions are the subjects of Part III's two chapters. While all of the volume's essays interrogate relationships between the past and present through built environments, these two do so through focused studies of sites whose use continues across the colonial-to-postcolonial transition. Interrogating prevalent conceptions of neocolonialism, Simon De Nys-Ketels, Johan Lagae, Kristien Geenen, Luce Beeckmans, and Trésor Lumfuankenda Bungiena address the appropriation of, and limitations imposed by, extant Belgian colonial-era hospital infrastructure in today's economically stratified Kinshasa. India has inherited both the British colonial penal system and many of its dilapidated and now overcrowded prison buildings, according to Mira Rai Waits. Her chapter, the final in Part III, offers compelling insight into the contemporary role played by these symbolically loaded sites of power in terms of both punishment and anti-colonial commemoration.

Part IV of the volume addresses the expansion or transformation of inherited colonial-era spaces for new uses in concert with contested globalization processes, which Held et al. view to be "a widening, deepening and speeding up of world-wide inter-connectedness in all aspects of contemporary social life, from the cultural to the criminal, the financial to the spiritual."[44] The flow of capital may follow paths established through historical imperialism, taking advantage of infrastructural, political, and linguistic, connections. Processes of globalization can thus build upon, reinforce, or obliterate historical networks, while at the same time providing those in power with opportunities to bolster their positions in an arguably homogenizing world.[45] In this way competitive globalization can operate hand-in-hand with neocolonialism, to both extend and counteract it. Chapters in

Part IV investigate the influences globalization can have on the modification and reuse of inherited colonial-era built environments in both Africa and Asia. Daniel E. Coslett does so first though a presentation of Tunis' iconic Bardo Museum, whose recent World Bank-backed expansion illustrates the influence of NGOs and a strong reliance on tourism in Tunisia. The site's experience with terrorism in 2015 highlights the potentially destabilizing ramifications that can come from engaging the broader international community and its neocolonialist elements. Nancy Demerdash-Fatemi, in her chapter on the conversion of Moroccan houses into popular riads for visiting tourists, foregrounds continuities with French-era interpretations of Maghrebi domesticity, while also addressing the potentially invasive nature of contemporary tourism development within the historic urban core. The redevelopment of lands owned by the Taiwan Sugar Corporation for domestic and international tourism and nation-building — which often include sites represented in a manner arguably sympathetic to Japanese colonial-era history — is addressed by Justin Kollar in the section's final chapter.

THE FUTURE OF THE EVER-PRESENT PAST

The essays collected in the present volume bring to light many salient connections between the colonial past and the neocolonial present. Together they do not, however, offer an easily digested conclusion on the subject. Nor are simple solutions for evading neocolonialism tendered. The ultimate value of these case studies comes not from their conclusions, but from the manner in which they open opportunities for further discussion within the interrelated and developing fields of colonial/postcolonial built environments, neocolonialism, and heritage management. The volume extends the analysis of addressed sites from the realm of Nora's historic "sites of memory" into the more operational realm of contemporary neocolonialist activity. As such, the volume not only introduces previously marginalized content, but in its totality reveals erstwhile-unexplored connections that may inspire potentially novel reconsiderations of long-known material and processes elsewhere. As suggested by the volume's closing commentary offered by Vikramāditya Prakāsh, who considers potential escape from the neocolonialist situation in a meditation on self-reflection and the future of teaching and conceiving global architectural histories, much work remains to be done.

Moving forward, one might use the questions posed and methods adopted by the volume's authors in sites elsewhere in Africa, Asia, Europe, and beyond. An awareness of the active roles played by inherited built environments in neocolonialist processes — whether actual or suggested — may enrich one's understanding of the ever-present past. Such enhanced understanding may facilitate new possibilities for the future of postcolonial contexts wherein all parties may contribute with improved equity and agency to the process of decolonization. The essays gathered here therefore invite further questions and more critical assessment of issues related to inherited built environments, including heritage management and tourism, infrastructural development, toponymy and commemorative inter-ventions, globalization, and identity. Ultimately the volume is just a small part of a broader, necessary discussion with ample ground left to cover on the enduring influences of neocolonialist sites of memory around the globe.

NOTES

1   Dominik Geppert and Frank Lorenz Müller, "Beyond National Memory. Nora's *Lieux de Mémoire* Across an Imperial World," in *Sites of Imperial Memory*, ed. Dominik Geppert and Frank Lorenz Müller (Manchester: Manchester University, 2015), 1.
2   Ibid., 15.
3   Pierre Nora "Between Memory and History: *Les Lieux de Mémoire*," *Representations* 26 (1989): 7–24.
4   Jane Burbank and Frederick Cooper, *Empires in World History: Power and the Politics of Difference* (Princeton, NJ: Princeton University, 2011), 288.
5   Max Jones et al., "Decolonising Imperial Heroes: Britain and France," *Journal of Imperial and Commonwealth History* 42, no. 5 (2014): 792. The same source states that France's empire covered seven million square miles and encompassed fifteen percent of the world's population at that time. Ibid.
6   On the dissolution of France's empire and resulting institutions, see Robert Aldrich, *Greater France: A History of French Overseas Expansion* (London: MacMillan, 1996), 266–325.
7   Burbank and Cooper, *Empires*, 289.
8   Jones et al., "Decolonising," 792.
9   Anthony D. King, "Colonialism, Urbanism and the Capitalist World Economy," in *Writing the Global City* (New York: Routledge, 2016), 26–28.
10 Daniel E. Coslett, "(Re)creating a Christian Image Abroad: The Catholic Cathedrals of Protectorate-era Tunis," in *Sacred Precincts: The Religious Architecture of Non-Muslim Communities across the Islamic World,* ed. Mohammad Gharipour (Boston: Brill, 2015), 353–75.
11 Baker quoted in Tristram Hunt, *Cities of Empire* (New York: Metropolitan, 2014), 367
12 Gwendolyn Wright, *The Politics of Design in French Colonial Urbanism* (Chicago, IL: University of Chicago, 1992), 85–160.
13 Mia Fuller, *Moderns Abroad: Architecture, Cities, and Italian Imperialism* (London: Routledge, 2007); Sean Anderson, *Modern Architecture and its Representation in Colonial Eritrea: An In-visible Colony, 1890–1941* (New York: Routledge, 2017).
14 See, for example, Samira Hassa, "From 'Avenue de France' to 'Boulevard Hassan II': Toponymic Inscription and the Construction of Nationhood in Fes, Morocco," in *Place Names in Africa*, ed. Liora Bigon (New York: Springer, 2016), 79–91.
15 See, for example, the 2017 designation of the Italian colonial core of Asmara, Eritrea, as a tourist-friendly UNESCO World Heritage Site entitled "a Modernist City of Africa." "Decision 41 COM 8B.11: Asmara: A Modernist City of Africa (Eritrea)," UNESCO, 2017, accessed March 6, 2019, https://whc.unesco.org/en/decisions/6883. As Benedict Anderson says, "it is probably not too surprising that post-independence states, which exhibited marked continuities with their colonial predecessors, inherited this form of political museumizing." Benedict Anderson, *Imagined Communities: Reflections on the Origin and Spread of Nationalism* (London: Verso, 1991), 183.
16 Berny Sèbe's work considers the afterlife of imperial heroes — personalities lauded during the colonial era and celebrated through built monuments within the colonies, many of which outlived their respective empires — in postcolonial built environ-ments. Contentious struggles in the wake of independence have in many places

subsided, and the sustained presence of such sites may reflect "a more consensual approach to historical realities" today, he says. Berny Sèbe, "From Post-Colonialism to Cosmopolitan Nation-Building? British and French Imperial Heroes in Twenty-First-Century Africa," *Journal of Imperial and Commonwealth History* 42, no. 5 (2014): 947. Sèbe, in coining the term "neo-imperial sites of memory," is in turn borrowing from Geppert and Muller, *Sites of Imperial Memory*.

17 Nora, "Between Memory and History," 12.
18 Jones et al., "Decolonising," 804.
19 On terminology debates and distinctions see Anthony D. King, *Colonial Urban Development: Culture, Social Power, and Environment* (London: Routledge, 1976), 17; King, "Colonialism, Urbanism," 25–26; Anthony D. King, "Postcolonial Cities, Postcolonial Critiques," in King, *Writing*, 117–28.
20 Burbank and Cooper, *Empires*, 8.
21 Ella Shohat, "Notes on the 'Post-colonial'," *Social Text* 31/32 (1992): 99–113.
22 Ibid.; Chadwick Allen, "Who Put the 'Post' in Postcolonialism?," *Novel* 32, no. 1 (1998): 144–46.
23 Kwame Nkrumah, *Neo-colonialism: The Last Stage of Imperialism* (Camden, NJ: Nelson, 1965), ix.
24 Michael Hardt and Antonio Negri, *Empire* (Cambridge, MA: Harvard University, 2000), 345.
25 Ibid., 343–48.
26 Victor-Manuel Vallin, "France as the Gendarme of Africa 1960–2014," *Political Science Quarterly* 130, no.1 (2015): 79–101.
27 Kenya currently owes China US$5.3 billion. Eyder Peralta, "A New Chinese-Funded Railway in Kenya Sparks Debt-trap Fears," *National Public Radio*, October 8, 2018, https://www.npr.org/2018/10/08/641625157/a-new-chinese-funded-railway-in-kenya-sparks-debt-trap-fears. Similar situations have arisen in Asia as well. See, for example, Maria Abi-Habib, "How China Got Sri Lanka to Cough up a Port," *New York Times*, June 25, 2018, https://www.nytimes.com/2018/06/25/world/asia/china-sri-lanka-port.html. See also Derek Watkins, K.K. Rebecca Lai, and Keith Bradsher, "The World, Built by China," *New York Times*, November 18, 2018, https://www.nytimes.com/interactive/2018/11/18/world/asia/world-built-by-china.html.
28 See, for example, Mark Langan, *Neo-colonialism and the Poverty of "Development" in Africa* (New York: Palgrave MacMillan, 2018).
29 Laurajane Smith, *The Uses of Heritage* (New York: Routledge, 2006), 11–43. See also Michael A. DiGiovine, *The Heritage-scape: UNESCO, World Heritage, and Tourism* (New York: Lexington, 2009).
30 On the maintenance of colonial-era architectural pedagogies in postcolonial Asia and North Africa, for example, see Jyoti Hosagrahar, "South Asia: Looking Back, Moving Ahead-History and Modernization," *Journal of the Society of Architectural Historians* 61, no. 3 (2002): 355–69; Ali Djerbi and Abdelwahab Safi, "Teaching the History of Architecture in Algeria, Tunisia, and Morocco: Colonialism, Independence, and Globalization," *Journal of the Society of Architectural Historians* 62, no. 1 (2003): 110–20.
31 See, for example, Daniel E. Coslett, "(Re)branding a (Post)colonial Streetscape: Tunis's Avenue Bourguiba & the Road Ahead." *International Journal of Islamic Architecture* 6, no. 1 (2017): 59–96.
32 Shelley Baranowski quoted in Shelley Baranowski et al., "Tourism and Empire," *Journal of Tourism History* 7, no. 1–2 (2015): 29.
33 For example, a 2014 survey of the British public found that fifty-nine percent of those polled considered the British Empire something of which to be proud. Nineteen

percent expressed shame. Will Dahlgreen, "The British Empire is 'something to be proud of,'" *YouGov,* July 26, 2014, https://yougov.co.uk/topics/politics/articles-reports/2014/07/26/britain-proud-its-empire. See also Patricia M.E. Lorcin, "Imperial Nostalgia: Colonial Nostalgia: Differences of Theory, Similarities of Practice?" *Historical Reflections/Réflexions Historiques* 39, no. 3 (2013): 77–111.

34   For examples of the popularity of colonial-era imagery and spaces in postcolonial contexts, see Coslett, "(Re)branding"; Edward M. Bruner, "The Maasai and the Lion King: Authenticity, Nationalism, and Globalization in African Tourism," in *Tourists and Tourism: A Reader,* ed. Sharon Gmelch and Adam Kaul (Long Grove, IL: Waveland, 2018), 109–38; Tim Edensor and Uma Kothari, "Sweetening Colonialism: A Mauritian Themed Resort," in *Architecture and Tourism,* ed. D. Medina Lasansky and Brian McLaren (New York: Berg, 2004), 189–205.

35   The chapters that constitute the present volume are of course not the first published works that address the place of colonial-era built environments within the contemporary context. See, for example, Henry S. Grabar, "Reclaiming the City: Changing Urban Meaning in Algiers After 1962," *Cultural Geographies* 2, no. 3 (2014): 389–409; Tom Avermaete and Maristella Casciato, *Casablanca Chandigarh: A Report on Modernization* (Montreal: Canadian Centre for Architecture, 2014); Diana Wylie, "The Importance of Being at Home: A Defense of Historic Preservation in Algeria," *Change Over Time* 2, no. 2 (2012): 172–87; Robert Parks, "From the War of National Liberation to Gentrification: Conflicting Claims over Property in Algeria," *Middle East Research and Information Project,* August 10, 2018, accessed April 7, 2019, https://merip.org/2018/08/from-the-war-of-national-liberation-to-gentrification; Geppert and Müller, *Sites of Imperial Memory*; Coslett, "(Re)branding." On sculptural monuments in particular, see Jones et al., "Decolonising," 804–05; Paul McGarr, "'The Viceroys are Disappearing from the Roundabouts in Delhi': British Symbols of Power in Post-colonial India," *Modern Asian Studies* 49, no. 3 (2015): 787–831; Alain Amato, *Monuments en exil* (Paris: Editions de l'Atlanthrope, 1979); Sèbe, "From Post-Colonialism."

36   Jean-Louis Cohen, "Architectural History and the Colonial Question: Casablanca, Algiers and Beyond," *Architectural History* 49 (2006): 354.

37   Ibid.. 355

38   King, *Colonial Urban Development.*

39   Anthony King, *Spaces of Global Cultures: Architecture, Urbanism, Identity* (New York: Routledge, 2004), 62.

40   G.A. Bremner, "The Metropolis: Imperial Buildings and Landscapes in Brotain," in *Architecture and Urbanism in the British Empire*, ed. G.A. Bremner (Oxford: Oxford University, 2016), 125.

41   Jones et al., "Decolonising," 291–92.

42   Notable exceptions to this include Robert Aldrich, *Vestiges of the Colonial Empire in France: Monuments, Museums and Colonial Memories* (London: Palgrave Macmillan, 2005); Patricia A. Morton, *Hybrid Modernities: Architecture and Representation at the 1931 Colonial Exposition, Paris* (Cambridge, MA: MIT, 2000); Flavia Marcello, "Mussolini and the Idealisation of Empire: the Augustan Exhibition of Romanità," *Modern Italy* 16, no. 3 (2011): 223–47; Mark Crinson, *Empire Building: Orientalism and Victorian Architecture* (New York: Routledge, 1996); Mark Crinson, *Modern Architecture and the End of Empire* (Burlington, VT: Ashgate, 2003); Idesbald Goddeeris, "Colonial Streets and Statues: Postcolonial Belgium in the Public Space," *Postcolonial Studies* 18, no. 4 (2015): 397–409 ; Matthew G. Stanard, *The Leopard, the Lion, and the Cock: Colonial Memories and Monuments in Belgium* (Leuven: Leuven University Press, 2019); Robert Aldrich, "Putting the Colonies on the Map,"

in *Promoting the Colonial Idea: Propaganda and Visions of Empire in France*, ed. Tony Chafer and Amanda Sackur (New York: Palgrave, 2002), 211–23.

43   On forgetting and national identity creation, see Homi K. Bhabha, "DissemiNation: Time, Narratives, and the Margins of the Modern Nation," in *Nation and Narration,* ed. Homi K. Bhabha (New York: Routledge, 1990), 291–322.

44   David Held et al., *Global Transformations* (Stanford, CA: Stanford University, 1999), 2. See also King, *Spaces of Global Cultures*, 23–44.

45   While the increasingly complex flow of capital around the globe is undeniable, the degree to which a truly global culture has emerged is not entirely clear, nor is it certain that the current situation is entirely novel. King, for example, questions whether or not the label is used to describe dynamics that have long existed under other terms (perhaps cosmopolitanism, internationalism, or universalism). King, *Spaces of Global Cultures*, 24–27.

Part I
Colonial spaces in postcolonial metropoles

2

Old colonial sites and new uses in contemporary Paris

Robert Aldrich

The built landscapes of France, and other countries in Europe, bear both the visible and subliminal traces of colonialism and its legacy: dedicated colonialist buildings and others with a direct connection to the Empire, monuments, war memorials, statues, and graves, and architectural and design motifs. In the early twentieth century, France claimed the world's second largest overseas empire, encompassing eleven million square kilometers in Africa, Asia, and islands of the Caribbean, Indian Ocean, and Pacific, and French citizens and subjects numbered one hundred million. Promoters of colonial expansion and rule hoped that marking the country with stone, bronze, or marble testimonials to France's prowess in conquering an empire and its proclaimed "genius" in ruling the *outre-mer* and fulfilling its *mission civilisatrice* would galvanize popular support and manifest France's imperial vocation. The sites created ranged from the modest tombs of now largely forgotten explorers to grandiose purpose-built structures such as a colonial museum in Paris. A *flâneur* in Paris, and other cities, especially those linked with the colonies, such as Marseille, Bordeaux, Lyon, La Rochelle, Fréjus — and many other places — easily stumbles across reminders of the colonial past, both those that have survived from the colonial period and a few that have subsequently been erected.[1]

That colonial past has been much contested in recent years, though most of France's colonies had already gained independence by 1960. New revelations, around the year 2000, about torture during the Franco-Algerian War of 1954–62 ripped open scars left from one of the most divisive conflicts in French history. Debates about the place of Muslims in contemporary society and Islamic cultures in France (such as the practice of wearing Muslim headscarves and *burqas* by women) relate directly both to channels of migration from Africa established under colonialism and age-old French perceptions of the Muslim and Islamic world. Exhibitions, films and television programs, speeches, and public forums have brought the French face to face with a colonial record that many would have preferred to be quietly filed away. The activism of diasporic groups in France has linked contemporary problems of discrimination and xenophobia to colonial attitudes and behaviors, and politicians and activists of all stripes have tried to deploy the issue of colonialism to their advantage.[2]

Old and new sites connected with French overseas expansion and decolonization, not surprisingly, have become significant stakes in debates and public policy in the postcolonial age. One question was what to do with sites that no longer served their original function and whose triumphalist colonialist message and style became increasingly inappropriate and uncomfortable.[3] Some statues were shuffled off to obscure locations, others moldered away where they stood. Heritage considerations and architectural or artistic value have made it impossible to demolish especially significant sites, and they were often repurposed. For example, the former École Coloniale, built in the Moorish style just outside the Jardin du Luxembourg in the 1880s to train civil servants for the Empire, ceased to enroll new students in the early 1960s, and was later turned into a training institute for students from overseas, many from France's former colonies [Figure 2.1]. The vast ceiling painting in the institute's library, showing an allegorical figure of France receiving the homage of maidens representing various regions of the French Empire, remains as a reminder of the ideology behind the institute and of France's continued engagement, neocolonial or not, with its former possessions.[4]

This chapter explores in greater detail the "recycling" of three other sites in Paris, suggesting that efforts to repurpose them form part and parcel of France's difficult, and not always successful, attempt to come to terms with its colonial

Figure 2.1
The former École Coloniale, Paris (Yvon, 1895). Primary façade detail. Photograph 2014
Source: Daniel E. Coslett

past. The inventory from which the selection could be taken is a lengthy one, from the old colonial ministry in the Rue Oudinot (which still houses the ministry in charge of France's remaining *départements et territoires d'outre-mer*) to the seminary and chapel of the Société des Missions Étrangères in the Rue du Bac (still the headquarters of the missionary society founded in the mid-1600s, and host to a museum of French overseas evangelization) and many others, both imposing and diminutive.

THE JARDIN COLONIAL

In the *commune* of Nogent-sur-Marne, at the eastern edge of the Bois de Vincennes — the park where a grand Exposition Coloniale would take place in 1931 — the French at the very end of the nineteenth century set up the Jardin Botanique Colonial. Its mandate was to study plants from the French colonies to determine which ones might be profitably transplanted from one colony to another or acclimatized to the metropole. Tropical agricultural commodities pro-vided a mainstay of colonial business, with long-established markets for such products as sugar and coffee, and developing ones for others, like the rubber that was finding new value for bicycle and automobile tires. The colonial botanical garden also trained agronomists for colonial work, collecting specimens of trop-ical hardwoods in its *xylothèque* (wood specimen library) and avidly promoting France's colonial mission. The grounds of the garden included large greenhouses, laboratories, teaching rooms, a library, and administrative buildings. The garden had links with other scientific institutions, such as the Muséum National d'Histoire Naturelle (National Museum of Natural History), and groups within the "colonial lobby," the informal network of political, commercial, scholarly, and other figures who served as boosters for the French Empire.[5]

The Jardin Botanique Colonial fulfilled its function dutifully, and in 1907 organized a colonial exhibition that highlighted the wealth of the plant kingdom in France's colonies, the commodities (and financial returns) that tropical agri-culture brought to France and the Empire, and the agronomical research being undertaken by its staff and students. The fair, which followed a larger Exposition Coloniale held the previous year in Marseille — a city that prided itself on being France's "portal to the East" and self-appointed colonial capital — was one in a series of colonial fairs held in a number of French cities in the early twentieth cen-tury. The Vincennes fair drew on the Marseille precedent, and indeed some of the old pavilions from Marseille were disassembled and transferred to Paris. Another colonial exhibition in Marseille, in 1922, also produced the gift of disused buildings for the Vincennes site. With a star-and-crescent topped pavilion that had hosted Tunisia's display, another with vaguely Indochinese motifs, and a house in the style of equatorial Africa, the Jardin Botanique Colonial began to look more and more like a colonial theme park [Figure 2.2].

Many soldiers from the colonies fought and died for France in the First World War, and the botanical garden was commandeered as a hospital for the wounded

Figure 2.2
The Jardin Botanique
Colonial, Paris.
Photographs 2016. Sou
Daniel E. Coslett. The
1922 Tunisian pavilion a
statue of Eugène Étienr
(A, top). Fragments of
Belloc's monument "to
glory of French colonial
expansion" (B, bottom).

among them during the conflict; a (temporary) mosque set up for Muslims was one of the first officially recognized Islamic places of worship in France. The botanical garden thus seemed a suitable place to erect memorials in honor of the soldiers after the war. The most impressive was a Vietnamese *dinh*, a communal hall, constructed in Vietnam and transported to France, where it was placed within a copse of bamboo, facing a huge incense urn and ceremonial screen [Figure 2.3]; inside the edifice was a rescript from the Vietnamese emperor, who visited the site when he toured Paris in 1922.[6] Nearby was a memorial to Christian soldiers from Vietnam and Cambodia who had died for France during the First World War. An eagle stood atop the Malagasy memorial, symbol of the dynasty of the Imerina kingdom (which the French had abolished when they made Madagascar a colony during the 1890s). A large stone monument depicting a woman and child looking sadly towards the graves of their loved ones honored African soldiers, and there was also a stele in memory of the *tirailleurs sénégalais*, the troops from western Africa who had made a dramatic impression on the French with their valor during the war.

Over the next forty years, the botanists and agronomists at the Jardin Botanique Colonial continued their work, and old soldiers, military and colonial dignitaries, and representatives of diasporic communities regularly gathered for remembrance services at the memorials. The winding down of the Empire and the reorganization of research and teaching institutions, however, meant that many functions of the garden were transferred to other centers, and the garden lost its *raison d'être*. While some scientific work continued, the site from the 1970s suffered worsening disrepair. The old exhibition pavillons were left vacant and untended, though sometimes occupied by squatters. The Vietnamese *dinh* burned — though it is uncertain whether arson was involved or whether the conflagration was accidental. A hailstorm shattered roofs of the greenhouses. To a visitor in the early 2000s, the site seemed a dramatic representation of the ruins of empire. Toppled and broken statuary once meant to adorn a monument "to the glory of French colonial expansion" (which, in fact, was never erected) lay in the overgrown forest, buildings were decrepit with broken windows, sagging verandas and holes in roofs, and a statue of Eugène Étienne, the leader of the colonial lobby, stood forlornly surveying the remains of the garden and the vanished colonies [see Figure 2.2]. A Vietnamese memorial house had nevertheless been reconstructed, the striking vermilion walls of the small edifice standing against the green stands of bamboo offering an exotic and touching reminder of Indochine Française and the service of its soldiers in the world wars — though subliminally also an intimation of the long war of independence fought by a later generation of Vietnamese against the French. The whole garden remained unsignposted, so few visitors could reconstruct its history or even identify the buildings left standing.

As even greater degradation of the site threatened, authorities decided to act, although not without debates about who held responsibility — the veterans' ministry, the education ministry, the *ministère de l'outre-mer*, the municipal government of Nogent-sur-Marne or Paris, or some other agency. Finally, a fence was erected around the site, and signage was installed that informs visitors about its history. The garden was rebaptised the "Jardin Tropical de Paris," and now hosts several research institutes; temporary exhibitions have also been held in the garden. It is billed as a "campus for sustainable development, ecology and equity."[7]

The Nogent venue nevertheless remains a relatively little-known stop on the tourist itinerary, though one of the most evident, and poignant, reminders of France's colonial past. It does not offer a comprehensive, or critical, view of French colonialism, but such was not the objective of those responsible for its conservation and present-day use. An outdoor "museum" of colonial architecture and motifs, a collection of war memorials, a recollection of the scientific and commercial activities of the French overseas, and a visual elegy to the grand ambitions of the colonial lobby, the Jardin Tropical testifies to the triumph of French colonialism, the occlusion of the colonial past in the last decades of the twentieth century, and the more recent rediscovery and conservation of France's colonial history and heritage.

THE MUSÉE COLONIAL AND THE SITE OF THE 1931 EXPOSITION COLONIALE

The Exposition Coloniale Internationale, held over six months in 1931, attracted eight million visitors to Paris and was the greatest colonialist jamboree in France.[8] Organized by France's colonial elder statesman, Marshal Hubert Lyautey, and spread out over a vast area in the Bois de Vincennes in eastern Paris, the fair was designed to show off the French Empire, to stimulate colonialist sentiment and to revivify a working-class area of the city. Each of France's colonies and protectorates was represented, as were those of other colonial powers, from Denmark to the US, though the UK (which had held its own colonial fair at Wembley in 1924) declined to take part. Some pavilions displayed the art, architecture, and handcrafts of the colonies; others were organized by the French military, business organizations, missionary societies, and the press. A reproduction of one part of the grand temple at Angkor Wat was the most impressive edifice, flood-lit at night and the stage for performances of traditional Khmer dancing.

The displays, however, were also designed to showcase French "achievements" in political, economic, and social development in the colonies, to advertise the policy of *mise en valeur* (a phrase used for the "valorization" of human and natural resources through the building of infrastructure and socio-economic development) that had become a watchword in the 1920s, and to convince spectators of the invaluable benefits — primary products, commercial profits, land for settlers, geopolitical advantage, military bases, and manpower — that the colonies brought to France. On show, too, was the beneficence of French rule.

In short, the Exposition Coloniale was overtly designed as propaganda, providing edification, education, and entertainment as well. The public, by and large, proving responsive, took advantage of the possibility of "visiting the world in a single day" (as the publicity promised) and enjoyed the exoticism of West Indian cafés serving rum punch, a would-be sub-Saharan village complete with "natives" brought from Africa for the show, and a North African market.

Most of the buildings were temporary constructions, demolished at the end of the exposition. Among those that remained were the pavilions of Togo and Cameroon — constructed in West African style — which are now, somewhat improbably, temples that form part of the Buddhist International Centre in the Bois de Vincennes. Another structure, a Catholic church, was slated for demolition, but the Cardinal-Archbishop of Paris arranged for it to be dismantled and rebuilt in the Paris suburb of Épinay-sur-Seine. Notre-Dame des Missions, with Indochinese tile façade, a minaret-inspired bell tower, and other exotic motifs, as well as murals chronicling the history of French evangelization and martyrdom, remains a functioning parish. It was formally classified as a French "historical monument" in 1994.

The building explicitly meant to survive from the exposition was the Musée Permanent des Colonies — the name an indication of its intended use and perhaps also of hopes for the permanency of the Empire. After several years of refurbishing at the end of the fair, it reopened in 1935 as the Musée de la France d'Outre-Mer.[9] Constructed in modernist style just behind the western (city-side) entry to the Bois de Vincennes, the exterior boasted the world's largest sculpted bas-relief (by

Figure 2.4
The Musée Permanent des Colonies, Paris (Laprade, 1931). Photograph 2014. Source: Daniel E. Coslett.

Figure 2.5
The sculpted façade (by Alfred Janniot) of the Musée Permanent des Colonies, Paris (Laprade 1931). Photograph 201
Source: Daniel E. Coslet

Alfred Janniot), a panorama of the goods colonies gave to France, an extraordinary depiction of "natives," agriculture, fishing, mining, ports, and commerce [Figures 2.4 and 2.5]. Visitors were also greeted by a gilt statue of Athena wearing a Gallic helmet, executed by Léon Drivier, that stood on the building's front steps and represented French imperial mastery of art, industry, and war [Figure 2.6].[10] The four walls of the museum's great hall, the *salle des fêtes,* were covered in frescoes that,

...re 2.6
statue of Athena
éon Drivier, Paris.
...tograph 2014. Source:
...iel E. Coslett. Originally
...ed outside the entry
...he Musée Permanent
Colonies, the statue
...v overlooks a square
...icated to veterans of
war in Vietnam that
...s once the entry (Porte
...onneur) to the 1931
...osition.

complementarily, showed what France had given to the colonies, with images of doctors, educators, law-givers, and scientists [Figure 2.7]. Two grand reception rooms were filled with Art Deco furniture made from tropical woods, and murals evoking traditional African and Asian cultures and religions. Motifs throughout the building in stone, ironwork, painting, and sculpture were taken from the colonies. From its reopening until 1960, the building presented exhibitions of art from

the colonies, indigenous artifacts, and commercial products. Though the displays inevitably dated, and the number of visitors declined as the Empire unraveled, the museum remained a popular attraction, in particular because of the aquarium it housed.

In 1960 — the year of independence for most of France's sub-Saharan colonies and two years before the independence of Algeria — the Minister of Culture, André Malraux, decreed that the museum would be renamed and turned into the Musée des Arts Africains and Océaniens. The change was not just one of necessary re-branding, but an effort to indicate France's new policies towards and continued engagement with its formerly colonized territories in the Third World, as well as its continued appreciation of what had once been labeled the "primitive" art of Africa and Oceania. France proclaimed itself a mentor for newly liberated African countries, a privileged interlocutor between Europe and Africa, and a guardian of African artifacts that had arrived in France as booty of conquest, donations from colonials or purchases on the vibrant "primitive art" market in Paris. In Oceania, France continued to administer New Caledonia, French Polynesia, and Wallis and Futuna (as it still does), and thus the museum remained in a way a display of France's residual *outre-mer*.[11]

The development of the Musée des Colonies was intertwined with that of another institution, the Musée de l'Homme (Museum of Man), built in the Place du Trocadéro for another international exhibition, in 1936. The Musée de l'Homme replaced an earlier ethnographical museum established in a nearby site in the late nineteenth century, but was meant to be a more scientific presentation of global cultures in line with the anthropological perspectives of the inter-war years, though as Alice Conklin has shown, the museum retained much of

Figure 2.7
A portion of Bouquet's mural (restored in 2011) in the *salle des fêtes* of the Musée Permanent des Colonies, Paris. Photograph 2014. Five continents are allegorically represented surrounding a maternal France. North America is featured at right. Source: Daniel E. Coslett.

a colonial cast and a colonialist discourse.[12] While the Musée de l'Homme was meant to be scholarly and highlight the daily life and material culture of non-European societies, the Musée des Arts Africains and Océaniens focused, as its name indicated, on the plastic and aesthetic, rather than the functionalist, qualities of works from overseas.

From the 1960s onwards, the two museums, working in a relationship of fraternal rivalry, produced a noteworthy succession of exhibitions, though generally avoiding head-on reminders of colonialism. The Musée de l'Homme tried to distance itself from the colonial period and ideology in its displays, and the Musée des Arts Africains et Océaniens literally tried to hide its colonial past. It was not possible to cover up the exterior bas-relief, but the *salle des fêtes* was simply closed to the public, and used as a storeroom for the museum's large collection of art. "Colonialist art," the successor to the Orientalist art of the nineteenth century, including paintings and sculptures produced by French artists overseas, either travelers or those who settled in the colonies and sometimes taught in the art academies the French had founded in places such as Algiers and Hanoi, as well as works by indigenous artists trained in the European tradition. The works generally depicted the colonies in bucolic fashion with scenes of picturesque deserts and rivers, tidy villages, and colorful markets, in addition to attractive "typical" people. Some of the paintings and sculptures were only second-rate art, though still of historical interest, but others were highly accomplished works. However, not only did the generally academic style of the paintings become old-fashioned in the age of high modernism, abstract expressionism and other avant-garde movements, but the figurative exoticism and the implicit or explicit colonialism rendered their display increasingly awkward. The works were therefore mothballed out of sight, a hardly subtle way of hiding the history of French colonialism and artistic movements it engendered.[13]

From the 1970s on, French authorities embarked on a program of *grands projets* for the capital, created new museums in Paris — the Centre Georges Pompidou, the Musée d'Orsay, the Institut du Monde Arabe (Arab World Institute) — and made plans for the renovation and extension of the Musée du Louvre and the Asian arts museum, the Musée Guimet. The Musée de l'Homme and the Musée des Arts d'Afrique et d'Océanie (as the Bois de Vincennes institution was now called) also came up for discussion [Figure 2.8]. The former, up-to-date in the 1930s, was now considered out-of-date in both scholarly and museographical senses, despite its popularity with the public. The Musée des Arts d'Afrique et d'Océanie was in worse straits, losing its "clientele" of visitors, thought of as something of an exile by curators appointed to work there, and even an embarrassment in a France increasingly discomforted by its imperial record.

After much discussion, those who managed national museums decided on a radical plan, which, despite some protests from curators, scholars, and the public, was put into place. A new museum would be created for the arts of Africa, Oceania, and pre-Columbian America, the combination of geographical areas having no particular logic other than the now taboo "primitive art" compendium. The

Figure 2.8
The Institut du Monde Arabe (Arab World Institute), Paris (Nouvel 1987). Photograph 201▮
The building's iconic façade panels reference Arab *mashrabiya* patte▮
Source: Daniel E. Cosle

museum was thus named the Musée du Quai Branly because of its Paris location, with the name Jacques Chirac more recently added in honor of the former president and guiding force behind the museum.[14] The Musée de l'Homme would be turned largely into a museum of prehistory, and its other collections disbursed to the new Quai Branly museum and another new institution, the Musée des Civilisation de l'Europe et de la Méditerranée in Marseille, opened in 2013.[15]

Various suggestions were mooted for the Musée des Arts d'Afrique et d'Océanie — or as the building was renamed, the Palais de la Porte Dorée in honor of its address — once it was decided that its collection of artifacts and paintings would be shifted to the Musée du Quai Branly. One idea was that it become a museum of colonialism, though this gained little support (and a controversial plan for a colonial museum in Marseille came to naught).[16] Another was that it be turned into a museum of Art Deco, in line with the design of the building itself, or a more generalized museum of decorative arts. In the end, the decision was made that it would become the Cité Nationale de l'Histoire de l'Immigration (National Center for the History of Immigration), the word "*cité*" (also used for suburban housing estates populated by many migrants) chosen to indicate its wider brief as a research center and public forum rather than a simple museum. The new vocation was, at the least, curious. Though much of France's postwar immigration has come from the former colonies in the Maghreb and North Africa, historically there have been other large currents of migration — from Italy, Portugal, Poland, and other European and non-European countries. Moreover, displaying the history of the migration of North Africans, black Africans and West Indians in a décor that explicitly references colonialism (but fully avoids the depredations of colonialism) seemed questionable.

The plan nevertheless went ahead, and the Cité de l'Histoire de l'Immigration duly opened, though without fanfare because of the debates the project had incited about the repurposing of the old colonial museum in this way, in 2007.[17] It essayed new museographical techniques — increased use of audio-visual methods, a limited number of items on display rather than overcrowded vitrines, a more vernacular approach that curators hoped would draw into the museum a multicultural audience and people not usually counted among the cohort of museum visitors. An exhibition on *Les Étrangers au temps de l'Exposition Coloniale de 1931* (Foreigners at the Time of the 1931 Colonial Exposition) directly addressed the history of the building and colonialism, and there has also been an exhibition on Algerians in France during the Franco-Algerian War of 1954–62. Other exhibitions have covered such subjects as Italian, Polish, and Armenian migration to France, Franco-German relations, sacred sites in the Mediterranean, Ellis Island, immigration as seen in comic books, and photographs of "gypsy worlds."[18] Since opening, the institution has also changed its name to the Musée National de l'Histoire de l'Immigration and adopted a stylized image of the building for its logo [Figure 2.9].

THE CHARONNE MÉTRO STATION

Colonialism produced its opposite, but the state was hardly eager to consecrate sites of anti-colonialism. Ones that recall opposition to empire nevertheless exist in Paris, though often not signposted (or only recently so). An anti-colonial exposition of 1931 was held in the Place du Colonel-Fabien, now dominated by the headquarters of the French Communist Party. In the year of the colonial exhibition,

ure 2.9
advertisement for
e Musée National de
istoire de l'Immigration
the Paris Métro.
otograph 2014. Source:
niel E. Coslett. Note the
useum's architectural
go in the top left corner.

students at the Maison de l'Indochine (now the Maison des Étudiants de l'Asie du Sud-Est) demonstrated against the inauguration of the residential college in the Cité Universitaire because of the bloody repression of a rebellion in Vietnam. Outside of one of Ho Chi Minh's Paris residences a privately erected plaque pays tribute to the leader of the Vietnamese nationalist movement. In recent years, the French government has created a modest monument to the enslaved and the abolition of slavery in the Jardin du Luxembourg, and the Paris city council (in which Socialists held the majority of seats), more controversially, in 2001 affixed a plaque to a parapet bordering the Seine in memory of protestors against the Franco-Algerian War who were thrown into the river by police and drowned in October 1961 near the Place Saint-Michel [Figure 2.10]. It also named a square in the Latin Quarter after Maurice Audin, a young anti-war activist who died in police custody in Algiers in 1957.

One of the most potent anti-colonial sites is the Charonne Métro Station, where on February 8, 1962, police, under orders of the police prefect, Maurice Papon (who was convicted in 1998 for crimes against humanity because of his role in the deportation of French Jews to extermination camps during the Second World War), attacked a crowd of 30,000 Algerians protesting against the war. The march though Paris had been peaceful, carefully guided by its leaders, and with protestors unarmed. The police attack pushed the crowds down the stairway and into the entrance to the underground station, crushing many in the mêlée; nine died.[19] The action, though defended by authorities, helped turn French opinion more resolutely against a war that, since 1954, had pitted nationalist Algerians (and their French supporters) against the *Français d'Algérie* or *pieds-noirs*, the descendants of European settlers, and their defenders. The war was particularly

Figure 2.10
Massacre of 1961 memorial plaque at the Saint-Michel Bridge, Paris. Photograph 2014. Source Daniel E. Coslett. "To the memory of numerous Algerians killed during the bloody repression of the peaceful protest of October 17, 1961," reads the marker that was installed in 2001.

ugly. It was punctuated with bombings, assassinations, torture, and the mutilation of cadavers, and the violence had spread to the metropole, where President de Gaulle was wrestling with whether to pursue a war that France was losing, in a diehard move to protect the lives and property of the one million *pieds-noirs*, or to give independence to the seven million Algerians. Discord tore apart French and Algerian populations, and de Gaulle narrowly escaped an attempt by right-wing extremists to assassinate him in August 1962. The protests, such as those now commemorated by a plaque on the Seine mentioned above, manifested the divisiveness of what, officially, was not a war but law and order operations carried out in a territory that was, in constitutional terms, fully integrated into the French Republic.

The protestors at the Charonne Métro in 1962 enjoyed considerable support from the French Communist Party and its affiliated trades union, the Confédération Générale du Travail, which subsequently put up a plaque: "Here, on February 8, 1962, during a demonstration by the people of Paris for peace in Algeria, nine men and women workers, Communists, militants of the CGT, the youngest of whom was sixteen years old, died the victims of repression." There follow the names of the victims, who were buried in the Père-Lachaise cemetery near the Mur des Fédérés, an iconic site where thousands of supporters of the Commune of 1871 had been gunned down by government troops. The Charonne massacre has gained a place in the memory of the French left: a song was composed about the incident in 1968, and three years later the artist Ernest Pignon-Ernest painted the stairs of the station in memory of the protestors. Leftist associations often leave wreaths below the Charonne plaque, and a ceremony is held there each February.

Not until 1999 was the conflict in Algeria officially declared by the French parliament to have been a "war," and intellectual and political debates about the war and its repercussions have continued since that time. New monuments signify diverse perspectives. In 2002, a national memorial to the 23,000 soldiers and *harkis* (Maghrebi troops in the French armed forces) killed in North Africa, as well as civilian victims of the war, was unveiled by the French president on the banks of the Seine. The three stelae, with screens where the names of the war dead scroll down, are a minimalist and sober re-interpretation of traditional war memorials, devoid of the language of heroism and glory that characterize, for instance, many First World War memorials. Several right-wing groups meanwhile tried to erect memorials in the south of France to members of the Organisation Armée Secrète, a diehard colonialist group that used terror tactics to protest the "abandonment" of French Algeria — the renegade officer who was convicted and executed for his attempt on the life of de Gaulle was a particular figure of veneration. Showing a different point of view, in February 2007, the mayor of Paris, Betrand Delanoë, presided at the naming of a square at the intersection of the Rue de Charonne and the Boulevard Voltaire as the Place du 8 Février 1962, "date of the demonstration against the war in Algeria where nine demonstrators met their death at the Charonne Métro." Thousands of pedestrians pass by the street sign and the older plaque inside the underground station each day, though many of them probably know little about the events the signs recall.[20]

OLD AND NEW COLONIAL SITES

Throughout Europe, over the past twenty years, new monuments linked to the history of colonialism have been erected, such as the aforementioned modest abstract monument in the Jardin du Luxembourg dedicated to the enslaved and their emancipation, and similar memorials in other countries with a history of practicing slavery in their colonies. Older sites connected with colonial history have provoked much debate — among others, statues of Cecil Rhodes in Britain, a veteran Amsterdam monument to Dutch General J.B. van Heutsz (infamous for the bloody conquest of Aceh in the East Indies), the stone obelisk transported to Rome by Italian troops from Ethiopia in the 1930s (and not re-erected in Ethiopia until 2008).[21] Politicians and curators have faced the question of what to do with old colonial museums that celebrated European expansion and rule over foreign countries. The grand old Dutch colonial and ethnographic museum, Amsterdam's Tropenmuseum, has undergone several redesigns and now provides a critical perspective on Dutch colonialism. The Belgian colonial museum, the Royal Museum of Central Africa in the Brussels suburb of Tervuren, closed in late 2013 for major refurbishment and reopened in December 2018. A British Empire and Commonwealth Museum was established in Bristol in 2002, but had a controversial life and closed only six years later, with many of its artifacts shifted to a new municipal museum in Bristol.[22]

Colonial monuments new and old, buildings designed to celebrate colonialism, and other empire-related sites are legion in Europe. The question of what to do with such *lieux de mémoire* that have considerable historical references, and sometimes are themselves of heritage and aesthetic value, is a difficult one. Should statues of now compromised colonizing heroes, for example, be left standing, taken down, removed from public view and housed in museums, or perhaps have plaques and signposts amended to take account of present-day views of colonialism? Should new plaques be erected in commemoration of anti-colonialism and protests against empire? What to do in the case of architectural and design motifs that were once accepted but are now viewed as stereotypical and even racist? The debates about old sites, and the way that they can be "repurposed," for various uses, forms part and parcel of a colonial *Vergangenheitsbewältigung* (coming to terms with history, struggling to overcome or go beyond darker aspects or incidents of history) that has animated discussions in academia, among the political elite and throughout the public sphere.[23] Debate has exposed old wrongdoings and reopened barely healed wounds but also occasionally led to new sorts of reconciliation, if seldom providing "closure" — though "closure," if that means a shelving of discussion about colonialism or continued "amnesia" about the colonial past is an unlikely and undesirable goal in the eyes of many. Discussions, in particular in France, have also touched on contemporary issues concerning migration and cultural pluralism, "neocolonialism" in foreign policy and France's role in world affairs, and even the endurance of outright colonialism in France's remaining overseas territories.[24]

In many ways, the colonial past stands in relief in the landscape of Europe, blatant in such manifestations as old colonial museums, celebratory statues and war memorials, but also more or less visible in public sites and in private buildings and collections, such as the stately homes built with the profits of the slave trade or colonial commerce. The colonialist "sites of memory" have become sites for contestation of the colonial past. The question that still remains largely unanswered is whether and how the "recycling" of old sites (or indeed the creation of new ones) can aid in coming to terms with the colonial past.

NOTES

1   Robert Aldrich, *Vestiges of the Colonial Empire in France: Monuments, Museums and Colonial Memories* (London: Palgrave Macmillan, 2005), and an updated French edition, *Les Traces coloniales dans le paysage français: monuments et mémoires* (Paris: Société française d'histoire d'outre-mer, 2011). Among works on particular cities that explore "sites of memory," see Christelle Lozère, *Bordeaux colonial, 1850–1940* (Luçon: Éditions Sud-Ouest, 2007).

2   Robert Aldrich, "Apologies, Restitutions and Compensation: Making Reparations for Colonialism," in *The Oxford Handbook of the Ends of Empire*, ed. Martin Thomas and Andrew Thompson (Oxford: Oxford University, 2018), 714–32.

3   Although there have been some efforts undertaken to have several Parisian streets named for slave-traders renamed, there has not yet a large-scale movement on par with current efforts to see statues of Rhodes removed in the UK or Civil War memorials razed in the US.

4   Béatrice Grand, *Le 2 avenue de l'Observatoire: de l'École cambodgienne à l'Institut international d'administration publique* (Paris: La Documentation française, 1996).

5   Isabelle Levêque, Dominique Pinon, and Michel Griffon, *Le Jardin d'agronomie tropicale: de l'agriculture coloniale au développement durable* (Arles: Actes Sud/CIRAD, 2005).

6   Eric Jennings, "Remembering 'Other' Losses: The Temple du Souvenir Indochinois of Nogent-sur-Marne," *History and Memory* 15, no. 1 (2003): 5–48.

7   Léveque, Pinon, and Griffon, *Le Jardin,* 149.

8   Note that a more modest anti-colonial exhibition, held in the same year, attracted far fewer visitors, and left almost no traces in the landscape. See Alexander C.T. Geppert, *Fleeting Cities: Imperial Expositions in Fin-de-Siècle Europe* (London: Palgrave Macmillan, 2013), chap. 6 (and chap. 5 on the Wembley exhibition); Patricia A. Morton, *Hybrid Modernities: Architecture and Representation at the 1931 Colonial Exposition, Paris* (Cambridge, MA: MIT, 2000); Catherine Hodeir and Michel Pierre, *L'Exposition Coloniale* (Paris: Éditions Complexe, 1991). See also Robert Aldrich, "The The Difficult Art of Exhibiting the Colonies," in *Colonial Culture in France,* ed. Nicolas Bancel et al. (Bloomington, IN: Indiana University, 2013) 438–52.

9   The word *outre-mer* (overseas) was rapidly replacing what was considered the outdated nomenclature, "colonies" and "empire," in official parlance. Dominique Taffin, ed., *Du Musée colonial au musée des cultures du monde* (Paris: Maisonneuve et Larose, 2000), contains studies of the Paris museum and other colonial museums in Europe. The final published catalogue was *Le Musée des Arts d'Afrique et d'Océanie*

(Paris: MAAO, 2001). Several more detailed (and beautifully illustrated) studies were published before its closure: Germain Viatte and Dominique François, *Le Palais des colonies: Histoire du Musée des Arts d'Afrique et d'Océanie* (Paris: Éditions de la Réunion des musées nationaux, 2002); J. Eidelman, A. Monjaret, and M. Routan, *MAAO Mémoires* (with photographs by Bernard Plossu) (Paris: Marval, 2002).

10   The statue has been relocated to what was the fairground's original entry space, which is now a landscaped square — ironically enough — named in honor of French veterans of the Indochina War.

11   The museum became more reflective and critical in its examination of France's relationship with the colonies, for instance, in the exhibition and catalogue *Kannibals & vahinés: Images des mers du Sud* (Paris: Réunion des musées nationaux, 2002).

12   Alice Conklin, *In the Museum of Man: Race, Anthropology, and Empire in France, 1850–1950* (Ithaca, NY: Cornell University, 2013).

13   Some of the works were transferred to, and are on display at, the Musée des Années Trente in Boulogne-Billancourt. See Emmanuel Bréon and Michèle Lefrançois, *Le Musée des années 30* (Paris: Somogy Éditions d'Art, 1998).

14   Critical studies of the Quai Branly museum include Bernard Dupaigne, *Le Scandale des arts premiers: la véritable histoire du Musée du Quai Branly* (Paris: Mille et une nuits, 2006), and Sally Price, *Paris Primitive: Jacques Chirac's Museum on the Quai Branly* (Chicago, IL: University of Chicago, 2007). On the history of display of non-European art, see Sally Price, *Primitive Art in Civilized Places* (Chicago,IL: University of Chicago, 2001), and Benoît de l'Estoile, *Le Goût des Autres: de l'Exposition coloniale aux Arts premiers* (Paris: Flammarion, 2007).

15   For an astute critical analysis of this and other new museums, see Herman Lebovics, "The Future of the Nation Foretold in its Museums," *French Cultural Studies* 25, no. 3–4 (2014): 290–98.

16   The Musée de la Méditerranée that was built (on the site designated for a colonial museum) was, in a sense, a replacement for the aborted project.

17   Maureen Murphy, *Un Palais pour une cité: du Musée des colonies à la Cité nationale de l'histoire de l'immigration* (Paris: Réunion des musées nationaux, 2007).

18   Laure Blévis, et al., eds., *1931: Les étrangers au temps de l'Exposition colonial* (Paris: Gallimard/CNHI, 2008). The old aquarium still exists and is open to the public within the building.

19   Jim House and Neil MacMaster, *Paris 1961: Algerians, State Terror, and Memory* (Oxford: Oxford University, 2006).

20   There are, of course, various sites in Paris that hold particular significance for certain communities linked to France's colonial past. For North Africans, these include the 1926 Paris Grand Mosque (see Moustafa Bayoumi, "Shadows and Light: Colonial Modernity and the Grand Mosque of Paris," *Yale Journal of Criticism* 13, no. 2 (2000): 267–92), the Muslim cemetery in Bobigny (see Marie-Ange d'Adler, *Le Cimetière musulman de Bobigny: lieu de mémoire d'un siècle d'immigration* (Paris: Éditions Autrement, 2005), and the *quartiers* with a concentration of North Africans, around Barbès-Rochechouart, Belleville, and the Goutte d'Or.

21   See, e.g., Elizabeth Kowaleski Wallace, *The British Slave Trade and Public Memory* (New York: Columbia University, 2006), and J.R. Oldfield, *"Chords of Freedom": Commemoration, Ritual and British Transatlantic Slavery* (Manchester: Manchester University, 2007). See also Marcello and Carter's chapter in the present volume.

22   On colonial sites in some other European cities, see Ulrich van der Heyden and Joachim Zeller, *Kolonialmetropol Berlin: Eine Spurensuche* (Berlin: Berlin Edition, 2002); Ewald Vanvugt, *De maagd en de soldaat: Koloniale monumenten in Amsterdam en elders* (Amsterdam: J. Mets, 1998); Matthew G. Stanard, *The Leopard,*

the Lion, and the Cock: Colonial Memories and Monuments in Belgium (Leuven: Leuven University Press, 2019); Krystyna von Henneberg, "Monuments, Public Space, and the Memory of Empire in Modern Italy," *History and Memory* 16, no. 1 (2004): 37–85. See also the chapter on Berlin by Rozas-Krause in the present volume.

23   There is a growing literature on this subject. See among other works, Robert Aldrich, "The Colonial Past and the Post-Colonial Present," in *The French Colonial Mind*, Vol. *2: Violence, Military Encounters, and Colonialism*, Martin Thomas, ed. (Lincoln, NE: University of Nebraska, 2011), 334–56. Other works include *Histoires coloniales: Héritages et transmissions* (Paris: Éditions de la Bibliothèque publique d'information/ Centre Pompidou, 2007); Nicolas Bancel, et al., eds., *Ruptures postcoloniales: Les nouveaux visages de la société française* (Paris: La Découverte, 2010); Patricia Lorcin, ed., *Algeria and France, 1800–2000: Identity, Memory, Nostalgia* (Syracuse, NY: Syracuse University, 2006); and Kathryn Edwards, *Contesting Indochina: French Remembrance between Colonization and Cold War* (Berkeley, CA: University of California, 2016).

24   On these issues, see Alec G. Hargreaves, ed., *Memory, Empire, and Postcolonialism: Legacies of French Colonialism* (Lanham, MD: Lexington, 2005); Herman Lebovics, *Imperialism and the Corruption of Democracies* (Durham, NC: Duke University, 2012), as well as Ralph Ghoche's chapter in the present volume.

3

The Axum Obelisk

Shifting concepts of colonialism and empire in Fascist and 21st-century Rome

Flavia Marcello and Aidan Carter

Most known for its stunning ancient monuments, many of which attest to its seven centuries of ancient imperial achievements, Rome was also capital of a Fascist empire (1936–43) that included Greece's Dodecanese islands, Albania, Libya, and the Horn of Africa [Figure 3.1]. Rome harbors numerous remnants of this much smaller and shorter-lived Fascist empire, but they have been easily forgotten or ignored. The street names of the African Quarter (*Quartiere Africano*), created in the 1930s on the northern edge of Rome between Via Nomentana, Via Salaria, and the Aniene River, are all, as the name suggests, African.[1] Other perhaps less conspicuous examples include the *Cinema Impero* (Empire Cinema) in the outer suburb of Tor Pignattara and the Amedeo d'Aosta bridge, whose inscriptions still glorify the atrocities committed by the Duke during the African campaign and his time as Viceroy of Ethiopia. Other buildings, such as the Fascist Institute of Italian Africa that was once in Palazzo Brancaccio, and the African Museum in Via Aldrovandi, have changed use and the traces of empire wiped away.[2] Then there is famous series of marble empire maps along the Via dei Fori Imperiali (former Via dell'impero) narrating the five phases of Roman Empire from its origin in the eighth century BCE to Trajan in the second century with a fifth map showing the Fascist empire in the twentieth century that was removed in 1945.[3] There are bas-reliefs showing episodes of colonialism and conquest on the exedra buildings in the satellite suburb of EUR (from Esposizione Universale Roma, the failed world's fair from 1942) just next to a modern obelisk, a massive monument to Guglielmo Marconi, the "Father of Radio" at the center of a roundabout. EUR, in its original conception, was an expression of empire in and of itself, which can be seen in the layout of its streets and its monumental artworks.[4]

There are also what one may call more literal traces. The monument to the 1887 Battle of Dogali (Eritrea) boasting an Egyptian obelisk on a nineteenth-century base, the mosaics and inscriptions in the shadow of the Mussolini obelisk, which stands at the entry of Rome's major sporting complex, the Foro Italico, still incites debate. This chapter, however, focuses on the Axum Obelisk [Figure 3.2], brought to Rome as war booty after Italy's 1936 colonization of Ethiopia and finally returned

in 2005 and re-erected there in 2008. The story of this obelisk — a 24-meter granite grave marker dating to the fourth century — demonstrates that it was both a visual signpost in Rome's urban experience to orient people in the city and a historical signpost whose shifting symbolism tells of the difficult heritage of the Fascist period and the even more difficult heritage of Fascist Italy's colonialist project.

Debates around the legacy of Fascism in the built environment center on the Fascist regime as an interval of Italian history to be reviled and forgotten, or remembered and celebrated. Scholars, politicians, and the public agree that it deserves consideration so that the past can continue to inform the present and potentially act as admonishment for the future.[5] In the months following the fall of the regime in 1943, many symbols of Fascism were erased, destroyed, mutilated or "emasculated," but this process was far from systematic and many examples still survive.[6] The colonial aspect of the Fascist legacy has yet to be properly scrutinized and its remnants in the built environment have not been thoroughly interrogated from the perspective of Italy's reconciliation with its colonial past. For example, how is it that a mosaic depicting the former Ethiopian Emperor Haile Selassie (r.1930–74) with his

Figure 3.2
The Axum Obelisk (or
Rome Stele) in the
Archaeological Park
of Axum, Ethiopia.
Photograph 2009. Sour
Ondřej Žváček [Wikime
Commons].

right arm extended in the Fascist salute is still on public display at the Foro Italico sporting complex and was never raised as an issue when debates were afire on the continued presence of the Fascist oath's rendering in stone just a few meters away [Figure 3.3]? Why did the Italian government wait nearly seventy years to return the Axum Obelisk to its place of origin after the end of its short-lived empire?

ITALY AS COLONIZER

Italy began its economic expansion into Africa in 1869 with much smaller colonial enterprises compared to the global empires of France and Britain. After a

ure 3.3
saic of Haile Selassie
ting a Fascist soldier
ile the Lion of Judah
ws in submission, 1937.
me, Piazzale del Foro
ico. Photograph 2018.
rce: Flavia Marcello.

disastrous defeat at the Battle of Dogali in 1887, Eritrea was declared an Italian colony, Somalia was taken six years later and Libya became an Italian colony after the Italian-Turkish war of 1911–12. Eritrea and Somalia were relatively poor countries and Libya was a more strategic than a resource-driven conquest. Italy coveted Ethiopia, a country rich in mineral resources that had resisted colonialist forces and had resoundingly defeated Italy in the 1896 Battle of Adowa.[7] Italy's imperialism was both economic and imitative, a pursuit of prestige and glory that was, in the words of Prime Minister Francesco Crispi, a "necessity of modern life."[8] Fascist imperialism was a "hyperkinetic form of nationalism" combined with Italy's need to use African colonies as "receptacles for her excess population."[9] Fascist rhetoric regarding the conquest of Ethiopia was two-fold. First, it fit into the general climate of *romanità* (Roman-ness) characteristic of the Fascist period wherein the revival of the glories of ancient Rome was not just limited to the cultural realm of art, architecture and literature.[10] Empire was made an actual, geographic entity with its founder Mussolini as the contemporary reincarnation of Augustus, and the title of Emperor given to King Victor Emanuel III (*r.*1900–46). Second, it was about vengeance. By defeating Ethiopia, Fascist Italy had established itself as a "bellicose and virile nation" that had wiped away the shame of Adowa and recreated the Roman Empire, "the stain of blame" had been finally washed from the records of the Fatherland.[11]

The Italian invasion of Ethiopia began on October 3, 1935, but the capital, Addis Ababa, was not taken until May 5, the following year. Like the ancient Romans before them and their contemporary British and French counterparts, once Italian soldiers and Fascist leaders gained control of Ethiopia, they looted objects of both material and symbolic value in an explicit effort to remove symbols of Ethiopian independence from the country. Paintings from museums, the Ethiopian emperor's library, money from the Bank of Abyssinia, and highly significant monuments, such as a 1930s gilded bronze statue of the Lion of Judah, were brought back to Rome. The Lion of Judah, a symbol of the nation and the emperor, signified Ethiopia's pact with God. A particularly powerful symbol, this version was produced for Haile Selassie's coronation.[12] On the night of October 17, 1935, the equestrian statue of Emperor Menilek II (founder of modern Ethiopia, *r.*1889–1913) was taken down from its pedestal. Though rumors were spread that it had been taken to Rome along with many other items, it had only been hidden.[13] One of the famous Obelisks of Axum was dismantled and transported to Rome under Mussolini's personal orders where it was to be re-erected to celebrate the first anniversary of Italy's Fascist Empire.[14] The statues of Menelik and the Lion of Judah already carried their own national meaning for the Ethiopians, but Mussolini's choice to take this particular funerary monument from Axum to Rome as representation of Fascist conquest gave it another layer of symbolism for Ethiopians, one that only grew in power as the years wore on.

With the fall of Fascism in 1943 Italy's colonial territories were occupied by British and French forces and, under the terms of the 1947 Paris Peace Treaty, Italy was made to give up all of its colonies, including those it held before the Fascist era. In order to eliminate the stigma of Fascist crimes and be welcomed into the community of democratic nations, Italy's nascent republic had to put aside its notions of imperial dignity and swallow its colonial pride.[15] The long and drawn out story of the Axum Obelisk indicates that this recognition and symbolic penance was not easily achieved.

Until the early 1990s there was a persistent myth among Italians that their colonialism was somehow different, that it was more human, more enlightened, more tolerant than its British and French counterparts.[16] This myth of the Italian as the "noble soldier" was grounded in the many defeats suffered by Italian troops in Africa over the seventy-five years of its colonial presence there, but it conveniently glossed over the 100,000 dead in Libya, the 750,000 dead in Ethiopia, and the use of gas warfare in flagrant defiance of the 1925 Geneva protocol.[17] Italy was also unlike its British and French counterparts in that it has avoided any critical debate about its colonial past. This has been partly due to the fact that Italy forfeited its territories at the end of WWII and thus avoided debates inspired by the wars of independence, like the Franco-Algerian war, that characterized the 1950s and 1960s.[18] To some degree France, the UK, and Germany have all made efforts in reckoning with their colonial and Nazi pasts; Italy is yet to do so.

Until the mid-1970s the archives of the Italian Ministry of Foreign Affairs were inaccessible and large bodies of material concerning the African campaigns were effectively censored.[19] Italy's incapacity or unwillingness to deal with its colonial past reflects the same difficulties that the First Republic (1948–92) and the Italian people had in reconciling with their Fascist past. Dealing with the past does not just mean facing up to or reckoning with historical facts and events, it means coming to terms with their moral, emotional, and political resonance and the material traces these histories leave behind in the contemporary city. Although historians like Angelo Del Boca have long made the truths behind Italian colonialism known, these difficult truths have not necessarily translated into public memory or been properly explored within built heritage.

OBELISKS AND EMPIRES: THE DOGALI MONUMENT

The first obelisk connected to Italy's modern colonial past is part of its ancient colonial history: an Egyptian obelisk brought over by the Emperor Domitian (r.81–96) to adorn the new Temple of Isis in the Campus Martius. It was rediscovered not far from the Pantheon at about the same time that it was decided to erect a monument in the Piazza dei Cinquecento (Piazza of the Five Hundred) in front of Rome's central Termini Station to commemorate the five hundred Italians killed during Italy's first invasion of Africa at the Battle of Dogali (1887).[20] In 1925 it was moved to a small garden between the Baths of Diocletian and what is now Via Luigi Einaudi. Some say it was getting in the way of the new tramlines and preparation for the construction of a new station, while others claim that as a symbol of defeat its relocation to a less prominent spot was appropriate.[21]

The monument was given new status when a spirit of vengeance inspired the placement of the Lion of Judah statue, taken from Addis Ababa in May 1937, at its base [Figure 3.4]. Placing the symbolic representation of a (then vanquished) emperor at the base of a monument to Italian defeat connected the Battle of Dogali to the Battle of Adowa and was intended to further "humiliate" Ethiopia by placing its national symbol "at the feet of [Italy's] avenged heroes."[22] The Lion was removed from the Dogali monument by Allied troops soon after the fall of the regime and kept in storage. It was returned to Ethiopia in 1969 by then Minister for Foreign Affairs, Aldo Moro, whose visit to Ethiopia was more than just the usual diplomacy; it was an important step towards reconciliation between the two countries.[23] Although it remains, for the most part ignored, the obelisk is still there as a reminder of a nineteenth-century battle and a testimony to Italy's colonial past, though no trace of its role glorifying the Fascist defeat of Ethiopia remains.

The presence of the Dogali obelisk may have influenced Mussolini's decision to bring the Obelisk (or Stele) of Axum from Ethiopia as a trophy of war.[24] From its placement in 1937 to its return in 2005, its presence incited a range of feelings in citizens, tourists, and visitors: pride, shame, curiosity, denial, outrage, nostalgia, or no particular feelings at all. Those seventy years encompass a long and complex history of Fascist imperialism, postcolonialist denial, national shame, inflamed debate and just retribution that can be told through five principal episodes: the Axum Obelisk's arrival in Rome as war plunder and symbolic representation of conquest; the post-war treaties and the rocky diplomatic relations between Italy and Ethiopia; Abyssinian athlete Abebe Bikila's marathon victory in the 1960 Olympics and the reconciliation marked by Haile Selassie's visit in 1970; the resurrection of the campaign for its return during the Second Republic in the 1990s; and its final repatriation and reconstruction in the 2000s. The conclusion

concerns its non-presence, and how the monument remains in the imaginations and memories of both Italians and Ethiopians as a reference to the short-lived colonial experience that still needs to be reckoned with.

Figure 3.4
The Dogali Monument with the Lion of Judah at its base, Rome. Contemporary postcard c.1937. Source: Author's collection.

OBELISKS AND EMPIRES: THE PLUNDERED AXUM OBELISK
AND THE MINISTRY OF ITALIAN AFRICA

The idea to bring an Ethiopian obelisk to Rome belongs to the archaeologist and Egypt expert, Aristide Calderini. In a 1939 article in *Le Vie d'Italia* he declared:

> Like the emperors who brought the obelisks from Roman Egypt [to Rome] to decorate its circuses and buildings … so must Italy bring the tallest Axum Obelisk from Italian Ethiopia for its new *piazza* to continue an ideal of meaning and tradition between the ancient Imperial glory and the new glory [of today].[25]

Although originally intended to be a centerpiece for the *Esposizione Universale* (Universal Exposition) of 1942 (E42), the Axum Obelisk was installed at Piazza di Porta Capena, just south of the Circus Maximus. It was unveiled by the Governor of Rome on November 3, 1937, in front of crowds in serried ranks while colonial soldiers saluted from its pedestal.[26] Mussolini had wanted the obelisk in place for the Empire's first anniversary on May 9, 1937, but neither he, nor the governor, had foreseen the many problems that eventually delayed the inauguration. Firstly, the all-important bottom section did not reach Rome until mid-April. The foundations had to be dug much deeper to support the obelisk's estimated 170 tons, and archaeological finds unearthed during excavations further slowed the process. Missing sections had to be replaced with the right color of granite because it was not possible to get the original stone from Ethiopia. Finally, the travertine needed for the monument's steps took much longer than expected to be delivered.[27]

The obelisk was not just symbolic — it had an urban function as both a visual and symbolic signpost. The placement of the Axum Obelisk was determined by its visibility along newly created axes and vistas: the Via dei Trionfi (now Via San Gregorio) connecting the Circus Maximus to the Colosseum, and the Viale Africa (now Viale Aventino) that linked the Circus Maximus to the Pyramid of Caius Cestius [Figure 3.5]. The Governor of Rome, Filippo Colonna, wrote to Mussolini explaining that it would be clearly visible from the Arch of Constantine but not hinder the flow of traffic.[28] This idea built on the plans of sixteenth-century Pope Sixtus V, who had excavated and restored Augustus' obelisks and had them placed in front of the major pilgrimage churches to aid with orientation. By placing the Axum Obelisk at the beginning of the Via Imperiale that would lead from the city's ancient Augustan heart to E42, and thence to the Mediterranean Sea or *mare nostrum* of new conquests, Mussolini was continuing a tradition of overlaying concepts of colonial power onto the cultural heritage of the conquered lands.[29]

With what were then felt to be substantial territories throughout the African continent, the Ministry of African Colonies needed a new headquarters. On August 5, 1937, the Minister for Public Works wrote to Mussolini giving him a choice of six sites and outlining the pros and cons of each.[30] The Ministry of African Colonies, later named the Ministry of Italian Africa, would stand as an architectural symbol of both Italy's colonialist expansion into northern Africa and the continuation of the Fascist era.[31] A design competition announced in 1937 charged Italian architects and engineers with the task of designing the building, linking it to the site of the planned E42 campus and maintaining the imperial monuments and splendor of the zone at the starting point of the recently inaugurated Via Imperiale (now Via Cristoforo Colombo).[32] The competition's second round saw the addition of a new requirement; designers had to take into account the recently erected Axum Obelisk at the building's main entrance. When no clear winner emerged from this second round the Minister began to worry that construction would be further put off and sought permission from Mussolini to award the commission to his preferred entry by architects Vittorio Cafiero, Alberto Legnani, Mario Ridolfi, and Ettore Rossi with engineers Giulio Rinaldi and Armando Sabatini.[33]

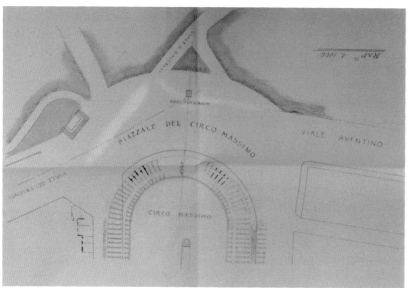

Figure 3.5
The Piazza di Porta Cap
with the Axum Obelisk
its planned location (to
Retouched photograph
1937. Site plan showin
visual axes to the Arch
Constantine (bottom). F
1937. Source: Archivio
Centrale dello Stato,
Rome.

Mussolini inaugurated the construction of the Ministry in August 1938 with much pomp and circumstance. On the site he made a couple furrows with a pick-axe to break the ground both for the construction of the Ministry and the new Via Imperiale.[34] The fall of the Fascist government in July 1943, however, meant the end of Fascist colonialism, the end of the Ministry of Italian Africa and the suspension of its headquarters' construction.[35] The complex's four buildings were far from complete: only the foundations had been poured for Buildings A and C, just five of Building B's planned eight stories had been built, and Building D had only its frames and internal wall divisions in place.[36] In the immediate post-war period there were appeals to the Ministry for Post-War Assistance to convert the

re 3.6
Axum Obelisk in
Fascist context with
erial Eagles on the via
Trionfi. Contemporary
tcard c.1939 (top)
The Axum Obelisk
ront of the newly
npleted FAO Building.
ntemporary postcard
960 (bottom). Source:
thor's collection.

ROMA - Obelisco di Axum e Via dei Trionfi

half-finished building into apartments for those whose homes had been destroyed during the war, but it was decided in August 1945 to move the Ministry of Post and Communications there and in 1950 for it to share spaces with the United Nations Food and Agriculture Organization (FAO) [Figure 3.6]. It took another eight years for Buildings B and D to be completed. It was not clear which ministry would pay for the construction and its completed spaces were used for furniture storage. The Ministry of Post and Telecommunications remained there while a new purpose-built suburban headquarters was built in EUR.[37] Throughout the 1960s and 1970s the postal department shared space with the headquarters of the FAO, who continued their move there in the early 1960s once Building D was completed. By 1980 the FAO became the building's sole occupant and it was thence simply known as Palazzo FAO.[38] Throughout the drawn-out construction process the Axum Obelisk towered over the worksite.

POST-WAR TREATIES AND REPATRIATION PROMISES

With WWII concluded, Italy agreed at the 1946/47 Paris Peace Conference, albeit begrudgingly, to return the Axum Obelisk, the Lion of Judah, and other pilfered objects to Ethiopia.[39] Although a portion of the paintings and other artifacts that were brought to Italy in 1936 were gradually returned, the Lion of Judah did not make it home 1969 and the Axum Obelisk remained in Rome until the beginning of the twenty-first century. After a much-publicized visit to Ethiopia by the known anti-Fascist Under Secretary for Foreign Affairs, Giuseppe Brusasca, diplomatic relations between Italy and Ethiopia were re-established, which led to arrangements for reparations and, eventually, to the 1956 Italo-Ethiopian Agreement.[40]

Alcide De Gasperi, then interim president of the board of the Ministry of the African Colonies,[41] may have complicated matters when he claimed that the items retained by the Italian government were nothing more than "six copper or golden-brass crowns garnished and retouched in various ways with no real value."[42] In addition, items on lists to be returned were "poorly described and therefore difficult to locate."[43] In the meantime, the Lion of Judah, from the Dogali monument's base, and the Axum Obelisk, in front of the newly completed Palazzo FAO, stood as reminders of colonial conflict that was far from resolved.

The 1956 agreement also proposed an indemnity for the return of the obelisk and items from the Emperor's library in the form of a new hospital or a place of worship to be built in Addis Ababa.[44] This suggestion and others — such as paying reparations in the form of economic projects and technology, instead of cash payments, would ensure that Italy could continue its *presenza* in Africa and keep its self-respect in the face of other "competing" nations.[45] Despite awareness on the part of the Italian authorities of the Axum Obelisk's psychological and symbolic value, the government did give the impression it wanted to repair the wrong. Claims were still being made that the obelisk was a gift to the Italian people and other more dubious pretexts such as the monument now symbolizing the unity of Italian and Ethiopian peoples were also used.[46] The then ambassador Giulio Pascucci-Righi maintained that the Ethiopians attached no sentimental, cultural, or economic value to its return, an impression bolstered by what Italians chose to see as Ethiopian Emperor Selassie's detachment from the whole affair. In fact, the continued presence of Lion and Obelisk in Rome was actually a barrier to any official return visit on his part.[47]

TWO ETHIOPIANS TRIUMPH IN ROME: ABEBE BIKILA AT THE 1960 OLYMPICS AND HAILE SELASSIE'S OFFICIAL VISIT

The political redolence of the Axum Obelisk was revived during the 1960 Olympic Games, which were hosted by Rome at its Foro Italico (ex-Foro Mussolini) and EUR sites, where little was done to reprogram the country's recent Fascist history.[48] The Olympics' most spectacular event — the marathon — took the athletes (and accompanying cameras) past the most representative symbols of ancient, national, Fascist, and Catholic *romanità* as well as its most obvious symbol of colonialism.[49] Starting at the Campidoglio, athletes ran through the ancient imperial fora, around the Colosseum, past the Axum Obelisk, and down Via Cristoforo Colombo through EUR, before taking a section of Rome's Grande Raccordo Anulare (ring road). The return route took contestants up the ancient Appian Way, through the ancient wall at the Porta San Sebastiano and past the Axum Obelisk again, before ending along a section of the ancient emperors' triumphal route at the Arch of Constantine. Ethiopian Abebe Bikila won the marathon in his bare feet. It is very likely that the irony of his triumph was not lost on him as he twice passed the symbol of his nation's humiliation [Figure 3.7].

Italian responses to Bikila's victory were varied. Newspapers reported that during the race someone from the crowd shouted "Go Selassie!" and the journalist suggested that his win recalled the first act of Verdi's *Aida* in which it is announced that the Ethiopian armies are marching towards Thebes.[50] It was also suggested that Bikila may have accelerated on passing the obelisk to break the world record at the triumphal Arch of Constantine.[51] Newspapers noted that Bikila was a member of Ethiopia's imperial guard who came from nowhere and

Figure 3.7
Abebe Bikila winning the marathon at the 1960 Rome Olympics. Photograph 1960. Source: Comitato organizzatore dei Giochi della XVII Olimpiade [Wikimedia Commons].

triumphed on the same path as the victorious emperors of antiquity. Compellingly, some reporters mention all the great monuments the runners passed on the marathon route, including the Roman Forum, the Circus Maximus, the Appian Way, the Arch of Constantine, but failed to list the Axum Obelisk.[52] The Italian national television company, RAI, was the first to transmit extensive coverage of the events with footage of the marathon showing suggestive views of the torch-lit Appian Way and the Arch of Constantine. The Axum Obelisk is hardly discernible in these images and may well have been intentionally left in darkness.[53] The only political comment of the time appeared in the weekly left-leaning political magazine *l'Espresso,* which published a satirical cartoon on the subject; two Fascists reading the headline — "An Abyssinian wins the marathon on the triumphal route" — note that Tambroni (the Christian Democrat who had recently ruled the country with the support of the far-right — essentially Fascist — Movimento Sociale Italiano party) would never have allowed it.[54]

Bikila's victory did not help the process of repatriating Ethiopia's displaced cultural heritage. In 1968 the Ethiopian Emperor took a stand by refusing to visit Italy until the obelisk was returned, leading to the suspension of trade and diplomatic relations between the two countries.[55] The Lion of Judah statue was returned in 1969, thanks to Moro's efforts, while the Axum Obelisk remained in Rome continuing its torment of the Ethiopian population both in Rome and in Africa. The Lion's return helped ease some of the tension and Selassie finally visited Rome in November 1970. Newspapers talked of reconciliation, friendship, and reciprocal trust. Selassie avoided any mention of "Fascist aggression" in the interests of peace and focused his speech on Italy's contribution to Africa's economic development.[56]

It appeared that neither side wanted to consider the thorny questions of pillage and violence that come with colonialism. The topic of the obelisk's continued presence in Rome was generally avoided during Selassie's visit. Although newspapers insisted that the return of the obelisk remained a moral issue, the government played down its legal and political aspects.[57] The issues were merely technical and a commission composed of archaeologists and architects would need to investigate.[58] If it were found that the obelisk could not be safely moved, then it would be up to Italy to pay its "debt" in another way — by building a hospital, for example, and to provide Ethiopia with a substantial loan of US$50 million.[59] The official newsreel reported on the win-win situation that this deal afforded, noting that "the sick would have a refuge and the Nationalists would be able to keep their monument."[60] When the commission found that technical issues prevented the obelisk's return it seems that Selassie agreed to exchange a symbolic monument for something that was seen as practical.[61] The *Corriere della Sera* summed up the visit as a "solemn and official closing of the pages of Italy's Fascist and pre-Fascist colonial history."[62] Acknowledging the difficulty of reconciling with this past, only the left-wing weekly *L'Espresso* spoke openly of those dark pages.[63]

THE 1990S: NEW CAMPAIGNS FOR THE OBELISK'S RETURN

Fresh demands to return the obelisk surfaced in 1991 with a push by academics and the official declaration of Axum as a UNESCO World Heritage Site. Although the granting of material aid owing to the "technical impossibility" of its return was used to justify the obelisk's extended stay in Rome, Luca Acquarelli has argued that its endurance reflects a convenient act of forgetting. Unlike Augustus' obelisks that Sixtus V had re-erected during the sixteenth century, which were adorned with plaques detailing the Pope's intervention, the Axum Obelisk received no such plaque explaining its original or applied meaning.[64] During the Fascist period its symbolism was determined by the political context and accompanying rhetoric woven around it through the various channels of propaganda. The meaning for a late-twentieth-century Italian, he contends, disappeared with the explicitly Fascist colonial context — a convenience for the government of the First Republic that repeatedly reneged on promises of its return.[65] If most people did not know what it meant or why it was there, they could hardly protest its presence. The obelisk thus remained outside Palazzo FAO in direct contradiction to its occupants' work at ameliorating hunger in Africa.

Ethiopia, however, had not forgotten and did protest. In 1996 the Ethiopian parliament held a special hearing that resulted in a unanimous resolution for the Ethiopian government to, once again, request the obelisk's immediate return.[66] This led to a formal promise on the part of Italian President Oscar Luigi Scalfaro during a state visit to Ethiopia in November of the same year. On March 4, 1997 the Italian government declared that the obelisk would be returned by year's end. Italy could fulfill its obligation and at the same time end the constant postponement that had caused the embarrassed country to lose face (the dreaded *brutta figura*).[67] Scalfaro did eventually apologize for the atrocities of Italy's colonial history.[68] The Ethiopian government was so sure that the obelisk would come home that it issued a series of commemorative stamps to mark the occasion, but the logistics of its return rendered the release premature and there was another decade-long delay.[69]

THE 2000S: THE OBELISK'S RETURN AND RECONSTRUCTION

On May 27, 2002 the obelisk was struck by lightning, posing further risk to dismantlement and transportation.[70] The strike did spark productive debates in parliament that confronted the country's colonial past and the monument's delayed repatriation head-on. To give back the obelisk meant to close the dark chapter of Italy's colonial history, it was said. At the same time, left-wing members of parliament managed to turn the discourse around to their own sense of superiority by stating that returning the obelisk would restore Italian dignity as a civilized nation by honoring treaties they made so long ago. It was acknowledged that although Italy was not legally obligated to return the obelisk, it was ethically bound to do so because it remained war booty obtained by illegal means. Commenting on the dispersal of ancient Roman antiquities throughout the world, it was said as well that Italy, of all countries, should understand what it means to have its heritage "ransacked," and thus ought to be sympathetic to Ethiopia's demands.[71] Arguments for the retention of the obelisk reiterated those deployed previously: the obelisk was a gift and had been exchanged for a hospital in Addis Ababa. Other justifications were more strident but less solid: Ethiopia would not look after it properly or because Ethiopia was part of Italy at the time of the monument's removal, it was rightfully an Italian monument.

Ultimately the campaigns organized by Italian, Ethiopian, and British intellectuals achieved their aims and in 2003 the Italian government began in earnest to organize the obelisk's return, but not without residual protest.[72] Members of the far-right (and thinly veiled neo-Fascist) party, Alleanza Nazionale, reputedly chained themselves to the obelisk while a retired school teacher in Addis Ababa criticized the decision stating that "educated Ethiopians [we]re not in favor" and would prefer that US$8 million in transport costs be spent on food security and tourism.[73]

Although Giorgio Croci, from Rome's Sapienza University, supervised the obelisk's dismantlement in July 2004, conditions in Ethiopia were not conducive to easy repatriation and restoration.[74] As the roads between Axum and the port of Massawa were no longer suitable for transporting the massive monument, it was deemed necessary to break it into three 60-ton pieces and fly it in a Russian built Antonov 124 cargo plane.[75] Progress was again stalled when it was determined that the runway at Axum airport was too short and roads and bridges to the airport would need reinforcing to carry the obelisk's weight.[76] Whilst these factors were beyond the control of the Italian government, the delay increased the emotional cost to the Ethiopian people. The dismantled obelisk thus remained in storage at Rome's Leonardo Da Vinci airport until April 19, 2005 when the first piece finally arrived in Ethiopia, with the second and third pieces arriving less than a week later.[77] It would not be until July 31, 2008 that the obelisk would be fully restored in the archaeological park of Axum and the "long controversy between Italy and Ethiopia" would be put to rest.[78]

Despite the grumblings of a few, in the weeks before the obelisk's arrival in Ethiopia, "euphoria seized much of the nation [with] parading school children … and dancing Axumites … broadcast daily on Ethiopian television"[79] as the nation anticipated its return. Ethiopia's economic issues notwithstanding, the recovery of the sacred Axum Obelisk allowed Ethiopia to restore the integrity of its rich history, relocate its symbolic dimensional identity, and look towards its future.[80] At the September 4 unveiling, a solemn ceremony marked the occasion and commemorative souvenirs were distributed [Figure 3.8].[81]

CONCLUSION

The Axum Obelisk was brought to Rome to carry out both a symbolic and an urban function. It inserted Mussolini into the genealogy of great imperial leaders like Augustus and Constantine, it marked the site of his new Ministry

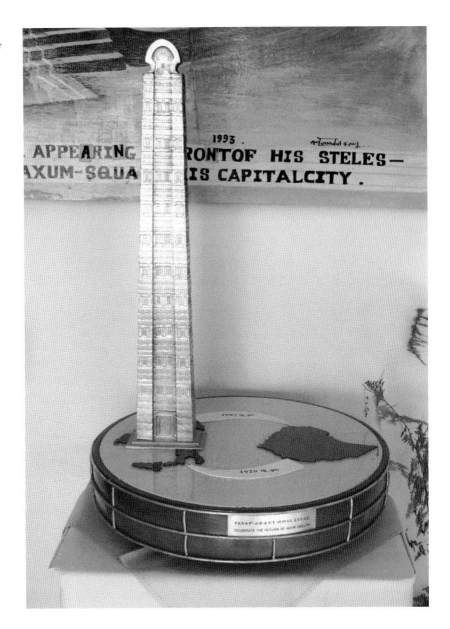

of Italian Africa and linked the ancient Rome of the Caesars to the new Rome of Fascism.

Unlike its ancient counterparts (the Egyptian government has not demanded the repatriation of its obelisks) the Axum Obelisk was a recurrent cause of significant political tension. This occurred both locally between left- and right-wing groups and in the international arena between Italy and Ethiopia drawing into its orbit both the United Nations and UNESCO. The long and drawn out conflict that led to suspended diplomatic relations and stood as a painful memory of Italian occupation among the Ethiopian people, continued to remind Italy — though perhaps less effectively — that it needed to reckon with its colonial past. Despite the fall of Fascism, the obligations of the Paris Peace Conference, and the damage it caused to Italian-Ethiopian relations, the obelisk remained in Rome as a constant and painful reminder of the Italian occupation of Ethiopia and the horrors that had been perpetrated there. The Axum Obelisk remained invisible to those who did not know its meaning, it was ignored by those who preferred not to engage with its meaning and it stood as a constant reminder of an unreconciled past to those who wanted its meaning to spur resolution. Italy oscillated between being totally blind to its colonial past and shining a glaring spotlight on it.

Today, the traces of the Axum Obelisk outside the Palazzo FAO are non-existent [Figure 3.8]. In October 2002, colonial historian Del Boca, Rome's Superintendent of Archaeology Eugenio della Rocca, and other left-wing groups campaigned for a new, smaller obelisk or plaque to be placed on the site. Something simple, inscribed with dates of massacres, deportations, the creation of concentration camps accompanied by names of Ethiopian patriots who died defending their land.[82] On the other side of the spectrum, groups of fervent neo-Fascist nostalgics have campaigned for a plaque to be placed on the spot to commemorate the Italian soldiers who died during the African campaign.[83] Arguments for replacing it with nothing were put forth by famous architects including Massimiliano Fuksas and Leonardo Benevolo, and even the left-wing urban historian Italo Insolera. Some claimed "it's a false problem," "Rome already has enough obelisks," and "no one ever noticed it while it was there so no one will notice that it is gone."[84]

There is a monument on the site today, but not one dedicated to colonialism or Africa. Rather, two fragmentary column shafts and a plaque honor those who died in the September 11, 2001 attack on the World Trade Center [Figure 3.9]. Acknowledging the innocent deaths of 9/11 in distant New York — an event that had little to do with Italy as a nation — was felt to be more important than acknowledging the hundreds of thousands of innocent deaths caused by Italian

Figure 3.9
View down via San Gregorio towards the FAO without the obelisk June 2018 (L). Monumen to the victims of the September 11, 2001 terrorist attack, near the former obelisk site (R). Photographs 2018. Sourc Flavia Marcello.

imperialism. The re-inscription of the site has perhaps displaced the site's potential to act as a catalyst in the public imagination to gain a better understanding of Italy's colonial past.

Rome is still riddled with vestiges of its colonial past, but Italy's current relationship with Ethiopia is still portrayed as positive. Premier Giovanni Conte was the first European leader to visit after the peace accord between Ethiopia and Eritrea in July 2018, and Italy still plays a significant — arguably neocolonialist — role in Ethiopia's economic development. Still, reporting on official visits obfuscates significant issues, such as the ongoing refugee crisis, and current media reports make no reference to dealing with Italy's colonial past, instead referring to the relationship between the countries as "long-standing."[85] Perhaps Italy presenting itself as the purveyor and supporter of peace is an oblique way of apologizing for its past aggression, but in the words of Ethiopian writer Igiaba Scego, Italian colonialism remains a "wound that has not healed, a wound poorly stitched up, a memory erased."[86]

NOTES

1   On empire-related street names in European metropoles, see the chapter on Berlin by Valentina Rozas-Krause in the present volume as well as Robert Aldrich, "Putting the Colonies on the Map," in *Promoting the Colonial Idea: Propaganda and Visions of Empire in France*, ed. Tony Chafer and Amanda Sackur (New York: Palgrave, 2002), 211–23.

2   Igiaba Scego and Rino Bianchi, *Roma negata. Percorsi post-coloniali nella città* (Rome: Ediesse, 2014), 28–32, 41, 99–104, and 130–32.

3   Heather Hyde Minor, "Mapping Mussolini: Ritual and cartography in public art during the second Roman Empire," *Imago Mundi* 51, no. 1 (1999): 155. The Padua version of the map is present amongst other plaques commemorating fallen Paduans in Italy's various military campaigns — including its colonial wars.

4   See Flavia Marcello, "All Roads Lead to Rome: the Universality of the Roman Ideal in Achille Funi's incomplete fresco cycle for the Palazzo dei Congressi in EUR, 1940–43," in *Civiltà romana. Rivista pluridisciplinare di studi su Roma Antica e le sue Interpretazioni*, III (Rome: Edizione Quasar, 2016), 151–77; Flavia Marcello, "The Norme of 1932 and the Fascist Concept of Monument. Publio Morbiducci's *The History of Rome Through Its Built Works*," in *The Venice Charter Revisited: Modernism & Conservation in the Post-War World*, ed. M. Hardy (Newcastle upon Tyne: Cambridge Scholars', 2009), 187–97; Flavia Marcello, "The Idea of Rome in Fascist Art and Architecture: The Decorative Program of the Palazzo dei congressi in EUR, Rome," *Interspaces: Art and Architectural Exchanges from East to West*, University of Melbourne, August 20–22, 2010; Borden W. Painter Jr., *Mussolini's Rome: Rebuilding the Eternal City* (New York: Palgrave Macmillan, 2005).

5   See, for example, Sharon Macdonald, *Difficult Heritage: Negotiating the Nazi Past in Nuremberg and Beyond* (New York: Routledge, 2009); Tim Benton, ed. *Understanding Heritage and Memory* (Manchester: Manchester University, 2010); *Modern Italy* 24, no. 2 (2019), special issue: "The Difficult Heritage of Italian Fascism." See also Håkan Hökerberg, "The Monument to Victory in Bolzano: Desacralisation of a Fascist Relic," *International Journal of Heritage Studies* 23, no. 8 (2017): 759–74; Hannah Malone, "Legacies of Fascism: Architecture, Heritage and Memory in Contemporary Italy," *Modern Italy* 22, no. 4 (2017): 445–70; Lucy

Maulsby, "Drinking from the River Lethe. Case Del Fascio and the Legacy of Fascism in Postwar Italy," *Future Anterior* 9, no. 2 (2014): 18–39; Joshua Samuels, "Difficult Heritage: Coming to Terms with Sicily's Fascist Past," in *Heritage Keywords: Rhetoric and Redescription in Cultural Heritage*, ed. Trinidad Rico and Kathryn Lafrenz Samuels (Boulder, CO: University Press of Colorado, 2015), 111–28.

6   See Tim Benton, "From the Arengario to the Lictor's Axe: Memories of Italian Fascism," in *In Material Memories: Design and Evocation*, ed. Marius Kwint, Christopher Breward, and Jeremy Aynsley (New York: Berg, 1999), 199–218.

7   Angelo Del Boca, *L'Africa nella coscienza degli Italiani: miti, memorie, errori, sconfitte* (Rome: Laterza, 1992), 111–12; Greg Blake, "Ethiopia's Decisive Victory at Adowa," *Military History* 14, no. 4 (1997): 62. For more on the Italian colonialism in Libya see: Muhammad T. Jerary, "Damages Caused by the Italian Fascist Colonization of Libya," in *Italian Colonialism*, ed. Ruth Ben-Ghiat and Mia Fuller (New York: Palgrave Macmillan, 2005), 203–08; Eileen Ryan, "Violence and the Politics of Prestige: The Fascist Turn in Colonial Libya," *Modern Italy* 20, no. 2 (2015): 123–35; Amedeo Osti Guerrazzi, "Italians at war: war and experience in Fascist Italy," *Journal of Modern Italian Studies* 22, no. 5 (2017): 587–603.

8   Christopher Seton-Watson, "Italy's Imperial Hangover," *Journal of Contemporary History* 15, no. 1 (1980): 170.

9   Robert Gale Woolbert, "Italian Colonial Expansion in Africa," *Journal of Modern History* 4, no. 3 (1932): 430.

10 Marla Stone, "A Flexible Rome, Fascism and the Cult of *Romanità*" in *Roman Presences: Receptions of Rome in European Culture, 1789–1945*, ed. Catherine Edwards (Cambridge: Cambridge University, 1999), 205–20.

11 Seton-Watson, "Italy's Imperial Hangover," 170; Giampaolo Calchi Novati, "Italy in the Triangle of the Horn: Too Many Corners for a Half Power," *Journal of Modern African Studies* 32, no. 3 (1994): 370.

12 Scego and Bianchi, *Roma negata*, 61. See also Sven Rubenson, "The Lion of the Tribe of Judah Christian Symbol and/or Imperial Title," *Journal of Ethiopian Studies* 3, no. 2 (1965): 75–85.

13 Richard Pankhurst, "Ethiopia, the Aksum Obelisk, and the Return of Africa's Cultural Heritage," *African Affairs* 98, no. 391 (1999): 234–35.

14 Suzette Scotti, "Do Unto Others as You Would Have Them Do Unto You: The Axum Obelisk," *Journal of Arts Crime* 10 (2013): 90.

15 Seton-Watson, "Italy's Imperial Hangover," 171–72 and 177; Ben-Ghiat and Fuller, *Italian Colonialism*, xvii-xviii; Novati, "Italy in the Triangle of the Horn," 371–73.

16 Del Boca, *L'Africa nella coscienza degli Italiani*, xii.

17 The worst proponent of massacres and cruelty in the Ethiopian war was Pietro Badoglio who justified the use of mustard gas as retaliation against what he termed as Ethiopian "atrocities" and was able to avoid both public condemnation by effec- tively taking over leadership after the fall of Mussolini and trial for war crimes thanks to support from London and Washington. See Del Boca, *L'Africa nella coscienza degli Italiani*, 112–19; Alberto Sbacchi, "Poison Gas and Atrocities in the Italo-Ethiopian War (1935–1936)," in Ben-Ghiat and Fuller, *Italian Colonialism,* 47–56.

18 Paolo Jedlowski,"Memoria pubblica e colonialismo italiano," *Storicamente* 7, no. 34 (2011): 1–3.

19 Del Boca, *L'Africa nella coscienza degli Italiani*, 114 and 119–20. For a full review of Italian historiography on Italy's colonial past, see ibid., 121–27.

20 For the use of obelisks in ancient Rome, see Susan Sorek, *The Emperors' Needles: Egyptian Obelisks and Rome* (Exeter: Bristol Phoenix, 2010), xiii. See also Jeffrey Laird Collins "Obelisks as Artifacts in Early Modern Rome: Collecting the Ultimate

Antiques," in *Viewing Antiquity: The Grand Tour, Antiquarianism, and Collecting*, ed. Louis Marchesano and Carole Paul (Rome: Carucci, 2000), 49–68.

21 Cinzia dal Maso, "La piazza dei Cinquecento eroi caduti a Dogali, in terra etiope," *Specchio romano. Rivista telematica di Cultura*, March 2, 2004, accessed November 27, 2018, http://www.specchioromano.it/fondamentali/Lespigolature/2004/Marzo/La%20piazza%20dei%20Cinquecento%20eroi%20caduti%20a%20Dogali,%20in%20terra%20etiope.htm; Scego and Bianchi, *Roma negata*, 61.

22 Arturo Gemmiti, "Scoperto il Leone di Giuda portato da Addis Abeba," Istituto Nazionale Luce, Giornale Luce B / B1094, 12/05/1937. The Lion is now gone and tourists sit at the monument's base with little idea of its colonialist meaning. See Francesco Conte, "A Roma c'è un monumento al colonialismo che non dovremmo ignorare," Termini TV, January 26, 2016. https://www.internazionale.it/video/2016/01/26/monumento-colonialismo-termini-roma. The rhetoric of vengeance was further bolstered by propaganda songs about Adua now being "free," "conquered," and "avenged." Scego and Bianchi, *Roma negata*, 62. In June 1938, the effect of the national symbol of the Ethiopian Emperor at the foot of a monument honoring Italian soldiers was too much for young Eritrean interpreter, Zerrai Deress, who after prostrating himself before the lion was approached by a Fascist police officer. Zerrai drew his sword wounding the officer and several onlookers. Although Zerrai was arrested and interned in a psychiatric asylum, the event saw him elevated to the status of hero of Ethiopian independence. Éloi Ficquet, "La stèle éthiopienne de Rome Objet d'un conflit de mémoires," *Cahiers d'Études Africaines*. Special edition: Réparations, restitutions, réconciliations: Entre Afriques, Europe et Amériques 44, no. 173/174 (2004): 375–76.

23 "The Lion of Judah Returns" in *Addis Reporter,* April 11, 1969, cited in Richard Pankhurst, "Ethiopia and The Loot of the Italian Invasion: 1935–1936," *Présence Africaine, Nouvelle série* 72 (1969): 85–95. See also Dal Maso, "La piazza"; Scego and Bianchi, *Roma negata*, 65.

24 Ann Thomas Wilkins, "Augustus, Mussolini and the Parallel Imagery of Empire" in *Donatello Among the Blackshirts: History and Modernity in the Visual Culture,* ed. Claudia Lazzaro and Roger J. Crum (Ithaca, NY: Cornell University, 2005), 63.

25 Aristide Calderini, "Un simbolo dell'Etiopia: gli obelischi di Axum," in *Vie d'Italia* 7 (1939): 456. Cited in Luca Acquarelli, "Sua altezza imperiale. L'obelisco di Axum tra dimenticanza a camouflage storico," *Zapruder. Storie in movimento. Rivista di storia della conflittualità sociale* 23 (2010): 61.

26 Arturo Gemmiti, "L'obelisco di Axum," Istituto Nazionale Luce, Giornale Luce B / B1194, 03/11/1937. Acquarelli cites October 31 as the inauguration date to coincide with the fifteenth anniversary of the March of Rome, which was in fact October 28, in Acquarelli, "Sua altezza imperiale," 60.

27 Letter to Mussolini from Piero Colonna, dated April 20, 1937. Archivio Centrale di Stato, Segreteria Particolare del Duce, B985, f. 174.330 "Roma. Obelisco di Axum. 1937 Collocamento."

28 Letter to Mussolini from Piero Colonna, dated March 6, 1937. Archivio Centrale di Stato, Segreteria Particolare del Duce, B985, f. 174.330 "Roma. Obelisco di Axum. 1937 Collocamento."

29 Wilkins, "Augustus, Mussolini," 61.

30 Letter to Mussolini from Giuseppe Cobolli Gigli, dated August 5, 1937. Archivio Centrale di Stato, Presidenza del Consiglio dei Ministri, 1937–39, B2117, f. 1/1-3 2366 "Costruzione del nuovo Ministero dell'Africa Italiana."

31 Mario Zanetti, "Concorso per il Ministero dell'Africa Italiana," *Architettura* (November 1939): 665.

32 Zanetti, "Concorso per il Ministero dell'Africa Italiana," 665; Arturo Gemmiti, "Mussolini inaugura i lavori per la costruzione della nuova sede del Ministero dell'Africa italiana," Istituto Nazionale Luce, Giornale Luce B / B1370, 08/09/1938.

33 Letter to Mussolini from Giuseppe Cobolli Gigli, dated July 27, 1938. Archivio Centrale di Stato, Presidenza del Consiglio dei Ministri, 1937–39, B2117, f. 1/1-3 2366 "Costruzione del nuovo Ministero dell'Africa Italiana."

34 Arturo Gemmiti, "Mussolini inaugura i lavori per la costruzione della nuova sede del Ministero dell'Africa italiana," Istituto Nazionale Luce, Giornale Luce B / B137008, 08/09/1938.

35 The Ministry of Italian Africa was not officially suppressed until 1953. L 430, April 29, 1953. *Gazzetta Ufficiale* 135, June 16, 1953.

36 "Sistemazione delle sedi delle amministrazioni centrali." Archivio Centrale di Stato, Presidenza del Consiglio dei Ministri, 1944–47, B3466, f. 10506/7.2.

37 "Nuova sede del Ministero dell'Africa italiana – Viale Aventino – Trasformazione in alloggi per sinistrati." Archivio Centrale di Stato, Presidenza del Consiglio dei Ministri, 1944–47, B3474, f. 55915/7.2; Memorandum from Ministry of Public Works to Ministry of Post and Telecommunications, April 16, 1945, "Sistemazione delle sedi delle amministrazioni centrali," Archivio Centrale di Stato, Presidenza del Consiglio dei Ministri, 1944–47, B3466, f. 10506/7.2.

38 Council of the Food and Agriculture Organization of the United Nations, Item 8 of Provisional Agenda "Headquarters agreement with the Government of the Republic of Italy," September 22, 1961, FAO Archives, Rome; Ralph Phillips, *FAO: Its Origins, Formation and Evolution, 1945–1981* (Rome: Food and Agriculture Organization of the United Nations, 1981), 48. Italy had already agreed to house the FAO on the site in 1951 and share space with the Ministry of Post and Telecommunications. Legge 9, January 9, 1951, "Approvazione ed esecuzione dell'Accordo fra l'Organizzazione delle Nazioni Unite per l'alimentazione e l'agricoltura ed il Governo della Repubbilca Italiana riguardante le sede centrale dell'Organizzazzione delle Nazioni Unite per l'alimentazione e l'agricoltura concluso a Washington il 31 Ottobre 1950," *Gazzetta Ufficiale della Repubblica Italiana*, January 27, 1951.

39 The Italian government was obliged to agree to return the Axum Obelisk to Ethiopia according to Article 37 of the Peace Treaty that stated that all objects removed from Ethiopia since October 3, 1935 were to be returned within eighteen months, cited in Patrizia Palumbo, *A Place in the Sun: Africa in Italian Colonial Culture from Post-unification to the Present* (Berkeley, CA: University of California, 2003), 21.

40 Giampaolo Calchi Novati, "Re-establishing Italo-Ethiopian Relations after the War: Old Prejudices and New Policies," *Northeast African Studies* 3, no. 1 (1996): 33–34.

41 De Gasperi was also on the board of the Museo Africano, which was an anthropological museum located in Rome that was dedicated to the people and culture of Italian Africa until its closure in 2011.

42 De Gasperi cited in Massimiliano Santi, *La stele di Axum da bottino di guerra a patrimonio dell'umanità* (Milan: Mimesis, 2014), 93.

43 Novati, "Re-establishing Italo-Ethiopian Relations," 39.

44 Santi, *La stele di Axum*, 92–94; Novati, "Re-establishing Italo-Ethiopian Relations," 37–38.

45 Ibid., 40.

46 Ibid., 40–41. See also "La stele di Axum," *Gazzetta del Popolo*, June 12, 1954.

47 Scego and Bianchi, *Roma negata*, 71–72.

48 For more on the politics of the 1960 Olympics see Simon Martin, "Rebranding the Republic: Rome and the 1960 Olympic Games," *European Review of History: Revue*

Européenne d'Histoire 24, no. 1 (2017): 59–61; R.J.B. Bosworth, *Whispering City: Modern Rome and Its Histories* (New Haven, CT: Yale University, 2011), chapter 10. On the mosaics at the Foro Mussolini, see Michael Tymkiw, "Floor Mosaics, *Romanità*, and Spectatorship: The Foro Mussolini's Piazzale dell'Impero," *Art Bulletin* 101 no. 2 (2019): 109–32.

49 Bosworth, *Whispering City*, 258; "Incidenti al Foro Italico per la cancellazione delle scritte," *Corriere della Sera*, September 11, 1960, 1; "L'ordine di Folchi," *Paese Sera*, August 10/11, 1960, 1.

50 Alberto Cavallari, "Un abissino dai piedi scalzi ha reincarnato Filippide," *Corriere della Sera*, September 11, 1960, 14.

51 Federico Cataldi, "Roma 1960: Abebe Bikila," Rai Storia, undated, accessed December 7, 2018, http://www.raistoria.rai.it/articoli-programma-puntate-roma-1960-abebe-bikila/23134/default.aspx.

52 Paese Sera, "Sulla Via dei Trionfi. Bikila maratoneta scalzo," *Paese Sera*, September 13, 1960, 7; C. V., "La maratona vinta dall'etiopico Abebe," *Corriere della Sera*, September 11, 1960, 1; Paolo Conti, "Abebe Bikila e il trionfo a piedi nudi. Roma scoprì la 'Grande bellezza'," *Corriere della Sera*, January 15, 2016, https://roma.corriere.it/notizie/cronaca/16_gennaio_14/abebe-bikila-trionfo-piedi-nudi-roma-scopri-grande-bellezza-cc264c78-bae7-11e5-8d36-042d88d67a9f.shtml.

53 Rai, "1960: le Olimpiadi della Tv," March 19, 2015, accessed December 7, 2018, http://www.teche.rai.it/2015/03/1960-le-olimpiadi-della-tv; Istituto Luce, "Olimpiadi: vince la maratona l'atleta etiope Bikila Abebe La Settimana Incom / 01972."

54 Anon., "Certo che Tambroni non l'avrebbe permesso," *L'Espresso*, September 18, 1960, 4; Martin, "Rebranding the Republic," 71. Italian news reports from 2016 that reflect on that day with a sense of historical distance stress the importance of the marathon route's taking Bikila through EUR, the heart of Fascist Rome, and twice past the obelisk that should have been returned to his country a decade earlier. Radio Rai, "10 Settembre - Abebe Bikila vince la maratona alle Olimpiadi di Roma del 1960," September 9, 2016, accessed October 19, 2018, http://www.rai.it/dl/portaleRadio/media/ContentItem-21f32b15-1ac4-4b68-bdcd-1f8bf4626b79.html.

55 Ian Limbach, "The Axum Obelisk Returns, but Some Still Grumble," *Achaeology* 58, no. 4 (2005): 10; Palumbo, *A Place in the Sun*, 22

56 Anon., "Saluti e brindisi nel primo giorno del Negus a Roma," *Paese Sera*, November 7, 1970, 16; Dino Frescobaldi, "Il Negus accolto da Saragat," *Corriere della Sera*, November 7, 1970, 2. His meeting with Pope Paul VI also required a measure of acknowledgement of the Vatican's tacit approval of Fascism's colonial enterprise. See Lillo Spadini, "L'imperatore d'Etiopia questa mattina dal Papa," *Paese Sera*, November 7, 1970, 6.

57 Dino Frescobaldi, "Il Negus conferma a Roma la sua linea di mediazione," *Corriere della Sera*, November 8, 1970, 2.

58 Anon., "Per l'obelisco di Axum solo 'problemi tecnici'," *Paese Sera*, November 9, 1970, 2.

59 Dino Frescobaldi, "Il Negus a Orvieto," *Corriere della Sera*, November 9, 1970, 2; Anon., "L'Italia presta all'Etiopia altri 50 millioni di dollari," *Paese Sera*, November 10, 1970, 2.

60 Corona cinematografica, "Roma: Visita dell'imperatore di Etiopia Hailé Sellassié," Cinemondo / CN138, 01/1970.

61 Acquarelli, "Sua altezza imperiale," 69.

62 Frescobaldi, "Il Negus accolto da Saragat," 1.

63 Paolo Pavolini, "E alla fine ha vinto lui," *L'Espresso*, November 8, 1970, 11.

64 Acquarelli, "Sua altezza imperiale," 64.

65   Luca Acquarelli, "L'obelisco di Axum tra oblio e risemantizzazione," *E/C. Rivista online dell'Associazione italiana di studi semiotici* (April 2010): 2–4.

66   Pankhurst, "Ethiopia, the Aksum Obelisk," 239.

67   Anon., "L'obelisco di Axum torna in Etiopia," *La Repubblica*, July 19, 2001, http://www.repubblica.it/online/cronaca/axum/restituzione/restituzione.html.

68   Anon., "Scalfaro chiede scusa all'Etiopia," *La Repubblica*, November 25, 1997, https://ricerca.repubblica.it/repubblica/archivio/repubblica/1997/11/25/scalfaro-chiede-scusa-all-etiopia.html.

69   Ficquet, "La stèle éthiopienne," 369.

70   Acquarelli, "Sua altezza imperiale," 71.

71   Cosimo Ventucci (Undersecretary, Presidenza del Consiglio), Titti De Simone (Rifondazione Comunista), Mauro Bulgarelli (Misto-Verdi), Aldo Perrotta (Forza Italia) — who highlighted that countries like France and Britain should be giving other works back to Italy — and Luigi Borrelli (Democratici di Sinistra – l'Ulivo) XIV LEGISLATURA, Assemblea, seduta n. 201, 9 ottobre 2002. Interpellanze e interrogazioni (Svolgimento), Restituzione all'Etiopia della Stele di Axum – nn. 2-00432, 3-00589, 3-01439 e 3-01440, accessed November 27, 2018, https://storia.camera.it/video/20021009-aula-seduta-201/deputato/$%7BdeputatoSlug%7D#iframeWebtv.

72   Limbach, "The Axum Obelisk Returns," 10

73   Anon., "La telenovela dell'obelisco di Axum: per Sgarbi, resta qui," *Corriere della Sera*, July 7, 2001, 41; Limbach, "The Axum Obelisk Returns," 11.

74   Giorgio Croci, "From Italy to Ethiopia: The Dismantling, Transportation and Re-erection of the Axum Obelisk," *Museum International* 61, no. 1–2 (2009): 61–67.

75   Ibid., 62–63; Limbach, "The Axum Obelisk Returns," 10–11.

76   Scotti, "Do Unto Others," 95.

77   Ibid., 94–95.

78   Paolo Conti, "L'obelisco conteso rinasce ad Axum," *Corriere della Sera*, May 26, 2008, https://www.corriere.it/cronache/08_maggio_26/l_obelisco_conteso_rinasce_ad_axum_6f8d4c02-2aec-11dd-9793-00144f02aabc.shtml.

79   Limbach, "The Axum Obelisk Returns," 10.

80   Haile Mariam, "The Cultural Benefits of the Return of the Axum Obelisk," *Museum International* 61, no. 1–2 (2009): 51.

81   Scotti, "Do Unto Others," 96

82   Angelo del Boca, "Ora la verità sulle atrocità coloniali," *Associazione politico-culturale Marx XXI*, April 20, 2005, accessed November 21, 2018, http://www.marx21.it/index.php/fr/42-articoli-archivio/4193-ora-la-verita-sulle-atrocita-coloniali.

83   See for example, Federale Littorio, "È stata brutalmente spezzata e rimossa la stele di Axum distruggendo il ricordo ed infangando il sacrificio dei nostri militi in Africa!," *Il Foro Mussolini*, November 6, 2003, accessed November 27, 2018, http://foroitalico.altervista.org/secondapagina.htm.

84   Scego and Bianchi, *Roma negata*, 96–98.

85   Paolo Lambruschi, *Conte in Etiopia ed Eritrea. La pace nel Corno d'Africa ha bisogno anche dell'Italia*, *Avvenire*, October 11, 2018, https://www.avvenire.it/opinioni/pagine/la-pace-nel-corno-dafrica-ha-bisogno-anche-dellitalia; Africa – Rivista del Continente Vero, Italia – Conte arriva in Etiopia, *Africa – Rivista del Continente Vero*, October 11, 2018, https://www.africarivista.it/italia-conte-arriva-in-etiopia/130073; Raffaella Scuderi, Conte primo leader europeo in Etiopia per celebrare la pace con l'Eritrea, *La Repubblica*, October 11, 2018, https://www.repubblica.it/esteri/2018/10/11/news/conte_primo_leader_europeo_in_etiopia_per_celebrare_la_pace_con_l_eritrea-208752204.

86   Scego and Bianchi, *Roma negata*, 18.

4

Postcolonial Berlin

Reckoning with traces of German colonialism

Valentina Rozas-Krause

While Holocaust memorials are a ubiquitous sight in Berlin, no memorial exists to the victims of the Herero and Nama genocide, which was carried out by Germany in today's Namibia from 1904 to 1908. As the capital of the German Empire, Berlin was the center of an expansive colonial system that used violence, genocide, usurpation, and political trickery to assure Germany's position in the African continent. The German Army's brutal conquest of what became known as German South West Africa, which led to the murder of thousands of natives in present-day Namibia, has been largely hidden beneath the veil of colonial amnesia. Yet, recent demands for an official German apology to Namibia, alongside the reconstruction of the Berlin Palace to house the Humboldt-Forum, a museum for an ethnography collection that includes stolen artifacts and human remains, have allowed obscured memories to resurface. This upsurge of colonial consciousness is manifested in public debates around reparations, provenance research, stolen artworks and cultural objects, racist and colonial-revering street-names, as well as annual commemorative marches and protests.[1] At the same time, these colonial memories, and to a much lesser degree, those who foster them, have entered museums, exhibitions, and private collections, in the center as well as in the periphery of Berlin.[2] In an effort to capture the current state of this process of recollection and memorialization, this chapter attempts to pin down this citywide phenomenon through a focused analysis of one corner of the center of Berlin, the intersection of Wilhelmstraße and a small street called An der Kolonnade [Figure 4.1]. Like many other places in the world, the corner of Wilhelmstraße and An der Kolonnade is being claimed by more than one memorial culture. The stillness and innocuous nature of the space fail to convey the intensity of the ongoing memorial dispute between its meaning as the symbolic heart of German colonialism and as the epicenter of the Third Reich. Following the interest of postcolonial scholarship in revealing the two-sidedness of colonialism, this chapter focuses on this intersection in Berlin, in order to reveal how entangled the European metropoles were — and still are — with their ex-colonial counterparts.[3]

BERLIN AS COLONIAL METROPOLE

Berlin became the center of a soon-to-be world empire with the founding of the German Reich in 1871. Germany's official entrance in the infamous "scramble for Africa," as the British newspaper *The Times* called it, occurred in 1884 with the organization of the Berlin Conference.[4] Yet, even before that, Berlin, as the capital of Prussia, had been the seat of early efforts by the Duke of Prussia — Friedrich Wilhelm the Great Elector (1620–88) — in establishing colonial trading posts in Africa and the Caribbean during the seventeenth century. Anticipating nineteenth-century German colonial conquests in Africa, Friedrich Wilhelm founded the Brandenburg African Company and established Großfriedrichsburg (in 1682), a small West African colony in the Gulf of Guinea, in present-day Ghana. The rivalry with other European colonizers, the harsh living conditions for German colonial entrepreneurs, and the resistance of the local population quickly rendered overseas trading unprofitable. In order to save its business, however, the Brandenburg African Company became involved in the slave trade, deporting and selling between 10,000 and 30,000 African natives.[5] Even though Prussia abandoned Großfriedrichsburg in 1717 and sold it to the Dutch in 1721, it was celebrated as a forbearer for the nineteenth-century colonial conquests of the Prussian-ruled German Reich.[6]

It was under Chancellor Otto von Bismarck's rule (1871–90) that Berlin became a colonial metropole, and this transformation left indelible marks in

Figure 4.1
Corner of Wilhelmstraße and An der Kolonnade. Photograph 2017. Sourc Valentina Rozas-Krause.

the city. All the colonial administrative institutions had their headquarters in Berlin: the colonial section of the Foreign Ministry and the high command of the Schutzgruppen (the colonial military forces) were particularly important in determining colonial policies. Berlin was also the seat for colonial societies and companies, as well as numerous colonial advocacy groups. Most scientific institutions involved with colonial investigations were also established in Berlin, including the Robert Koch Institute and the Kaiser Wilhelm Society (later Max Planck Society). The inauguration of a colonial museum at Lehrter Station in 1899, and the organization of large open-air colonial exhibitions and native peoples shows, reveal the degree to which colonialism was incorporated and spectacularized within the imperial city. The Empire was represented in Berlin's built environment not only by the presence of these institutions and events, but also by the commemoration of colonial ambitions through monuments and honorific street names.[7]

Despite the persistence of references to colonialism well past the demise of Germany's empire after WWI, in Berlin as well as in other German cities, the colonial past has been overlooked for decades.[8] This colonial amnesia reflected the marginal part that German colonialism has played in broader colonial histories and postcolonial theory. Overlooked because of its short duration (1884–1919) and, as George Steinmetz argues, because by the time of the later period of decolonization by European powers during the 1950s and 1960s Germany had no colonies, and, thus, no direct cultural exchange with African diaspora intellectuals from its former colonies.[9] After WWII East and West Germany each had a distinct approach towards Germany's colonial past, yet in both cases Nazi-dominated reparation and memory politics overshadowed critical engagement with Germany's colonial experience.[10] The recent resurgence of colonial memories has attempted to restore these vanished traces of Berlin's past, mainly through academic publications and guided colonial city tours.[11] Ulrich van der Heyden and Joachim Zeller's publication *Kolonialmetropole Berlin: Eine Spurensuche*, is an outstanding example of the ongoing efforts to reveal the two-sidedness of colonization in the German capital. More than fifteen years after Heyden and Zeller's 2002 publication, the demands to deal with Berlin's colonial past have moved beyond words, not only re-examining controversial street names, but also demanding a more palpable transformation of the city's built environment.

WILHELMSTRAßE AND AN DER KOLONNADE

The contrast between the remembrance of Germany's imperialism and totalitarianism is most palpable in the surroundings of the Topography of Terror, an indoor/ outdoor WWII history museum dedicated to the acts of Nazi perpetrators, located in the centre of Berlin. Only a couple of blocks away from the documentation centre of the Gestapo's headquarters, a modest plaque commemorates the site where the Berlin Conference (also known as the West Africa Conference and the Congo Conference) was held in 1884–85, marking the entrance of Germany

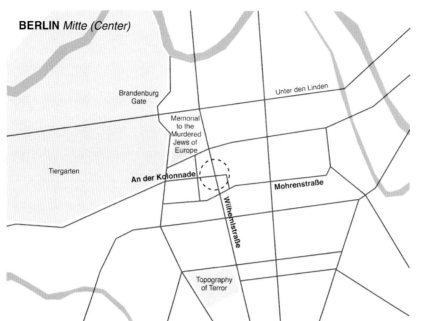

BERLIN *Mitte (Center)*

Brandenburg
Gate

Unter den Linden

Memorial
to the
Murdered
Jews of
Europe

Tiergarten

An der Kolonnade

Mohrenstraße

Wilhelmstraße

Topography
of Terror

Figure 4.2
Map of the Berlin's cen
highlighting the sites
referenced in this chap⸢
Plan c.2019. Source:
Daniel E. Coslett.

into the colonial conquest of Africa. The site of the plaque, at the intersection of Wilhelmstraße and An der Kolonnade, is perhaps the most puzzling memory site in Berlin today [Figure 4.2]. This corner is a remnant of the Wilhelmplatz, a plaza that housed the most important seat of power during the German Empire and the Third Reich, the old Reich Chancellery, which was later covered by new buildings under the German Democratic Republic (GDR).[12] Both Reich Chancellors, Otto von Bismarck and Adolf Hitler (who expanded and transformed the structure in significant ways), used the same building located at Wilhelmstraße 77/78 (right in front of *Wilhelmplatz*) as their official headquarters.[13] Before Hitler's time, two emblematic events had served to inaugurate the newly refurbished building after the unification of the German Empire: the Congress of Berlin in July 1878 (convened to determine the future of Eastern Europe after the Russo-Turkish War), and the Berlin Conference in 1884–85 (convened to decide the fate of Africa during the colonial "scramble"). On a conceptual level, the building's continuity might serve to enlighten the relationship between Bismarck's and Hitler's expansionist programs, yet the actual site of the former Reichskanzlei, at the intersection of Wilhelmstraße and An der Kolonnade, speaks of the conflict between the memories of both reigns.[14]

At first look, this intersection does not say much, surrounded by a 1980s GDR housing project, a brutalist building which houses the Embassy of the Czech Republic, a Chinese restaurant, and posted advertisements at various scales. So composed, it is innocuous, like any vernacular corner in a typical global city.[15] Yet, looking more closely, a handful of plaques, a large sculpture, sentences written on the pavement, and several other memorial interventions add visual complexity to

Figure 4.3
The two plaques of Wilhelmstraße standing side by side. Photographs 2017. Source: Valentina Rozas-Krause.

an otherwise essentially site. Ultimately, as it turns out, the site is filled with seemingly random objects and littered with memories [Figure 4.3].

One plaque, which belongs to a larger 1997 intervention on Wilhelmstraße entitled "Geschichtsmeile Wilhelmstraße" (Wilhelm Street Memory Mile) and curated by the Topography of Terror Foundation, informs passersby about the history of the building at Wilhelmstraße 77.[16] Words and historic images are combined to support a narrative that begins with the construction of the building in the eighteenth century as a noble palace. Focusing on Hitler's takeover of the Reichskanzlei in 1933, the panel ends with the building's demolition after WWII. While the plaque mentions Bismarck's Berlin Conference and the establishment of the German Republic in 1918 as two of the building's milestones, it omits the site's function supporting the colonization of the African continent.[17]

A second plaque, similar in size but different in shape, just a few feet away briefly describes the context, participant nations, and outcomes of the 1884–85 Berlin Conference in three different languages [see Figure 4.3]. Under the title "Remembering, Reconciling. Bearing United Responsibility for Our Future," this 2004 installation fills in the content void of the Wilhelm Street Memory Mile plaque. The curved panel includes historic images of the building during Bismarck's reign, a drawing of the main conference room, and a photograph of a group of Herero prisoners during the colonization of German South West Africa. Highlighting what is presented as the gruesome outcome of the conference, a brightly colored map of Africa, complete with its colonial subdivisions, adorns the center of the plaque. This map serves as an illustration of the last passage of the plaque's text, which asserts that "the Conference marks the turning-point from the stepwise expansion of diverse colonies to the total dividing-up of Africa [...]."[18] The continent's division, however, is more complex than the relatively concise text might suggest, as the meaning of the Berlin Conference has been subject to heated debates. While early African critics, like Mojola Agbebi, have regarded the event as the symbol of European imperialist exploitation, historians, like John D. Hargreaves, have argued that the Berlin Conference was the last attempt to regulate the African continent according to internationalist, civilized, free-trade principles aimed at establishing freedom of trade amongst the European and non-European imperial forces, and the well-being of the native populations.[19] Thus, it is important to distinguish between the actual historical event and what it symbolizes in retrospect. Within the context of the memory politics of this contested corner, these two dimensions of the Berlin Conference are easily conflated. With disregard to the political purpose of Bismarck's conference — a unilateral conference convened to decide the future of Africa without the involvement of a single African representative — the Berlin Conference has become the symbol of the genocidal imperialist politics that were implemented in its aftermath.

The authors of these two plaques differ significantly. On the one hand, the Topography of Terror Foundation is a federally and state-funded organization created in 1992 to manage and preserve the nearby site (the former headquarters of the Gestapo, Schutzstaffel (SS), Sturmabteilung (SA), and Sicherheitsdienst (SD) — later the Reichssicherheitshauptamt or RSHA during the Third Reich) which explains its temporal focus.[20] On the other hand, Africa-Forum, the organization behind the second plaque, is a non-governmental organization based in Berlin and created in 1996 to promote the dialogue between Africa and Europe.[21] Similar to the first plaque's omission of the Berlin Conference, the Africa-Forum plaque avoids any mention of Hitler's use of the building, focusing only on the relevance of the site for the advancement of the European colonization of Africa. It seems like the spatial proximity of these two plaques has not contributed to their mutual understanding. Yet, this is only partially true, because the more recent Africa-Forum plaque is a response to the first plaque. In the German tradition of the *Gegendenkmal,* or counter-memorial, these two plaques work together, filling each other's omissions. Counter-memorials emerged as an alternative to the removal of existing Nazi and militaristic monuments after the end of WWII. Instead of eliminating obsolete memorials, in these cases a second memorial was added in order to create a field of debate between the old and the new interpretations of the past. Conflictive pasts were thus made visible in the built environment.[22]

That parallel plaques present the two-fold history of Wilhelmstraße 77 is not an exception in Berlin. On the contrary, it has become more common as the memory of Germany's colonial past has unsettled memorial conventions regarding the Holocaust. Moreover, the two-folded approach is not particular to the treatment of Germany's colonial past, but has its roots in the fact that Germany's reckoning with its Nazi past coincided with the Cold War. Postwar memories divided along Cold War political interests shaped two distinct approaches to the Nazi past. Jeffrey Herf describes the emergence of two distinct memory cultures in East and West Germany: while in West Germany the "Jewish question" became the center of postwar memory politics, in East Germany the fight against fascism became the narrative around which memories were organized.[23] Although the reunification of Germany allowed western memory politics to prevail, visible traces of the anti-communist versus anti-fascist two-fold approach to the past remain ingrained in memory sites erected in former East Germany, and particularly in Berlin as the symbol and center of Cold War disputes. After the reunification of Germany in 1990 another highly controversial and publicly debated pair of two-fold pasts emerged within German memory culture: a theory of double dictatorships (*Totalitarismustheorie*) that equated the East German Sozialistische Einheitspartei Deutschlands (SED) and Nazi regimes. For the purpose of an official *Vergangenheitsaufarbeitung* (confrontation with the past) for the crimes of the SED regime, two inquiry commissions of the German Parliament founded a series of institutions to deal with the SED past in light of lessons learned from the difficult reckoning with the country's Nazi history.[24] Many critics, in particular Eberhard Jäckel and Salomon Korn, have voiced their rejection to equating the Nazi and the SED dictatorships. Besides pointing out the historical distortions that this parallel brings forward, Jäckel and Korn question the exalted SED-reparation policy that has derived from the double dictatorship theory.[25] Jäckel's critique of the two-folded nature of the German past is particularly interesting. Although he is not speaking about the parallel between German colonialism and Nazism, his position can shed light on the significance of the two plaques on the corner of Wilhelmstraße and An der Kolonnade, he argues that:

> Certain things cannot be said. Instead of comparing phenomena they get equated. [...] Whether the National Socialist murder of the Jews was unique or not, could only arise from a comparison with other mass murders. Yet, this is how the Germans are now dealing with their double past: avoiding comparison, certainly not confronting it, which would be immoral, all this in order to be able to equate even more self-evidently.[26]

As it stands today, the Wilhelmstraße/An der Kolonnade corner can be said to be yet another manifestation of a distinctly German Cold War-inspired two-fold memory policy that equates pasts instead of allowing analytical comparisons. Again, this is only partly true. Yes, the Wilhelmstraße plaques invoke two simplified versions of the multiple layers of history present at the site. Yet, unlike the separate memory policies of East and West Germany, or the double dictatorship theory, the plaques predate an official memorial policy about the colonial past and its relationship to Nazi Germany. These plaques still hold the potential of the *Gegendenkmal.*

Their power lies in the space between both narratives, as in the visitor who sees the plaques and draws her or his own conclusions. The question remains whether future memorial policies regarding German colonialism will follow the two-fold history precedents, or if they will be able to integrate, analyze, distinguish, and compare the multiple episodes of violence of the past more complexly.

M*STRAßE

The Africa-Forum plaque is not the only sign of postcolonial struggles in contemporary Berlin, indeed, it stands in the center of an increasing effort to put the traces of German colonialism in the built environment into question. Members of Berlin's black and African diaspora community, and its many supporters, demand that Mohrenstraße be renamed because it includes a discriminatory foreign designation for black people, the word "moor."[27] The so-called M*straße is an east-west thoroughfare and an important eighteenth-century avenue in the center of Berlin. Stretching from Hausvogteiplatz to Wilhelmstraße, it ends near the Wilhelmstraße/An der Kolonnade corner. Thus, the memorial meaning of this very confusing intersection is not only being shaped by the two incomplete, yet complementary, plaques, but it is also determined by the unresolved request to change the name of the adjoining M*street.

When exactly, and more importantly, why this street was named Mohrenstraße, are questions that have been subject to a heated debate, prompting at least one historian to argue that the word moor was not used in a derogatory sense when the street was dedicated.[28] Yet, given the street's eighteenth-century origin, one can reasonably attribute its name to early Prussian colonization in Africa. In the context of the German involvement in the transatlantic slave trade, African natives were taken to Berlin to serve in the court and in the army of the Brandenburg Elector and the Prussian aristocracy. Often underage, these slaves were known as "Hofmohren" or "Kammermohren" (court-moors). Thus, at the height of the transatlantic slave trade the image associated with the M-word was that of uncivilized slaves. In the twentieth century this racist image solidified around the character of the Sarotti-Mohr, a caricature of a black African native who for almost a century (1918–2004) was used as the German chocolate brand Sarotti's logo.[29]

Every August 23, in memory of the International Day for the Remembrance of the Slave Trade and its Abolition, an alliance of different activist groups called "Decolonize Mitte" (Decolonize the Center) organizes a street-renaming festival on M*street.[30] Political speeches, poetry readings, performance acts, and music create a spectacle that attracts activists, families, politicians, and residents alike. Every year the event culminates with the symbolic renaming of M*street, during which the existing sign is crossed off with a red stick, while a new sign is hung under the defaced original [Figure 4.4].

The M*street festival is both a celebration and an act of resistance against the backlash of historical relativists and political conservatives who want to

preserve the street name, and the inaction of the city council. Despite the event's popularity and publicity surrounding the symbolic renaming, the Berlin-Mitte city council has opposed every attempt to re-name M*street. One is perhaps left wondering how more than a decade of serious efforts to see colonial street-names like M*street change has so far failed.[31] The words of Götz Frömming, speaker of the parliamentary faction of the far-right party AfD (Alternative für Deutschland), capture the underlying threat that the name changes present. These are more than just names, he argues:

> Today it is the "Mohrenapotheke" in Frankfurt, which is to be renamed, and Eugen Gomringer's poem at the Alice Salomon University in Berlin, which is to be painted over [...] *but what will it be tomorrow?* Perhaps the many Goethe-Streets, just because there are anti-Semitic passages in Goethe's "Das Jahrmarktsfest zu Plundersweilern" [1773/8]!? Or the Aristotle-Street in Berlin, because Aristotle says that some are meant to command and the others to obey? *Where does it stop? Where does it lead!? There is probably nothing and nobody from earlier eras who would not be accused of anything if the moral gaze of today is focused on it* (emphasis added).[32]

Frömming reveals cracks in the façade of the fragile "cultural intimacy" that holds German national identity together.[33] The AfD is not alone in this position, some residents of the nearby African Quarter, a predominantly white working-class neighborhood in northwest Berlin, also fear an avalanche of cultural re-examinations will leave no German legacy standing, as one of them said in an interview with journalist Silvia Longo.[34] The Berlin-Mitte city council has recently approved the renaming of three colonial street-names in the African Quarter to honor African independence fighters instead of colonial pioneers. The city council's decision was met with strong opposition amongst local residents, which has delayed the actual renaming.[35] Within this heightened attention on colonial toponymy, to be against the renaming of M*street in particular, and colonial honoring streets in general, is a proxy for standing against political correctness, immigration, globalization, and even gentrification. This position must be read within a broader political shift in Europe, which the AfD has capitalized in Germany. Those who oppose the renaming of M*street organized themselves as "Initiative Pro Mohrenstraße" and argue that it would be a defilement of history to remove the name.[36] That the same district office has approved the renaming of three streets in the nearby African Quarter, while disapproving the renaming of M*street, is perplexing. Yet, behind this decision lie key factors like localization, income, and accessibility. Situated in what once was an industrial periphery, the working-class African Quarter presents less of a threat to the cultural intimacy, than the central M*street. Beyond class and location, there is another factor that can help to explain the resistance to renaming M*street; M*street is a taboo within a taboo, because it inevitably foregrounds German involvement in slave trade. German colonial amnesia has been slowly melting away thanks to the tireless work of postcolonial activists and scholars. Within this reckoning with the colonial past, however, German involvement in slavery still remains a contentious topic.

GEDENKMARSCH

Every February, for the past twelve years, a memorial march called "Gedenkmarsch" moves between M*straße and Wilhelmstraße, taking as its launching point the intersection of Wilhelmstraße and An der Kolonnade. The Africa-Forum plaque serves as a center around which more and more people gather every year to demand recognition and an apology for the crimes committed against black people and people of African descent. After a commemorative wreath laying in front of the Africa-Forum plaque, the march continues along M*street, passes the Foreign Ministry, and terminates at the gardens of the former City-Palace, the new Humboldt-Forum. This route intentionally stitches together sites that reveal the past and present role of Germany in Africa [Figure 4.5]. Under the motto "the duty to remember, the right to remember," the Committee for the Construction of an African Memorial in Berlin (KADIB, for its German initials) has chosen February 26th as the memorial day for the "African victims of enslavement, trade with enslaved people, colonial occupation and racist violence" to march in commemoration of the end of the Africa Conference.[37] Muchtar B. Kamara, a Berlin-based activist and organizer of the memory march, says that the idea originated from the Cameroonian scholar Kapet de Bana, the co-founder of the

ure 4.5
e 2018 Gedenkmarsch.
otograph 2018. Source:
ristian Demarco.

World Council of the Pan-African Diaspora and the Inter-African Association for Human Rights.[38] De Bana believed that given its role as a site of state-perpetrated crimes — from which Africa was arbitrarily divided — Berlin should have a memorial in remembrance of the victims of the continent's colonization. This demand has been at the core of the memory march and February 26th events. Yet, twelve years ago, when de Bana proposed the memorial, Kamara and the members of the then newly created Committee believed that before building a memorial a cultural shift needed to be initiated. The demands for recognition, apology, and reparation have thus become central in the activism of the Committee.[39] As James E. Young argues, it is the building up towards the memorial — in this case plaques, marches, protests, commemorative days, exhibitions, and performances — which is actually doing the critical "memory work."[40] However, this critical reflection would be impossible without the motivation of the actual building of the memorial.

MEMORIAL INFLATION

The Wilhelmstraße/An der Kolonnade corner, then, is not only the location of a clash between two historic interpretations of an absent building, but the starting point of the annual memorial march, and the site chosen for a future memorial for the African victims of colonization. Interviews with memory activists from the black community in Berlin have revealed that although the form and nature of the memorial is still open to debate, most agreed that the location for the memorial should be Wilhelmstraße 77 (currently number 92), the site of the Africa Conference.[41] Its historicity and centrality make it the ideal location for a memorial in a city that has erased most of its colonial traces. There is one caveat, however — there already is a memorial on the corner of Wilhelmstraße and An der Kolonnade.

A 56-foot sculpture rises high above the cars, trees, and information panels at the intersection. LED-illuminated, its steel frame shape mimics the profile of an unrecognizable man [Figure 4.6]. A nearby plaque, similar in shape and size to the other two plaques, explains that the depicted man is Georg Elser, a carpenter from Württemberg who in 1939 failed in his attempt to assassinate Hitler [Figure 4.7]. Long-forgotten and recently rediscovered, Elser was caught fleeing across the Swiss border. He was imprisoned, interrogated and tortured before being taken to the Dachau concentration camp, where he was murdered shortly before the war's end in 1945.[42] Quotations from Elser's confessions written on steel frames embedded in the nearby sidewalk add a third element to the memorial ensemble

Figure 4.6
Berlin's Georg Elser
Memorial (Klages Desig
2011). Photograph
2017. Source: Valentina
Rozas-Krause.

re 4.7
n's Georg Elser
morial (Klages Design,
1) plaque. Photograph
7. Source: Valentina
as-Krause.

created by the Berlin-based artist Ulrich Klages in 2011.[43] The memorial has been criticized for its indiscernible formal reference, but also compelling is its location in front of what used to be Hitler's as well as Bismarck's Reichskanzlei.[44] Rolf Hochhuth, a well-known German playwright and initiator of the idea for the Georg Elser Memorial, argued that its placement counter-balances Hitler's nearby bunker, a place of Nazi pilgrimage.[45] Still, it seems questionable whether this was the right place for this privately commissioned and publicly funded memorial, especially when considering that there are already more than sixty streets and plazas named after Elser, as well as thirteen memorials throughout Germany.[46] The memorial's site-specificity to the historic event, a key aspect in the construction of most memorials in Berlin, acquires a misleading meaning on the site of the former Reichskanzlei. Here, a memorial is necessary not to remember, but to neutralize the symbolic value of traces of the past.

As it stands today, the Wilhelmstraße/An der Kolonnade intersection thus presents a multiplicity of isolated memorials that rather than remember, reveal the limitations of contemporary German memory culture regarding sites of Nazi acclamation and traces of the country's colonial past. The Holocaust as a "limit event" has occluded events that came before, with a number of unsettling consequences.[47] One could conclude that, at the Wilhelmstraße/An der Kolonnade location, Elser stands in the way of an African memorial, or in other words, the Holocaust stands in the way of African memory, obscuring the latter's commemoration.

CONCLUSION

Finally, given the existing memorial landscape found at the intersection of Wilhelmstraße and An der Kolonnade, one wonders where the forthcoming memorial to the victims of Africa's colonization might fit in? This question's relevance transcends the intersection, as it applies to the larger issue of emergent postcolonial memories' place in memorial landscapes largely shaped by atonement for the Holocaust. This is particularly significant considering that some Namibian tribes are currently suing Germany for their colonial genocide in a US court.[48] Although some German officials have individually acknowledged the genocide of the Nama and Herrero, an official apology has yet to occur, and possible reparation terms have not been reached.[49] In this context, Berlin's 2016 ruling coalition-agreement of SPD, Die Linke, and Bündnis 90/Die Grünen parties included a statement regarding somehow coming to terms with the city's colonial past. A future memorial and the renaming of some streets are expected to be part of eventual reparations offered for Berlin's role as the seat of Germany's colonial empire.[50]

The place of future memorialization of German colonialism in a memorial landscape that has ignored its existence remains a challenging and contentious one. By commenting on events overlooked in the other, the first set of complementary plaques presented above, offer one alternative for this relationship between colonialism and WWII. As a political tactic, the memorial march is more confrontational because it temporarily re-appropriates the center of Berlin, exposing its colonial-era history in potentially unsettling ways. Indeed, when the march's route passed Peter Eisenman's iconic Memorial to the Murdered Jews of Europe a few years ago, it sparked a huge controversy. Black activists were accused of misappropriating a space and past that did not belong to them, while Holocaust activists were accused of covert racism by acknowledging only the loss of white lives on European soil.[51]

Ultimately, the Wilhelmstraße/An der Kolonnade corner reveals how mid- and early twentieth-century crimes have been pitted against each other in a position of rivalry, physically fighting for symbolic terrain in the same public space. Which memory will prevail in the intersection of Wilhelmstraße and An der Kolonnade? Will Bismarck, Hitler, Elser, or that of the colonized dominate? Must any one supersede the others though? This intersection in particular, and Berlin in general, have the potential to facilitate a necessary dialogue between different periods of Germany's past, in the vein of what Hannah Arendt proposed in her book *The Origins of Totalitarianism*. If we follow Arendt's argument, the Nazi regime cannot be understood without the camps and massacres that preceded it, and German colonialism cannot be understood in isolation from the violent colonial elite who pursued Germany's imperialist expansion first in Africa and later in Europe.[52] This does not mean that the political forms underlying these histories are equal. As a thorough distinction-maker, Arendt sought to illuminate the causal relationships, but also the differences between imperialism and totalitarianism. This is a particularly important lesson to be learned, considering the current double dictatorship theory that shapes reparations for the SED and Nazi past, as well as the resistance to comparisons of the Holocaust with other genocides.[53] The study of actual built environments, such as the one undertaken in this chapter, reveals that in a city like Berlin, pasts are inevitably superimposed. Such complex layering can lead to a wide array of responses, from omission and selection, to comparison and distinction. The Wilhelmstraße/An der Kolonnade corner presents opportunities for reckoning with the past, absent or present, commemorated or obscured, in an era of globalization and neocolonialism. Just as the Holocaust cannot be forgotten so that such an atrocity may not be repeated, so too must colonialism be remembered and understood in order to aid in the prevention of future state-enacted racism and exploitation. The current state of this corner, with its multiplicity of plaques and markers, is part of a fleeting present. Indeed, once official German colonial memory policies get set in stone, the Wilhelmstraße/An der Kolonnade corner will likely change and settle its competing narratives. In its current state, however, it has the potential to reveal compelling continuities between imperial and Nazi histories, as well as to inspire reflections of past and present racism in German culture.

ACKNOWLEDGEMENTS

The author wishes to extend sincere thanks to Yonas Endrias and Kristina Leko, and to the participants of the *"A Memorial in the African Quarter?"* course at the Afrika Akademie/Schwarze Volkshochshule and the Institut für Kunst im Kontext der Universität der Künste, Berlin. Special thanks to interviewees Josephine Apraku, Tahir Della, Muchtar B. Kamara, and Christian Kopp. Thanks must also go to Andrew M. Shanken, Greg Castillo, Julia Bryan-Wilson, and Paul Rabinow for their continued support and advice, and to Barry Trachtenberg and Richard J.

Bernstein for their comments on early drafts of this chapter. This chapter presents the preliminary results from dissertation research supported by CONICYT/Becas Chile 72150057, the German Academic Exchange service — DAAD, the Holocaust Educational Foundation at Northwestern University, the Institute of International Studies at the University of California (UC), Berkeley, and the UC Office of the President MRPI funding MR-15-328710.

NOTES

1   Kwame Opoku et al., *No Humboldt 21! Dekoloniale Einwände Gegen Das Humboldt-Forum* (Berlin: No Humboldt 21!, 2017); "Auf Safari Durch Den Wedding," *Der Tagesspiegel*, November 14, 2013, http://www.tagesspiegel.de/berlin/lern-und-erin nerungsort-afrikanisches-viertel-im-wedding-auf-safari-durch-den-wedding/ 9076962.html; "Neue Namen Für Drei Straßen in Wedding Geplant," *Der Tages spiegel*, May 31, 2017, http://www.tagesspiegel.de/berlin/afrikanisches-viertel-in-berlin-neue-namen-fuer-drei-strassen-in-wedding-geplant/19877344.html; "Postkolonialer Aktivismus und Die Erinnerung an den Deutschen Kolonialismus — Phase 2," accessed June 17, 2017, http://phase-zwei.org/hefte/artikel/postkolon ialer-aktivismus-und-die-erinnerung-an-den-deutschen-kolonialismus-134; Oumar Diallo and Joachim Zeller, eds., *Black Berlin: Die Deutsche Metropole und Ihre Afrikanische Diaspora in Geschichte und Gegenwart* (Berlin: Metropol, 2013); Ulrich van der Heyden and Joachim Zeller, eds., *Kolonialmetropole Berlin: Eine Spurensuche* (Berlin: Berlin Edition, 2002).
2   See, for example, Deutsches Historisches Museum, ed., *Deutscher Kolonialismus: Fragmente Seiner Geschichte und Gegenwart* (Darmstadt: Theiss Verlag, 2016); Schöneberg Museum, *Kolonialgeschichte in Tempelhof und Schöneberg – Eine Sonderausstellung*, May 4, 2017, accessed August 16, 2018, https://www.berlin.de/ ba-tempelhof-schoeneberg/aktuelles/pressemitteilungen/2017/pressemitteilung. 587714.php; *Zurückgeschaut: 1896 – Treptower Park – Erste Deutsche Koloniala usstellung*, Exhibition, October 13, 2017, accessed August 21, 2018, http://zurueckges chaut.de.
3   George Steinmetz and Julia Hell have developed this idea visually. See George Steinmetz and Julia Hell, "The Visual Archive of Colonialism: Germany and Namibia," *Public Culture* 18, no. 1 (2006): 183.
4   Horst Gründer, "Der 'Wettlauf' um Afrika und die Berliner Westafrika-Konferenz 1884/85" in *Kolonialmetropole Berlin: Eine Spurensuche*, ed. Ulrich van der Heyden and Joachim Zeller (Berlin: Berlin Edition, 2002), 19.
5   Ulrich van der Heyden, "Das brandenburgische Kolonialabenteuer unter den Großen Kurfürsten," in *Kolonialmetropole Berlin: Eine Spurensuche*, ed. Ulrich van der Heyden and Joachim Zeller (Berlin: Berlin Edition, 2002), 15–18.
6   This early colonial past left toponymic traces in the city. For example, Mohrenstraße, Guineastraße, and the former Gröbenufer (now May-Ayim-Ufer) are some exam-ples of Prussia's colonial legacy in contemporary Berlin. See Van der Heyden, "Das brandenburgische Kolonialabenteuer unter den Großen Kurfürsten"; Ulrich van der Heyden, *Auf Afrikas Spuren in Berlin: Die Mohrenstraße und andere koloniale Erblasten* (Berlin: Tenea Verlag, 2008).
7   Van der Heyden and Zeller, *Kolonialmetropole*.
8   For more on colonial traces in Germany, see Ulrich van der Heyden and Joachim Zeller, eds., *Kolonialismus Hierzulande: Eine Spurensuche in Deutschland* (Erfurt: Sutton, 2008).

9   George Steinmetz, *The Devil's Handwriting: Precoloniality and the German Colonial State in Qingdao, Samoa, and Southwest Africa* (Chicago, IL: University of Chicago, 2007), 509–10.

10   Winfried Speitkamp, "Kolonialherrschaft und Denkmal. Afrikanische und deutsche Erinnerungskultur im Konflikt," in *Architektur und Erinnerung*, ed. Wolfram Martini and Formen der Erinnerung (Göttingen: Vandenhoeck & Ruprecht, 2000), 165–90.

11   Such publications include Van der Heyden, *Auf Afrikas Spuren in Berlin*; Horst Gründer, "In Der Zentrale Der 'Weltmacht'," in *Kolonialmetropole Berlin: Eine Spurensuche*, ed. Ulrich van der Heyden and Joachim Zeller (Berlin: 2002), 19–23; Van der Heyden and Zeller, *Kolonialismus Hierzulande*; Oumar Diallo and Joachim Zeller, eds., *Black Berlin: Die Deutsche Metropole Und Ihre Afrikanische Diaspora in Geschichte Und Gegenwart* (Berlin: Metropol, 2013). Different organizations offer colonial city tours, including Berlin Postkolonial, Institut für diskriminierungsfreie Bildung (IDB), and Berliner Spurensuche.

12   The Ministry of Finance, the Kaiserhof Grand Hotel, and most importantly, the old Reich Chancellery flanked the French-style landscaped rectangular plaza named after King Frederick William I of Prussia. See Laurenz Demps, *Berlin-Wilhelmstraße: Eine Topographie preußisch-deutscher Macht* (Berlin: Ch. Links Verlag, 2010).

13   Wilhelmplatz was a place for Nazi celebration, it is here that large crowds cheered for Hitler, who celebrated his ascent to power standing on the balcony of the Reichskanzlei. Like many other places of Nazi-triumphalism post-war politics of amnesia erased Wilhelmplatz from the map of Berlin, as well as the severely bombed Reich Chancellery. The building location is now technically Wilhelmstraße 92. On the Reichskanzlei, see Angela Schönberger, *Die Neue Reichskanzlei von Albert Speer. Zum Zusammenhang von nationalsozialistischer Ideologie und Architektur* (Berlin: Gebrüder Mann Verlag, 1991).

14   An der Kolonnade is a newer, small street laid out after the erasure of Wilhelmplatz following WWII.

15   Maoz Azaryahu, *Von Wilhelmplatz Zu Thälmannplatz: Politische Symbole Im Öffentlichen Leben Der DDR*, ed. Shulamit Volkov and Frank Stern, trans. Kerstin Amrani and Alma Mandelbaum (Gerlingen: Bleicher Verlag, 1991).

16   Topography of Terror Foundation, ed., *Die Wilhelmstraße 1933–1945. Aufstieg Und Untergang Des NS-Regierunsgviertels* (Berlin: Stiftung Topographie des Terror, 2014).

17   An additional plaque, also belonging to the "Geschichtsmeile Wilhelmstraße," is located in close proximity to the first one. It details Hitler's expansion of the old Reichskanzlei into the adjacent lot located on Wilhelmstraße 78. Topography of Terror Foundation, Wilhelmstreet 77 and 78 plaques, 1997. Observed in 2017.

18   Africa-Forum e.V., Wilhelmstraße plaque, 2005. While the first plaque includes texts only in German and in English, this second plaque incorporates German, English and French translations.

19   John D. Hargreaves, "THE BERLIN WEST AFRICA CONFERENCE: A Timely Centenary," *History Today* 34, no. 11 (November 1984): 16. For the actual conference treaty, and a WWI-era interpretation, see Arthur Berriedale Keith, *The Belgian Congo and the Berlin Act* (Oxford: Clarendon, 1919).

20   Matthias Haß, *Das Aktive Museum und die Topographie des Terrors* (Berlin: Hentrich und Hentrich Verlag Berlin, 2012).

21   Afrika-Forum, "Gedenktafel," accessed August 16, 2018, http://www.afrikaforum.net.

22   Two types of counter-memorials can be distinguished within this tradition: coun-ter-memorials that confront existing monuments, and counter-memorials that defy the conventions of memorialization. Both emerged in Germany during the 1980s. See Dinah Wijsenbeek, *Denkmal und Gegendenkmal: Über den kritischen Umgang*

mit der Vergangenheit auf dem Gebiet der bildenden Kunst (Munich: Peter Lang, 2010); Jana Scheele, "Denkmal und Gegendenkmal. Kommunikationsraum der Generationen," *Hamburger Journal für Kulturanthropologie (HJK)* 1, no. 4 (2016): 73–85; James E. Young, "Memory, Countermemory, and the End of the Monument," in *At Memory's Edge: After-Images of the Holocaust in Contemporary Art and Architecture* (New Haven, CT: Yale University, 2000), 90–119; James E. Young, "Memory Against Itself in Germany Today," in ibid., 120–51; James E. Young, "Memory and Counter-Memory," *Harvard Design Magazine*, Fall 1999, http://www. harvarddesignmagazine.org/issues/9/memory-and-counter-memory.

23 Jeffrey Herf, *Divided Memory: The Nazi Past in the Two Germanys* (Cambridge, MA: Harvard University, 1997).

24 Anselma Gallinat, "The Local Aufarbeitung (Re-Working) of the SED-Dictatorship: Governing Memory to Save the Future," *European Politics and Society* 18, no. 1 (2017): 96–109; Deutscher Bundestag, "Errichtungsgesetz Bundesstiftung Zur Aufarbeitung Der SED-Diktatur," § 33 (1998), https://www.bundesstiftung-aufarbei-tung.de/errichtungsgesetz-1081.html.

25 Eberhard Jäckel, "Die Doppelte Vergangenheit," *Der Spiegel*, December 23, 1991, http://www.spiegel.de/spiegel/print/d-13492255.html; Evelyn Finger, "Deutsche Geschichte: Diktaturenvergleich jetzt! Neuer Streit um die Gedenkpolitik: Was unter-scheidet NS-Verbrechen von DDR-Unrecht? Ein Interview mit Salomon Korn," *Die Zeit*, November 19, 2007, https://www.zeit.de/2007/47/Gedenkstaetten.

26 Jäckel, "Die Doppelte Vergangenheit," 41.

27 Ken Münster, "Aktivisten laden zur Umbenennung der Mohrenstraße," *Der Tagesspiegel*, August 23, 2017, http://www.tagesspiegel.de/berlin/symbol-isches-fest-in-berlin-mitte-aktivisten-laden-zur-umbenennung-der-mohren-strasse/20223702.html; Uta Schleiermacher, "Verbrechen der deutschen Kolonialzeit: Protest gegen die Mohrenstraße," *Die Tageszeitung: taz*, August 22, 2017, http://www.taz.de/!5435267. The first person to draw attention to the offensive and derogatory meaning of Mohrenstraße was the Afro-German poet and activist May Ayim (1960–96).

28 Endrias (interview). Legal proceedings were taken against the historian, who artic-ulated his controversial position in numerous publications, including: Heyden, *Auf Afrikas Spuren in Berlin*.

29 Berliner Entwicklungspolitischer Ratschlag, in cooperation with Berlin Postkolonial and Initiative Schwarze Menschen in Deutschland (ISD-BUND), "Stadt neu lesen. Dossier zu kolonialen und rassistischen Straßennamen in Berlin" (Berlin: Berliner Entwicklungspolitischer Ratschlag, 2016); Decolonize-Mitte, "Hintergrundinformationen zur Umbenennung der ,M-Straße'," *decolonize-mitte* (blog), August 24, 2015, accessed August 17, 2018, http://decolonize-mitte. de/?p=238.

30 United Nations, "Slave Trade and Its Abolition," UNESCO, accessed July 10, 2018, http://www.unesco.org/new/en/unesco/events/prizes-and-celebrations/celebrations/international-days/slave-trade-and-its-abolition; Berlin Postkolonial e.V., "decolonize-mitte | Dekolonisierung von Berlin-Mitte," *decolonize-mitte | Dekolonisierung von Berlin-Mitte* (blog), August 23, 2015, accessed January 22, 2018, http://decolonize-mitte.de.

31 As of summer 2018, the only successful postcolonial street-name change in Berlin has been the renaming of Gröbenufer to May-Ayim-Ufer in the Berlin-Kreuzberg district (2010).

32 Götz Frömming, "Umbenennungspraxis ist zutiefst kolonialistisch," *Alternative für Deutschland* (blog), January 29, 2018, accessed August 17, 2018, https://www.afd.

de/goetz-froemming-umbenennungspraxis-ist-zutiefst-kolonialistisch. Frömming goes so far as to accuse proponents of name changes of reverse colonialization.

33 The term "cultural intimacy" is being used here in the sense used by Michael Herzfeld, *Cultural Intimacy: Social Poetics in the Nation-State* (New York: Routledge, 2005).

34 Silvia Longo, Conversation with a Journalist Living in the African Quarter, interview by Valentina Rozas-Krause, June 17, 2017.

35 The colonial street names in question are: Lüderitzstraße, Nachtigalplatz, and Petersallee. In 2017, after a first jury of black members belonging to organizations like Berlin Postkolonial, the Institut für diskriminierungsfreie Bildung (IDB) and the Initiative Schwarze Menschen in Deutschland (ISD) suggested three names to honor African independence fighters, a second jury of academic experts was appointed to identify new names. It follows that, according to the political agreement of the city council's majority coalition, Lüderitzstraße is to be named Cornelius-Frederiks-Straße in honor of a leader of the resistance war of the Nama in former German Southwest Africa, Nachtigalplatz will take the name of the Bell family who fought against German colonial oppression in Cameroon, and Petersallee will be divided in two — one section to be named after the Herero independence fighter Anna Mungunda and the other after the Maji-Maji Rebellion against Germany's occupation of German East Africa. On the history of the African Quarter see Alexander Honold, "Afrikanisches Viertel. Straßennamen als kolonialer Gedächtnisraum," in *Phantasiereiche: Zur Kulturgeschichte des deutschen Kolonialismus*, ed. Birthe Kundrus, 1st ed. (Frankfurt/Main: Campus Verlag, 2003), 305–21. On the African Quarter toponymic debate see Laura Hofmann, "CDU-Fraktion legt Beschwerde gegen Umbenennung der Petersallee ein | Namen & Neues | Tagesspiegel LEUTE Mitte," *Tagesspiegel*, May 4, 2018; Gerhard Lehrke, "Kommentar zum Afrikanischen Viertel: AfD relativiert Untaten des Kolonialismus," *Berliner Zeitung*, February 28, 2018; Hannah El-Hitami, "AdK-Veranstaltungsreihe Koloniales Erbe: "Schlimmste Verbrechen"," *Die Tageszeitung: taz*, January 21, 2018; Pro Afrikanisches Viertel, "Noch keine Veröffentlichung im Amtsblatt," accessed August 16, 2018, https://www.pro-afrikanisches-viertel.de.

36 Van der Heyden, *Auf Afrikas Spuren in Berlin*; Ulrich van der Heyden, "Namensstreit: Warum an der Mohrenstraße nichts schlecht ist," *Berliner Zeitung*, August 21, 2017, https://www.berliner-zeitung.de/politik/meinung/namensstreit-war-um-an-der-mohrenstrasse-nichts-schlecht-ist-28196006; Philipp Hartmann, "Diskussion um die Mohrenstraße: Initiative fordert Namenserhalt," *Berliner Woche*, August 24, 2017, https://www.berliner-woche.de/mitte/c-verkehr/diskussion-um-die-mohrenstrasse-initiative-fordert-namenserhalt_a131339.

37 Komitee für die Errichtung eines afrikanischen Denkmals in Berlin (KADIB), *Facebook*, accessed September, 2018, https://www.facebook.com/Komitee-f%C3%BCr-die-Errichtung-eines-afrikanischen-Denkmals-in-Berlin-1404186889821403.

38 Muchtar B. Kamara, of the Committee for the Construction of an African Memorial in Berlin (KADIB), interviewed by Valentina Rozas-Krause, November 2017.

39 KADIB, *Facebook*.

40 James E. Young, *The Texture of Memory: Holocaust Memorials and Meaning* (New Haven, CT: Yale University, 1993).

41 To this date, there is no formal design proposal for the future memorial. Kamara (interview); Kopp (interview); Della (interview); Apraku (interview); Endrias (interview).

42 Peter Steinbach and Johannes Tuchel, *Georg Elser: Der Hitler-Attentäter* (Berlin: Be.bra Verlag, 2010).

43 Klages Design, "Preisträger des Kunstwettbewerbs 'Denkzeichen Georg Elser' …," accessed August 17, 2018, http://www.klages-design.de/kunst02.html.

44   Birgit Walter, "Neues Denkmal: Ehrung Eines Helden," *Berliner Zeitung*, November 9, 2011, https://www.berliner-zeitung.de/kultur/neues-denkmal-ehrung-eines-helden-10673700.

45   Anon., "Gedenken an Hitler-Attentäter: Georg-Elser-Denkmal in Berlin Eingeweiht," *Spiegel Online*, November 8, 2011, http://www.spiegel.de/kultur/gesellschaft/gedenk-en-an-hitler-attentaeter-georg-elser-denkmal-in-berlin-eingeweiht-a-796600.html.

46   On streets named for Elser see Anon., "Georg Elser: 64 Straßen und Plätze," accessed August 17, 2018, http://www.georg-elser-arbeitskreis.de/texts/strassen. htm. On the thirteen memorials to Elser, see Anon., "Georg Elser: 13 Denkmale und Gedenktafeln," accessed August 17, 2018, http://www.georg-elser-arbeitskreis.de/texts/denkmale.htm.

47   As a limit event, the Holocaust has not only been conceived as the most radical rupture with the Western Enlightenment tradition and human kind in general, but it has also shaped post-Holocaust politics and identities across the world. See Simone Gigliotti, "Unspeakable Pasts as Limit Events: The Holocaust, Genocide, and the Stolen Generations," *Australian Journal of Politics & History* 49, no. 2 (2003): 164–81; A. Dirk Moses, "Conceptual Blockages and Definitional Dilemmas in the 'Racial Century': Genocides of Indigenous Peoples and the Holocaust," in *Colonialism and Genocide*, ed. A. Dirk Moses and Dan Stone (New York: Routledge, 2007), 149–80.

48   Christoph Schult and Christoph Titz, "Völkermord: Herero Und Nama Verklagen Deutschland," *Spiegel Online*, January 6, 2017, http://www.spiegel.de/poli-tik/deutschland/voelkermord-nachkommen-der-herero-und-nama-verkla-gen-deutschland-a-1128885.html.

49   Andreas Kynast, "Völkermord an Herero: In Namibia wächst die Wut auf Deutschland," *ZDF*, January 14, 2018, https://www.zdf.de/uri/e8f9f5b5-0a7d-4832-b2ed-96ac06a1355f; Anon., "Herero Massacre: General's Descendants Apologize for 'Germany's First Genocide,'" *Spiegel Online*, October 8, 2007, http://www.spiegel.de/international/world/herero-massacre-general-s-descendants-apol-ogize-for-germany-s-first-genocide-a-510163.html; Michelle Faul, "Germany's Return of Namibian Skulls Stokes Anger," *MSNBC*, October 4, 2011, http://www.nbcnews.com/id/44778704/ns/world_news-africa/t/germanys-return-namib-ian-skulls-stokes-anger; Andrew Meldrum, "German Minister Says Sorry for Genocide in Namibia," *The Guardian*, August 15, 2004, https://www.theguard-ian.com/world/2004/aug/16/germany.andrewmeldrum; Jason Burke and Philip Oltermann, "Germany Moves to Atone for 'forgotten Genocide' in Namibia," *The Guardian*, December 25, 2016, https://www.theguardian.com/world/2016/dec/25/germany-moves-to-atone-for-forgotten-genocide-in-namibia.

50   Sozialdemokratische Partei Deutschlands (SPD) Landesverband Berlin, Die Linke Landesverband Berlin, and Bündnis 90/Die Grünen Landesverband Berlin, "Koalitionsvereinbarung 2016–2021," 2016, accessed August 17, 2018, https://www.berlin.de/rbmskzl/regierender-buergermeister/senat/koalitionsvereinbarung.

51   Kamara (interview).

52   Hannah Arendt, *The Origins of Totalitarianism* (San Diego, CA: Harcourt Brace, 1979). See also Jürgen Zimmerer, *Von Windhuk nach Auschwitz?: Beiträge zum Verhältnis von Kolonialismus und Holocaust* (Berlin: Lit Verlag, 2011).

53   Jäckel, "Die Doppelte Vergangenheit."

Part II
Between postcolonial metropoles and postcolonies

5

Erasing the Ketchaoua Mosque

Catholicism, assimilation, and civic identity in France and Algeria

Ralph Ghoche

"Touche pas à mon église" ("Don't touch my church") reads the cover of the July 2015 issue of *Valeurs actuelles*, a French conservative news magazine. The slogan, and the movement that it sparked, were devised in response to comments made by Dalil Boubakeur, the rector of the Paris Grand Mosque, in a televised interview a month earlier. Asked whether disused churches in France could be transformed into mosques, Boubakeur had paused momentarily and answered: "Why not? It is the same God. The rites are similar, fraternal. I think that Muslims and Christians can coexist."[1] The reply generated controversy, as it seemed to feed conspiracist suspicions, fueled by the growing power of identitarian movements, that a grander cultural displacement of the white, Christian population by Arab Muslims was underway.[2] So fierce was the backlash that Boubakeur published a retraction soon after the interview.[3]

The author of the *Valeurs actuelles* article, Denis Tillinac — though himself a conservative Catholic — performed some masterly sleights of hand as he shifted the ground of debate from religion to cultural values, from Christianity to such French Republican convictions as secularism and freedom of speech. He spoke of churches less as objects of Christian worship than as sites for the preservation of national identity, rooted in cultural landscapes and historical memory. The slogan "Don't touch my church" too was deceptive and calculated as it co-opted the famous anti-racist slogan "Touche pas à mon pote" ("Don't touch my buddy") that issued from marches in the mid-1980s condemning a wave of race-based violence against adolescents of North African descent residing in France. Tillinac included a petition with the article, and while it garnered 25,000 signatures within a day, its first signatory attracted the most attention: the center-right former president Nicolas Sarkozy.[4] Indeed, the issue gained popular support and cut across political lines in France; polling revealed that sixty-seven percent of the public were supportive of measures that restrict the conversion of churches into mosques.[5]

What is the neocolonial present? The debate over the conversion of churches into mosques in France, not to say the veritable restrictions over the construction of minarets and new mosques in Germany, Switzerland, and Italy, point to a renewed backlash against more inclusive models of European citizenship advanced in prior decades. Indeed, in recent years, the heads of state of France (Sarkozy), UK (David Cameron), Germany (Angela Merkel), and Spain (José Maria Aznar) have all proclaimed the failure of multiculturalism. While politicians may declare the end of multicultural policies — policies that most governments in Europe have never instituted nor endorsed — the multicultural reality of life in Europe's urban centers is more difficult to deny.[6] In France, where multiculturalism has been treated with significant antipathy across the political spectrum, the visibility of ethnic and racial minorities on the "street" is not reflected in the nation's laws and constitution. Indeed, French legislators have tended to set citizenship against personal identity, and have asserted republican values over and against the recognition of minority groups.[7] For example, Article 1 of the French constitution has pitted the "equality of all citizens before the law" against any "distinction of origin, race or religion" since 1946, thus rendering these minority distinctions juridically invisible.[8] As Achille Mbembe has explained, "the perverse effect of this indifference to difference is thus the relative indifference to discrimination."[9]

In the wake of the professed failure of multiculturalism, prominent politicians and scholars have urged that we return to an idea with a long and fraught history: assimilation.[10] Those, like Sarkozy, who have sought to rehabilitate the term, stress the responsibility of immigrants and their descendants to demonstrate their public attachment to French values while suppressing their cultural and religious heritage or relegating them to the private sphere. Attempts to rebrand the concept of assimilation run parallel to recent governmental efforts at curtailing discussion of France's colonial legacy.[11] Indeed, issues of minority visibility and cultural integration always seem to come back to the question of colonialism. Once the byword for colonial policies of cultural violence, mechanisms of assimilation in the nineteenth century aimed to erase the socio-religious identities of colonial subjects and absorb them into French singularity. But if these policies were previously directed at colonial subjects located on territory d'outre-mer, that is to say, beyond Continental Europe, discussions of assimilation today have centered on citizens and permanent residents of mainland France.

This chapter looks back to the French colony of Algeria in the opening decades of the modern colonial era, in the period between 1830, the year of France's conquest of Algiers, to 1870, just before the consolidation and mass colonization of Algeria under the government of the Third Republic.[12] It was during these years that the modern concept of colonialist assimilation was forged. If the question of assimilation today has run parallel to debates on visible markers of Islam in the public sphere, in nineteenth-century Algiers assimilationist policies also helped forge the architectural identity of the city. As with today's debates over the consensual conversion of disused churches, forcible conversion emerged as a key tactic by French administrators to reshape urban life in colonial Algeria. Indeed, between 1830 and 1862, buildings serving Muslim religious needs in occupied Algeria were reduced from 172 to 47.[13] In Algiers alone, at least three of its five Catholic churches, including the Cathedral of Algiers (formerly the Ketchaoua Mosque), were housed in mosques that had been expropriated.[14]

What is clear is that architecture has always been an important instrument in the process of framing citizenship and identity. This is something that the "Touche pas à mon église" movement knows all too well. Indeed, a close reading of Tillinac's polemic shows that it centers, above all else, on the fear that the re-signification of churches into mosques would have a disruptive effect on national culture. In other words, at the very center of these debates is the concern that architecture might come to represent a differentiated form of citizenship rather than reproduce majoritarian norms, practices, and traditions, some long since eroded of meaning.

ARCHITECTURE AND ASSIMILATION

If Tillinac's movement today has insisted on the relative historical purity of France's architectural heritage as a way of enforcing cultural integration, an altogether different tactic was introduced in nineteenth-century Algeria in order to ensure the "pacification" and submission of the Algerian population: architectural hybridity and eclecticism. Even the famous neo-Gothic architect, Eugène-Emmanuel Viollet-le-Duc, who waged a long campaign to uphold a purified account of the rise of the Gothic that was free of foreign influences, transformed his architectural vocabulary in a radical way in Algeria, where he infused his design for a commemorative monument with stylistic idioms drawn from Islamic and North African architectures.[15] In fact, Viollet-le-Duc went further in his bid to see colonial Algeria populated by architectural hybrids. As *architecte des Édifices diocésains*, he appointed students from the most radically eclectic *atelier* in Paris, the atelier of Simon-Claude Constant-Dufeux, to head major church building projects in Algiers.

In the hands of the Catholic Church, architectural eclecticism emerged in mid-nineteenth-century Algiers as a style of forcible assimilation, one geared towards France's new expansionist footing.[16] Style in the nineteenth century was an intensely political and ideological phenomenon. In France, Romantic architects erected buildings with hybrid conjunctions of styles as a way to convey their sense of history's past and future trajectory. Buildings such as Henri Labrouste's Sainte-Geneviève Library, for example, portrayed France as the rightful heir of the westward migration of knowledge from Asia Minor, to Greece and Rome.[17] Visitors moved through the pre-classical entrance hall, up the Renaissance staircase and into the modern, iron-supported reading room; in other words, as they moved through physical and geographical space, they also proceeded through historical time.

Transplanted to Algerian soil, the worldview that animated Romantic architects — and produced some of Paris' most celebrated landmarks — would serve as a mandate for the appropriation and destruction of the cultural heritage of a people. Romantic architects looked at the territory as a zone of experimentation to test their architectural formulations for a healthy social order, even as these dominated or excluded the existing populations. The buildings they erected recombined architectural elements in such a way as to validate France's expansion into North Africa, a conquest that was based on the premise of bringing civilization back to its original cradle in the "Orient."[18] Here was an architecture of assimilation, in so far as it aimed to absorb and integrate the architectural heritage of Algeria — as foreign and alien as it might have been — into the consummate body of French identity.

Scholars have seen the practice of incorporating local and Arabic building forms into French colonial architecture as a phenomenon that emerged in the late nineteenth century and culminated in the rise of the so-called "Style Jonnart." The style was named after the governor general of Algeria, Charles Jonnart, who mandated the use of *néo-mauresque* elements in the design of public buildings in the first decade of the twentieth century. At first glance, the *néo-mauresque* buildings in Algeria appear to operate as reconciliatory images, elaborate and alluring displays suggesting the co-existence of two cultures: French and Algerian. This is the way they have tended to be interpreted. In *Arabisances*, an exhaustive study of *néo-mauresque* architecture in North Africa, François Béguin located the origins of such stylistic hybrids in the 1865 Arab kingdom policy of Napoleon III (*r.*1852–70) and in the new conservationist ethos of the Second Empire. The process of "arabization" of colonial architecture, therefore, reflected an interest in presenting France's "protecting" and "paternal" influence in the colonies, which led to new attempts to safeguard "ancestral forms of habitat and urban customs" and marked a shift from "armies and wars" to "political and psychological action."[19]

Some fifty years before Jonnart's policies were put into effect, however, the Catholic Church, working in conjunction with Romantic architects, spearheaded the deployment of such architectural hybrids in Algiers. Buildings such as Saint-Philippe Cathedral, the Bishop's palace, the Great Seminary at Kouba, and the Basilica of Notre-Dame d'Afrique were among the first colonial edifices in Algeria to integrate elements drawn from building traditions in the Middle East, North Africa, and Islamic Iberia [Figure 5.1]. Arguably the spate of religious buildings erected in Algiers in the mid-nineteenth century complicates the view that the introduction of arabizing elements into French colonial architecture served as conciliatory gestures. Looked at through the lens of the assimilationist theories of the age, particularly those propagated by church figures in Algeria, the reading proves as deceptive as it is dangerous.

Assimilation, as a set of practices and policies in French colonial history, has complex history. Most scholars chart the prevalence of assimilationist policies in French colonies as running parallel to the extent to which governmental administrations adhered to republican values. Modern assimilationist ideas emerged with the rise of Enlightenment ideals and were first applied as state policy by the National Convention a few years after the Revolution of 1789.[20] These policies were curtailed significantly during Napoleonic rule and the Bourbon Restoration although the "spirit of assimilation" remained among certain segments of the government leading to the introduction of modest assimilationist

ure 5.1
e Church of Notre
me d'Afrique (Our
dy of Africa), Algiers
an-Eugène Fromageau,
72). Photograph c.1880.
urce: Jean Geiser,
lotre Dame d'Afrique,"
Souvenir d'Algérie
1880) [Getty Institute].

policies during the liberal constitutional monarchy of Louis-Philippe (*r.*1830–48).[21] With the Republican revolution of 1848, assimilationist policies resurfaced in a much more overt way, most notably with the Constitution of November 4, 1848 which stated that the colonies were an integral part of French territory. The constitution led to the division of Algeria into three departments (Alger, Oran and Constantine) with representatives elected to the French parliament.[22] Policy shifted again during the last decade of the Second Empire, in this case toward a new colonial ideal, albeit a contradictory one, which purported to respect the institutions of native Algerians while supporting the gradual acculturation of Algerians to French social norms.[23] "France has not come to destroy the nationality of a people," Napoleon III exclaimed on his tour of Algiers in 1865. Addressing Algerians directly, he continued: "I want to increase your well-being, include you more and more in the ruling of your country as well as the benefits of civilization."[24]

In comparison to the fluctuating levels of governmental interest in instituting assimilationist policies in Algeria during the nineteenth century, the Catholic Church wavered little in its resolve to assimilate the Algerian population. In private channels, Church leaders employed the established term for such practices: religious conversion. In more public forums, however, terms like "assimilation" and "education" were used to convey the same message in a veiled way. The duplicity was the result of a prohibition on proselytizing to non-Christians by the Minister of War in Paris, which administered religious affairs in Algeria until 1848. The parts of Algeria that were "pacified" in the first dozen years of French rule were relatively small and largely urban, and French administrators sought to quell tensions with inhabitants. Moreover, anti-clericalism still pervaded military ranks during the July Monarchy.[25] The first bishop of Algiers, Antoine-Louis-Adolphe Dupuch, was forced to resign in 1845 as a result of his missionary zeal, which had put him somewhat at odds with the Minister of War, and especially with Thomas Bugeaud, the governor general of Algeria.

The Algerian Church was still in its infancy when Dupuch was obliged to leave the bishopric. While priests and chaplains were on board the first ships to dock in Algiers during the invasion of 1830, the Catholic Church was only officially installed in the territory in 1838, with the signing of a papal bull establishing a diocese in Algiers. The Church's arrival in Algeria was celebrated as a reconquest of territory that had been Roman and Christian before the spread of Islam across North Africa. Dupuch played a central role in propagating the impression of French colonialism in Algeria as a historic revival of the spirit of Augustinian Christendom. In 1847, two years after his resignation, he published *Essai sur l'Algérie chrétienne, romaine et française* which incorporated long translated excerpts from *Africa Christiana* (1816–17) by the Italian Jesuit scholar and epigraphist Stefano Antonio Morcelli. The book summed up Dupuch's vision of Algeria. The first half was dedicated to Morcelli's account of the ecclesiological geography of Algeria before the spread of Islam, while the second half returned to these same sites in the present day, incorporating detailed descriptions of each Christian parish and its relevance to the ancient Christian history of North Africa.

Relations between the Church and colonial administrators improved significantly with the removal of Dupuch and the installation of Louis-Antoine-Augustin Pavy, who presided over the diocese from 1846 to 1866.[26] Pavy was more delicate than his predecessor in his dealings with officials in the government. His efforts were rewarded as funding for Church building projects measurably increased during his tenure.[27] But little advancement was made on the issue of the conversion of Algerians as governmental officials in Algeria and Paris remained firmly opposed. As one of his biographer explained, on this issue Pavy's "hands were tied."[28]

Despite government prohibitions, Pavy was no less committed to evangelization than was Dupuch, though he employed tactics that were less conspicuous. In public, Pavy presented Christianity in much the same way as the government had, as a tolerant religion that promoted universal values. But in private channels, he maintained that the ultimate goal of the Church remained the conversion of Algerians.[29] These aims were laid out in the statutes governing the new diocese that were distributed to the clergy in Algeria. In the chapter titled "Relations with the Infidels" in the 1849 edition of the statutes, Pavy reminded priests to "never lose sight of our mission towards the Indigenous and neglect nothing that hastens the desired moment of their conversion."[30] Given the government ban on religious conversion, Pavy recommended that clergymen spend time "learning Arabic, the Koran and the habits and culture of the Indigenous in order to insinuate themselves more easily into the inner being ("esprit") of Algerians and even to show them, on occasion, the wrongheaded and immoral nature of their beliefs."[31] Children, Pavy continued, should be particular targets of evangelization; he recommended luring them into churches and schools where they could be more effectively re-educated.

While Pavy's recommendations may have been discreet enough to go unnoticed among the general population, some of the tactics employed by other clergymen in Algeria awakened the attention of governmental officials. Such was the case with Joseph Girard, appointed by Pavy as Superior General of the Great Seminary in Kouba on the outskirts of Algiers. Girard had rounded up a dozen impoverished children from the streets of Algiers, bringing them to the seminary where he saw to it that they be "gradually initiated … into this true civilization that scripture has brought the world."[32] Details of these bold efforts at religious conversion were published in *l'Atlas*, a newspaper out of Oran, leading to an order from Paris to dismiss Girard.[33]

Pavy's recommendations also emboldened Abbé Loyer, a priest in the Saharan town of Laghouat, who published *De l'assimilation des arabes* in 1866. The book was written as a rebuttal of Napoleon III's project for an "Arab Kingdom" inaugurated during the emperor's second visit to Algeria the year earlier. If the so-called Arab Kingdom policy urged respect for Algerian society and sought coexistence — albeit an unequal one — between French settlers and Algerians, Loyer advocated for the elimination of Algerian cultural institutions. What was needed to solve the "Arab question," he argued, was a two-pronged strategy: first the destruction of "Arab nationality," to be followed by its reconstitution into French identity. The final goal, Loyer explained, was for "the Arab to no longer be what he has been and for him to become what he is not yet, that is, French."[34]

Loyer recommended a number of tactics, each more devious than the last. Brute force, he claimed, had not achieved assimilation, neither had soft-power approaches like the creation of the Bureaux Arabes (institutions formed as links between the Algerians and the French) and the introduction of the Spahis (French military regiments composed of Algerians). Moreover, Loyer criticized the first bishop of Algiers for his overt methods of converting Algerians to Catholicism. What were needed were "clandestine" means.[35] He laid out two such tactics. First, he called for members of the clergy to remake themselves into *marabouts* (the Maghrebi term for a Muslim religious leader) in order to penetrate Algerian society and gain the trust of tribal members. Second, he proposed that French juvenile delinquents and orphans — boys and girls — be embedded, primarily through marriage, into Algerian tribal families.

The tactics recommended by Loyer, as those by Pavy before him, all involved some form of hybridization, whether through inter-marriage or through the deliberate adoption of local language, custom, and dress. The ultimate aim, both men made clear, should not be misinterpreted: assimilation was an instrument of counter-insurgency and of conquest ("to render insurrections nearly impossible," Loyer writes) and it entailed the destruction of Algerian culture and not the creation of a new, syncretic society.[36] For Loyer, the "Arab" needed to be "absorbed into us," "melted," "melded," made "submissive," and "pacified." The most pressing threat to France's colonial mission, Loyer claimed, was "the arabization of the Frenchman;" assimilation was clearly conceived to act in one direction only.[37]

TRANSFORMING THE KETCHAOUA MOSQUE

If mechanisms of assimilation entailed the destruction of Algerian cultural institutions, at an urban scale they involved the demolition, conversion, and re-
signification of buildings, landscapes, and monuments. Saint-Philippe Cathedral
was the most glaring example of such aims put into practice. At its origin, the
church was the product of the forcible Christianization of one of the most revered
Ottoman-era buildings in Algiers, the Ketchaoua Mosque [Figure 5.2]. The conversion of the building was carried out in a particularly brutal way: at noon on
December 18, 1832, two years following France's military conquest of the city,

Figure 5.2
The interior of the
Ketchaoua Mosque,
Algiers. Lithograph 183
Source: *Lessore et Wyld*
Voyage pittoresque dan
régence d'Alger, pendar
l'année 1833 (Paris: Ch.
Motte, 1835) [Bibliothè
Nationale de France].

French troops stormed the mosque which had been barricaded by 4,000 worship-pers amassed inside in order to stop its conversion.[38] At the time the Ketchaoua Mosque was among the most prestigious of Algiers' religious buildings and stood at the center of the city adjacent the former palace of the Ottoman Dey, which was now home to the French governor of Algiers. The order to forcibly convert the mosque was given by the governor who understood the symbolic importance of appropriating the seats of governmental and religious power and acted in contravention to a clause in the instrument of Algiers' surrender that guaranteed that Muslims would retain their places of worship. The brazen violation caused consternation even among some French officials.[39] The Christian cross and the

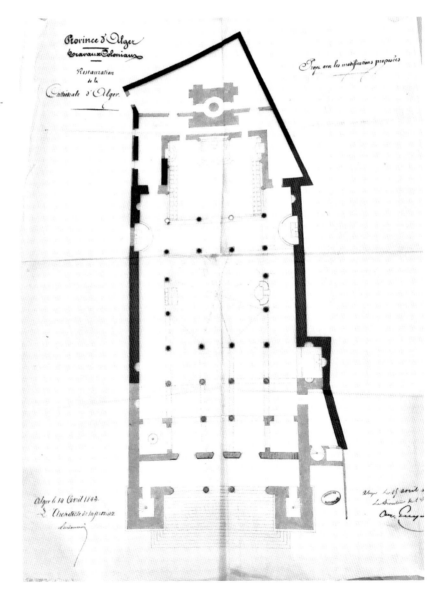

ıre 5.3
ı of the restoration of
Cathedral of Saint-
ippe, with the domed
ɨrior of the former
ɨsque integrated into
scheme, Algiers (Pierre-
ɡuste Guiauchain).
ıwing 1843. Source:
hives Nationales
ınce), CP/F19 7593.

Figure 5.4
The Cathedral of
Saint-Philippe before
its completion in 1886,
Algiers. Photograph be
1886. Source: © InVisu
(CNRS-INHA).

French flag were immediately hoisted up on the building and canons fired from
a nearby naval flotilla in celebration. The first mass held in the building was celebrated on Christmas Eve, just a week later, after modest transformations were
undertaken adding a Christian altar and incorporating a statue of the Virgin Mary
into the mihrab niche. The church was officially upgraded to cathedral status with
the creation of the Diocese of Algiers in 1838 and was dedicated to the French
king, Louis Philippe.

The year following the creation of the diocese, French military administrators,
in conjunction with religious authorities, embarked on a decades-long process

e 5.5
uilt scheme for the
de of the Cathedral
aint-Philippe, Algiers
nain Harou-Romain).
wing 1856. Source:
linistère de la Culture
nce), Médiathèque
architecture et du
imoine, diffusion
N-GP, 80-123-2003.

of transforming the cathedral in order to accommodate the growing number of officials, merchants, and colonists settling in Algiers (there were 117,366 Europeans in Algeria in 1848). By the end, no visible part of the original mosque building remained. Pierre-Auguste Guiauchain, the first of many architects to work on the project, presented plans for the reconstruction of the building in 1842, 1843, and 1848. As drawings of the retrofit show, initial work on the building encapsulated (or quite literally swallowed up) the old mosque within a new shell. The architect's intention to salvage the interior of the mosque was clearly rendered in the first drawings of the project, as was his aim to provide a new façade that reflected the

Islamic character of the original mosque and its setting [Figure 5.3]. Construction began on the façade, a choir, and the base of a new tower soon after Guiauchain's final design was prepared in 1848 [Figure 5.4].

Following Pavy's appointment as Bishop of Algiers in 1846, relations with the architects, which had been strained under Dupuch, improved significantly as Pavy began to play a more prominent role in the process of planning the renovation.[40] This, along with important changes in governance in the late 1840s, assured the Catholic Church greater control over the design of the cathedral.[41] Indeed, a report on the state of the cathedral in 1853 by the Parisian architect Léon Vaudoyer made specific mention of the close collaboration between diocesan architects working on the cathedral and Pavy. Vaudoyer singled out a design by Romain Harou-Romain, Guiauchain's successor, as having been produced "under the inspiration of the bishop" [Figure 5.5].[42] The drawing bears the marks of the bishop's admiration. "It is with the rarest satisfaction that I have seen and studied the drawing of the façade planned for my cathedral" is scrawled next to the signature of Pavy.[43]

The design reworked Guiauchain's façade, with its subdued incorporation of local forms, into a frenzied mergence of elements drawn from Islamic and Christian architectural traditions. Stone surfaces were rendered into intricate geometric latticework that evoked Byzantine and Moorish patterns, corbels were remodeled into muqarnas, and multifoil arches recalling archways in the Córdoba Mosque (a fitting image given the building's conversion during the Iberian *reconquista*) were introduced above the entrance portico. A bishop's balcony was added at the center of the composition, flanked by representations of Saint Augustine, the fourth century Christian theologian and bishop of Hippo Regius (Bône until 1962, now Annaba), and Cyprian, a third century Berber convert and Bishop of Carthage.

If the composite nature of the scheme might seem to gesture towards the reconciliation of the two central religions in colonial Algeria, it is more likely that it reflected Pavy's assimilationist ideals that proposed employing the outward expressions of Algerian culture as a clandestine measure to destroy Algerian religious identity. Indeed, while the scheme was never realized — and Guiauchain's façade remained unchanged until 1886 — the architects who replaced Harou-Romain continued the strategy of intermixing Christian and Islamic elements, albeit in a less ostentatious way. Under Jean-Baptiste-Pierre-Honoré Féraud, starting in 1852, the last traces of the mosque were demolished, including the impressive octagonal dome and the surrounding marble columns and cupolas, and replaced with a barrel vault. Under Jean-Eugène Fromageau some years later, a dome was erected over the new choir and a crypt installed beneath [Figure 5.6]. The destruction of the Ketchaoua Mosque was followed by the building's reconstitution in a hybridized form. The dissonant effect produced by the juxtaposition of Islamic architectural elements topped with Christian religious symbols was not accidental, for it aimed to break the cultural association between the form of the building and its spiritual function in Islamic and Algerian society; in other words it aimed

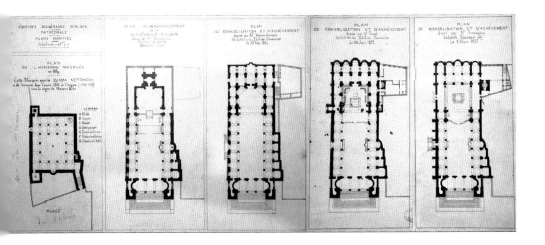

ure 5.6
nned alterations to the
thedral of Saint-Philippe
m 1838 to 1857,
iers (Jean-Eugène
mageau). Drawings
50. Source: Archives
tionales (France), CP/
9 7596.

to make clear to onlookers that the French held ultimate mastery and control over the culture of the colonized.

The particular way in which the two architectonic vocabularies were conjoined likewise expressed French supremacy over its Muslim colonial subjects. The architects of the cathedral reconfigured the prevailing narratives that saw the Romanesque and the Gothic as emerging from Islamic building traditions in such a way as to make the Romanesque appear as the progenitor of Islamic architecture. This is most clear in the way that the Romanesque buttresses that line the lateral wall of the church quite literally support the Islamic cupolas [Figure 5.7]. The subtle misconstrual reinforced conventional European ideas regarding Arab architecture that characterized it as excelling in decoration, but as indifferent to structural expression. These orientalist assumptions reflected more widespread prejudices that saw the West as masculine and rational and the "Orient" as feminine and passive.

Situated between the Casbah and the port, in an area subjected to major building and demolitions, the cathedral presented a dramatic contrast to the austere neoclassicist buildings rising up in parallel formation around it. Indeed, in the first decades of the colonial occupation, there were no imposing Christian buildings and the few places of Christian worship that did exist in Algiers were housed in repurposed buildings without notable exterior expression. The absence of visible markers of Christianity in the city concerned Church leaders who believed that, if native Algerians lacked respect for their colonizers, it was because they perceived them to be insufficiently religious. They cited, for example, the criticisms of Emir Abd-el-Kader, the Algerian religious and military leader who led a rebellion against the French occupation. "Your religion? But you do not have a religion," Abd-el-Kader reportedly exclaimed during the signing of the Tafna Treaty in 1837, adding that "if you were Christians as you pretend to be, you would have priests, churches, and we would be the best of friends."[44] The renovation of Saint-Philippe Cathedral was thus envisioned as a monumental expression of Catholicism's importance in the life of the colonizers and as a definitive statement

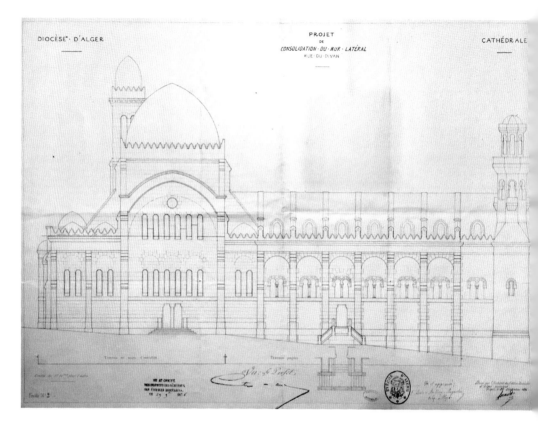

of the Church's renewed presence in North Africa. It operated as a piece of architectural seduction, aggrandizing the Church's presence in Algiers in order to gain the respect of Algerians, while "indigenizing" Christianity within foreign soil.

Figure 5.7
The lateral façade
of the Cathedral of
Saint-Philippe, Algiers
(Jean-Eugène Fromageat
Drawing 1860. Source:
Archives Nationales
(France), CP/F19 7595.

POSTCOLONIAL REAPPROPRIATION OF THE KETCHAOUA MOSQUE

The cathedral remained much the same way as it was in the nineteenth century when on July 5, 1962, the day of Algerian independence from France, a group of 800 men and women rushed inside and reclaimed it as the central mosque of the city. The Ketchaoua Mosque officially reopened on the anniversary of the outbreak of the Algerian Revolution a few months later.[45] While the building was entirely transformed since it last served Algerian worshippers, the towers, horseshoe arches, geometric tile work and countless other details from Islamic building traditions made for a natural fit for revived Muslim prayer.

The mosque has suffered damage from earthquakes and neglect in recent years, forcing its closure in 2006. The building reopened in April 2018, upon the conclusion of a four-year restoration project funded by the government of Turkey [Figure 5.8]. If the cathedral functioned as something of a monument to independence following its reconversion in 1962, that status has been complicated given the Turkish imprimatur on the recently renovated building. Indeed, French

ure 5.8
e Ketchaoua Mosque
ring the 2014–18
storation funded by
e Turkish government,
giers. Photograph 2017.
ource: Daniel E. Coslett.

settler colonialism replaced Ottoman rule over Algiers in 1830 and, before its demolition and reconstruction by French architects, the Ketchaoua Mosque was an architectural relic of the Ottoman period. Beyond the altruistic motivations that may inform Turkey's largesse, the gesture seeks to summon the city's distant past as the Ottoman Regency of Algiers while ensuring the maintenance of Turkish national and religious power across the Muslim world.[46]

Most recently, the Ketchaoua Mosque has re-entered public consciousness in the wake of the debates regarding Islamic spaces of worship in France. Critics of the "Touche pas à mon église" movement have seen the building, and its double conversion from a mosque to a church and back into a mosque, as presenting an instructive parallel to the recent polemic.[47] If today the suggestion to convert certain disused churches into mosques in a consensual manner has ignited public opinion, the indignation is at best disingenuous given the forcible conversions that haunt French colonial history. Indeed, the conversion of religious buildings was a key instrument of colonial domination during the initial decades of the French conquest of Algeria. Assimilation, as a tactic employed by the Catholic Church in Algeria in the nineteenth century, entailed nothing less than the destruction of Muslim cultural and religious institutions and the re-signification of its urban fabric and identity. While the return to notions of assimilation in recent years may bear little in common with the violence endured by Algerians before independence, for Muslim minorities in France, the current hostility toward the consensual conversion of certain empty churches into mosques is part of the continued struggle for visibility. From the standpoint of multiculturalism, it is unjustified to see recent mosque building and suggestions of church conversions as evidence of Muslim rejection of French identity, and at worst, as a ploy to subvert the founding principles of Western civilization. Rather, the gradual increases in places of Muslim worship should be seen as a positive endeavor and as a manifestation of the desire of once colonized and displaced populations to establish themselves in France and express themselves more openly in the civic sphere.

NOTES

1   The interview appeared on Europe 1 the day that it appeared on television. See "Dalil Boubakeur: des églises pour servir au culte musulman? 'Pourquoi pas'," Europe 1, June 15, 2015, http://www.europe1.fr/societe/dalil-boubakeur-le-ramadan-devrait-demarrer-jeudi-1355686. All translations into English are my own unless stated otherwise.

2   Thomas Chatterton Williams provides a good overview of the rise of "the grand replacement" idea in France and its recent impact on American white nationalist movements. Thomas Chatterton Williams, "The French Origins of 'You Will Not Replace Us'," *The New Yorker* 93, no. 39 (December 4, 2017): 24–30.

3   It should be noted that very few churches have been transformed into spaces for Islamic prayer in France. An article on the "Touche pas à mon église" controversy in the newspaper *L'Obs* cites four conversions across France and highlights their relative rarity. Sarah Diffalah, "Transformer les églises abandonnées en mosquées, pourquoi pas?," *l'Obs*, June 18, 2015, https://www.nouvelobs.com/societe/20150617. OBS0987/transformer-les-eglises-abandonnees-en-mosquees-pourquoi-pas.html.

4   Denis Tillinac, "Je signe l'appel de Denis Tillinac pour sauver nos églises," *Valeurs actuelles*, July 15, 2015, https://www.valeursactuelles.com/node/16673.

5   Polling was conducted by the Institut Français d'Opinion Publique and covered by multiple media outlets. A detailed breakdown of the poll numbers was provided in *L'Express*. See "'Ne touchez pas à nos églises!': Sarkozy cosigne un appel dans Valeurs Actuelles," *L'Express*, August 7, 2015, https://www.lexpress.fr/actualite/politique/ne-touchez-pas-a-nos-eglises-sarkozy-cosigne-un-appel-dans-valeurs-actuelles_1697271.html.

6   Queen's University (Canada) has produced a helpful online Multiculturalism Policy Index that compares multicultural policies across the Western democracies: "Multicultural Policies in Contemporary Democracies," Queen's University, https://www.queensu.ca/mcp/immigrant-minorities/evidence, accessed July 15, 2018.

7   As Charles Taylor has argued, "nonrecognition or misrecognition can inflict harm, can be a form of oppression, imprisoning someone in a false, distorted, and reduced mode of living." See Charles Taylor, "The Politics of Recognition," in *Multiculturalism: Examining the Politics of Recognition*, ed. Amy Gutman (Princeton, NJ: Princeton University, 1994), 25.

8   "Constitution of 4 October 1958," Constitutional Council of the French Republic, http://www.conseil-constitutionnel.fr/conseil-constitutionnel/root/bank_mm/anglais/constitution_anglais.pdf, accessed July 15, 2018. The recognition of racial and ethnic

minorities has been further eroded recently: on July 12, 2018, the French National Assembly voted unanimously to eliminate the term "race" from article 1 as part of a larger set of constitutional revisions. Members of visible minorities are thus caught in a contradictory state of affairs in France: they are rarely considered fully French by the population at large, and yet their background and cultural differences are left unrecognized by the state. See Jean Beaman, *Citizen Outsider: Children of North African Immigrants in France* (Oakland, CA: University of California, 2017).

9   Achille Mbembe, "Provincializing France?" *Public Culture* 23, no. 1 (2011): 93.

10 Charles Jaigu, "Sarkozy fait à nouveau l'éloge de l'assimilation," *Le Figaro,* September 16, 2015, http://www.lefigaro.fr/politique/2015/09/16/01002-20150916ART-FIG00395-sarkozy-fait-a-nouveau-l-eloge-de-l-assimilation.php.

11 One such measure was the Law on Recognition by the Nation and National Contribution in Favour of the French Repatriates of 2005 which contained an article (Article 4) that stipulated that school programs should "introduce all young French to the positive role France played overseas." While the article was eliminated the following year, attempts at curtailing criticism of France's colonial legacy have persisted. See Jan Jansen, "The Politics of Remembrance, Colonialism and the Algerian War of Independence in France," in *A European Memory?: Contested Histories and Politics of Remembrance*, ed. Małgorzata Pakier and Bo Stråth (New York: Berghahn, 2010), 286–88.

12 The literature on colonial Algeria in the nineteenth century is vast. Recent book-length studies in English include Jennifer E. Sessions, *By Sword and Plow: France and the Conquest of Algeria* (Ithaca, NY: Cornell University, 2011); William Gallois, *A History of Violence in the Early Algerian Colony* (New York: Palgrave Macmillan, 2013).

13 Darcie Fontaine, *Decolonizing Christianity: Religion and the End of Empire in France and Algeria* (Cambridge: Cambridge University, 2016), 38.

14 "Bâtiments affectés aux cultes, 1850," Archives Nationales d'Outre Mer, GGA 2N/43. The document also records that a total of eleven mosques were converted into Catholic churches throughout Algeria before 1850. The total number of expropriated mosques is much higher than what is documented in these files as many mosques were simply closed or converted to other functions.

15 For a discussion of Viollet-le-Duc's designs for the monument in Algiers, see Zeynep Çelik, "Commemorating the Empire: from Algiers to Damascus," in *Edges of Empire: Orientalism and Visual Culture*, ed. Jocelyn Hackforth-Jones and Mary Roberts (Malden, MA: Blackwell, 2005), 20–37; Martin Bressani, *Architecture and the Historical Imagination: Eugène-Emmanuel Viollet-le-Duc, 1814–1879* (Burlington, VT: Ashgate, 2014), 413–15.

16 The architecture of the Catholic Church in North Africa has been largely neglected by scholars. One notable exception is an essay by the editor of this volume. See Daniel E. Coslett, "(Re)creating a Christian Image Abroad: The Catholic Cathedrals of Protectorate-era Tunis," in *Sacred Precincts: The Religious Architecture of Non-Muslim Communities across the Islamic World*, ed. Mohammad Gharipour (Boston, MA: Brill, 2015), 353–75.

17 Henri Labrouste's decision to have Raphael's fresco, *The School of Athens*, repainted on the staircase wall of the library exemplifies this desire. In essence, Labrouste repurposed Renaissance Rome's own appropriation of ancient Greek wisdom in such a way as to suggest a direct lineage and continuity between classical Greece, Renaissance Rome, and modern France.

18 On the French conquest of Algeria as a return to a Roman and Christian past, see Nabila Oulebsir, "Rome ou l'Orient? Exploration, appropriation, recomposition

(1830–1880)," in *Les usages du patrimoine: monuments, musées et politique coloniale en Algérie (1830–1930)* (Paris: Maison des sciences de l'homme, 2004), 25–157.

19 François Béguin, *Arabisances: Décor architectural et tracé urbain en Afrique du Nord, 1830–1950* (Paris: Dunod, c.1983), 14–16.

20 Raymond Betts points to the Constitution of Year III as a pivotal document enshrining the ideas of assimilation. See Raymond F. Betts, *Assimilation and Association in French Colonial Theory, 1890–1914* (New York: AMS, 1970), 13.

21 Ibid., 18.

22 Ibid.

23 Napoleon III's idea of an "Arab Kingdom" emerged in the 1860s and replaced the government's previous position which encouraged the ruthless assimilation of Algerians and the destruction of their cultural and religious institutions. See Saliha Belmessous, *Assimilation and Empire: Uniformity in French and British Colonies, 1541–1954* (Oxford: Oxford University, 2013), 22.

24 Charles-Robert Ageron, *Histoire de l'Algérie contemporaine* (Paris: Presses universitaires de France, 1964), 31.

25 Marcel Emerit, "Le lutte entre les généraux et les prêtres aux débuts de l'Algérie française," *Revue africaine* 97 (1953): 68.

26 On the tensions between the French military authority in Algeria and the clergy, see Emerit, "Le lutte."

27 The number of official parishes increased from 29 to 187 during Pavy's tenure. See Kyle Francis, "Catholic Missionaries in Colonial Algeria: Faith, Foreigners, and France's Other Civilizing Mission, 1848–1883," *French Historical Studies* 39, no. 4 (October 1, 2016): 696.

28 Abbé Loyer, *Mgr Pavy, évêque d'Alger. Simple esquisse* (Paris: Callamel ainé, 1867), 34.

29 According to Pavy's biographer, L.-C. Pavy (no apparent relation), the bishop hoped to see the Church and military combine their forces towards the common goal of converting Algerians to Christianity. L.-C. Pavy explained: "Such is, in effect, the dominance of the military on the Arab populations and on the tolbas [religious students] and marabouts, that the day that the military will seriously commit to missionary work, we shall see the resistance of the *indigènes* (natives) weaken and we will be able to work reasonably and productively … on their conversion." L.-C. Pavy, *Monseigneur Pavy, sa vie et ses oeuvres ou la nouvelle église d'Afrique*, v. 1 (Paris: Lecoffre, Fils et Cie., 1870), 330.

30 Louis-Antoine-Augustin Pavy, *Statuts du diocèse d'Alger* (Alger: Imprimerie du Gouvernement, 1849), 52.

31 Pavy, *Statuts*, 34.

32 L.C. Pavy, *Monseigneur Pavy,* v. 1, 36.

33 The order was rescinded. Upon hearing of Girard's immanent dismissal, Pavy stormed into the Palace of the Governor General and convinced Aimable Pélissier not to follow through with the orders. Pavy, *Monseigneur Pavy,* v. 1, 492.

34 Abbé Loyer, *De l'assimilation des Arabes* (Paris: Challamel ainé, 1866), 2.

35 Loyer described the tactics to subdue the Algerian population as "occulte plutôt qu'apparente." Ibid., 105.

36 Ibid., 99.

37 Ibid., 140.

38 For a contemporaneous account of the incident, see Florian Pharaon, *Episode de La Conquête. Cathédrale et Mosquée* (Paris: A. Lahure, 1880).

39 The conversion of the mosque was criticized by government officials and colonial administrators. The civil intendant of Algiers, Baron Pichon, tried to dissuade René

Savary, Duc de Rovigo, working back channels to secure a less notable mosque for conversion. "You have been given the most poorly located and least venerated mosque in the city. I don't want it! I want the most beautiful [mosque]!" the Duc de Rovigo was reported to have replied. Jean-de-Dieu Soult, the Minister of War, fired off a letter from Paris stating that, while he shared the belief that principles of Christianity "needed to run parallel to military efforts at progressing civilization," he warned that such drastic measures as the expropriation of Algiers' central mosque could "alienate the French from Muslim populations." ANOM F/80/1627.

40   The Catholic priest Jules Tournier noted that Dupuch often complained about the architects working on the cathedral. See Jules Tournier, *La conquête religieuse de l'Algérie 1830–1845*. 6th edition (Paris: Librairie Plon, 1930), 111–12.

41   The most important change occurred in 1848, after the establishment of the Second Republic. First, the military's hold over religious affairs was significantly lessened as governmental decrees transferred oversight of Christian and Jewish religious affairs from the Minister of War to the Minister of Public Instruction and Religion (Ministère de l'Instruction Publiques et des Cultes). In addition, oversight of the cathedral was transferred from the Service des bâtiments civiles in Paris to the Service des edifices diocésains, which was newly established in the colony.

42   Léon Vaudoyer, Rapport de l'Inspecteur générale des édifices diocésains en 1853. Archives nationales, F/19/*/1822, F/19/*/1823.

43   Romain Harou-Romain, Elévation de la façade principale. Médiathèque de l'architecture et du patrimoine, 80/123/2003.

44   Quoted in Emerit, "Le lutte," 66–67.

45   Darcie Fontaine, "After the Exodus: Catholics and the Formation of Postcolonial Identity in Algeria," *French Politics, Culture & Society* 33, no. 2 (Summer 2015): 106.

46   There are thinly concealed geopolitical motivations at work in Turkey's involvement with the renovation of the Ketchaoua Mosque. For a detailed analysis Turkish investment in the construction of mosques across the Muslim world, see chapter 1 in Kishwar Rizvi, *The Transnational Mosque: Architecture and Historical Memory in the Contemporary Middle East* (Chapel Hill, NC: University of North Carolina, 2015).

47   See Chems Eddine Chitour, "Les lieux de culte musulman en France: La quadrature du cercle," *Réseau international,* July 26, 2015, http://reseauinternational.net/les-lieux-de-culte-musulman-en-france-la-quadrature-du-cercle; Sarah Diffalah, "Transformer les églises abandonnées en mosquées, pourquoi pas?," *l'Obs*, June 18, 2015, https://www.nouvelobs.com/societe/20150617.OBS0987/transformer-les-eglises-abandonnees-en-mosquees-pourquoi-pas.html.

6

All empire is a stage

Italian colonial exhibitions in continuum

Stephanie Malia Hom

"It is not about a parallel universe, a double universe, or even a possible universe — neither possible, impossible, neither real nor unreal: *hyperreal* — it is a universe of simulation, which is something else altogether."

Jean Baudrillard

"Like reality at the world exhibition, the world's political truths are never presented, they are only ever represented."

Timothy Mitchell

The land that expands south of Rome is flat and salty, crisscrossed with canals, artichoke fields, industrial warehouses, and razor-straight roads. Humidity clings to the body, the sea breeze the only occasional relief. The sun is both harsh and diffuse. There is a solemn beauty to this land, which, until the 1920s existed as an uninhabitable marsh. Malaria flourished here. The Romans called it *Pomptinae Paludes*. In Italian, it is known as the Agro Pontino (Pontine Marshes). There were many unsuccessful attempts to drain this land, yet it was only with Mussolini's ambitious program of land reclamation, known as the *bonifica integrale* (total reclamation), that the marshes were transformed into agricultural fields and modern towns.

In the 1930s and early 1940s, the Agro Pontino emerged as the apotheosis of Fascist architecture as well as urban and rural planning. The *bonifica* (reclamation) became a model to emulate throughout the country and in the Italian colonies. During this time, tens of thousands of impoverished farmers were relocated here from northern Italy. They were given a *podere* (homestead), a plough, and several hectares. They were charged with growing crops in this former marsh, or in the parlance of the times, helping the soil meet its fertile destiny. The resettlement of northern Italians to the Agro Pontino was one of the most extensive programs of internal colonization ever undertaken in twentieth-century Europe, and one that remains little known outside Italy.[1]

Today, the Museo Storico Piana delle Orme (Historical Museum of Piana delle Orme, henceforth called the *bonifica* museum), near the regional capital of Latina, has as its self-declared goal the celebration of the Agro Pontino's modern history, including its pastoral culture, agricultural transformation, and site as combat zone during World War II. (Allied Forces famously landed at nearby Anzio and Nettuno in 1944.) Opened in 1997, it accomplishes this vis-à-vis life-size dioramas housed in twelve airplane hangars. Within them, thousands of tractors and mannequins, among other things, are staged in various scenes of heroic action. Half of the museum's hangars recreate an agricultural utopia of the *bonifica*, and the other half, the battles and events of WWII.[2]

Clearly, the *bonifica* is a point of pride for the museum. Its founder, Mariano De Pasquale (1938–2006), spent decades collecting early twentieth-century memorabilia from the region, particularly technologies of agriculture. These artifacts mark the Agro Pontino's singularity as a site of exceptional engineering, land reclamation, and planning. The museum's dioramas materialize a perfectly Fascist order predicated upon internal colonization. Put another way, the debris of Italy's domestic colonial project — pickaxes, threshing machines, ploughs, tractors — is re-organized here as hyperreal display. It is an imperial simulation par excellence.

The museum's present-day simulacra have an antecedent in Italian colonial Libya at the Fiera di Tripoli, or Tripoli Trade Fair. This was a colonial exhibition staged annually from 1927–39 in the city of Tripoli proper. (Libya was an Italian colony from 1911–43.)[3] Its pavilions, like the hangars of the museum, contained within them the stereotypical best that Italy's overseas colonies had to offer. On the surface, the Fiera di Tripoli appeared similar to other colonial expositions like the famous 1931 Exposition coloniale internationale in Paris that had as its architectural mission: "to make concrete inherent differences between Europe and the colonies and to represent Europe's *mission civilisatrice*."[4] Likewise the Fiera spatialized a colonial utopia in plaster and mortar, a contrived space that offered visitors the best of colonial everything in the right place and the right order. Indigenous inhabitants, too, were put on display, like the potter at work near the fake Arab *suq*, or the Bedouin shepherds enclosed with their camels in a treeless corral. The hyperreal displays at the Tripoli Trade Fair showcased not imperial debris per se, but rather objects from existing colonial everyday life. Things like spears, leopard skins, and woven rugs punctuated the Fiera's universe of simulation with material reminders of a "real" life outside its walls. In such a way, the Tripoli Trade Fair was simultaneously colonial and hyperreal, or in the words of Jean Baudrillard, "something else altogether."[5]

This chapter focuses attention on the exhibition as something else altogether, not only as the built expression of Italian colonial ideals and hierarchical relations of power, but also the unacknowledged colonial heritage of what have been often characterized as postmodern phenomena, that is, simulacra and simulation. To situate the operations of simulation in the colonial context is to expand our thinking on the hyperreal. Too often simulacra are thought to be devoid of human connections, they are but "models of a real without origin or reality."[6] At the Tripoli Trade Fair of the past and the *bonifica* museum of the present, human connections are paramount, taking form along the uneven hierarchies of colonizer and colonized.[7]

The Tripoli Trade Fair and the *bonifica* museum — which one may classify together under the rubric of "exhibition" — are expressions of the same imperial formation that engages simulation to hold at bay the coercive violence of one population subjugating another in the name of colonialism.[8] The museum stands at the site of the largest internal colonization movement in Europe, the Agro Pontino, and the fair was built within the territory of Italy's most prized colony, Libya. These were colonial simulacra created by Italians for Italians.

The exhibition presents the illusion of cohesion of Italy's colonial enterprise. It spatializes a *via positiva* of smiling subjects, fertile pastures, and unfettered progress that runs counter to the actually existing *via negativa* playing out on the ground.[9] Mobility also governs the exhibition. Like their postmodern counterparts (e.g., Disneyland), the Tripoli Trade Fair and the *bonifica* museum control *who* can move through their spaces as well as *how* they move through them. Everything is deliberate. Visitors see and experience only what is presented to them. At the same time, the exhibition immobilizes "dangerous" subjects by putting them on display. Think Bedouin confined in a fake corral or Somali warriors restricted to a tent. Here, pavilions and dioramas take the place of stocks and gallows. Yet what haunts one most are the ways in which the exhibition uses simulacra and simulation to suspend disbelief about the brutalities of Italian colonization, which, in the case of the Tripoli Trade Fair, included the genocide occurring in the Italian-built concentration camps outside its very walls.[10]

THE COLONIAL AND THE HYPERREAL

As laboratories of modernity, inventories of the world, and shrines to progress, world's fairs simultaneously articulated and embodied complex historical moments and cultural contexts.[11] Walter Benjamin famously declared them: "sites of pilgrimages to the commodity fetish."[12] The scholarship on world's fairs is extensive, much of it concerned with exhibitions as battlegrounds of signifying practices.[13] Of course, colonial exhibitions were the most ideologically charged subset of these fairs.[14] They imparted the appearance of colonial order and staged opportunities for visitors to imagine their mastery of that order.[15]

Almost all colonial exhibitions were built in Europe between 1880 and 1940, the height of European colonial imperialism, with the aim of expanding trade between metropole and colony, and increasing domestic support for such efforts. Often, quotidian colonial life was recreated there — be it architecturally, as in the reconstruction of a Cairo street at the 1931 Exposition coloniale internationale in Paris; or, commercially, as with demonstrations of labor at the pavilions of agriculture, industry, and commerce at the 1914 *Mostra coloniale* (colonial exhibition) in Genoa; or, even ethnologically, with the *Völkerschauen* (people displays), *villages nègres* (Negro villages), and human zoos that were commonplace at almost all colonial fairs.[16] In such ways, millions of visitors experienced an "exotic" world brought from outside, which, when ordered and framed in the built environment of the exhibition, became a world rendered object-like and thus ready for domination.[17]

Moreover, such fairs referenced a world, inert and permanent, outside the exhibition. According to Timothy Mitchell, the effect created by staking the colonial exhibition on such fixity:

> would always appear as though it were a conceptual structure … as an order of meaning or truth existing somehow before and behind what would now be thought of as mere 'things in themselves.' Political authority itself would now more and more reside in this effect of a prior ordering truth.[18]

Yet in these colonial exhibitions, Mitchell adds, authority presided without ever really being present, and the political order(s) expressed were never quite accessible, always remaining on the outside. Novelty came in the new ways in which the exhibitions rendered abstractions of authority into entwined representational realms of objects and order.

These colonial exhibitions were thus simulacra: copies of an "original" artificially resurrected under the auspices of the "real." Here, Mitchell writes that:

> everything both imitates and is imitated — there is no simple division into an order of copies and an order of originals, of pictures and what they represent, of exhibits and reality, of the text and the real world, of signifiers and signified.[19]

These processes of denaturalization and simulation were especially pronounced at the Tripoli Trade Fair.[20]

What began as a series of temporary installations along Tripoli's seafront esplanade transformed into a sprawling 50,000 square-meter fairground of permanent pavilions in the new, Italian-built neighborhood west of Tripoli's medina [Figure 6.1]. Its wide boulevards, high walls, entryway fountains, and triumphal arch contrasted with the relatively undeveloped land surrounding it. (N.B. Today the fairgrounds remain the site of an international trade show, the Tripoli International Fair, and visitors still enter through the same arch). Similar to the exhibitions staged in the metropole, the Fiera recreated the architectures of quotidian colonial life in situ.[21] Visitors to the fair would observe this cleansed and curated colonial order of appearance, and then, unlike the exhibitions in Paris or Naples, they would walk outside the fair's boundaries to observe the colonial "reality" with their own eyes.

Yet Tripoli's actual built environment had not escaped major intervention; it had been entirely re-constructed — or, technically "re-cleansed" (*ripristino*) — by Italian architects. The streets, buildings, monuments, and indeed, the entire plan of the "real" city had been completely manipulated and reformed by Italian colonial regime since the 1910s.[22] Architects and administrators alike worked to rebuild Tripoli, in part, to conform to an ideal of an Orient that, in fact, never existed.[23] The city itself no longer had a relation to any reality — in a way, it was its own simulacrum. Together, the relation between the Tripoli Trade Fair and the city

of Tripoli proper was that of two simulated environments bound up in an infinite calculus of figural exchanges. This was a universe of simulation, an immanent Italian empire.

Figure 6.1
View of central esplanad
and pavilions of the Trip
Trade Fair in Tripoli, Liby
Photograph c.1930.

COLONIES WITHIN A COLONY

Mise en abyme structured these simulacra, too. A French term often used in literary criticism and art history, mise en abyme denotes a hierarchical mirroring of two elements. At the Fiera di Tripoli, things were not just mirrored, mimicked, or doubled here, but perpetually multiplied and enframed ... and misrecognized.[24] The Fiera flaunted all the trappings of successful empire: pacified natives, high-quality exports, domestic industry, modern buildings, geopolitical reach, etc. The mise en abyme — the Tripoli-as-exhibition within the Tripoli-as-city — normalized the appearance of a rational, domesticated, and productive order. Visitors only saw the benefits of colonialism, which reinforced the impression that Italians had of themselves as good colonizers, or *brava gente* (good people).[25]

Yet mise en abyme only amplified the misrecognition of Italian colonial order. The "reality" on the ground in Libya (and elsewhere in the Italian colonies) was entirely different than the idealized world presented at the trade fair. Gunfire still reverberated from skirmishes outside Tripoli. The construction of infrastructure suffered long delays. The province of Cyrenaica remained in a constant state of civil unrest. The simulation on display at the Fiera only gave the appearance of Italian control over its colony.

Today, mise en abyme also structures, in part, the *bonifica* museum south of Rome. Several of its thematic pavilions depict life in the Agro Pontino during the time of internal colonization. The displays are "perfect reconstructions that reproduce environments and systems of work."[26] One of the first dioramas shows the clearing of swampland and construction of canals. Mannequins with pickaxes and shovels load rocks onto a trolley while a sign nearby announces the scene: *Bonifica di Littoria.* (Littoria was another name for the town of Latina.) Still another display shows dozens of mannequins — men, women, and children — disembarking from a train. They represent the thousands of colonists re-settled from northern Italy, mostly from the Veneto region, to "reclaim" the land through agriculture [Figure 6.2].

The museum's artificial canals exist adjacent to real ones nearby. Fake *poderi* (homesteads) are mere kilometers from the actual extant *poderi* built during the Fascist era. Like the Tripoli Trade Fair, the *bonifica* museum gives the impression of the Agro Pontino as a rational, domesticated, and productive (internal) colonial order. When visitors to the Fiera stepped outside the walls and into the city of Tripoli already manipulated by Italian planners, so, too, do present-day visitors to the museum. These visitors step outside into the "real" *bonifica*. They step into the lands of Fascist new towns that have been extensively manipulated by Italian

planners, architects, and engineers just like the urban fabric of Tripoli itself. Real and hyperreal collide once again.

Whereas the *bonifica* inspired the museum, Mussolini's visit to Libya in 1926 inspired the creation of the Tripoli Trade Fair. The then governor of Tripolitania, Emilio De Bono, decided that a colonial exhibition would best announce Italy's arrival as a colonial power on the world stage. He subsequently funded the fair, which opened the next year in 1927.[27] Yet the Fiera was hardly a static entity. It was always evolving in structure and scope. Its central premises, however, remained consistent: to demonstrate the economic and political value of the colonies to Italian visitors, and to market the civic benevolence of Italy and Italians to "natives." Economic value was first and foremost, with the showpiece being the *valorizzazione* (valorization) of Italy's most prized colony, Libya, above all. Political value was second, with the Fiera making the case for Italian colonialism as a benevolent enterprise.

The unique geographical position of the Fiera — as a colonial exhibition staged within a colony — was not lost on the fair's organizers. In his detailed history of the Tripoli Trade Fair, Angelo Pìccioli, a teacher and school superintendent in Libya, wrote that the Fiera stood apart from exhibitions on the Continent precisely because it was mutually constitutive with its colonial setting:

> The Tripoli Trade Fair, in fact, cannot be studied and explained with the same criteria that are valid for the exhibitions of the Continent. A fundamental element essentially distinguishes the colonial Fiera from its related sisters in Europe, and that element is the very diverse commercial receptiveness of the environment in which the one and the others are respectively held.[28]

For Pìccioli, a colonial exhibition staged within a colony was unequivocally distinct from those staged in the European metropole. He implied the Fiera was an intentional simulacrum, a cleansed-and-ordered Tripoli imported inside exhibition walls: "Ordered and cleansed, Arab and Jewish Tripoli, the Tripoli of tradition is transported inside the enclosure of the Fair, to make a beautiful show of itself."[29] This Tripoli was a tableau vivant inhabited by obedient subjects who knew their places and performed their roles. Pìccioli added:

> It was a living fragment of the old Muslim Tripoli — houses and workshops, men and beasts — transplanted as if by a spell to the middle of that city of machines and mechanisms. The Bedouin tent, all patched and mended, rose on the shores of an artificial lake: document of the nomad life.[30]

The Fiera was meant to give the "exact sensation" of life in the Italian colonies.[31]

The old Muslim Tripoli, however, was one that Italian planners and architects had already manipulated in such a way as to fulfill their own (ambiguous) Orientalist fantasies. Buildings like the Grand Hotel or the Bank of Italy with their Euro-Moorish ornamentation represented a layered enmeshment of forms, which Mia Fuller described as characteristic of the Italian colonial city.[32] Those formal fantasies were likewise re-territorialized within the walls of the Fiera. Indeed, the city and the fair so mutually constituted one another that several Italian architects of the era complained that "Tripoli resembled a European fairground rather than a North African city."[33]

These simulated spaces of the Fiera estranged identities from their territories, replacing the fluid identifications of the Bedouin, the Arab, the Somali, et al. with cultural stereotypes. Much like the tourist guidebook, the Fiera emptied the landscape of its people and replaced them "an improbable typology [that] serves to mask the real spectacle of conditions, classes, and professions."[34] Whereas the guidebook suffered from "the disease of thinking in essences" in *text*, the Fiera suffered from the disease of thinking in essences in *space*.[35] The Bedouin was a nomadic shepherd. The Eritrean was an *askari* warrior. The Italian was a benevolent colonizer. Indeed, the real spectacle of conditions at the Fiera was that of the uneven power and violence of Italian colonialism. It not only actualized the notions that certain territories and people required domination but also displayed how such dominated territories and people could be made productive.[36] Such colonial productivity was measured in material goods as well as subjugated "natives."

In its first two years, 1927–28, the Fiera pavilions were built out of wood. When it moved to bigger fairgrounds in 1929, the pavilions were re-made in brick and stone. In 1934, however, organizers re-adopted wood as the preferred material of the fair.[37] This return to ephemeral building materials at the Fiera may belie an (unconscious) insecurity toward the Italian colonial project generally, as if the organizers somehow sensed the enterprise was finite. The Fiera never did rest on solid ground.

This insecurity was made plain in governor De Bono's speech on the Fiera's opening day in 1927. The exhibition, he noted, would convince Italians that Libya was not a giant sandbox but rather a fertile land ready for cultivation: "On this fourth shore of our sea, there are no arid lands, there are no seas of sand, but there are fertile plots that eagerly await the arms of our good farmers."[38] At the same time, the Fiera would show "natives" the benevolence of the Italian state even if couched in the threat of violence. De Bono announced:[39]

> I appeal especially to the natives of this land blessed by God, our beloved subjects, who love Italy that, yes, governs them with an iron fist but also protects them. This exhibition, which opens today, is a test of how the heart of Italians and their minds are turned towards you [natives]. Entering these enclosures, you will see that Italy as a power is second to none in that which reflects production, for everything represents the latest in modern progress. You will convince yourselves that in Italy you can find everything that is necessary for increasing your wellbeing and your civilization. Here you will find the most effective and real expression of what Italy knows and wants to do.

According to De Bono, Italy was the apogee of modern progress and civilization, and the Fiera the consummate expression thereof. De Bono's speech was an uncommon instance of a European colonial power trying to convince the already-subjugated of its very worth as a colonizer. Piccioli also described "natives" traveling from afar to visit this first Fiera and their experience of being awed by Italian machinery:

> While the Europeans lingered in the folkloristic zone, the natives paused for hours and hours before the stands of railcars and pumps … For the first time, many of them had come to Tripoli; and they set out again for the solitude of Jafara and toward the slopes of the Jabal with their eyes dazzled by new wonders.[40]

Yet the Fiera was a space of simulation, of loose signifying distances, of colonial hyperreality — a space where the insidious violence and brutal realities of Italy's colonial project were entirely disavowed. It was a space of temporary permanence that stayed pointedly on message: Italians were good colonizers, *brava gente*, whose presence only benefited the lands and people with which they came in contact. Of course, this was not actually the case.

UNREAL SUBJECTS OF THE COLONIAL HYPERREAL

A grainy photo from the May 1929 issue of the magazine *Italia Coloniale* shows a dirt corral surround by high walls.[41] Two Bedouin tents line its perimeter but the eye is drawn to a group of men in burnooses (hooded cloaks) sitting with their camels in the center [Figure 6.3]. The walls, asylum-white and several meters high, dwarf man and beast. In this place, there are no trees, no shade, and seemingly no escape. The caption reads "a corner of the Arab village," and it becomes clear that this enclosure is part of the simulated environs of the Tripoli Trade Fair. The photograph, a high-angle shot taken from atop one of the walls, diminishes the subjects at its center, making them appear small, submissive. With the wall framed in the foreground, it imparts the gaze of an overseer, or perhaps a warden, looking down at the men below. They are Bedouin in a cage.

However, this cage was not yet the barbed-wire one described by anthropologist E.E. Evans-Pritchard of Italian-built concentration camps in Cyrenaica.[42] Construction on those "cages" would begin later that same year. In four years, 1929–32, the Italian colonial regime built sixteen camps into which they forcibly dispossessed, displaced, and interned more than 100,000 Bedouin. At least 40,000 people died in these camps, with some historians putting the death toll even higher.[43] If mentioned at all, the camps are but footnotes in the studies of European imperialisms. These were sites of abject horror, what Libyan poet Rajab Hamad Buwaish al-Minifi, himself a survivor of the camp at El-Agheila, described as places where "evil leaned hard on good, dominant."[44] At the apex of the concentration camps' use in 1931, more than 53,000 visitors toured the Tripoli Trade Fair and were exposed to the narrative of Italy's benevolent colonization, a far cry from the actually existing conditions on the ground in nearby camps at the very same time.[45]

Rather, the *villaggio arabo* (Arab village) at the Fiera was a cage born of imperial simulation. It was a pure simulacrum housing a *suq* (market), a café, weaving

ure 6.3
douin sequestered with
nels in the so-called
ab village at the Tripoli
ade Fair. Photograph
29. Source: Istituto
ce.

displays, houses, and a paddock with tents, Bedouin, and apparently, camel rides. The space reflected the city that was just outside the walls in microcosm, where copy and original collapsed into one another to create an "uninterrupted circuit without reference or circumference."[46] Put another way, the Fiera proved to be the unspoken model for the cage — the precession of simulacra — that opened space for the forced sedentarization, dislocation, and dispossession of Bedouin and other colonial subjects. In their lockdown in the simulacrum, the Bedouin and others on display became subjects of (and subjected to) the colonial hyperreality of the Fiera. They became hyperreal subjects that were simultaneously themselves and never resembled themselves again. They were something like clones born of colonization.

Following Baudrillard's logic, hyperreal subjects are inherently haunted by this thwarted resemblance. Yet this is not always the case. Baudrillard writes, "When the double materializes, when it becomes visible, it signifies imminent death."[47] Over the twelve years of the Fiera, doubles steadily materialized: the Bedouin in the corral, the Somali warrior, the Arab metalworker, among many others. More precisely, imminent death was everywhere. These colonial hyperreal subjects — doubles who were almost the same but not quite — signified the imminent death of the "real" subjects at or after the fair. Indeed, this theoretical death through simulation at the Fiera, preceded the real death of the actually existing Bedouin, Somalis, Arabs, et cetera. In the pure simulacrum of the Fiera, hyperreal subjects became "unreal," or better yet, always-already dead. They were corpses in a simulated cage.

If the "natives" were always-already figured as dead within the walls of the Fiera, logic holds that it would become much easier to perpetrate a genocide against them outside of that space, as happened upon the plains of Cyrenaica just a few months later. Here at the fair, simulation acted the sovereign, making dead and letting live the clone-like subjects of an Italian colonial hyperreality. It materialized the figurative biopolitical limits — real and unreal, death and life, inclusion and exclusion — that would be carried to their most extreme conclusions within the barefaced walls of the concentration camp.[48] Not only did the Fiera loosen, mask, denature, and dissipate the tenuous bonds between representation and reality in Italian-occupied Libya, but it also opened up a hyperreal space to be filled up with the myth of Italians as good colonizers, and the bodies of Bedouin killed in its name. What appeared to be innocuous spaces — pavilions, houses, cafés, markets, corrals — were hardly at all, for they materialized an idealized, state-sanctioned, and domesticated colonial order. They embodied forms of colonial dominance but did so by way of imperial simulation executed within the territorial bounds of the colony itself.[49]

Yet colonial life and colonial subjects were not the only things simulated here, so too were metropolitan life and its subjects. From the outset, an equal amount of space was given over to the pavilions of Italian regions and industries at the Tripoli Trade Fair. To do so showcased Italian modernization to both international tourists as well "natives" visiting the Fiera.[50] For example, the region of Calabria had its own pavilion. The region of Puglia sponsored an elaborate product display featuring objects like wheelbarrows and pickaxe handles. The automobile company, FIAT, also built an exhibit. Even the National Institute of Insurance (Istituto Nazionale delle Assicurazioni, known today as INA Assitalia) had its own structure.[51] Italy's metropolitan and colonial pavilions served as a counterpoint to the ones sponsored by other colonial powers like Belgium and France, which began to exhibit at the Fiera from 1934 onward. While most of the metropolitan pavilions were filled with photographs, signage, and specialty products, some of them even had "native Italians" on display, most often in the form of mannequins. Seen another way, even the ostensible colonizers — "Italian" subjects of a colonial hyperreality — were immobilized here, and as mannequins, existed in a state of a figurative death.[52] Thus, the subjects of the Italian state, like the Bedouin in the corral, ran up against a biopolitical limit in the pure simulacrum that was the Fiera. It was a limit that rendered these Italians "unreal." They, too, were corpses in a simulated cage.

Today, at the *bonifica* museum near Latina the simulated Italians on display are also "unreal." They are all mannequins. In one of the museum's self-declared faithful reproductions, for instance, a woman is painted with arms outstretched beside the corpse of a man who recently died of malaria. She is drawn into the scene against a backdrop of expansive swampland, with Monte Circeo, the promontory that marks Agro Pontino's southern limit, in the distance. Another captures a moment of everyday life in one of the region's *borghi* (villages), smaller settlements such as Borgo San Michele, where the museum itself is actually located. In this one, three men sit around a café table with a jug of wine. Their faces and bodies are roughly hewn and out-of-proportion. In another diorama nearby, Italian military commanders gather in the simulated sands of El-Alamein. They are dressed in iconic imperialist garb, including pith helmets and khaki uniforms. One points to a map of Egypt marked with Italian troop positions. Yet unlike the men at the café (or, for that matter, all other civilian figures at the museum) these soldiers have no faces. Their visages are blank, flesh-colored, empty. In fact, virtually every soldier depicted at the *bonifica* museum lacks a face [Figure 6.4]. This transformation from civilian to soldier — and from face to faceless — is shown at a scene that recreates an army recruitment office. Two young men, with dark hair and five o'clock shadows, pick up their uniforms from a faceless soldier. They presumably go on to become one of the faceless soldiers in the next diorama. It was as if they gave up their individual subjectivity — marked by something as personal as one's face — to literally become part of a faceless military mass.

At the *bonifica* museum, the degree of these Italian subjects' "reality" is gradated at best. Some of them, like the woman in the swamp, are two-dimensional paintings or cut-outs. Others are three-dimensional mannequins of the sort found

in department stores. Still others are homemade versions with imperfect and roughly cut features like the men at the café. And still others have no faces at all. They are all figures that are identifiable as Italian subjects but are not quite whole. The double has not materialized fully in this imperial simulacrum. The figurative clones remain incomplete.[53] They do not necessarily signify imminent death, but perhaps only a wound or laceration? Perhaps they mark the tattered-but-still-existing sinews of empire that connect the Italian subjects of the Tripoli Trade Fair in the past and those of the *bonifica* museum in the present? Perhaps such imperial formations connect most powerfully in the sphere of the hyperreal?

THE CAMP AS REMAINDER

In early March 2013, a brand new diorama opened at the *bonifica* museum. Alongside its simulated homesteads and battlefields, there now exists a display dedicated to the *deportati* (deportees), that is, people who were sent from Italy to Nazi concentration camps in the early 1940s. The diorama centers on a replica of Rome's Tiburtina train station. All is stark in faux white marble and Fascist linearity. Plastic *fasces* line the walls, as does the relief of an eagle that gives the date of the scene: A.XIX.E.F. ("Year 19 of the Fascist Era," or 1941). A poster signed by Nazi field marshal Erwin Rommel announces the German occupation of Italy. Full-size train cars line both sides of the platform.

Jewish deportees fill one boxcar — mannequins with rough-hewn faces frozen in varying states of indifference and incomprehension. They are dressed in thick scarves and winter coats. Barbed wire covers the railcar windows. The coach next to this one is empty save for a pile of battered leather suitcases. Its interior walls are covered with names, presumably of those condemned to the camps. The destination, Poland, is etched in cursive outside.

Across the platform, German officers shepherd Italian soldiers into another coach. These mannequins have downtrodden faces and threadbare uniforms, arms hanging limply at their sides. Either captured or surrendered in battle, these prisoners of war were re-classified as *Internati Militari Italiani* (Interned Military Italians) in 1943, a change in juridical status that allowed for their internment in Nazi camps. If they did not die of starvation or disease, POWs were usually put to hard labor in mines, factories, foundries, and the like. According to the signage at the diorama, more than half of 100,000 Italian military internees perished in the camps. The sign laments: "It is one of the aspects that, unfortunately, has been neglected in the major studies about the victims of the Nazi lager."

Beyond the soldiers' coach lays the most surreal boxcar of all. An open door reveals two-dimensional figures tightly packed together and dressed in the striped uniforms of the camp [Figure 6.5]. Each one bears a classification symbol on their left breast: a black triangle, yellow Star of David, violet triangle, et cetera. A smoke machine periodically releases a cloud that lends an eerie theatricality to the proceedings. Unlike the faceless figures in the other cars, the mannequins have faces

...re 6.5
...v of boxcar with
...ortees en route to a
...ılated Auschwitz at the
...orical Museum Piana
...e Orme. Photograph
...3. Source: Stephanie
...a Hom. The camp's
...rative guard tower and
...e with its in famous
...an, *Arbeit Macht Frei*
...rk Sets You Free),
...arely visible in the
...ance.

here, caught in a moment of horror. They all bear the same nude, plastic visage of Edvard Munch's *The Scream*.

One hundred meters from the boxcars and the platform, the train tracks run out toward a grassy field and a windbreak of eucalyptus trees. A military truck used for troop transport is parked between the tracks, and nearby, an elevated wooden guardhouse. The gate behind the truck is easily overlooked as it blends into the trees. It is also easy to miss the metal lettering above the gate, which reads: *Arbeit Macht Frei* (Work Sets You Free). While this slogan was commonly placed at the entrance of many Nazi concentration camps, the gate at the *bonifica* museum is a simulation of the infamous gate at Auschwitz, where the words curved in a slight parabola and the "B" of *Arbeit* was inverted. The phrase hangs above a lower gate of reticulated metal. Here in the Agro Pontino, deep in the marshlands reclaimed by the Fascist regime, every boxcar is figuratively heading toward Auschwitz.

Thus, the circuits of imperial simulation materialized by the Fiera di Tripoli in the 1920s and 1930s come full circle at the *bonifica* museum today. The former reflected Italy's *external* colonizing enterprise vis-à-vis simulacra located within an external colony (Libya). The latter represented Italy's *internal* colonizing enterprise vis-à-vis simulacra located at the site of internal colonization (Agro Pontino). The fair and the museum are therefore expressions of the same imperial formation that engages simulation to hold at bay the coercive violence of one population subjugating another in the name of colonialism. Rather, in the unreal signifying distances of simulation that collapse limits into a zone of indistinction, these spaces suspend the brutalities and banalities of Italian colonization.

In the past, at the Fiera in Italian colonial Libya, this collapse opened way to the real space of the concentration camps in Cyrenaica. It gave way to spaces, in the words of Giorgio Agamben, where "the most absolute *conditio inhumana* that has ever existed on earth was realized."[54] The camp had no meaning outside of itself for which it could be exchanged. It was an absolute limit: the Ursprung (origin) of pure, absolute, and impassable biopolitical space. There was no equivalent to the camp but the camp itself. Thus, the concentration camp was founded on what Baudrillard would call an impossible exchange.[55] This was an eccentric state of existence, wherein the sphere of the real was no longer exchangeable for the sphere of the sign. Both lost their force. It was a state in which illusion was the fundamental rule and discontinuity alone was probable.

In contemporary Italy at the *bonifica* museum, the collapse of distinctions wrought by imperial simulation also open up to a hyperreal concentration camp. Illusory and incomplete, this simulation stays a slender existence at the edges of the museum, its presence only intimated in metal gates and railroad ties. It is there and yet it is not. Here, the remnants of Auschwitz are imperial remains, yes, but they are also something else altogether: the simulation of an impossible exchange. As such, the camp-as-simulacra must remain unseen and unfinished, haunted as it is by the impossibility of spatializing the absolute *conditio inhumana* of the camp. This is imperial debris. The quantum void of simulation. The remainder of the hyperreal.

And this debris, this void, this remainder expands the museum's deliberately crafted narrative. No longer is the museum just a space that advances a "comprehensive understanding of [Fascist] ruralization as the creator of a society that is simultaneously modern and modernizing, natural and naturalizing," it is also a space in which difference in flattened and immanent knowledge emerges from simulation.[56] Walking along the train platform and into the boxcars, visitors stand among the deportees and inhabit their very spaces. We become every one of them. Thus, the museum renders the experience of deportation personal, as if we were all destined for the camp and are indeed still haunted by it. This is exactly the point: the heritage of the concentration camp belongs to all of us.[57] It still persists in the longue durée. It is a hyperreal remainder that reminds us never to forget.

NOTES

1   On the development of Fascist new towns in the Agro Pontino, see Federico Caprotti, *Mussolini's Cities: Internal Colonialism in Italy, 1930–1939* (Amherst, NY: Cambria, 2007); Alda Dalzini, *La terra promessa: breve storia della bonifica delle paludi pontine* (Latina: Museo Piana delle Orme, 2005); Mia Fuller, "Tradition as a Means to the End of Tradition: Farmers' Houses in Italy's Fascist-Era 'New Towns'," in *The End of Tradition?*, ed. Nezar AlSayyad (London: Routledge, 2004), 171–86; Diane Ghirardo, *Italy: Modern Architectures in History* (London: Reaktion, 2013). Mia Fuller's unpublished manuscript in progress, *Mussolini Threshing Still: Inertia Memoriae, Italy, and Fascist Monuments*, explores the symbolic legacy of these Fascist new towns in Italy and beyond.

2   Suzanne Stewart-Steinberg, "Grounds for Reclamation: Fascism and Postfascism in the Pontine Marshes," *differences* 27, no. 1 (2016): 94–142. My observations on the Museo Storico Piana delle Orme are based on three field visits I made to the *bonifica*

museum and the Agro Pontino region in March 2013, December 2014, and March 2016.

3   Italy's official tenure as a colonizing power lasted approximately fifty years from 1890 to 1943. In chronological order, Italian forces occupied Eritrea (1890); a small concession in Tianjin, China (1900); Libya (1911–12); Rhodes & the Dodecanese Islands in Greece (1911–12); Somalia (1927); Ethiopia (1936); and Albania (1939). On Italy's colonial legacy, see also the chapter by Flavia Marcello and Aidan Carter in this volume.

4   Patricia A. Morton, *Hybrid Modernities: Architecture and Representation at the 1931 Colonial Exhibition, Paris* (Cambridge, MA: MIT, 2000), 7.

5   Jean Baudrillard, *Simulacra and Simulation*, trans. Sheila Faria Glaser (Ann Arbor, MI: University of Michigan, 1994), 125.

6   Ibid., 1.

7   Stephanie Malia Hom, "Simulated Imperialism," *Traditional Dwellings and Settlements Review* 25, no. 1 (2013): 25–44.

8   Ann Laura Stoler and Carole McGranahan, "Introduction," in *Imperial Formations*, ed. Ann Laura Stoler, Carole McGranahan, and Peter C. Perdue (Santa Fe, NM: School for Advanced Research, 2007), 3–42.

9   On the *via negativa* spatialized in the form of the camp, see Bülent Diken and Carsten Bagge Laustsen, *The Culture of Exception: Sociology Facing the Camp* (London: Routledge, 2005), 18. On the spaces conditioned by the *via negativa* of Italian imperial formations, see Stephanie Malia Hom, *Empire's Mobius Strip: Historical Echoes in Italy's Crisis of Migration and Detention* (Ithaca, NY: Cornell University, 2019).

10 *Romanità* (Roman-ness) emerged as a key trope for justifying Italy's colonizing project in the Mediterranean, particularly in Libya. Rome, as both city and imaginary, assumed a place of prominence at the Fiera di Tripoli. Architect Alessandro Limongelli designed a Roman arch as the entrance to the fairgrounds in 1929. The colonial press hailed it as a triumphal arch under which every visitor had to walk to enter the Fiera's hyper-reality beyond. Rome was simultaneously a space of passage and point of historical fixity, *caput mundi* and *caput exhibitionis* in one. On *romanità*, see Sean Anderson, "The Light and the Line: Florestano di Fausto and the Politics of *Mediterraneità*," *California Italian Studies* 1, no. 1 (2010): 1–13; Joshua Arthurs, *Excavating Modernity: The Roman Past in Fascist Italy* (Ithaca, NY: Cornell University, 2012); Mia Fuller, *Moderns Abroad: Architecture, Cities, and Italian Imperialism* (London: Routledge, 2007), 40–41; Brian L. McLaren, *Architecture and Tourism in Italian Colonial Libya: An Ambivalent Modernism* (Seattle, WA: University of Washington, 2006), 158; Krystyna Von Henneberg, "Public Space and Public Place: Italian Fascist Urban Planning at Tripoli's Colonial Trade Fair," in *Italian Colonialism*, ed. Ruth Ben-Ghiat and Mia Fuller (New York: Palgrave, 2005), 158. For a representative example of positive colonial press coverage of the Fiera, see Anon., "Il padiglione di Roma alla III Fiera di Tripoli," *L'Italia Coloniale* 6, n. 5 (1929): 85.

11 Cristina della Colletta, *World's Fairs Italian Style: The Great Exhibitions in Turin and Their Narratives, 1860–1915* (Toronto: University of Toronto, 2006), 3.

12 Walter Benjamin, "Paris, Capital of the Nineteenth Century," *Reflections: Essays, Aphorisms, Autobiographical Writings*, ed. Peter Demetz, trans. Edmund Jephcott (New York: Schocken, 1978), 151.

13 On exhibitions generally, representative scholarship includes: Paul Greenhalgh, *Ephemeral Vistas: The Expositions Universelles, Great Exhibitions and World's Fairs 1851–1939* (Manchester: Manchester University, 1988); Patricia Mainardi, *Art and Politics of the Second Empire: The University Expositions of 1855 and 1867* (New Haven, CT: Yale University, 1987); Robert W. Rydell and Nancy Gwinn, eds., *Fair Representations: World's Fairs and the Modern World* (Amsterdam: VU University,

1994); Robert W. Rydell, *World of Fairs: The Century-of-Progress Expositions* (Chicago, IL: University of Chicago, 1993).

14 Timothy Mitchell, *Colonising Egypt* (Berkeley, CA: University of California, 1991), 34–62. See also Morton, *Hybrid Modernities*, 16–95.

15 Ibid., 1–33. On colonial exhibitions, see also Alexander C.T. Geppert, *Fleeting Cities. Imperial Expositions in Fin-de-Siècle Europe* (New York: Palgrave Macmillan, 2010); Nicola Labanca, ed., *L'Africa in vetrina. Storia di musei e di esposizioni coloniali in Italia* (Treviso: Pagus, 1992).

16 Raymond Corbey, "Ethnographic Showcases, 1870–1930," *Cultural Anthropology* 8, no. 3 (1993): 338–69; Anne Dreesbach, "Colonial Exhibitions, 'Völkerschauen,' and the Display of the Other," *European History Online*, March 3, 2012, accessed September 19, 2018, http://www.ieg-ego.eu/en/threads/models-and-stereotypes/the-wild-and-the-civilized/anne-dreesbach-colonial-exhibitions-voelkerschauen-and-the-display-of-the-other.

17 Mitchell, *Colonising Egypt*, 33.

18 Ibid., 178.

19 Ibid., 61.

20 Rare was the colonial exhibition staged on colonial soil. Aside from the Tripoli Trade Fair, the only other case seems to be the 1914 *Koloniale Tentoonstelling* held in Semarang (Java, Indonesia), which aimed to "give a comprehensive picture of the Dutch Indies in their present prosperous condition attained since the restoration of Dutch rule in 1914." Anon., "Calendar," *The Independent,* July 13, 1914: 49, accessed September 19, 2018, http://archive.org/stream/independen79v80newy#page/n53/mode/1up. On the Tripoli Trade Fair specifically, see McLaren, *Architecture and Tourism*, 26–27 and 57–59, and his "The Tripoli Trade Fair and the Representation of Italy's African colonies," *The Journal of Decorative and Propaganda Arts* 24 (2002): 171–97; Von Henneberg, "Public Space," 155–65.

21 McLaren, *Architecture and Tourism*, 132–34.

22 Fuller, *Moderns Abroad*, 151–70; Von Henneberg, "Public Space," 160–61.

23 In the Italian metropole, too, Fascist architects and planners recreated spaces to conform to ideals that never existed; for example, the "medievalization" of the Tuscan town, Arezzo. On this, see D. Medina Lasansky, *The Renaissance Perfected: Architecture, Spectacle and Tourism in Fascist Italy* (University Park, PA: Pennsylvania State University, 2005), 107–43.

24 Homi Bhabha, "Of Mimicry and Man," in *The Location of Culture* (London: Routledge, 1994), 126. On mise en abyme, see Lucien Dällenbach, *The Mirror in Text*, trans. Jeremy Whitely (Chicago, IL: University of Chicago, 1989).

25 Angelo Del Boca, *Italiani, brava gente? Un mito duro a morire* (Vicenza: Neri Pozza Editore, 2005), 44–51; see also a brochure produced by Ente Autonomo Fiera di Tripoli, *Tripoli* (Roma: Ente Autonomo Fiera di Tripoli, 1935): 1. Since the Fiera di Tripoli's main purpose was to justify Italy's colonizing project, especially to Italians themselves, the Fiera became a popular subject of propagandistic newsreels produced by Istituto Luce in the 1930s. See Ruth Ben-Ghiat, *Italian Fascism's Empire Cinema* (Bloomington, IN: Indiana University, 2015), 299–300. For a representative example of a newsreel about the Fiera, see "Tripoli: La Decima Fiera Campionaria di Tripoli alla presenza di Balbo," March 13, 1936, Newsreel B0850. Istituto Luce, accessed September 19, 2018, https://www.youtube.com/watch?v=Y2DqUJm073U.

26 DVD, "Museo Piana delle Orme" (Borgo Faiti, Latina, Italy: Museo Piana delle Orme, n.d.). See also Stewart-Steinberg, "Grounds for Reclamation," 122–28.

27 Angelo Piccioli, "La Fiera di Tripoli," *Gli Annali dell'Africa Italiana* 1, no. 2 (August 1938): 496–566.

28   Ibid., 498.

29   Ibid., 505.

30   Ibid., 505–06.

31   Giuseppe Borghetti, "Alla III Fiera di Tripoli: la svolta economica," *L'Italia Coloniale* 6, no. 5 (May 1929): 83.

32   Fuller, *Moderns Abroad*, 153.

33   Ibid., 155.

34   Roland Barthes, "The Blue Guide," *Mythologies*, trans. Annette Levers (New York: Hill and Wang, 1972), 75.

35   Ibid., 75.

36   Rhiannon Welch, *Vital Subjects: Race and Biopolitics in Italy, 1860–1920.* (Liverpool: Liverpool University, 2016).

37   Piccioli, "La Fiera," 542.

38   Ibid., 501.

39   Ibid., 501–02.

40   Ibid., 504.

41   "La terza Fiera Campionaria di Tripoli: nell'interno della mostra," *L'Italia Coloniale* 6, no. 5 (May 1929): 112–13.

42   E.E. Evans-Pritchard, *The Sanusi of Cyrenaica* (Oxford: Clarendon, 1949), 189.

43   Yusuf Salim al-Barghathi, "The Concentration Camps and the Harm Resulting from the Italian Invasion of Libya," in *'Umar al-Mukhtar, nashatuhu wa-jihaduhu min 1862 ilá 1931: dirasat fi harakat al-jihad al-Libi: a'mal al-nadwah al-'ilmiyah allati 'aqadaha Markaz Dirasat Jihad al-Libiyin Didda al-Ghazw al-Itali* ('Umar Al-Mukhtar—His Early Life and his Jihad from 1862 to 1931, Studies in the Libyan Jihad Movement: Proceedings of the Scientific Session Convened by the Center of the Study of the Jihad of Libyans against the Italian Invasion), ed., 'Aqil Al-Barbar et al. (Tripoli: al-Markaz, 1981), 113–49.

44   As cited in Ali Ahmida, *Forgotten Voices: Power and Agency in Colonial and Postcolonial Libya* (London: Routledge, 2005), 50–51.

45   Piccioli, "La Fiera," 524 and 527.

46   Baudrillard, *Simulacra and Simulation*, 6.

47   Ibid., 95.

48   Giorgio Agamben, *Remnants of Auschwitz: the Witness and the Archive*, trans. Daniel Heller-Roazen (Stanford, CA: Stanford University, 1999).

49   Mia Fuller, "Building Power: Italian Architecture and Urbanism in Libya and Ethiopia," in *Forms of Dominance: On the Architecture and Urbanism of the Colonial Enterprise*, ed. Nezar AlSayyad (Aldershot: Avebury, 1992), 211–39; Von Henneberg, "Public Space," 156.

50   Based on ticket sales, the Fiera had 81,000 visitors in its first year, 1927, and by its last year, 1939, had 180,000 visitors. Piccioli, "La Fiera," 503 and 562.

51   Anon., "La IV Fiera di Tripoli," *L'Italia Coloniale* 7, no. 2 (February 1930): 66–69.

52   Hom, "Simulated Imperialism," 38–41.

53   Baudrillard, "Simulacra and Simulation," 95–97.

54   Giorgio Agamben, *Homo Sacer: Sovereign Power and Bare Life*, trans. Daniel Heller-Roazen (Palo Alto, CA: Stanford University, 1998), 166.

55   Jean Baudrillard, *Impossible Exchange*, trans. Chris Turner (Paris: Éditions Galilée, 1999 repr. London: Verso, 2012). 5.

56   Stewart-Steinberg, "Grounds for Reclamation," 95.

57   Agamben, *Homo Sacer*, 175–78.

7

The legacy of colonial architecture in South Korea

The Government-General Building of Chosŏn revisited

Suzie Kim

South Korea offers a rich source for the study of modern architecture in formerly colonized territories. Throughout the Japanese colonial period, from 1910 to 1945, Japan sought to legitimize and signify its imperial Pan-Asian ambition and its coercion of Korea by constructing "modern" architectural landmarks in the Korean capital city of Kyŏngsŏng (Keijō in Japanese; now Seoul). Various Western styles of architecture were idealized as symbols of modernity, an ambition Japan had been promoting at home since the Meiji restoration in 1868. That ideal was brought to Korea starting in the 1910s, when Japanese architects began to shape the modern urban environment in the main districts of Kyŏngsŏng.[1] Even after the official end of colonialism, with the Japanese surrender to the Allies in August 1945, the Koreans struggled for a long time against the identities constructed for them by their former colonizers. Much of this effort was focused on reshaping the historic districts in the middle of the formerly colonized capital.

Applying the conceptual framework of postcolonialism to challenge dominant perspectives on inherited colonialist architecture in Seoul, this chapter re-evaluates the architectural style and historical context of the headquarters of the Japanese colonial administration (called the Government-General of Chosŏn), the Government-General Building of Chosŏn (GGB; constructed 1916–26), and discusses the current status of historic preservation in Korea [Figure 7.1].

To display the triumph of Imperial Japan over Korea, a highly symbolic site was chosen for the GGB, right at the Kyŏngbok Palace, the main palace of the last Korean imperial dynasty, Chosŏn (1392–1910). The Japanese dismantled and relocated the main gate Kwanghwamun, which led to the palace, and demolished 4,000 *kan* (a traditional Korean architectural measurement for the area framed by four pillars, approximately 5.76 square meters), including the residences of the king and queen, Kangnyŏngjŏn and Kyot'aejŏn. The GGB was built right in front of the Kŭnjŏngjŏn, the central hall of the palace where the Chosŏn kings were enthroned [Figure 7.2]. The concomitant destruction and relocation of Kwanghwamun in 1926 garnered heavy criticism from Japanese and Korean intellectuals at the time,

and from the mid-1980s the Korean government and Korean nationalist scholars condemned the placement of the GGB.[2]

Made of reinforced concrete, brick, and granite, the GGB was constructed as a five-story building with a basement. When it was finished in 1926, the massive building covered 7,336.25 square meters and included a total of 257 rooms.[3] It was executed in the Neoclassical style with barrel vaults, pilasters, stained glass, a protruding façade with decorative Corinthian columns, and an enormous Baroque dome on top. The interior of the main hall was furnished with two flights of stairs leading up to the second floor and two monumental mural paintings. It was reminiscent of contemporary Neoclassical or Beaux-Arts public architecture in Europe and America, as well as in select destinations in the Japanese Empire, including Taiwan, Manchuria, and of course Tokyo.

Discussing a building built by the colonial Government of Chosŏn as an icon of the Japanese occupation is a difficult task since the bitter memories of an older generation remain in both North and South Korea, and vehement, unresolved disputes about the colonial past still exist between Japan and Korea. The building's recent history reflects those difficulties and expresses its rhetoric: it was used as the government office of South Korea after independence from Japan

Figure 7.2
The former GGB seen
from the Kyŏngbok Pala▬
looking south towards
Seoul. Photograph 1995
Source: Canadiana
[Wikimedia Commons].

in 1945, was converted to the National Museum in 1986, and then was demolished between 1995 and 1997 [Figure 7.3].

However, as Michael Robinson argues, to understand the colonial period, we must neither reiterate the exploitative nature of Japanese imperialism nor focus on heroic Korean resistance.[4] Rather than debating whether the GGB should have been moved or preserved, or if it deserved to be demolished, revised postcolonial views have turned on recent scholarly research on the history of the GGB. Hyung-Il Pai's study examines the political intentions of former president Kim Young-sam (in office 1993–98) behind the destruction project, whereas Jong-Heon Jin's addresses the disruption of the nationalist discourse by investigating the transitional functions of the building.[5] Further qualitative studies on public responses to the demolition of the GGB have been conducted by Jung-Sun N. Han and Seung Ho Youn.[6] Instead of reiterating political ideologies and reception, this chapter focuses on the building itself, with a close investigation of the architectural form and its murals, all of which have been largely neglected in previous studies. It is important to acknowledge that the architectural experience and accumulated technical knowledge benefited both the colonizer and colonized in different ways, a perspective that is close to a revisionist view of postcolonialist theory.

Postcolonialists, starting with Edward Saïd and Bernard Cohn, have claimed that the European conquest over the colonies relied not only on their military and political strength but also on colonial knowledge.[7] They argue that the accumulation of colonial knowledge, which has been produced solely by the colonizers

ure 7.3
e demolition of the
mer GGB. Photograph
36. Source: The National
chives of Korea.

through their exploitation of the passive colonized, promised a better understanding of the colonized, resulting in supremacy over them.[8] Revisionists, such
as Eugene F. Irschick, Thomas R. Trautmann, and Philip B. Wagoner, agree with
the postcolonialist view that colonial knowledge contributed to the affirmation of
colonial rule. However, they advance the discussion by focusing on the transnational encounters between the colonizers and the local intellectuals and informants.[9] As Irschick argues, the dialogue between the colonizer and the colonized,
despite constant violence and issues of inequality, was deeply instrumental in the
construction of colonial knowledge.[10] Local individuals cached colonial knowledge as part of their expertise and used it later for their own advantage and
development. This "collaborationist" perspective, a term that has been coined
by Wagoner, is adopted here, positing that the construction of the GGB should
be understood as a synergic production of the colonizer and the colonized.
Furthermore, it is important to acknowledge that Koreans developed their own
"tactics" through the GGB, despite the severe oppression and tight military
rules placed on them by the Government-General of Chosŏn during this time.[11]
The term "tactics" is drawn from Michel de Certeau's study on the relationship
between the city and the individuals living in it. In his essay "Walking in the City,"
de Certeau viewed the city as a totalizing landmark generated by the strategies of
the government, other institutions, or power structures, while individuals or the
consumers are the walkers who try out, actualize, transform, or even abandon
the given urban space by using tactics. Thus, the walkers' divergent paths cannot

be reduced to a singular graphic trail on the map or to just accepting what was offered, but should be understood as an attempt to manipulate and diversify spatial organizations.[12]

The Japanese successfully demonstrated through the GGB that they were the sole rulers and commanders of the whole modernization process. At the same time, however, they also instilled skills in the first generation of young Korean architects and ordinary Koreans, who constituted the main construction work-force. While the Japanese learned from the local people how to handle native materials, such as granite and wood, the Koreans also learned how to use new construction materials that were imported from Japan, Europe, and America. Despite the oppressive structure and environment, the Korean architects soon found their own ways and solutions to continue the development of a distinctive modern architectural style in Korea during the late colonial period and after.

THE DEATH AND LIFE OF THE GGB

Against the vehement opposition of some professors, architects, and critics, the Korean government under President Kim Young-sam hastily scheduled the demolition of the GGB and a ceremony to connect that event to the fiftieth anniversary of independence from Japan, August 15, 1995.[13] The government regarded the building as the epitome of imperial belligerence and asserted that the demolition was both unavoidable and justifiable. In the demolition report of the GGB published in 1997, Song T'ae-ho, the Minister of Culture, Sports and Tourism, noted:

> The former GGB served as the symbol of Japanese colonialization over Korea and Korea's eternal dependency upon Japan … . This building had to be demolished to restore the Kyŏngbok Palace as a symbolic place of the nation, and to recover the nation's vital force [or spirit] and historical identity … . Even though the building doesn't exist anymore, we decided to publish an exact report of the demolition to remember our bitter history of the [colonial] past.[14]

After the building was completely deconstructed in 1997, most of the detritus was removed and discarded, but select remains, such as the Corinthian capitals, broken columns, the cornerstone, and the dome's lantern, were kept for commemorative political purposes. Some pieces were moved to the park of the Independence Hall of Korea, Ch'ŏnan, Korea and some were placed in front of the Seoul Museum of History [Figure 7.4]. In the park in Ch'ŏnan, the dome's lantern is displayed inside a crater, symbolizing burial. The other remains are chaotically dispersed through-out the park, to be overgrown with weeds. A label calls it "the gloomiest scene in history."

The life of this building tells a different story. The GGB — in theory a colonial building — was, in fact, used by Koreans for twenty-seven years longer than it was by the colonizers who built and first occupied it. Completed in October 1926, it housed the colonial-era Government-General of Chosŏn for approximately

Figure 7.4
Remains of the GGB
displayed in the Park of
the Independence Hall of
Korea, Ch'ŏnan, Korea.
Photograph 2018. Source:
Suzie Kim.

twenty years.[15] From September 9, 1945, when the Japanese flag in front of the Government-General building came down with the surrender of Japan, the building was used by the US Army Military Government in Korea until its withdrawal on August 15, 1948. At that time the independent Korean government started to use it for administration. The building was bombed during the Korean War, but it was soon restored and then continuously used by the government. With the beginning of the Fifth Republic of South Korea (1981–88), governed by President Chun Doo-hwan (in office 1980–88), the building was renovated and re-inaugurated on August 21, 1986, as the National Museum of Korea.[16] Soon after its opening to the public, harsh criticism was lodged against the content of the north and south mural paintings in the main hall [Figure 7.5]. Korean newspapers argued that the murals presented the political ideology of *Naisenittai* (内鮮一体, *Naesŏnilch'e* in Korean), a Japanese imperial assimilation policy that presented Japan and Korea as one entity, and that they needed to be torn down because they justified Korea's invasion by Japan. Despite the effort of some scholars who claimed that the murals should be preserved in situ within the repurposed GGB/museum building, they were removed from the walls just before the building was demolished in the mid-1990s. The detached murals remain in the archives of the National Museum of Korea, which has since 2005 been housed in a purpose-built structure in Seoul's Yongsan Family Park. The murals have been exhibited publicly only once, as a part of the *Tongyangŭl sujip'ada* (Collecting the East) exhibition, held from October 28, 2014 to January 11, 2015.

MAIN HALL MURAL PAINTINGS REVISITED

The murals in the main hall, by Japanese artist Wada Sanzō (1883–1967), visually denoted Japanese colonial policy as clearly as did the GGB's architecture. In the 1920s, the Government-General of Chosŏn sought traditional fairy tales that could be shared by both Koreans and Japanese. On the northern wall of the hall, Wada depicted a widely known Korean folktale of a woodcutter who helped a wounded deer and thereby discovered a place where fairies descended from heaven to bathe [Figure 7.6].[17] The artist depicted hunters tracking deer on the left panel. On the middle panel, a group of fairies bathe, with Mt. Kumgang (Diamond Mountain) in the background, while the woodcutter watches them from the right corner. He peacefully cuts wood on the right panel. For the hall's south wall, authorities selected the ancient Japanese *hagoromo* (a feathered robe that gives its name to the story) tale about a fisherman and a fairy. The fisherman, not identifiable as such from his garment or gestures, sits on a tree on the left panel. The relaxed fairies bathe at *Miho no Matsubara* (Miho Pine Grove) in the middle panel. The presence of Mt. Fuji in the background, as in the case with Mt. Kumgang on the north mural, establishes the story's setting. On the right is a peaceful gathering around a mother breastfeeding a child. Overall, the scenes, with their smooth pastel colors and soft contours, exude tranquility. The physiognomy of the figures does not indicate ethnicity. The pair of murals creates an imaginative story, and does not presume realistic renditions of local customs or true depictions of the traditional fairy tales.[18]

Figure 7.5
View towards the north side of the GGB's Main Hall (during its use as the National Museum of Korea). Photograph 198
Source: The National Archives of Korea.

ure 7.6
e GGB Main Hall murals
'ada Sanzō, 1926).
ith side mural (top) and
uth side mural (bottom).
e middle panel is 457
449 cm, and each side
nel is 414 x 395 cm.
ey are painted in oil on
per attached to canvas.
urce: The National
useum of Korea.

On October 18, 1986, *Dong-a Ilbo* (Dong-a Daily News) published an article titled "*Naesŏnilch'e* Mural on the Wall of the Main Hall at the National Museum of Korea Embellishes the Invasion of Japan."[19] The newspaper article harshly criticized the museum directors for being unaware of the content of the murals and their connection with the *Naesŏnilch'e* doctrine that had been taught to Koreans by the Japanese as part of their colonial policy, and it strongly argued for the murals' removal. In response to Koreans outraged by this news, Yi Kyŏng-sŏng, former director of the National Museum of Modern and Contemporary Art, and three professors from the Seoul National University and Chungang University met with Han Byŏng-sam, former director of the National Museum of Korea, on November 2, 1986.[20] The scholars claimed the murals should be preserved because, they argued, Wada had painted an allegorical representation of life and hope rather than realistic renditions of the two fairy tales or the imperialist ideas of *Naesŏnilch'e*.

Perhaps the scholars were correct. But neither they nor the public realized that the mural painting could be justifiably criticized as a careful conceptualization of the idea of the noble savage. The noble savage idea, popularized by philosopher Jean-Jacques Rousseau (1712–78), considered the original "man" to be free from sin, appetite, or the concept of right and wrong, and that this "savage" was not brutal, but honorable. The noble savage came to imply the intrinsic goodness of the colonized who had not yet been exposed to the corrupting influences of civilization. In the mural, the idyllic and nostalgic pastoral scenes of women and children, hunters and woodcutters fulfilling their duties, and the uncivilized, mysterious mountains in the background aligned well with the pastoral, romanticized countryside scenes. A notion of the noble savage to construct mythification was prevalent in the art scene during the colonial period. The so-called "local color" (*hyangt'osaek*) paintings that, like the mural, depicted calm and romanticized rural scenes, were preferred by the Japanese judges at the Chosŏn Art Exhibitions held in Kyŏngsŏng from 1922.[21] A nostalgic view of Korea's past legitimized Japan's imperial pan-Asian ambition and its occupation of Korea. Aware of this, and to amplify the effect of the GGB's architectural style, the Government-General of Chosŏn sought to add a mural with a topic intended to "provide a soft but deep impression on the audience."[22] It carefully omitted local customs and assimilated distinct national traditions, and thereby reflected the ruler's gaze — imperial custodianship of a colony's naïve past and a devaluation of the identity of the colonized.

LOOKING TO THE WEST: ARCHITECTURAL STYLE OF THE GGB

Whereas the GGB's murals articulated the rhetoric of colonial policies, its architectural style, which imitated recently constructed governmental buildings of the West, provided a profound research opportunity for both Japanese and Koreans. Iwai Chōzaburō (d. 1943), the chief architect of the Government-General of Chosŏn from 1921 to 1929, stated that the classical style and the use of granite would reflect the functional nature of the building.[23] The *Government-General of Chosŏn New Construction Report* (1929) simply described its style as "*kinseifukkōshiki* (Early Modern Revival)."[24] *Kinseifukkōshiki* was thus a style that would accommodate Japan's ambitions to make the building a symbol of the state's imperial power over Korea. Previous studies of the building, however, have not identified precisely to what "Early Modern Revival" referred. Neoclassical, neo-Baroque, and neo-Renaissance have been suggested, but without much argument.[25] The disagreement on even which stylistic period to assign the building reveals an even more fundamental problem, namely, that no detailed comparison with specific buildings that might have served as models has yet been undertaken. Most scholars have accepted the brief narrative found in the GGB demoliton report, that the prototypes were the City Hall in Singapore (constructed 1926–29, still extant), designed by the British architects A. Gordon and F.D. Meadows; the former Hongkong and Shanghai Banking Corporation Building (constructed 1921–23; now the Shanghai Pudong Development Bank) by the British architecture firm Palmer & Turner Architects and Surveyors; the National Museum of Taiwan, built by the colonial government in Taipei (constructed 1915); and the former Viceroy's House in New Delhi, India (constructed 1913–30, now the Indian president's residence), by British architect Sir Edwin Lutyens (1869–1944).[26] However, as the GGB was planned before, or while, these buidings were constructed, they cannot be treated properly as direct models. A connection to Lutyens's Viceroy's House is particularly tenuous at best. Lutyens's preliminary studies in 1920 of the exterior for the Viceroy's House include detailed sketches of the massive, and simple, dome in the middle and a colonnaded portico.[27] The Viceroy's House has a dome that is smooth and hemispherical, like a Buddhist stupa, but the GGB has a much smaller-scale dome and external ribs.[28] Formal similarities between the GGB and the other proposed models are also limited to more general and stylistically common attributes, thus rendering dubious the suggested connections. It would be more accurate to say that the GGB loosely shared the Neoclassical/Beaux-Arts style of architecture exhibited by these British and Japanese colonial buildings, generally symbolizing imperial power and sovereignty.

The changing leadership of the GGB's construction makes it difficult to assign sole authorship of the building. The first chief architect, a Prussian designer named George (Karl Adolph Guido) de Lalande (1872–1914) died two years after the project was initiated. After his death, Japanese architects Kunieda Hiroshi (1880–1943) and Nomura Ichirō (1868–1942) took over the project.[29] In addition to de Lalande's rich experience in Europe, China, and Japan, Kunieda's research trip to the United States and Europe in 1912 augmented the project team's competence in the construction materials, facilities, and structures of significant government buildings of the time. Kunieda traveled from Japan to Honolulu on April 18, 1912, and from there visited major cities in America, England, France, Switzerland, Italy, Austria, Hungary, Germany, and Russia before his return to Japan on December 2, 1912.[30] His itinerary makes it highly probable that British and American buildings were used as the models for the GGB. The GGB lacks any heavy decorative patterns on the exterior that were prominent in Baroque buildings of the seventeenth century, so one could argue that it followed the Grand Manner style, later called Edwardian Baroque in Britain. Edwardian Baroque buildings presented classical elements in a simple but delicate manner and drew from older significant buildings that furnished a uniquely national style, such as St. Paul's Cathedral (1675–1710) in London or Blenheim Palace (1705–22) in Blenheim, Oxfordshire, England.[31] The Edwardian Baroque typified the British imperial style of architecture of the late nineteenth and early twentieth centuries, and is illustrated in works by William Young (1843–1900), John Brydon (1840–1901), Herbert Baker (1862–1946), and Sir Arnold Thornely (1870–1953). It served as a symbol of the British conquest and assimilation of the colonies, a symbolism that aligned well with Japanese imperialist theory, which sought to build new infrastructure (such as the GGB) to evoke the image of colonized people being drawn into a burgeoning imperial community dominated by the Japanese.[32]

For a more direct parallel to the GGB, we might look to the Port of Liverpool building (formerly Mersey Docks and Harbour Board Offices, more commonly known as the Dock Office) in Liverpool, England, which was a typical Edwardian Baroque-style building, designed by Sir Arnold Thornely and constructed in 1903–07 [Figure 7.7]. Kunieda must have had the opportunity to explore this building on his way from London to Edinburgh in July 1912. It and the GGB have some identical features, namely, the rustication on the first floor, the origin of the

Figure 7.7
The Port of Liverpool
Building (Sir Arnold
Thornely, 1903–07).
Photograph 2012. Sou
Rept0n1x [Wikimedia
Commons].

Corinthian columns on the upper floors rather than the ground, and the Baroque-style copper dome with external ribs and base decorated with posts and columns. Most importantly, both buildings have segmented arches on the side of the four corners. Every segmented arch has a cornice on each end which is supported by an entablature and Corinthian columns. In the GGB, the segmented arch has been implemented directly into the four corners rather than on the side, but the other details are strikingly similar [Figure 7.8].

Likewise, American public buildings were also thoroughly researched by Kunieda during his visit to Washington, DC June 26–28, 1912. The Thomas Jefferson building of the Library of Congress, completed in 1897, was a direct model for the GGB, as evidenced by similar massings and plans [Figure 7.9]. Indeed, both make use of flat-roofed, square pavilions at their four corners, as well as rectangular floorplans with main halls and central domes bisecting their courtyards.[33] Fujioka Jūichi directly mentions in his 1925 *Chosen to Kenchiku* (Chosŏn and Architecture) article that the style of mosaic pattern and brass on the marble floor in the main hall of the GGB was copied from the main floor of the Library of Congress building.[34] In contrast to the harmonized, simple, and austere exterior of the GGB, its additional ornamentation was more experimental. The dome's lantern and the ornamental elements used to flank the exterior windows in the four corners, for example, featured an innovative style drawn from new and developing architectural trends in Central and Eastern Europe in the 1920s — Art Nouveau, Art Deco, Viennese Secession, and German Jugendstil [see Figures 7.8 and 7.10]. Fujioka noted at the beginning of his 1925 article that the materials used for decorations, such as stained glass for the dome, were meant to

reflect contemporary trends in the West.[35] He thought that using new materials and ornamentation would provide a great opportunity to try out and examine their quality and style. The GGB's architects were thus open to experimenting with materials and decorations, and were not beholden to strict classical stylistic norms.

THE INVOLVEMENT OF KOREAN ARCHITECT PARK GIL-RYONG

Even though the GGB was planned and constructed chiefly by European and Japanese architects, the workers were all Korean and Chinese.[36] In total, Koreans

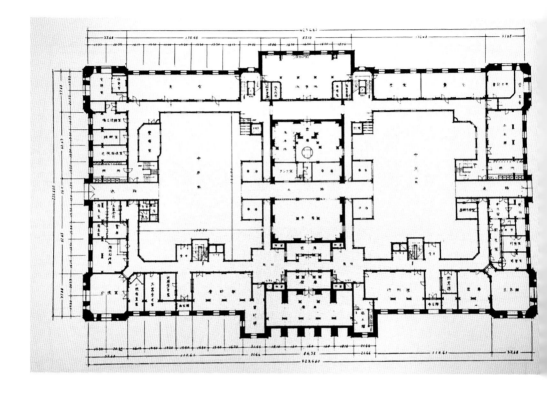

worked approximately 2 million worker days on this project.[37] Not all of the architects and engineers associated with the GGB were European or Japanese, however. In a letter written for the ceremony that commemorated the raising of the
ridge beam to complete the framework of the roof (*sangnyangje*) on May 17,
1923, Korean architect Park Gil-ryong (1898–1943) was credited as a junior engineer (*kisu*). Park, one of the first Korean graduates from the architecture department at Kyŏngsŏng College of Engineering in 1919, worked as a junior engineer
at the Ministry of Communications, where he practiced while assisting Japanese
architects. The college, established by the Japanese Government-General of
Chosŏn in 1916, accepted seven students in the architecture department, but
the courses were limited to draftsmanship and engineering. However, as Ahn
Chang-mo notes, the school should be considered the first institution to provide
a professional architectural curriculum identical to other engineering colleges in
Japan.[38] Park was promoted to Chief Engineer in 1932, and he opened his own
architecture firm in Kongp'yŏng-dong, Seoul that same year. Park's educational
pedigree and practical experience informed his design approach, which combined
the typical Neoclassicism of the GGB with modernist principles of plain, simple
formalism devoid of ornamentation. After being involved in the construction of
the GGB — the largest Western structure visible in Kyŏngsŏng — he applied his
knowledge to the design of the Namdaemun branch office building of Dong-il
bank in 1931, the first notable public structure designed by a Korean during
the colonial period. Even though it was much smaller in scale, he applied to the

Figure 7.9
The plan of the GGB's fi
floor. Plan 1929. Source
The National Archives of
Korea.

136 □

...e 7.10
...GGB's dome lantern
...display in the Park of
...Independence Hall of
...ea, Ch'ŏnan, Korea.
...tograph 2018. Source:
...e Kim.

bank building the GGB's style of copper dome with external ribs and pilasters. Park's design for the Hanchông Building (1935), with its ground-floor shopping arcade, gave way to a classicizing treatment, but the flat roof, the use of rein-forced concrete, and the rhythmic curtain walls decorated with uniform windows are typical of nondecorative modernist architecture. His preference for a mixture of a more classical Western style with modern trends was seen in his six-floor reinforced concrete masterpiece, the Hwashin Department Store (1937), where the current Chong-ro (Jongno) tower stands. Park Gil-ryong's designs should not be viewed as simply European or Japanese imports, but as a mediated type of colonial modernism, one that integrated native traditions and expectations with Japanese modernism. Unlike the Japanese architects, Park Gil-ryong recognized and employed local geography, language, and the people of Korea, and he also suggested a way to meld Western and Japanese style houses and urban *hanok* (Korean traditional houses).[39]

The desire to reconstruct the urban landscape using modern, Western-style architecture shows one of the many variable forms of colonial knowledge that the first generation of postcolonial Koreans contributed to and benefited from. The construction material, technique, and architectural style of the GGB marked a significant change in the history of Korean modern architecture, especially because Korean architects in the early twentieth century had few opportunities to study abroad in Europe and America, unlike the Japanese, and they could learn practical skills only by working as junior engineers for the colonial government or by studying under Japanese professors. Once liberated from Japanese rule, they soon found their own taste, and they amalgamated Western architectural elements with Korean ones.

CONCLUSION

The preservation of architectural works in postcolonial Korea has engaged some complicated issues due to the country's colonial past. In 1962, the Cultural Heritage Protection Act provided the legal framework that currently governs heritage preservation. The Cultural Heritage Administration (CHA) of the Republic of Korea recognizes five categories of heritage: state-designated heritage, city/province-designated heritage, cultural heritage material, registered cultural heritage, and undesignated cultural heritage. Starting from 2002 — late compared to other nations — the CHA designated architecture constructed from the late nineteenth century to the mid-1940s as "registered cultural heritage," the category for "architectural structures or monumental facilities of early modern or modern times, that have significant values and thus need to be preserved."[40] Korea's heritage preservation system clearly adopts UNESCO's international standards of heritage management, but not all of the colonial buildings remaining in Seoul have been registered.[41] The number of registered cultural heritage properties reached a total of 755 as of June 5, 2019. It includes significant buildings built by the Japanese architects during the colonial period, such as the Kyŏngsŏng Municipal Hall building by Iwai Chōzaburō in Jung-gu, Seoul (1925–26, registered cultural heritage property no. 52, now the Seoul Library). On June 25, 2018, the CHA announced that it will approve districts the size of townships (*myeon*) as registered cultural heritage zones. To begin with, CHA will approve the historic districts of Kunsan and Mokp'o, which served as significant port cities during the Japanese colonial period and recently became major tourist destinations due to their extant colonial-era architecture. This recent change signifies a positive move in expanding historic preservation. However, there remain a large number of noteworthy commercial buildings and residences built during the colonial period that have not yet been approved, despite their historical significance. Many have been razed, particularly in the Chong-ro and Yongsan areas of Seoul, to make space for new skyscrapers. This means that any buildings that are reminders of Japanese imperial dominance and are not registered as protected cultural heritage may suffer the same fate as that of the GGB, unless there is a reassessment and reconsideration of how such buildings might be interpreted as meaningful instructional tools worthy of historic preservation.

One recent example is particularly salient. In 1920, the Japanese removed parts of the Tŏksu Palace, in present-day Chŏngdong, Seoul, about a kilometer and a half south of Kyŏngbok Palace. In the process, they destroyed the Sŏnwŏnjŏn compound, a significant part of the Tŏksu Palace complex, which once held historic portraits of several Chosŏn kings. At the site of the compound, in 1938, the Japanese erected the residence for the old Chosŏn Savings Bank's president. Later home to the Vice-Ambassador of the United States, the house was one of the very few remaining Japanese style *bunka jutaku* (culture house) in Seoul, and for the last eighty years it has been extremely well preserved. On June 19, 2018, the CHA started a massive restoration project to rebuild the demolished parts of the Tŏksu Palace. The aim of this whole project, which is scheduled to be finished by 2038, is to cultivate Korea's unique cultural heritage, to inspire within citizens a pride for their national culture, and to convert the capital into one of the top global metropolises to proudly preserve the icons of its traditional culture.[42] The government decided to demolish all of the buildings adjacent to the Tŏksu Palace to make space to rebuild the Sŏnwŏnjŏn compound. So with very little notice, just three months after the launch of the project, in September 2018 the *bunka jutaku* was completely demolished, with no regard for its historical importance and not even allowing time for anyone to submit a proposal to register this remarkable building as cultural heritage. The decision is highly questionable and seems to be a political attempt to appropriate and erase the colonial past in the name of contemporary cultural nationalism, showing the current Korean government's inability to act fast enough to preserve all of its culturally significant architecture, including that which was built during the colonial period.

The GGB intrinsically embodied Korea's modernization process. As the new country sought out a national identity and struggled to reconcile that identity with its experience under the Japanese, the GGB had to be addressed. Japanese colonial policy had stressed the achievements of new infrastructure and monumental architecture to draw the colonized into a burgeoning imperial community dominated by the Japanese. At the same time, the new architecture, in a completely Western style, was Japan's creation of a new form of colonial knowledge that demonstrated and furthered its imperialist ambitions. Despite the GGB's contentious location, its politically charged murals, and the exploitative policies of the Government-General, it should not be forgotten that George de Lalande, Kunieda Hiroshi, and Nomura Ichirō's combined project introduced a groundbreaking landmark in Western art and architectural forms into the urban fabric of Kyŏngsŏng.

Through the exploration of the newly introduced architectural style of the GGB, just like any other architecture built in Seoul during the colonial period, the first generation of Korean architects could figure out multiple ways in the structured colonial space to gain knowledge, to draw inspiration, and to shape the modern urban environment under Korean self-determination. Its demolition offers relevant lessons for the future of historic preservation in Korea and Korea's full adherence to internationally recognized standards of heritage management.

NOTES

1   For the colonial history of Korea, see Hyung-Gu Lynn, ed., *Critical Readings on the Colonial Period of Korea, 1910–1945* (Leiden: Brill, 2013); Kyung Moon Hwang, *A History of Korea: An Episodic Narrative* (New York: Palgrave Macmillan, 2010).
2   Japanese scholar and art critic Yanagi Muneyoshi (1889–1961) and Korean Seol Eui-sik, possibly a pseudonym, criticized the demolition and relocation of Kwanghwamun. Koen de Ceuster, "The Changing Nature of National Icons in the Seoul Landscape," *The Review of Korean Studies* 3, no. 2 (2000): 93–98.
3   *Chōsensōtokufuchōshashineishi* (Government-General Building of Chosŏn New Construction Report), published in 1929, claimed that the building constituted 7,336.25 square meters. However, it was found to be 7,722.04 square meters when it was remeasured in 1997. Measurements retrieved from *Ku Chosŏnch'ongdokpu kŏnmul shilch'ŭk mit ch'ŏlgŏ pogosŏ* I (Government-General Building of Chosŏn Measurement and Demolition Report I) (Seoul: Ministry of Culture, Sports and Tourism and the National Museum of Korea, 1997), 114–15.
4   Michael Robinson, *Korea's Twentieth-Century Odyssey* (Honolulu, HI: University of Hawai'i, 2007), 4. For more on colonial modernity or colonial modernism in Korea, see Inha Jung, *Architecture and Urbanism in Modern Korea* (Honolulu, HI: University of Hawai'i, 2013), 3; Gi-Wook Shin and Michael Robinson, "Introduction," in *Colonial Modernity in Korea*, ed. Gi-Wook Shin and Michael Robinson (Cambridge, MA: Harvard University, 1999), 1–18.
5   Hyung-Il Pai, *Constructing "Korean" Origins: A Critical Review of Archaeology, Historiography, and Racial Myth in Korean State-Formation Theories* (Cambridge, MA: Harvard University Asia Center, 2000); Jong-Heon Jin, "Demolishing Colony: The Demolition of the Old Government-General Building of Chosŏn," in *Sitings: Critical Approaches to Korean Geography*, ed. Sallie Yea and Timothy R. Tangherlini (Honolulu, HI: University of Hawai'i, 2008), 39–58.
6   Jung-Sun N. Han, "Japan in the Public Culture of South Korea, 1945–2000s: The Making and Remaking of Colonial Sites and Memories," in *Imagining Japan in Post-War East Asia: Identity Politics, Schooling and Popular Culture*, ed. Paul Morris, Naoko Shimazu, and Edward Vickers (New York: Routledge, 2013), 106–26; Seung Ho Youn, "The Impact of Colonial Architectural Heritage on South Koreans' National Identity" (Ph.D. diss., University of Surrey, 2014).
7   Edward Saïd, *Orientalism* (New York: Routledge, 1978); Bernard S. Cohn, *Colonialism and Its Forms of Knowledge: The British in India* (Princeton, NJ: Princeton University, 1996).
8   Phillip B. Wagoner, "Precolonial Intellectuals and the Production of Colonial Knowledge," *Comparative Studies in Society and History* 45, no. 4 (2003): 783–84.
9   Eugene F. Irschick, *Dialogue and History: Constructing South India, 1795–1895* (Berkeley, CA: University of California, 1994); Thomas R. Trautmann, "Inventing

the History of South India," in *Invoking the Past: The Uses of History in South Asia*, ed. Daud Ali (London: Oxford University, 1999), 36–54; Wagoner, "Precolonial Intellectuals," 783–814.

10 Irschick, *Dialogue*, 8–9.

11 The independence movement and major upheavals in 1919 forced the colonial government of Chosŏn to switch to a more tolerant policy known as Cultural Rule (*bunka seiji*). Under this policy, the Japanese strategically allowed Korean elites to contribute to the decision-making and administrative process but, in reality, the surveillance system became even stronger, since the number of police stations increased fourfold. Robinson, *Korea's Twentieth-Century Odyssey,* 43–51.

12 Michel de Certeau, "Walking in the City," in *The Practice of Everyday Life*, trans. Steven Rendal (Berkeley, CA: University of California, 1984), 91–110.

13 On the strategic planning of the demolition by the Kim Young-sam government, see Hyung-Il Pai, *Constructing "Korean" Origins*, 237–243.

14 *Ku Chosŏnch'ongdokpu kŏnmul shilch'ŭk mit ch'ŏlgŏ pogosŏ* I, 3.

15 The closed and sacred ceremonial sites of the Kyŏngbok Palace were turned into public sites when the Government-General of Chosŏn hosted the Korean Industrial Exhibition (*Chosŏn mulsan kongjinhoe*) from September 11 through October 31, 1915. Jong-Heon Jin, "Demolishing Colony," 42.

16 *Ku Chosŏnch'ongdokpu kŏnmul shilch'uk mit ch'ŏlgŏ pogosŏ* I, 48–54.

17 The Government-General also suggested adding two murals beneath the south mural to represent the daily life of both countries. These were prepared, but were lost during the Korean War and thus were replaced with stuccos of the symbolic Korean national flower. *Changgwanbogosŏ chunganghol pyŏk'wa* (Ministry Report on the Murals in the Main Hall) (Seoul: Department of Management, Secretariat of the National Museum of Korea, Ministry of Culture and Tourism, 1986, report no. BA0756759), 6 (National Archives of Korea).

18 Kim Jung-sun suggested that the motifs do not present the original story and that the vague style of the clothing were intended to create a new fairy tale that would symbolize the unification of Japan and Korea, meaning that the two nations come from the same ancestors and share the same tradition. Kim based her argument on her in-depth research on other *hagoromo* paintings and Japanese mural paintings that followed the mural painting traditions by French artist Pierre Puvis de Chavannes (1824–98). Kim Jung-sun, *"Chosŏn ch'ongdokpu pyŏk'wae taehan koch'al — naesŏnilch'e p'yosangesŏ kŭndae pyŏk'waro"* (The Study of the Mural Painting of Japanese Government-General of Chosŏn: With a Focus on the Japanese Modern Mural Painting), *Misulsa nondan* (Art History Forum) 26 (2008): 141–70.

19 Anon., *"Kungnip chungangbangmulgwanŭi chunganghol pyŏge ilchech'imnyak mihwahan naesŏnilch'e pyŏk'wa"* (Naesŏnilch'e Mural on the Wall of the Main Hall at the National Museum of Korea Embellishes the Invasion of Japan), *Dong-a Ilbo* (Dong-a Daily News), October 18, 1986.

20 *Changgwanbogosŏ chunganghol pyŏk'wa* (Ministry Report on the Murals in the Main Hall), 6.

21 Youngna Kim, *20th Century Korean Art* (London: Laurence King, 2005): 106–23.

22 Iwai Chōzaburō, *"Sōtokufu shinchōsha no keikaku to jisshi ni tsuite"* (The Planning and Implementation of the New Government-General Building), *Chosen* (Keijō: Chosen Sōtokufu [Government-General of Chosŏn], April 1926), 19–20. Text quoted in Kim, *"Chosŏn,"* 142.

23 Iwai Chōzaburō, "*Shinchōsha no keikakuni tsuite*" (About the Plan of the New Government Building) *Chosen to Kenchiku* (Chosōn and Architecture) 5, no. 5 (1926): 6.

24 *Chōsensōtokufuchōshashineishi* (Government-General Building of Chosōn New Construction Report), trans. Kim Dong-hyeon (Seoul: National Museum of Korea, 1995), 57.

25 See *Ku Chosōnch'ongdokpu kŏnmul shilch'ŭk mit ch'ŏlgŏ pogosŏ* I; Tanigawa Ryūichi, "*Nihon shokuminchi to sono kyōkai ni okeru kenzōbutsu ni kansuru rekishiteki genkyū: 1867–1953 no nihon to chōsenhantō o chūsin toshite* (Historical Research on Japanese Colonies and the Buildings on the Border: Japan and Chosen Continent 1867–1953)" (Ph.D. diss., Tokyo University, 2008); Kim Jeong Dong, *Namainnŭn yŏksa sarajinŭn kŏnch'ungmul* (Remaining History, Vanishing Architecture) (Seoul: Daeweon-sa, 2012); Yasuhiko Nishizawa, "A Study of Japanese Colonial Architecture in East Asia," in *Constructing the Colonized Land: Entwined Perspectives of East Asia around WWII*, ed. Izumi Kuroishi (Burlington, VT: Ashgate, 2014), 11–42.

26 *Ku Chosŏnch'ongdokpu kŏnmul shilch'ŭk mit ch'ŏlgŏ pogosŏ* I, 38. For more on Lutyens's dome in New Delhi, see Aman Nath and Amit Mehra, *Dome over India: Rashtrapati Bhavan* (Mumbai: India Book House, 2002).

27 Images of the preliminary studies for the Viceroy's House are available through the online image library of the RIBA collections (see image nos. RIBA29671 and RIBA97592).

28 The dome with a square base seen in the 1918 plan was switched to a cylindrical drum with four piers wrapped around it.

29 *Ku Chosŏnch'ongdokpu kŏnmul shilch'ŭk mit ch'ŏlgŏ pogosŏ* I, 34–37. De Lalande, born in Prussia in 1872, completed his undergraduate studies at the Royal Institute of Technology, Charlottenburg (today the Technical University of Berlin) in 1894. After graduation, he worked in the planning department of Wrocław and Głogów, Poland, and later at architectural offices in Vienna and Berlin. In 1901, he moved to Shanghai and Tianjin, China, and worked under German architect Richard Seel (1854–1922). After two years, he moved to Yokohama, Japan, and upon his return to Germany he took over the Seel office. The appointment of de Lalande as chief architect of the GGB was secured not only because of the need for a person of significance but because of his close relationship with Terauchi Masatake (1852–1919), the first Japanese Governor-General of Korea. Tanigawa, in his study of the building, argued that de Lalande finished the design of the exterior; Kunieda was in charge of the overall structure, material, facilities, and construction; Nomura decided the design of the space and layout; and Fujioka Jūichi added some final touches to the interior design and provided final construction supervision. Tanigawa, *Nihon*, 343–45.

30 Kunieda visited Chicago, New York, Washington, DC, London, Edinburgh, Glasgow, The Hague, Brussels, Paris, Lucern, Milan, Geneva, Rome, Pompeii, Naples, Florence, Venice, Vienna, Budapest, Leipzig, Berlin, Hamburg, St. Petersburg, Moscow, and Vladivostok, according to Tanigawa. This information was retrieved from the forty postcards that Kunieda sent to his brother Kunieda Susumu. The postcards were kept by Kunieda's daughters Yamane Yōko and Hukami Reiko. Ibid., 330–31.

31 G.A. Bremner, "The Metropolis: Imperial Buildings and Landscapes in Britain," in *Architecture and Urbanism in the British Empire*, ed. G.A. Bremner (Oxford: Oxford University, 2016), 125–58.

32 Todd Henry, "Respatializing Chosŏn's Royal Capital: The Politics of Japanese Urban Reforms in Early Colonial Seoul, 1905–1919," in *Sitings: Critical Approaches to Korean Geography*, ed. Sallie Yea and Timothy R. Tangherlini (Honolulu, HI: University of Hawai'i, 2008), 15–38.

33 However, the veranda/hallway, added later and not present in the 1918 plan, was certainly modeled after the Government-General Building of Taiwan, since Nomura, who was in charge by then, had served before as the chief architect for the Government-General Building of Taiwan.

34 Fujioka Jūichi, "*Chōsha no sōshoku to kōgei*" (The Ornamentations and Crafts of the Government Building), *Chosen to Kenchiku* (Chosŏn and Architecture) 5, no. 5 (1925): 31–38.

35 Ibid., 31.

36 Iwai noted that using stones on the exterior of the GGB might exceed the cost of the Government-General Building of Taiwan, which used bricks, but the cheap labor provided by Korean and Chinese workers would keep the cost lower than what had been estimated in Japan. Iwai, "*Shinchōsha*," 6.

37 *Chosŏnch'ongdokpuch'ŏngsa kwallyŏn kirongmulch'ŏl* (Compilation of Records on the Government-General Building of Chosŏn) (Seoul: Account Department of the Government-General, document nos. CJA0012788, 1937 and CJA0012932, 1937–38), 4 (National Archives of Korea).

38 Ahn Chang-mo, "*Ilcheha kyŏngsŏng godŭng gongŏphakkyo wa kŏnch'uk kyoyuk*" (A Study on Kyôngsông College of Engineering and Architectural Education), *Taehan'gŏnch'uk'ak'oe nonmunjip – kyehoekkye* (Journal of the Architectural Institute of Korea – Planning & Design) 14, no.6 (1998): 35–46.

39 On Park Gil-ryong's reformation theory of dwelling, see Woo Dong-sun, "On Park Gil-ryong's Discovering, Understanding, and Designing of Korean Architecture," in *Constructing the Colonized Land: Entwined Perspectives of East Asia around WWII,* ed. Izumi Kurioshi (Burlington, VT: Ashgate, 2014), 193–214; Kim Myung-Sun, "*Pakkillyongŭi ch'ogi chut'aekkaeryanganŭi yuhyŏnggwa t'ŭkching – Chapchie shilsaenghwal e 1932–3 nyŏn palp'yohan 10 p'yŏnŭi chut'aekkyehoeganŭl chungshimŭ-ro*" (The Improved Plans of Korean Traditional Houses by Gil-ryong from Late 1920s to Early 1930s – Ten Floorplans Published in the Magazine "Real Life(實生活)" in 1932–3) *Taehan'gŏnch'uk'ak'oe nonmunjip – kyehoekkye* (Journal of the Architectural Institute of Korea – Planning & Design) 27, no. 4 (2011): 61–70.

40 The Cultural Heritage Association (Republic of Korea), "Heritage Classification," accessed October 1, 2018, http://english.cha.go.kr/html/HtmlPage.do?pg=/classfication/classification.jsp&mn=EN_02_01.

41 The rules follow the UNESCO "Convention Concerning the Protection of the World Cultural and Natural Heritage," from 1972. In the Convention text, cultural heritage monuments are defined as "architectural works, works of monumental sculpture and painting, elements or structures of an archaeological nature, inscriptions, cave dwellings and combinations of features, which are of outstanding universal value from the point of view of history, art or science." See United Nations Educational, Scientific, and Cultural Organization (UNESCO), "Convention Concerning the Protection of the World Cultural and Natural Heritage," 2, accessed October 31, 2018, https://whc.unesco.org/archive/convention-en.pdf.

42 *Tŏksugung sŏnwŏnjŏn pogwŏnjŏngbi kibon'gyehoek* (Fundamental Planning for the Restoration of Tŏksu Palace Sŏnwŏnjŏn) (Seoul: Cultural Heritage Administration, 2014), 10.

Part III

Inherited colonial-era spaces in contemporary postcolonies

8

Spatial governmentality and everyday hospital life in colonial and postcolonial DR Congo

Simon De Nys-Ketels, Johan Lagae, Kristien Geenen, Luce Beeckmans, and Trésor Lumfuankenda Bungiena

THE HOSPITAL AS AN AMBIVALENT COLONIAL/POSTCOLONIAL INSTITUTION

At the time of this chapter's writing, in May 2018, the Democratic Republic of the Congo (henceforth Congo) was, alas not for the first time, enduring an outbreak of the Ebola virus. This time the disease had appeared near Mbandaka, a city situated in the part of the country that Joseph Conrad famously described as the "Heart of Darkness."[1] Together with the ongoing armed conflict in the country's eastern regions and the political turmoil in the southern Kasaï province, this latest crisis strengthens the highly mediatized image of Congo as a country torn by war, poverty, and disease. According to all international monitoring sources, vulnerability and poverty indicators in Congo, including health, are "catastrophic."[2] The resulting mass-migration, both internal and to/from neighboring territories, has had a devastating impact on healthcare in the rural areas.[3] Though Ebola has most recently struck in rural areas, the situation in Congo's major urban centers is equally troublesome. In a 1984 description of the situation in the country's capital, Kinshasa, doctor Zam Kalume provides an early, bleak account of what has become today an everyday reality for most Congolese: a complete lack of social welfare programs, the decrepit state of a totally insufficient healthcare infrastructure, and insurmountable difficulties in obtaining reliable medication.[4] Illness in Congo, so Kalume writes, is a "luxury" that only a few can afford. Hospitals have been infested by an *"économie de la 'débrouille'"* ("economy of making do"), meaning that in the absence of regularly paid salaries, medical staff charge patients directly or prefer to provide healthcare services in private offices, which in local parlance are referred to as *"polycliniques de fortune"* ("good luck polyclinics").[5] More recent surveys among Kinshasa's population indicate that the situation has not improved, revealing that, surprisingly enough, households in fact do not even list healthcare among their top concerns, as they see themselves confronted with other, more urgent challenges.[6] For quite some time important efforts have been made via humanitarian aid programs, multilateral agencies, and non-governmental organizations (NGOs) with regard to the treatment of HIV, Malaria, and Ebola, resulting in a medical landscape increasingly shaped by transnational flows of expertise and resources. Congo is now experiencing what scholars have defined as the emergence of a "global health" paradigm in Africa.[7] Recent decades have also seen a strong proliferation of healing churches of all kinds, selling the promise of a better future — often at high cost — while introducing new forms of solidarity. Under the reign of Joseph Kabila, the situation has not substantially changed, despite the fact that healthcare was one of the spearheads in his "Cinq Chantiers" ("Five Building Sites") plan launched during the 2006 presidential campaign.[8] In 2019, the situation for the average Congolese, and in particular for the Kinois (inhabitants of its capital city, Kinshasa), thus remains very much consistent with the situation described in 2004 by Persyn and Ladrière wherein "healthcare is no longer perceived as a basic public service, but as a free-market commodity."[9]

The current state of healthcare services is often used to depict today's Congo as a "failed state."[10] Both apologists for colonialism seeking to counter rising critiques of Belgian colonial rule, and Congolese lamenting the incompetence and greed of the current political elite, tend to contrast the current "failure" with an often nostalgic discourse on healthcare services in Congo on the eve of independence, when the efforts made by the Belgian government in the medical domain afforded the Belgian Congo an international reputation as a successful *colonie modèle* (model colony). Compared to the situation in other colonized territories, the number of urban general hospitals, neighborhood dispensaries, and rural health centers constructed in the context of the *Ten Year Plan for the Economic and Social Development of the Belgian Congo* (1949–59) was admittedly impressive. Yet, this whole operation remained an extremely paternalistic act. Just before independence, for instance, not one Congolese had graduated as a doctor, even if a large and very competent workforce of medical assistants had been trained.[11] Postcolonial scholarship moreover has already clearly revealed the reverse of the philanthropic discourse of colonialism, demonstrating that the provision of healthcare and the development of medical knowledge in Africa was not only a crucial instrument used to safeguard the wellbeing of the colonizer in a territory considered "a white man's grave," but, perhaps more importantly, to secure the productivity of African labor much needed for a successful economy of exploitation. Drawing on Foucault's ideas, several scholars have described public healthcare as a specific form of biopolitics — which Achille Mbembe in the context of colonial rule provocatively redefined as "necropolitics"[12] — in which race was instrumentalized to "decide who would live and who would die."[13]

This chapter interrogates this contrast between a claimed colonial success and the alleged incapability of the current Congolese authorities in the domain of healthcare via another angle. More specifically, it draws on the notion of "governmentality" (introduced by Michel Foucault in his later writings)[14] to blur such distinction between the colonial past and the postcolonial present. Rather than drawing on the Panopticon,[15] a Foucauldian reference commonly used in spatial analyses of colonial hospitals targeting the colonized population,[16] this chapter begins with "governmentality," or the "art of government" and the way it relates to the design and use of space, both architectural and urban as a powerful entry point. Such an approach allows one to counter the assessment of colonial hospital sites as strictly disciplinary environments aimed at "creating economically efficient yet politically docile subjects."[17] Extending the use of this notion of governmentality to postcolonial healthcare practices enables one to entail a more nuanced discussion of how past and present relate and whether terms like "neocolonial" and "neoliberal" can really help in defining the contemporary conditions in Congolese hospitals. In the specific case of Congo, one may conclude that they may not, as practices and policies of healthcare, just like in other policy domains, may be better be described in terms of what some scholars have started to call "hybrid governance."[18]

Towards these ends the present chapter focuses on the Hôpital Provincial Général de Kinshasa (Provincial General Hospital of Kinshasa), a large medical complex situated in the city center of Congo's capital city [Figure 8.1]. Originally conceived as the first major hospital for Africans, with construction work starting in 1922, the hospital has been expanding throughout the decades. Often referred to by the name it acquired during president Mobutu's reign (1965–97), Hôpital Mama Yemo, it still functions today as one of the major sites of public healthcare in a city currently accommodating (according to official, and unreliable, surveys) twelve million inhabitants. Discussing how this site was subject to forms of spatial governmentality over time — thus paying attention to "micropolitics of power" at work on site and confronting this with an, albeit incomplete, inquiry of the

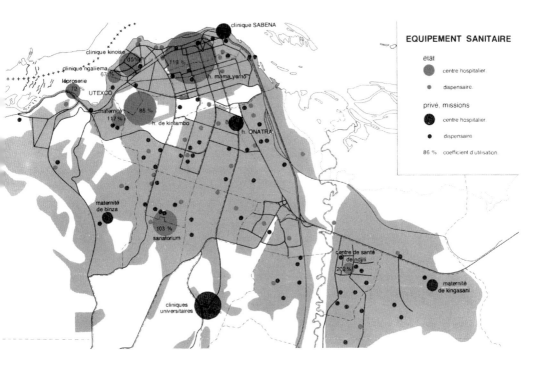

everyday life that actually occurred within its boundaries — highlights moments of failure, conflict, and tension which at times profoundly unsettled colonialist pursuits of order and discipline. Such an approach facilitates an understanding of healthcare facilities less as instruments of a dominant power, but rather as the product of a constant negotiation between a multitude of actors including doctors, nurses, patients and their families or relatives, local authorities, neighboring communities, and, in more recent decades, foreign experts and consultants. It is arguably this ambivalence that forms a pattern of continuity from colonial to postcolonial contexts, and nuances the alleged contrast between a successful colonial healthcare system and a failing postcolonial one sketched above. Indeed, even within the *colonie modèle* context, authorities regularly struggled to provide sufficient healthcare, and dealt with situations reminiscent of some of the deplorable scenes seen in today's Congolese hospitals. Such a focus on ambivalence thus reminds one of the limits of power that seem absent in current discussions of hospitals as biopolitical institutions, both in the colonial past and what is sometimes too narrowly defined as a neocolonial present.

HEALING THE COLONIAL CAPITAL CITY

In 1909, only one year after the international campaign against the colonial "red rubber" regime in Congo had forced Belgium's King Léopold II (*r.*1865–1909) to cede the Congo Free State (erstwhile a personal possession) to the Belgian state, the then Prince (and soon to become king) Albert visited the territory. As a noted advocate of labor reform, he lamented "the detestable sanitary state" of the capital and criticized the previous politics of exploitation of the Congo Free State. Eager to shed the stigma inherited from the earlier Free State period, the new Belgian colonial administration quickly established a colonial medical service and additional government agencies. These focused no longer mainly on the sanitary condition of the white colonizer, but from 1911 onwards increasingly emphasized the "well-being" of the Congolese.[19] Delayed in part by World War I, however, the first comprehensive program for hospital infrastructure was not developed until the early 1920s, as part of a large building campaign also including road, rail, and waterway infrastructure. In keeping with general segregationist policies, the program developed separate facilities and services for the European and African populations.

The city of Kinshasa, known at the time as Léopoldville and destined to become the capital city of the Belgian Congo in 1923, had been in dire need of new and modern medical facilities. The existing hospital for Africans had become particularly dilapidated and overcrowded because of a rural exodus from the surrounding regions. Patients were often forced to stay outdoors because wards were fully occupied, the contagious sick were often not separated from non-contagious patients, and those who had broken "in house" rules were simply chained to a tree.[20] Realizing the urgent need for additional medical infrastructure for Africans, colonial authorities designed and built a new Hôpital des Noirs

(Hospital for Blacks). Run by white personnel but almost exclusively serving African patients, the new hospital opened its doors in September 1924, counting three wards for around seventy patients. The complex grew rapidly with the addition of several new pavilions and offered medical care to over 320 patients. The expanded Hôpital des Noirs quickly became one of the showpieces of Belgian Congo's public healthcare propaganda. Contemporary reporters applauded the way the hospital wards facilitated a neat division by sex, religion, and pathology, and praised its overall comfort and cleanliness, which was said to surpass "numerous Belgian provincial hospitals, which are not as well-equipped."[21]

Designed according to the pavilion typology model [Figure 8.2], the new Hôpital des Noirs seems to epitomize Foucault's description of a *"machine à guérir"* (healing machine),[22] a biopolitical disciplinary institution, which, by "ordering and regimenting space,"[23] simultaneously sought to cure and discipline its patients. Providing separated and well ventilated wards for each pathologically distinct illness, and connecting these by a series of covered corridors, this particular architectural typology facilitated a strict sanitary regime aimed at maximizing the healing potential of the sick. At the same time, however, the isolated pavilions and the internal design of the wards not only allowed medical observation, pathological classification and the collection of biostatistics. Also noteworthy, the hospital's design facilitated the surveillance and disciplining of Congolese patients, as the quarters for the *gardes de nuit* (night guards) strategically overlooked the hospital's circulatory spaces and main entrances [Figure 8.3].

DISCIPLINARY REGIMES AND THEIR LIMITS

It is tempting to interpret the Hôpital des Noirs as a classical example of the biopolitical Panopticon.[24] However, a combined spatial analysis on the scale of the complex and its immediate surroundings, and an investigation of everyday hospital life — traces of which surface in archival sources — demonstrate that the Hôpital des Noirs differed significantly from the ideally sanitized and disciplined space which a Foucauldian perspective suggests. Real conditions proved much more complicated and far less precisely managed. When viewed on the urban scale, the medical facility unsettled the colonial order, as the Hôpital des Noirs did not fit the strict binary and sanitary logics of the colonial city, the spatial planning of which was, according to widespread practices in Sub-Saharan Africa, based on the principle of racial segregation.[25] When the white personnel of the Hôpital des Noirs welcomed its first African patients in 1924, the complex was situated in an ambiguous zone, a strip of land where the European residential area of Léopoldville gradually transitioned into the African part of town.[26] In the early 1930s, when the Belgian colonial administration sought to enforce a more strict segregation, this strip was transformed into a neutral zone (*cordon sanitaire*), in order to neatly separate the European *ville* (city) from the African *cité indigène* (native town). The implementation of this *cordon sanitaire* saw the Hôpital des Noirs (as well as the marketplace and the police camp) positioned on the wrong, that is to say European, side of

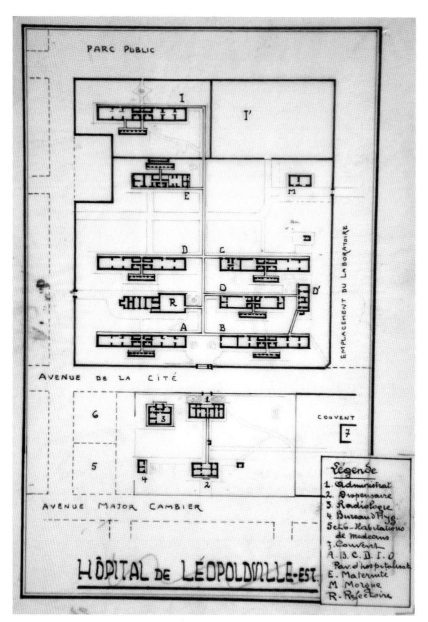

Figure 8.2
The pavilion-type Hôp
des Noirs, Kinshasa.
Plan c.1933. Source:
"Les Hôpitaux pour
Européens et Indigène
construits ces dernière
années à Léopoldville,
Assistance Hospitalière
1 (1934), 12 [Library
Faculty of Engineering
and Architecture, Ghe
University, TW01.TS.H

the neutral zone [Figure 8.4]. The "out-of-place" location of these public facilities sparked fears of contamination and promiscuity amongst European inhabitants and colonial administrators, generating a long-lasting polemic among colonial officials regarding a possible relocation of the hospital.[27]

On a more general note, these discussions reveal how medicine, urban planning, and racial segregation were closely intertwined in the African colonial context, as contemporary preconceptions of hygiene pathologized the African body in the tropics.[28] Indeed, calling for a relocation of the hospital, the head of the local

Public Works Department argued that urban hygiene was impossible to safeguard while "maintaining the Hôpital des Noirs at its current location."[29] Simultaneously, many Europeans occupying parcels adjacent to the Hôpital des Noirs complained about the unhygienic conditions triggered by the African patients and their numerous visitors at the hospital. Despite these tensions, the hospital was never relocated, mainly because this would have entailed too high a cost at a time when the colonial government struggled with an economic recession. In an attempt to reassure the European population in the vicinity of the hospital, the provincial governor committed in 1929 to heightening the complex's existing enclosure wall to "conceal the medical facilities and the life of its users to passers-by and neighbors" [Figure 8.5].[30]

Reflecting an obsession with visual regimes of control among colonial officials, the wall turned the medical complex into an enclave divorced from its European surroundings. The wall did not, however, hermetically shield European passers-by from the smells, sounds, and germs associated with the presence of sick African bodies. More striking even, was the location of the hospital's main entrance, situated at the northern side of the complex. Ironically providing easy access from the European quarter, it was placed at the largest possible distance from the African neighborhood, thereby necessitating a flow of sick Africans who, in seeking treatment, had to cross the neutral zone by way of the European area. This practice completely nullified the medical purpose of the *cordon sanitaire*. The unsatisfactory situation was addressed in 1937 when a new, southern entrance was planned in order to open up the hospital site directly to the "native town" it was intended to serve.[31] It would take more than ten years to complete even this modest adaptation to the hospital's infrastructure.

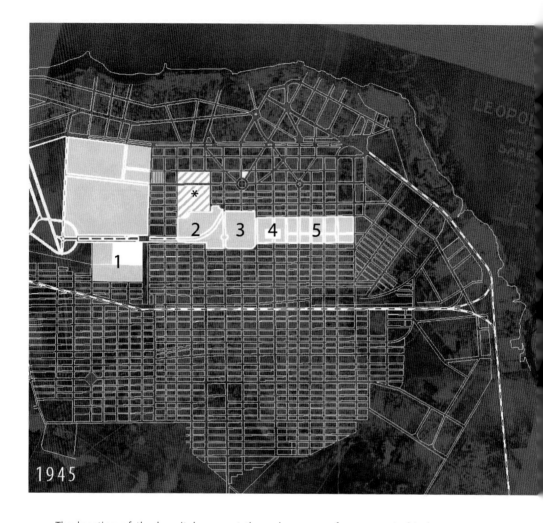

The location of the hospital was not the only source of concern. Archival sources from the late 1920s and 1930s provide ample evidence that within its perimeter wall, too, the medical complex was far from the sanitary, regimented, and disciplinary institution an ideal biopolitical Panopticon presupposes.[32] While the original design of the hospital foresaw a strict compartmentalization according to sex, social class, and disease type, in reality, the hospital management determined the actual use of the wards on the spot, often resulting in a pragmatic mixing of categories. Original intent was disregarded for other reasons as well. For example, in the early stages, the European nursing nuns were accommodated within one of the pavilions intended for Africans, as funds were insufficient for the construction of their convent. Testifying to the building's less than ideal condition, in 1931 the head of the local medical service described its hygienic state as an "unequalled danger."[33] The smell of the kitchen was said to be unbearable and the laundry room, in which cement (rather than easily cleanable tiles) had been used to cover the floor, lacked a properly functioning disinfection unit. Other high-ranking

Figure 8.4
Kinshasa with the location of the Hôpital des Noirs (indicated by asterisk) and the *cordon sanitaire* (indicated in grey), c.194 Plan 2012. Source: Ruth Kennivé, Rebekka Van Coster, and Johan Lagae (aerial photo from 1931) Also highlighted are an area for urban gardening (5), the market (4), the Parc de Bock (3), a zoo (2 The new police camp (1) is located just south of th *cordon sanitaire.*

officials also criticized the hospital's deplorable sanitary circumstances, lamenting for instance the intolerable unhygienic state of its toilets, its failing sewer system, and the staff's poor waste management practices. A decade later, this waste problem had still not been resolved, as it was noted that medical personnel littered the grounds with garbage due to an insufficient number of waste bins.[34]

These sanitary problems were exacerbated by the flood of African migrants relocating to the city during the 1920s and 1930s. As the largest part of the growing African population sought healthcare in the Hôpital des Noirs, the medical facility quickly lacked sufficient beds, despite the addition of several new pavilions to the existing structure. The overcrowding of the Hôpital des Noirs, however, was also due to the fact that its management had started allowing Congolese family members to cook for their relatives within the hospital during mealtimes. Close reliance on family members for personal medical care was a practice with precolonial origins,[35] but both European doctors and African nurses regarded the practice of Congolese accompanying hospitalized family members with suspicion, as they felt it hindered the hospital's efficiency. Over time however, the medical staff turned a blind eye to such practices and even facilitated them, taking a pragmatic attitude towards problems they were unable to tackle themselves because of limited resources. After Congolese patients had repeatedly complained about the "European" food made by the nurses, the management of the Hôpital des Noirs, for instance, decided to construct sheds as *cuisines indigènes* ("native kitchens"), allowing African wives to cook for hospitalized and attendant family members. Such emerging alternative forms of governance prefigure the present-day situation in Congolese hospitals, with patients now always being accompanied by so-called *gardes-malades*, one or more relatives who not only cook, but also take care of other logistic tasks such as the purchase and administration of medications.

As these instances of everyday life unveil, the Hôpital des Noirs in Kinshasa was far from a strictly regulated Panopticon, where a dominant colonial government unambiguously succeeded in realizing a rigidly zoned, sanitized, and well-surveilled space. Instead, the hospital's out-of-place location, unhygienic circumstances, overcrowded facilities, and the agency of patients and their guests to influence the hospital's procedures and built environment, bear witness to the colonial administration's continuous struggle to rigorously implement a strict regime of hygiene and discipline.

Problems continued to plague the Hôpital des Noirs throughout the postwar period, when the colonial government's healthcare ambitions reached their pinnacle. A 1955 newspaper article, tellingly titled "Les femmes dorment sur le sol" (Women are sleeping on the floor),[36] not only echoes situations described in sources of the early decades of the Hôpital des Noirs, but it also foreshadowed current mediatized scenes of today's Congolese hospitals.

POSTWAR AND POST-INDEPENDENCE WELFARE AMBITIONS

In 1947 the Belgian colonial government decided to design and construct a new and vast medical complex for Congolese to complement the existing overcrowded Hôpital des Noirs.[37] This was also the time when preparation for the *Ten Year Plan for the Economic and Social Development of the Belgian Congo* (1949–59) was underway, and a general consensus had been reached among colonial officials that important investments in public healthcare were to be made, if only to assuage growing international criticism of European colonialism in Africa. Reflecting the welfarist turn in the postwar policies of the Belgian Congo, this new hospital was to become an important urban landmark in Kinshasa. The Brussels-based architect and urbanist Georges Ricquier — who in 1948–49 would author a monumental, imperialist masterplan for "Le Grand Léo" — was tasked with the design.[38] Consistent with recommendations by officials in the colonial medical service, Ricquier renounced the pavilion typology, which, although still widespread throughout the colony, had become outdated in Belgium. Instead, he opted for the more up-to-date planning principle of the *hôpital en bloc*, designing a complex in which a number of multistory wings (*blocs*) accommodated different functions (patients' wards, operation rooms, technical services, etc.) [Figure 8.6]. The most important aspect of his project, however, concerned the hospital's location. Ricquier situated the new hospital complex far south of the *cordon sanitaire* which had been implemented during 1930s, in close proximity of the new "native towns" that were being planned and built from the late 1940s onwards, thus

taking into consideration future expansions of the city and bringing public health-care much closer to the majority of African patients. Most importantly, however, his proposal demonstrated a clear break with the "out-of-place" siting of the existing Hôpital des Noirs, and a return to neat race-based spatial segregation. At a time when prominent colonial medical experts were starting to question the reasoning behind the *politique de la peau* ("politics of the skin") in the domain of healthcare, as well as the placement of healthcare facilities for Europeans and Africans in separate parts of the city, Ricquier's plan for the new hospital, as well as his urban masterplan, explicitly aimed to restore the segregationist principle of the cordon sanitaire.[39]

Ricquier's *pièce de résistance* was, however, never realized. His original hos-pital design proved too costly, forcing the colonial government to downgrade the design several times. After long and tiresome negotiations, causing many delays — despite the urgent need for new healthcare facilities — Ricquier was replaced with architects from the colonial administration who drew up less expensive final plans. In the end, the cornerstone of the new hospital for Africans was eventually laid in 1958.[40] On January 4, 1959, bloody riots broke out in Kinshasa, shattering all remaining hopes for a harmonious coexistence among colonizer and colonized. Just eighteen months later, on June 30, 1960, Congo became independent.[41] The new hospital project languished amid the violence and the excitement of inde-pendence, and in the end it remained an unexecuted project on paper.

The first post-independence years were marked by political turmoil and Congo became a battleground of Cold War politics when Joseph-Desiré Mobutu (1930–97) seized power in 1965. He quickly initiated a nation-building project with the aid of foreign donors and drew on the expertise from abroad, particularly in the fields of education and healthcare. A number of studies indicate that Zaïre (the country's name during much of the Mobutu era) succeeded in maintaining the public healthcare system until the late 1970s, and even counted as an example for Sub-Saharan Africa. In 1980, the country signed the *African Charter for Health for All by the Year 2000*.[42] Still, a significant gap existed between ambitions and reality. Although a major number of Congolese medical assistants had received an excellent six-year training during the colonial period, they had never been granted, let alone allowed to pursue, an official degree as doctor. In the immediate postwar years, many physicians needed to be recruited from elsewhere to run the hospitals. In 1968, the American doctor William Close, for instance, became director of the Hôpital des Noirs, which remained the main healthcare facility in the capital city but was now renamed Hôpital Mama Yemo for President Mobutu's mother.[43] Today several Congolese staff members of the hospital tell what seem to be nostalgic stories about "la belle époque" of the Hôpital Mama Yemo under the administration of Close, but in fact reveal complex modes of remembering past futures.[44]

This alleged period of prosperity was short-lived. Due to divergent opinions about the future of the hospital and a presumed lack of financial means to run it properly, Close quit the institute in 1976. A survey the following year confirmed that the situation in the Hôpital Mama Yemo had become "catastrophic," with occupation rates up to 178 percent in some services and an alarming lack of pharmaceutical products.[45] Despite many efforts, Close's successor, Pol Jansegers, did not succeed in organizing a substantial expansion of the complex to respond to the needs of a rapidly growing urban population.[46] Until the late 1980s, a number of ad hoc additions were made to the crowded structure, which lead to a strong densification of the hospital site [Figure 8.7]. More importantly, because of the expanding city's territory away from the hospital, its location became increasingly peripheral with regard to its target audience.

The nationalization of Congo's economy in 1973, the changing geopolitics, and the end of the Cold War contributed to the isolation of president Mobutu, which resulted in major reductions of foreign investments and donor aid during the early 1990s.[47] The overall picture of public healthcare became increasingly gloomy; buildings and equipment were no longer repaired or replaced, and infrastructure became increasingly dilapidated. More than ever, being ill in Congo was a "luxury" that most Kinois could no longer afford.

A POROUS URBAN ENCLAVE

Today, the Hôpital Mama Yemo blatantly demonstrates the commodification of medical care. The "*économie de la débrouille*" ("economy of making do") is apparent in almost every corner of the struggling medical complex. During fieldwork, it was established that as many as 2,400 employees, ranging from doctors and nurses to cleaning personnel, laundrymen, engineers, and security guards, provide healthcare to an average of about 600 patients each day.[48] Adding considerably to the number of people on site, most patients are joined by a growing number of family members serving as personal caretakers or *gardes-malades*.[49] As state funding has diminished, the public institution increasingly struggles to provide even the

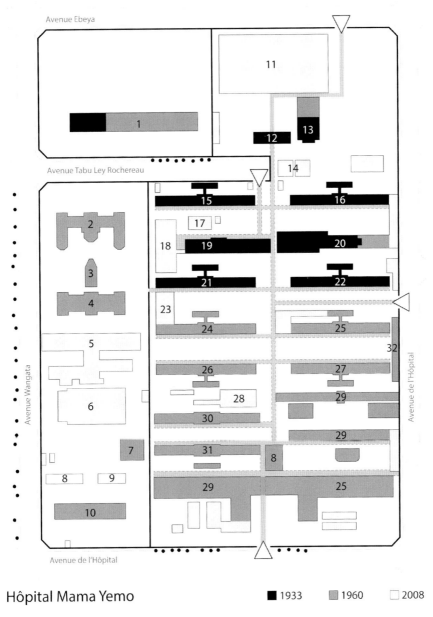

Hôpital Mama Yemo   ■ 1933   ■ 1960   □ 2008

Figure 8.7

Plan of the Hôpital Mama Yemo, Kinshasa. Plan 2018. Source: Simon de Nys-Ketels and Johan Lagae (based on a 2008 plan kept in the archives of the Hôpital Mama Yemo). Illustrating are the results of a pragmatic building history that saw additions made to pavilion-type complex executed without an overall design plan, and highlighting building campaigns completed through 1933, 1960, and 2008. Plan, 2018. Key: 1. Convent / 2. Laboratory / 3. Conference Hall / 4. Administration / 5. Dispensary & Physiotherapy / 6. Radiology / 7. Morgue / 8. Prenatal counseling / 9. Forensics / 10. Dentistry / 11. Pharmaceutical depot / 12. Emergency and registration / 13. Surgery / 14. Operating rooms / 15. Ophthalmology / 16. Orthopedics / 17. Sterilization / 18. Main operating room / 19. Intensive care / 20. Laundry room: 21. Surgery / 22. Internal Medicine: Women's / 23. Blood bank / 24. Internal Medicine: Men's / 25. Pediatrics / 26. Dermatology / 27. Urology / 28. Respiratory care / 29. Maternity / 30. Gynecology / 31. Delivery room / 32. "Cuisine indigène" ("native kitchen"). The dots indicate informal food stalls set up in the streets surrounding the hospital.

most basic services such as food, medication, and bed linens to its patients, and the hospital management now expects every patient to bring along at least one family member or friend as a private nurse. These *gardes-malades* are not only supposed to cook for their relatives, but also to wash and nurse their patients, and even remove and renew bandages. They spend the night in the hospital, either on the floor next to the bed of the patient, or on the veranda of one of the pavilions, and have claimed, adapted and reshaped some of the spaces available in the hospital. Spreading out a matrass or a piece of clothing, the *gardes-malades* have transformed the verandas of several pavilions into temporary living spaces [Figure 8.8]. Green spaces between the pavilions are used to dry laundry, wash dishes, burn litter, and prepare meals. Strikingly, the pavilion typology hospital, originally designed as a strictly sanitized, regimented, and easily surveilled space, provides an adequate arena for such informal activities. Its spatial organization has proven surprisingly resilient, capable of accommodating changing social practices over time, now as during the colonial era.

Moreover, several thousands of employees, patients, and *gardes-malades* attract additional crowds. Countless food vendors, medical clothing shops, funeral homes, and drugstores have set up stalls just outside the medical complex, offering a wide variety of services the hospital can no longer afford to provide. Apart from these fixed market booths, various semi-ambulant vendors arrive at dawn. Putting up moveable wooden stalls at the streets around the hospital, they sell funeral wreaths, provide phone credit, and offer photocopy services. These retailers are joined by various peddlers vending jewelry, chocolate cakes, and plastic bags of clean water, who, in turn, attract additional vagrants, street children,

Figure 8.8
Contemporary view of one of the pavilions of the Hôpital Mama Yemo Kinshasa, illustrating the conversion of a veranda to accommodate multip informal functions. Photograph 2010. Sourc Marc Gemoets.

and prostitutes. This myriad of vendors, all trying to make ends meet at the bustling medical site, have turned the public hospital institute into a free market of commodified healthcare.[50]

These dynamics of small-scale economies have not only drastically altered the use of space within and around the medical complex, but they have also redefined the complex's perimeter wall altogether. The Hôpital Mama Yemo enclosure, a remnant of 1930s segregationist urban planning policies, has become quite porous, and is now subject to intense fluxes of people coming and going, including, most remarkably, shortcutting pedestrians who capitalize on the busy gates to slip through and avoid a time-consuming detour around the complex on their way from Kinshasa's central market to one of the city's main bus terminal sites.[51] During the colonial period the perimeter wall had failed to hermetically seal off the medical complex, and today the numerous people crossing the gates have rendered it even more permeable. What was initially conceived and developed as a clearly delineated enclave in the center of the colonial city has now become an interwoven part of the public urban tissue and the epicenter of unexpected urban dynamics that defy the intentions of both its original design and its underlying ideology of colonial biopolitics.

BEYOND BIOPOLITICS, PAST AND PRESENT

Kinshasa's current healthcare landscape has become quite diversified and now includes new facilities like the Hôpital de l'Amitié Sino-Congolaise (Hospital of Chinese-Congolese Friendship) in the Ndjili neighborhood and the Hôpital du Cinquantenaire, situated near the city's Boulevard Triomphale. The latter was a prestige project of president Joseph Kabila, which opened its doors in 2014 and, in a highly medialized campaign, was presented as "the best-equipped in the DRC."[52] As an example of a public-private partnership project, it testifies of the emergence of a "global health" logic in Congo's policies, as it was built with the help of Chinese investments and as the management, the provision of equipment and the recruitment of medical staff was outsourced to Padiyath Health Care, an Indian private group specializing in "luxury hospitals" in Dubaï and Abu Dhabi.[53] Largely the product of a neoliberal present, in which crucial public services become transformed as a result of economic and political liberalization and globalization, the Hôpital du Cinquantenaire, somewhat ironically, has proven to be a complete failure of the Kabila's promised Révolution de la Modernité (Revolution of Modernity),[54] and largely a mismatch with the local context, as it is a place that most Kinois seeking care and treatment deliberately avoid. Despite the introduction of a series of measures intended to lower entrance fees, the fact that the Indian medical staff only speaks English (in a Francophone country) has essentially blocked access for the largest part of the Kinois.[55] Due to the passing away of a patient in February 2015, after alleged mistreatment by the medical staff (an event which received widespread media coverage), the Hôpital du Cinquantenaire quickly became the subject of distrust and mockery among Kinshasa's population.

Less than three years after its opening, the shiny new complex — in fact a major renovation and upgrade of an existing structure built during Mobutu's reign — became dilapidated.[56]

The Hôpital Mama Yemo thus remains a crucial healthcare facility in Congo's capital city, even if some parts of it are by now almost a century old. Discussions continue as to whether the largely dilapidated infrastructure should be replaced, at least partially, with new buildings. A 2013 visit by President Kabila reignited debate, but nothing has yet materialized.[57] How is one to interpret its status within this changing medical landscape, where services are either provided within a "global health" framework or the alternative that healing churches are now offering, with mounting success, to the Kinois? Has it shifted from a public to a neoliberal institution, as a multitude of non-state actors are now actively involved in helping run the hospital, be it by financing renovation works or by offering training for its staff?[58] If so, how then does one account for the everyday function-ing of the complex, which is highly dependent on the outsourcing of basic services to the *gardes-malades* that accompany patients?

When viewed using the entry point of "spatial governmentality," this par-ticular hospital can be seen to have been simultaneously functioning and dys-functional over time, from its origin in the 1920s, through the heyday of the colonial welfare state, and into the ongoing postcolonial development era. By investigating the resilience of the spatial organization of this pavilion-type hospi-tal and how it has accommodated, both within its perimeter and in its immediate urban surroundings, a multitude of "informal" practices, what comes to the fore is a continuous process of negotiation between a myriad of actors, both official and non-official, which testify to alternative forms of governance. This analysis of the Hôpital Mama Yemo thus aligns with a plea made by some political scientists working on conflict and development in Congo, namely that it is time to shift the narrative from critiques on an alleged "absent," "failing," or "good" gov-ernance towards investigations that focus on "arrangements that work" without romanticizing what are in the end often coping strategies to deal with desperate situations instead of socially accepted practices.[59] Such scholarship on "hybrid governance," that is now appearing in literature on other African contexts as well, suggests that a notion like "neocolonial" fails to account for the complexity of the current situation, just like scholarship on global health in Africa equally invites us to think beyond sometimes "bland caricatures" of neoliberalism, as a recent edited volume by Paul Wenzel Geissler suggests.[60] This chapter argues that it is also useful to extend such a perspective to historical research, and acknowledge that the exercise of colonial power and biopolitics was, at times, much more indi-rect, multilayered, and messy, than postcolonial scholarship has sometimes been willing to acknowledge.

Consistent with current scholarship on "policing" in colonial contexts, in which it is argued that even moments of repressive surveillance and severe vio-lence executed by colonial police forces can testify to the "essential weakness of colonial empires," making "colonial policing" at the same time "dirty" and "tragic,"[61] the study of the design and function of colonial hospitals offers, it is here argued, a powerful lens for unveiling the limits of colonial disciplinary and sanitary regimes. If one accepts that the postcolonial present is indeed to some extent informed by the colonial past, in particular with regard to how colonial-era architectural heritage shapes today's cityscapes, then it is the task of (architectural) history to demonstrate that such linkages need not be direct or simple, and, inversely, that an ethnographic inquiry of the complexities of the present might in fact also be helpful in gaining a more nuanced historical understanding of the spatial governmentalities produced under colonialism.

ACKNOWLEDGEMENTS

The chapter is based on investigations conducted in the context of a four-year research project (FWO n°G045015N) entitled "Urban landscapes of colonial / postcolonial healthcare. Towards a spatial mapping of the performance of hospital infrastructure in Kinshasa, Mbandaka and Kisangani (DR Congo) from past to present (1920–2014)". It ran from 2015 to 2018 under the supervision of Johan Lagae, Koen Stroeken, Luce Beeckmans (Ghent University), and Jacob Sabakinu Kivilu (Université de Kinshasa). Simon De Nys-Ketels and Laurence Heindryckx, as well as anthropologist Kristien Geenen, have worked as the main researchers on the project, while the Congolese architect Trésor Lumfuankenda Bungiena (Ph.D. candidate at the Université Libre de Bruxelles) has also been directly associated with it. The authors thank all involved in the project, especially the staff and informants of the Hôpital Mama Yemo, and Jacob Sabakinu Kivilu, whose help in facilitating fieldwork has been very significant.

NOTES

1   Joseph Conrad, "Heart of Darkness," *Blackwood's Magazine*, February, March, and April, 1899.

2   Theodore Trefon, *Congo Masquerade: The Political Culture of Aid Inefficiency and Reform Failure* (London: ZED, 2011), 2.

3   Médecins sans frontières, *RD Congo: Silence on meurt. Témoignages* (Paris: L'Harmattan, 2002).

4   Zam Kalume, "Le luxe d'être malade," *Autrement* (special issue "Capitales de couleur. Dakar – Abidjan – Lagos – Douala – Kinshasa") 9 (1984): 182–87.

5   Isodore Ndaywel è Nziem, "Le territoire médical à l'épreuve de l'informel. 'Survivre' comme infirmière aux Cliniques Universitaires de Kinshasa," in *Manières de vivre. Économie de la « débrouille » dans les villes du Congo/Zaïre,* ed. Gauthier De Villers, Bogumil Jewsiewicki and Laurent Monnier (Brussels: Institut Africain-CEDAF, 2002), 141–69.

6   When asked "What causes you the most concern?," only 6.6 percent of the inhabitants of the Kindele neighborhood in Kinshasa listed healthcare as the primary challenge. More urgent concerns indicated were, in diminishing order of importance, the bad governance of the country, the schooling of one's children, work related issues, and the provision of food. See Léon de Saint-Moulin, ed., *Kinshasa, Enracinements Historiques et Horizons Culturels* (Paris: L'Harmattan, 2012), 258. See also Francis Lelo

Nzuzi, Claudine Tshimanga Mbuyi, and Léon de Saint-Moulin, *Pauvreté Urbaine à Kinshasa* (Kinshasa: CORDAID, 2004), 135–44.

7 Paul Wenzel Geissler, ed. *Para-States and Medical Science. Making African Global Health* (Durham, NC: Duke University, 2015).

8 For an official account, written by one of Kabila's closest advisors, see Pierre Kambila-Kankwende, *Construire le Congo. Les cinq chantiers* (Paris: L'Harmattan, 2010).

9 Peter Persyn and Fabienne Ladrière, "The Miracle of Life in Kinshasa: New Approaches to Public Health," in *Reinventing Order in the Congo: How People Respond to State Failure in Kinshasa*, ed. Theodore Tréfon (London: ZED, 2004), 65–81.

10 Despite this common depiction, several scholars, especially from the political sciences, have countered this perspective of a "failed state" with evidence of more hybrid cooperation between state and non-state actors. See Koen Vlassenroot and Timothy Raeymaeckers, *Conflict and Social Transformation in Eastern DR Congo* (Ghent: Academia, 2004); Kristof Titeca and Tom de Herdt, "Real Governance Beyond the 'Failed State': Negotiating Education in the Democratic Republic of the Congo," *African Affairs* 110 no. 439 (2011): 213–31.

11 Jacob Sabakinu Kivilu, "Paul-Gabriel Dieudonné Bolya: De l'assistant médical à l'homme politique," in *La mémoire du Congo. Le temps colonial*, ed. Jean-Luc Vellut (Tervuren: Musée Royale De L'Afrique Centrale, 2005), 235–39; Pieter G. Janssens et al., "L'enseignement medical," in *Médecine et hygiène en Afrique centrale de 1885 à nos jours,* ed. Pieter G. Janssens, Maurice Kivits, and Jacques Vuylsteke, 83–160 (Brussels: King Baudouin Foundation, 1992), 161–93.

12 Achille Mbembe, "Necropolitics," *Public Culture* 15, no. 1 (2003): 11–40.

13 Stephen Legg, "Beyond the European Province: Foucault and Postcolonialism," in *Space, Knowledge and Power, Foucault and Geography*, ed. Jeremy W. Crampton and Stuart Elden (New York: Ashgate, 2007), 268.

14 Foucault originally introduced this notion of "governmentality" around 1978 in his lectures at the *Collège de France* around 1978. For an in-depth discussion of this notion and its usefulness for investigating colonial contexts, see Stephen Legg, *Spaces of Colonialism: Delhi's Urban Governmentalities* (Malden, MA: Blackwell, 2007).

15 Michel Foucault, *Surveiller et punir: Naissance de la prison* (Paris: Gallimard, 1976).

16 See, for example, Jiat-Hwee Chang, *A Genealogy of Tropical Architecture: Colonial Networks, Nature and Technoscience* (New York: Routledge, 2016).

17 Legg, *Spaces of Colonialism*, 8.

18 Kate Maeger, Tom de Herdt, and Filip Titeca, "Unravelling Public Authority: Paths of Hybrid Governance in Africa" (Wageningen: IS Academy on Human Security in Fragile States, 2014), 1–8.

19 For a detailed historical survey of healthcare policy in the Belgian Congo, see J. André and J. Burke, "Développement des services de santé," in *Médecine et hygiène en Afrique centrale de 1885 à nos jours,* ed. Pieter G. Janssens, Maurice Kivits, and Jacques Vuylsteke (Brussels: King Baudouin Foundation, 1992), 83–160.

20 Henry Carton de Wiart, *Mes Vacances au Congo* (Brussels: Piette, 1923).

21 Ministry of Colonies, "Les hôpitaux pour Européens et Indigènes construits ces dernières années à Léopoldville," *L'Assistance Hospitalière* 3 (1934): 3–21. See also a synthesis of contemporary accounts provided by Whyms (pseudonym of journalist Hélène Guilaume) in her exhaustive unpublished manuscript from 1956 entitled *Chronique de Léopoldville 1885–1956* (Archives of the History Department, Royal Museum for Central Africa), 1404.

22 Michel Foucault, *Les machines à guérir: aux origines de l'hôpital moderne* (Brussels: Pierre Mardaga, 1979).

23 Sven-Olov Wallenstein, *Biopolitics and the Emergence of Modern Architecture* (New York: Princeton Architectural, 2008).

24 For similar interpretations of hospitals, see Wallenstein, *Biopolitics*; Chang, *Genealogy*.

25 Carl H. Nightingale, *Segregation: A Global History of Divided Cities* (Chicago,IL: University of Chicago, 2012).

26 Luce Beeckmans and Johan Lagae, "Kinshasa's Syndrome-planning in Historical Perspective: From Belgian Colonial Capital to Self-constructed Megalopolis." in *Urban Planning in Sub-Saharan Africa: Colonial and Post-colonial Planning Cultures*, ed. Carlos Nunes Silva (New York: Routledge, 2015), 201–24.

27 Johan Lagae, Luce Beeckmans, Ruth Kennivé, and Rebekka Van Coster, "Vers une radioscopie de la ville coloniale: Episodes dans la génèse de l'avenue Kasa-Vubu, Kinshasa," in *La Société Congolaise Face à la Modernité (1700–2010): Mélanges Eurafricains Offerts à Jean-Luc Vellut*, ed. Mathieu Zana Etambala and Pamphile Miabiala Mantuba-Ngoma (Paris: L'Harmattan, 2016), 309–43.

28 Chang, *Genealogy*; Nightingale, *Segregation,* 159–91.

29 Note from the Head of the Public Works Department, March 8, 1929, Africa Archives, Ministry of Foreign Affairs, Brussels (AA MFA, Brussels), AA/GG 14927.

30 Letter from the Provincial Governor to the Governor General, May 1929, AA MFA, Brussels, AA/GG 15816. The lower perimeter wall had been planned in 1923 on the basis of the argument that "racial promiscuity" was not to be feared. Letter from Provincial Governor to Governor General, May 1, 1923. AA/GG 14927. It was built in 1924.

31 Letter from the Chef de Province to the Governor General, June 14, 1937, AA MFA, Brussels, AA/GG 20458.

32 Such traces of everyday life in the Hôpital des Noirs have been found in several archival dossiers in both Belgium and Congo, including: Africa Archives, Ministry of Foreign Affairs, Brussels: AA/GG 911; AA/GG 14927; AA/GG 20458; AA/GG 22451; Documentation and Research Center on Religion, Culture and Society (Kadoc), Leuven: BE/942855/1696; Archives Nationales du Congo (ARNACO), Kinshasa, GP108/449.

33 AA/GG 732, November 20, 1931, Note from Head of the Medical Service Dr. Trolli to Governor General.

34 See the annual report for the year 1941 of the *Service de l'Hygiène de la Ville* [of Léopoldville/Kinshasa], AA/RA/MED 46.

35 Maryinez Lyons, "Sleeping Sickness Epidemics and Public Health in the Belgian Congo," in *Imperial Medicine and Indigenous Societies*, ed. David Arnold (Manchester: Manchester University, 1988), 105–24.

36 Anon., "Les femmes dorment sur le sol," in unknown newspaper, 1955, AA MFA, Brussels, AA/H 4472.

37 Letter from Governor General to provincial governor, September 30, 1947, AA MFA, Brussels, AA/Public Works Service (3DG).

38 On Ricquier's masterplan, see Bruno de Meulder, *Kuvuande Mbote. Een eeuw architectuur in Kongo* (Antwerp: deSingel, 2000), 159–69; Luce Beeckmans, "Making the African City. Dakar, Dar es Salaam, Kinshasa 1920–1980" (Ph.D. diss., University of Groningen, 2013). For a first in-depth analysis of Ricquier's hospital design for Kinshasa in the context of the broader healthcare policy in the Belgian Congo, see Koenraad Danneels, "Hospitalen en segregatie. Een analyse van de bouw van hospitalen en de medische invloed op stadsplanning en segregatie in het naoorlogse Belgisch Congo (1945–1960)" (MA thesis, Ghent University, 2014).

39 For first discussions of these shifts in discourse, see Johan Lagae, Sofie Boonen and Maarten Liefooghe, "Fissures dans le « cordon sanitaire ». Architecture hospital-ière et ségrégation urbaine à Lubumbashi, 1920–1960," in *Lubumbashi. Cent d'ans d'histoire*, ed. Maurice Amuri Mpala-Lutebele (Paris: L'Harmattan, 2013), 247–61; Danneels, *Hospitalen en segregatie*, 2014.

40 Internal note from Head of the Public Works Service E. Dangotte, January 13, 1958, AA MFA, Brussels, AA/3DG.

41 For a concise overview of this period of transition, see Isidore Ndaywel è Nziem, *Histoire générale du Congo. De l'héritage ancient à la République Démocratique* (Paris: Duculot, 1998), 499–560.

42 Persyn and Ladrière, "Miracle"; André and Burke, "Développement."

43 William T. Close and Malonga Miatudila, *Médecin de Mobutu: vingt ans au Congo parmi les puissants et les misérables*, trans. Charles Antoine De Trazegnies (Brussels: Le Roseau vert, 2007).

44 Interviews conducted in Kinshasa by Kristien Geenen and Simon De Nys-Ketels with staff members of the Hôpital Mama Yemo: an officier policier judiciaire 1, October 28, 2015; the secrétaire de la Direction, November 19, 2015; and laundry personnel 1, November 5, 2015. Memory in contemporary Congo is a complicated affair and since the mid-1990s scholars have been assessing this complexity with regard to the colonial and postcolonial past. See the work of Johannes Fabian, Bogumil Jewsiewicki, Danielle De Lame, Marie-Bénédicte Dembour, and Lieve Spaas, among others. For a more general discussion of remembering "past futures" in relation to (post)colonial healthcare policies, see Paul Wenzel Geissler et al., eds., *Traces of the Future: An Archaeology of Medical Science in Africa* (Bristol: Intellect, 2016).

45 Marc Pain, *Kinshasa: La Ville et la Cité* (Paris: Editions de l'ORSTOM, 1984), 83.

46 Janseghers' account of the postcolonial period in the Hôpital Mama Yemo, given dur-ing an interview with the authors in January 2016, differed significantly from Close's published description.

47 Persyn and Ladrière, "Miracle"; Harry Van Balen, "Les soins de santé au Zaïre," *La Nouvelle Revue* 3 (1989): 203–14.

48 During two three-month research trips (in 2015 and 2016), Kristien Geenen and Simon De Nys-Ketels conducted anthropological research in the Mama Yemo hospital, and completed historical research in the local national archives and the maintenance archives of the hospital. During the anthropological research, in-depth, open-ended interviews were carried out with seventy-two interviewees, including hospital guards, management staff, nurses and doctors, patients and their visiting or attending families. Trésor Lumfuankenda Bungiena has followed up on that field-work, and has held conversations on the management and renovation strategies applied on the hospital since the 1970s.

49 *Gardes-malades* are also common outside of Congo. See Marie Schnitzler, "Le rôle de l'entourage au sein de l'hôpital africain: Une thématique négligée?" *Sciences sociales et santé* 32, no.1 (2014): 39–64.

50 Fieldwork in other hospital sites in Kinshasa, conducted by Trésor Lumfuankenda Bungenia, suggests that such practices also occur elsewhere, but the general perception among all local informants is that they originated in the Hôpital Mama Yemo.

51 For a more in-depth discussion of the current situation in the Hôpital Mama Yemo, see Kristien Geenen and Simon De Nys-Ketels, "Pedestrian Itineraries: On Shortcuts, Permeable Walls and Welded Shut Gates in a Former Colonial Hospital," *Space and Culture* (September 2018).

52 "Kinshasa: Joseph Kabila inaugure l'hôpital du Cinquantenaire," *Radio Okapi*, March 22, 2014, https://www.radiookapi.net/actualite/2014/03/22/ kinshasa-joseph-kabila-inaugure-lhopital-du-cinquantenaire.

53 We are indebted here to Guillaume Lachenal from the University Paris-Diderot, who has started to investigate the Hôpital de Cinquantenaire in the larger context of the neoliberal present of global health in Africa.

54 Joseph Kabila launched the political concept of the "Révolution de la Modernité" in September 2011, promising a reconstruction of the DRC, but only a couple of years later it was already harshly criticized due to the lack of impact on the ground. See A.O. "Révolution De La Modernité En RDC – Un Concept Tronqué ?," *Le Congolais*, January 6, 2015, https://www.lecongolais.cd/revolution-de-la-modernite-en-rdc-un-concept-tronque.

55 Data gathered by Trésor Lumfuankenda Bungiena in 2017–18.

56 "RDC: décès dans des circonstances floues d'une étudiante à l'hôpital du Cinquantenaire," *Radio Okapi*, February 20, 2015, https://www.radiookapi.net/ actualite/2015/02/20/rdc-deces-dans-des-circonstances-floues-dune-etudiante-lhopital-du-cinquantenaire.

57 Data gathered by Trésor Lumfuankenda Bungiena in February 2018 at the *Direction des Etudes et Planification* of the Ministry of Health, Kinshasa.

58 Healthcare policies in Congo have been supported for several decades now by both bilateral and multilateral aid involving the World Bank, the European Union, the World Health Organization, the Banque Africaine du Développement, Coopération Technique belge, and China.

59 Maeger, de Herdt, and Titeca, "Unravelling." See also Tom de Herdt and Kristof Titeca, eds., *Negotiating Public Services in the Congo: State, Society and Governance* (London: ZED, forthcoming).

60 See Paul Wenzel Geissler, ed. *Para-States and Medical Science: Making African Global Health* (Durham, NC: Duke University, 2015).

61 Emmanual Blanchard, Marieke Bloembergen, and Amandine Lauro, eds., *Policing in Colonial Empires: Cases, Connections, Boundaries (c.1850–1970)* (Brussels: Peter Lang Verlag, 2017), 14.

9

Colonial mimicry and nationalist memory in the postcolonial prisons of India

Mira Rai Waits

As the clock neared midnight on August 15, 1947, India's future Prime Minister Jawaharlal Nehru (1889–1964) gave his "Tryst with Destiny" speech to the Constituent Assembly in New Delhi's Council House. Broadcast throughout India and reprinted in special edition newspapers, Nehru's stirring words celebrated the end of the British Empire in India, along with a vision of a new nation that would "awake to life and freedom."[1] Nehru, widely acknowledged as the architect of the modern Indian nation-state, spent the years leading up to this speech imagining independence from inside colonial prison cells [Figure 9.1].[2] Imprisoned nine times for a total of 3,259 days between the years 1922 and 1945, Nehru wrote his most well-known works — *Glimpses of World History* (1934), *Toward Freedom* (1941), and *The Discovery of India* (1946) — while incarcerated. In these works, he reflects on Indian history, philosophy and culture, as well as the myriad problems with British rule; among his many claims of British injustice is a discussion of the colonial prison system.

Brought to the subcontinent in the late eighteenth century, the colonial prison system provided an architectural means of distinguishing British East India Company (EIC) rule from that of its Mughal predecessors. Prisons were constructed within colonial cities and towns and had become permanent features of India's built environment by the late nineteenth century. In the first half of the twentieth century colonial prisons took on a new role — confining political prisoners opposed to colonial rule. Various displays of civil disobedience prompted the colonial state to imprison freedom fighters without trial under the Defence of India Act of 1915. Political prisoners wrote about their experiences while incarcerated, representing the prison as a space of dehumanization and corruption. Consequently, the prison became one of the most important symbols of colonial tyranny within Indian nationalist imagination. When the British left India in 1947, prison reform appeared to be a top postcolonial priority; numerous postcolonial jail committees were formed in the immediate aftermath of independence to overhaul the former colonial system. When it came to the subject of prison architecture, however, instead of redesigning or constructing new facilities, the vast majority of Indian

states continued to use the colonial buildings built in the late nineteenth and early twentieth centuries.[3]

This seemingly contradictory position — prisons as symbols of colonial tyranny, later reused by the postcolonial state — begs further interrogation. In the contemporary global world the practice of imprisonment persists as *the* paradigm of punishment. The continued reliance on imprisonment and prisons could be viewed as the inevitable consequence of the triumph of the modern nation-state, along with the related idea that modern political societies must be defined through their apparatuses of security.[4] However, in former colonies like India the continued use of prisons reveals a complex set of spatial negotiations whereby the postcolonial state must manage or "tame" architectural symbols from its colonial past in accordance with nationalist rhetoric, while simultaneously repurposing those symbols in the articulation of its modern identity.[5] This chapter explores the following questions to deepen our understanding of postcolonial spatial negotiation: Does the postcolonial prison system in India represent a rupture with the colonial past or a replication of colonial strategies of rule? If replication occurs should we interpret this as a form of internal neocolonialism? To what degree do prison buildings contribute to the perpetuation of colonial-era carceral practices and imagery? Lastly, what might these buildings represent in the public consciousness of past imperialism and control?

This chapter introduces a general history of the postcolonial prison system in India, followed by a brief examination of Indian prison architecture to address these questions. It concludes by focusing on the Alipore Central Correctional Home in Kolkata (colonial-era Calcutta), capital of the Indian state of West Bengal.

While the prison was built by the British in the early twentieth century, it remained operational under the postcolonial government and its presence in Kolkata functioned both as a memorial to nationalist resistance and as a space that testified to the long shadow of colonialism.

POSTCOLONIAL TRANSITION

When Lord Wavell, Viceroy of India, retired in February of 1947 he did so knowing that his plan to ease India into independence using a staged (province-by-province) withdrawal had failed.[6] There was no sign of compromise between the Indian National Congress and the Muslim League. As a result of this impasse, Lord Mountbatten stepped in as India's last viceroy and was "given a virtual free hand to decide on the time and settle the manner of British departure."[7] With "ruthless diplomacy" he imposed the partition of India in August of that year.[8] In a letter dated August 9, 1947, William Francis Hare, the last British secretary of state for India and Burma, congratulated Mountbatten on his efforts to efficiently orchestrate India's path to independence:

> It must be with a sense of great relief that you see the 15th August approaching and yet relief not untinged with regret at the ending of a great chapter and of concern at the thought of uncharted seas that lie ahead.[9]

India's looming independence seems to have signaled radical change even among the highest ranks of the British Empire. However, neither colonial officials nor the Congress leaders who took their place had any immediate plans to end or reform the system of imprisonment in India. In fact, as Ujjwal Kumar Singh has argued, the ideology of colonial governmentality remained firmly in place after independence; the nationalist elite at the helm of postcolonial power capitalized on the colonial theme of "inadequacy" to justify the necessity of certain practices, including imprisonment.[10]

The sole expression of rupture with colonial imprisonment amidst Independence Day euphoria was the release of thousands of political prisoners, along with the commutation of prison sentences. Although, as Yasmin Khan has shown, "blurred terminology and lack of clarity about the nature of the crimes" also resulted in widespread amnesty for non-political prisoners.[11] Thus the prison population appeared to "awake to life and freedom" in accordance with Nehru's vision, but little was done to the extant prison system beyond this gesture of amnesty. The postcolonial state went on to adopt an ambiguous position with regards to prisons and decolonization at large, perpetuating a kind of discursive colonization that internalizes the "framework of rational universality" inherited from former colonial masters, particularly in matters pertaining to crime and punishment, all the while criticizing the "exploitative" nature of foreign rule.[12]

Indeed, the vast majority of colonial jail rules were maintained after independence, while the few revisions concentrated on deleting obvious references to the former Empire. For example, in place of celebrations for the Emperor's birthday, rules mandated that postcolonial prisoners celebrate the birthdays of freedom fighters, such as Bal Gangadhar Tilak and Mahatma Gandhi, who were both incarcerated in colonial prisons.[13] Other revisions gestured to the legacy of Gandhian resistance, but continue to adhere to colonial policies, often adopting more stringent positions. During the early years of independence, Communist Party of India prisoners protested Mountbatten's resolution along with the nationalist elite's governance of India through hunger strikes — a tactic political prisoners had employed with frequent success in colonial prisons as a sign of resistance against the British.[14] The postcolonial state went on to criminalize prison protests to a greater degree than their colonial predecessors; a memo from Madhya Pradesh, a state in central India, defined hunger strikes as a "major jail offence," while equating mass hunger strikes to "mutiny."[15] The memo went on to encourage prison officers to give "as little publicity as possible" to hunger strikes.[16] Postcolonial penal errata thus presents the state's seemingly dichotomous position of celebrating the nationalist struggle, but criminalizing its tactics.

The main thrust of the postcolonial state's efforts to reform their inherited prison system was the convening of numerous jail reform committees beginning in 1948. National committees met with some frequency in the decade that followed.[17] The state also turned to the United Nations (UN) for assistance with their newly inherited penal system. The UN sent Dr. Walter C. Reckless, an American criminologist, to India in 1951 to assist with training jail officers, as well as provide new approaches to modernizing Indian penology.[18] Reckless was impressed with the "number and quality" of prison reform committees in India, but noted that their suggestions had rarely been implemented.[19] He published a report in 1953 titled *Jail Administration in India*, detailing the need for spatial reorganization. He was primarily concerned with housing women and juvenile prisoners away from adult males.[20] Reckless was also invited to review the blueprints for a new jail in Delhi that would later be known as the Tihar Jail, the largest jail complex in India today. He recommended designing and retrofitting prison buildings to perform specialized functions; prisons could become agricultural colonies, open Borstals (youth reformatory institutions), or provide medical, psychiatric, or vocational services.[21] Following Reckless's involvement, the All India Jail Manual Committee of 1957 published its *Model Prison Manual and Report*. This report was promptly circulated to every Indian state, but as late as 1980 only four (Andhra Pradesh, Karnataka, Kerala, and Maharashtra) adhered to the majority of its guidelines.[22]

Additional committees interested in the subject of prison reform convened with varying goals and functions in the decades that followed. Some noteworthy examples include the Government of India's 1972 working group to improve prisons, which recommended that prison administration be included in the nation's Five-Year Plan, as well as the 1980–83 India Committee on Jail Reforms. The latter committee, similar to Reckless, hoped to improve postcolonial prisons by renewing state interest in reforming juvenile offenders. The Juvenile Justice Act was passed in 1986 to ensure that juvenile prisoners would not be confined with adults. Concerns over safety also led to the convening of the All India Group on Prison

Administration-Security and Discipline that same year, and in 1995 the Government of India went on to create an agency known as the Bureau of Police Research & Development, which was tasked with the study of prisons and prison administration. Within the last twenty years, additional committees have formed, publishing manuals and drafting policies that strive towards further reform.[23]

Today the Government of India has adopted a position that frames their various prison initiatives as demonstrative of an increasing concern with human rights and a desire to elevate Indian jails to a more scientific standard that represents an intentional break with the colonial past.[24] Certainly changes such as the 1956 eradication of the colonial punishment of transportation (deportation for life) signal a shift to more humane modes of punishment. However, other decisions, as Mark Brown has argued — including the postcolonial Indian Government's re-branding of criminals, formerly classified under the 1931 Criminal Tribes Act, as habitual offenders under the 1952 Habitual Offenders Act — represent a more oppressive disciplinary model that suggests that "postcolonial actors often were no better prepared, and sometimes worse so, than their colonial predecessors for the task of giving effect to transcendent constitutional ideals of equality and freedom."[25]

Indeed the very foundation of the postcolonial government and its administration continues to bear imprints of colonial governmentality; laws, government services, and the court system, along with the police and army, were "expanded and not transformed" under the postcolonial state.[26] India's postcolonial constitution, which came into effect in 1950 under the chairmanship of social reformer Bhimrao Ramji Ambedkar, was influenced by the British model and bound within pre-existing colonial legal structures that privileged Hindu men.[27] Similarly, the Indian Penal Code, drafted during the colonial period (in 1860), remains significantly tied to its colonial origins in the classification of crime, despite frequent postcolonial amendments. This contradiction, as Upendra Baxi has argued, "continues colonial laws' repressive legacies and even innovates these through the regimes of security legislations … [but] installs a new order of representation of the national 'selfhood.'"[28] Consequently, the postcolonial nation-state, Baxi goes on to claim, "appears neocolonial to many groups whose understanding of struggle against colonialism was radically divergent from those who eventually capture state power and apparatus."[29]

Ultimately, with respect to penal governance in India, evidence of a rupture between the colonial and postcolonial is difficult to discern, what we discover instead is "an impressive continuity of practice and purpose," or more specifically a mimetic tendency towards reproducing colonial policies and practices.[30] The organization of postcolonial prison types, for example, adheres to a scheme similar to the one used by colonial officials; prisons were divided into three types (central, district, and sub-jails), which served different penal functions (although the term "correctional home" would eventually come to replace "jail" in official building titles).[31] Moreover, this mimetic tendency was ultimately unavoidable when it came to the spatial experience of postcolonial prisons; anti-colonial idealism could only take the system so far when the architectural reality of prison buildings left little opportunity for rupture. For example, the Tihar Jail, built in Delhi in 1958, incorporated Reckless's suggestion that prison buildings perform special functions; the jail was supposed to promote prisoner rehabilitation through an internal organization that resembled a college campus replete with green spaces, thereby representing a break with former colonial prison models.[32] However, in the decades that followed the prison's initial construction, overcrowding, sanitation issues, internal corruption, and lack of funds produced a problematic built environment that mirrored the colonial experience or was in some ways worse.[33] In cases where colonial buildings remained in use, the legacy of the colonial period was further realized in the day-to-day spatial experience of the postcolonial prisoner.

ARCHITECTURAL LEGACY

Contemporary prison reports document postcolonial efforts to reconcile the prison's colonial past with its postcolonial present. As lingering architectural symbols of that past, former colonial buildings still in use represent a significant challenge to overcome. Officials attempt to "tame" their continued reliance on these buildings, citing postcolonial building projects as proof of "development" and "modernization." For example, a 2013 issue of *The Metamorphosis*, a quarterly bulletin on "the changing lives in the Correctional Homes of West Bengal," celebrates recent developments in prison infrastructure.[34] Two new sub-correctional homes were added to West Bengal's existing list of fifty-six that year, while upgrades occurred within two former colonial prisons, known as the Jalpaiguri Central Correctional Home and the Burdwan District Correctional Home. Jalpaiguri, built in the northern region of Bengal in 1883, was characterized in the bulletin as maintaining "the British legacy in body and mind."[35] Consequently, eight new dormitory buildings were built with hygienic lavatories intentionally to contest this legacy. Similarly, Burdwan, the site of one of the oldest colonial prisons in British India built in 1797, was "modernized" through the construction of a three-story building for male prisoners, a separate enclosure for females, and renovated warders' barracks. To "tame" the colonial presence, the old administrative building was demolished, but the gallows were preserved as a heritage site.[36] Bulletins like *The Metamorphosis* suggest that the colonial legacy of the postcolonial prison can be erased through new construction. However, the perpetuation of a developmental history of prison architecture in India replicates the approach of colonial discussions.

Along with their collection of prison buildings, the British left behind a narrative strategy for thinking about prison architecture; the story colonial officials told about their institution was one of linear progress.[37] Early colonial prison buildings in India, as has been discussed elsewhere, were criticized by administrators for their lack of uniform architectural identity.[38] Many were converted from existing military, vernacular, and Mughal buildings, while purpose-built prisons were often unadorned single-story bungalows with sloping roofs and simple volumes. An 1865 plan of the Burdwan Jail provides a good example of an early colonial prison

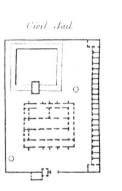

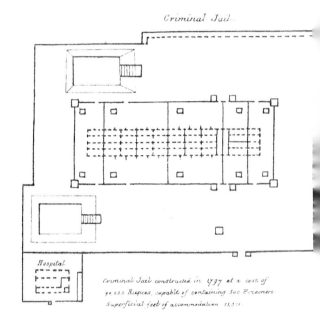

type [Figure 9.2]. A generic rectangular building, enclosed by a perimeter wall, served as main the prison space for up to 500 prisoners convicted of criminal sentences. While internal walls divided the main building into subsections that served as the wards, prisoners were for the most part housed communally. Nearby was a prison for those convicted of civil sentences. Built in 1817, this small prison had housing for up to 14 prisoners. Though fairly reproducible, this plan was determined to be too simple and inefficient by the late nineteenth century.[39] Colonial officials engaged in constant discussions about the inadequacy of early colonial prison buildings' locations, designs, security, and infrastructure, specifically with respect to ventilation and sanitation.

Officials began to push for more elaborate structures, known as central jails, to hold prisoners with long-term sentences. By the mid-nineteenth century plans for such jails were underway. Optimistic officials hoped that if their buildings adhered to more consistent patterns that incorporated rational design principles, such as identical housing spaces, an effective prison system would follow. The

Figure 9.2
The Burdwan Jail. Plan 1865. Source: F.J. Moua⸱ Annual Report on the Administration of Jails o⸱ the Bengal Presidency, 1864–65 (Calcutta: Alipc⸱ Jail Press, 1865), Appenc⸱ XVII [IOR, IOR/V/24/2066⸱ © The British Library Board].

ideal design was a radial plan that promised to help colonial officials order prisoners according to colonial notions of Indian crime. Officials determined that certain criminals were predisposed to crime; criminality, in other words, was seen as hereditary, as well as habitual. In the latter half of the nineteenth century one of the leading architectural objectives of colonial prison design was preventing different criminal types from mingling to mitigate the likelihood that prisoners with lighter sentences be corrupted by hereditary/habitual offenders. The prevailing opinion was that prisons could continue to house prisoners communally as long as prisoners were similarly classed. Consequently, Indian radial plans differed from Western counterparts, which employed cellular confinement to separate individuals from one another. A sample plan for the proposed European Penitentiary at Hazaribagh published in the same report as the Burdwan plan provides an example of the preferred design for future prison construction [Figure 9.3]. The plan represents a prison compound bound by a roughly 990-by-760-foot perimeter wall. In the center of the compound is a watchtower encircled by a covered passage from which the prison's identical barracks emanate. A vast majority of central jails that date from the second half of the nineteenth century were

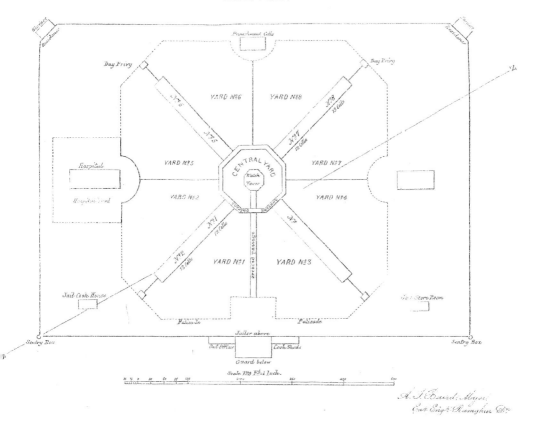

175 □

designed according to this basic ideal.[40] Though adherence to this spatial formation legitimized the colonial prison system in terms of homogeneity, radi-
ally planned prisons faced similar problems to older prisons after construction.
Nevertheless, the general consensus among officials was that radial plans represented a vast improvement over early models.[41] Despite this linear narrative of
progress, colonial prison buildings were rarely celebrated in circles outside the
prison bureaucracy as examples of innovative and appealing colonial architecture;
prison builders' goal was to design institutional buildings that were functional,
but not necessarily visually stimulating.

This attitude was maintained after decolonization; not only were former
colonial prison buildings still in use, but prison architecture occupied a peripheral
position in the imagination of the independent Indian nation-state, similar to its
marginal status in the colonial period. Instead of deliberating on the future of
the postcolonial prison's built environment, political leaders directed their atten-
tions to determining the appropriate architectural vocabulary for monumental
building projects, debating between "traditional" or "modern." Nehru's architectural vision, for example, favored the language of modernism to fuel industrial
and urban development.[42] Conversely, everyday public buildings, as Peter Scriver
and Amit Srivastava argue, were maintained by branches of the former colonial
Public Works Department and "were geared to a more measured and pragmatic
pace of development and progress that effectively sustained many of the familiar
design and planning norms, if not the forms, of the former colonial-modern tech-
nocracy."[43] This reluctance to shift the maintenance and construction program
of everyday public buildings away from the colonial formula persisted long after
India's initial declaration of independence.

This sustained development can be observed in Kolkata's Presidency
Correctional Home (hereafter Presidency) [Figure 9.4]. Dating to the early nineteenth century, the structure occupied a significant place in the city's memory;
its urban location led to its importance during both the colonial period and after
independence.[44] While a colonial jail, Presidency housed some of the most noto-
rious revolutionaries of the nationalist movement, including those arrested in
connection with the Alipore Bomb Case of 1908. This group included Aurobindo
Ghose who later documented the inhumane conditions he experienced.[45] During
the postcolonial period, this prison also served a critical role in the incarceration
of another group of political revolutionaries. Communist Party of India (Marxist)
prisoners affiliated with the Naxalite Movement, which began with an uprising
in the village of Naxalbari in West Bengal in 1967, were confined at Presidency.
Similar to colonial Defence of India rules, the West Bengal (Prevention of Violent
Activities) Act of 1970 and the Maintenance of Internal Security Act of 1971
led to increased instances of detention without trial. An Amnesty International
investigation from 1974 reported on some of the troubling experiences of
postcolonial prisons during this period and specifically found Presidency to be
vastly overcrowded.[46] Prisoners confined there had minimal access to clean
drinking water and the prison's sick ward. They were also allegedly kept in bar

fetters for fifteen days, after which further time shackling could be authorized; the report suggests that some prisoners spent several years in restraints.[47] The practice of fettering lingered from the colonial period, and its alleged use in West Bengal jails directly contradicted the UN Standard Rules for the Treatment of Prisoners.[48]

Today at Presidency prisoners are still housed communally and the correctional home contains both male and female prisoners. Numerous areas show signs of age and poor living conditions; the walls of barrack buildings are in need of repair, although prisoners make use of the rusty, grated window openings to store belongings [Figure 9.5]. The postcolonial prison administration has added some seemingly beneficial programming for prisoners to improve quality of life, but all of these activities occur within aged colonial-era walls, prompting one to consider whether or not the space of the correctional home appears neocolonial to the groups of prisoners confined within.[49]

Figure 9.5
View into the ward at
Presidency Correctiona
Home, Kolkata.
Photograph 2011. Sou
Mira Rai Waits.

For Mary Tyler — a British citizen arrested alongside her Bengali husband Amalendu Sen for alleged Naxalite activity — the miserable conditions of the post-colonial Indian prison certainly seemed to continue the "repressive legacies" of the colonial period. Confined in the Hazaribagh Central Prison for five years beginning in 1970, Tyler published a memoir in 1977 in which she described her experiences while incarcerated in vivid detail [Figure 9.6].[50] Illustrations appear alongside her reflections; an image of the cell where she spent part of her time supports her description of the deterioration of this former colonial jail, built in the 1870s not long after the aforementioned model plan was drafted [Figure 9.7]. The exposed brick in the illustration, coupled with her description of the "patchy" whitewashed walls "pock-marked high and low with holes of long-removed nails," and the "broken concrete and crumbling brickwork of the drains," represent Hazaribagh's

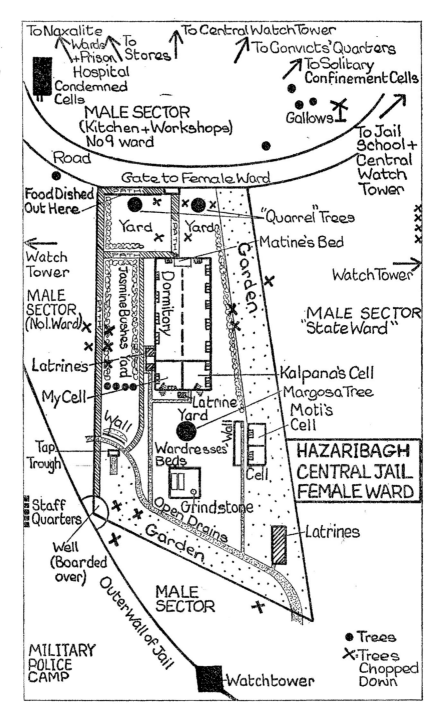

re 9.6
Hazaribagh Central
ale Ward. Plan c.1977.
ce: Plan by Dilip Ray
ary Tyler's *My Years in
ndian Prison* (London:
or Gollancz/Orion
ishing Group, 1977)
Mary Tyler].

Figure 9.7
Illustration of Mary Tyle
Cell in the Hazaribagh
Drawing c.1977. Sour
Illustration by Dilip Ray
Mary Tyler's *My Years i*
an Indian Prison (Lond
Victor Gollancz/Orion
Publishing Group, 197
[© Mary Tyler].

architectural age and decay.[51] Her memoir also emphasizes prisoners' suffering, reiterating the findings of Amnesty International on the use of bar fetters in Indian jails. Held without trial in a crumbling former colonial building, Tyler's experience implies the worst about the postcolonial prison system's inability to break away from its past both physically and ideologically.

Within the discourse of the many postcolonial jail committees, the continued reliance on extant colonial buildings, such as Hazaribagh, had long been a subject of critique. A meeting of the national finance commission in 1978 determined that there had been no improvements to the "physical environments" of Indian jails and that "improvements in amenities in respect of water supply, sanitary facilities, electrification" were of utmost importance.[52] Many problems plaguing colonial prisons, such as limited resources to confine women and juveniles in separate facilities were likewise at the heart of discussions about reforming postcolonial prison space. Even within the last fifteen years official reports have continued to allude to problematic physical conditions, citing overcrowding and congestion, along with the failure to provide hygienic conditions and other basic amenities, which echo colonial officials' complaints from over a 150 years ago.

There are a few postcolonial examples of prison spaces that seem to demonstrate a radical re-thinking of the role of prison buildings. The Lalgola Open Air Correctional Home, located 160 miles from the city of Kolkata, is one such space. Established in the district of Murshidabad in 1987, Lalgola, along with several other correctional homes in India, is premised on the idea of an "open institution."[53] Male prisoners — who have been sentenced to seven years or more, have already served two-thirds of their sentences, and have a consistent good jail record — can be relocated there. While in residence they are permitted "complete freedom of movement" and can leave the correctional home premises for most of the day to pursue vocations.[54] Their families also reside with them in cottages provided by the government.

Lalgola, hailed as the government's experiment in "reformation theory," seems strikingly revolutionary; the government teaches prisoners trades, so they can earn money, buy property, such as goats and cows, and be better equipped to work upon release.[55] Lalgola also appears to represent a break with colonial penal practice; in conceiving of a prison's boundaries as permeable the postcolonial state alters the idea of punishment as enclosure. Yet the government's interest in the reformative potential of prisoner labor — an essential idea of an open-air correctional home — has ties to the colonial period. Colonial officials also turned to prisoner labor as a reformative behavior. Colonial patterns of jail organization sought to maximize prisoner labor by including spaces of manufacture within the boundaries of the radial plan.[56] Under the colonial system remunerative prison labor was used to offset some of the exorbitant costs of managing an empire, as well as to provide the system with a modern purpose, promising to transform unproductive native criminals into efficient laboring bodies. Though Lalgola differs from colonial prisons in the spatial freedoms it affords to prisoners, the ideology informing the attention to labor and its centrality to the broader experience of the Indian prisoner ought to be examined in the context of the prison's colonial origins. Today in India prison labor continues to be celebrated as part of the prison's linear narrative of progress.[57] At Presidency, for example, prisoners manufacture candles, oil, clothing, and leather goods to earn a small wage, and such efforts are represented as pioneering projects of reform.[58]

While a deeper investigation into the ethical ramifications of contemporary prison industrial systems is beyond the scope of this chapter, in drawing parallels between the idea of reformative labor during the colonial and postcolonial periods, this chapter's goal is to suggest that the "framework of rational universality" that gave meaning to the colonial system was indeed replicated after independence. Not only are many colonial buildings still used, but the lived spatial experiences of postcolonial prisoners and the postcolonial system's broader rationale connect to its colonial past. Thus the majority of postcolonial prisons still bear an imprint, either physical or ideological, of the colonial regime. As mimetic spaces, these prisons reproduce the practices and policies of the colonial state but have found ways of "taming" this replication by invoking nationalist memory.

ALIPORE CONTRADICTION

Postcolonial prisons remained deeply tied to their pasts, not only on account of their origin as colonial buildings, but also because of their connection to the larger landscape of former colonial cities and towns. Contemporary Kolkata is one such Indian city that is haunted by colonial memory. Kolkata, which began as a fortified trading station of the EIC on the east bank of the Hooghly River, quickly grew in the eighteenth and nineteenth centuries into the capital of the British Empire in India — a designation held until 1911 when the British moved the capital to New Delhi. Today tension exists throughout city between its colonial past and its postcolonial present. This tension can be clearly observed in the treatment of city monuments. After independence numerous colonial monuments and streets were replaced with nationalist figures and names, respectively. Along with this reimagining of the city, there was, as Partha Chatterjee has argued, a "parallel awareness of the need to preserve the architectural and aesthetic heritage of what was once a colonial city."[59] There are different forms this awareness takes, such as the transformation of the colonial governor's former residence into a national library or investing sites throughout the city with "new nationalist historical narratives" through the erection of additional markers.[60] However, institutional buildings were not as easily re-branded; the city's prisons could not be replaced or shut down, so officials chose to appropriate particular spaces within to "tame" their colonial origins in way that validated national identity.

One of the most important prisons in Kolkata, in addition to the aforementioned Presidency, both during the colonial period and at present, was the Alipore Central Correctional Home (hereafter Alipore). Nestled within the elite Alipore district, the buildings that comprise Alipore were initially constructed in the early part of the twentieth century. The jail opened in 1913 near the Kalighat Temple, which has longed served as an important landmark in city.[61] Built with a red-brick façade that mirrored other colonial buildings such as the Calcutta High Court, the prison was organized according to a radial plan, employed to produce a more secure prison facility for a city that had become especially politically charged during the growing turbulence of the nationalist movement. In addition to its modern design, Alipore's construction was also tied to the early twentieth-century colonial reimagining of the city. Queen Victoria's death in 1901 prompted Lord Curzon, Viceroy of India, to call for a memorial to be built in Kolkata in the Queen's honor to reinforce the British presence in the city. The Victoria Memorial was to be built in the Maidan, which necessitated that one of the city's existing jails be shut down. This older jail, that at the time held the designation of Presidency Jail, was demolished and Alipore's construction began.[62]

Alipore would go on to serve a central role in the detention and execution of prominent political prisoners during the nationalist period, and continued to function as an important penal space long after the British left, confining major figures (both men and women) of the Naxalite Movement, as well as carrying out executions that drew national attention.[63] In 2019 Alipore was shut down and numerous prisoners were moved to a facility in the nearby city of Baruipur. The construction of high-rises in the immediate vicinity of Alipore precipitated this decision, as the high-rises provided views into Alipore making security and surveillance more difficult to maintain.[64] The Government of West Bengal has plans to turn Alipore into a heritage site to commemorate the nationalist history of India's prison system. Such plans would consolidate the extant sites of commemoration within the prison, established during the postcolonial period, into a singular memorial.

A printing press building located inside Alipore is one site of commemoration. Containing one of the oldest presses in India, this heritage site celebrated Alipore's long history with industry. The prison press was an early colonial initiative put in place at Alipore to reform prisoners through labor. The press was considered a colonial success story that published numerous documents for the colonial government while simultaneously teaching prisoners a trade. The press stayed open in the postcolonial period and continued to print documents for the government. In commemorating the press, prison officials seem to both preserve and celebrate the productive colonial heritage of their prison system.

Other physical markers scattered throughout the exterior and interior were intended to legitimize the representation of Alipore as symbol of colonial tyranny within collective nationalist memory. The names of nationalist martyrs executed by the British, for example, appeared on a plaque on the exterior of Alipore's entrance in an effort to attach the memory of sacrifice to the site. Other heritage sites inside include decommissioned wards, which were left to stand in memorial to the famous nationalist prisoners once housed within. While for much of the year these cells remained closed to the public, commemorative events, such as the offering of flowers, took place at the cells in conjunction with the numerous martyrs' days celebrated throughout the year.

Known as the Nehru Bhavan (building), the single-story ward containing the cell where Nehru was incarcerated from February 17 to May 7, 1934, serves as a good example of Alipore's internal commemorative project [see Figure 9.1]. While Alipore was operational, the ward was closed off from the lived spaces of the jail but was regularly landscaped and kept tidy. In the center of the cell is a painted black bust of the prime minster resting atop a stool [Figure 9.8]. As the only object within, the likeness attempts to capture Nehru's incarceration for posterity, a physical reminder of the years he spent imagining independence.

While clearly tied to the representation of a "national selfhood," this heritage site also gestures to the complicated nature of commemorative space within the postcolonial landscape. Convicted prisoners confined to Alipore had little to do with the site; visitors could only access it with permission of the superintendent outside of martyrs' days. Thus while the site co-exists within a space shared with convicted prisoners, its message is directed at a public detached from the everyday realities of the postcolonial prison system and the "repressive legacies" of the colonial period. The site's purpose was to serve as an analogue of nationalist memory for India's non-criminal population, but its hidden nature differs from traditional built memorials from the Raj period or even memorials constructed after independence, which were intended to be seen by large numbers in visible and accessible public spaces. The site's potency was instead premised on the selective remembrance of the few who visited it and a willingness on behalf of those visitors to forget its larger spatial context within an operational correctional home. In repurposing this cell as memorial, the postcolonial government of India attempted to "tame" their inherited carceral space and downplay its mimetic nature as a relic of the former colonial system. Inspiring nostalgia and reverence for the past, Alipore as a memorial suggests

Figure 9.8
View into Jawaharlal
Nehru's cell at the Alip
Correctional Home,
Kolkata. Photograph 2
Source: Mira Rai Waits

that colonial prisons are colonized by the political agency of freedom fighters to counter a view of the postcolony as forever colonized by colonial institutions.

CONCLUSION

The postcolonial prison system in India remains tied to colonial history in terms of policy, practice, and spatial experience. The image of the prison as nationalist symbol, manufactured through heritage sites, is meant to diffuse the prison's colonial origins, as well as mitigate the postcolonial state's continued reliance on prisons to punish within a select public consciousness.

India is not alone in sustaining this contradiction. The former Sŏdaemun Prison in Seoul, South Korea, is today a museum that commemorates Korean anti-colonial activists who were martyred at the hands of Japanese colonial officials. However, as Russell Burge has recently argued, the nationalist narrative is complicated by how the prison was used as a space of political suppression, even after the fall of the Japanese Empire until it was finally decommissioned in 1987.[65] In South Africa prison memorials function in a similar way to the prisons of India. The Kgosi Mampuru II Correctional Centre (formerly the Pretoria Central Jail) commemorates the numerous anti-apartheid martyrs who were hanged within prison walls, while the prison itself remains operational.[66] Meanwhile, prisons in Latin America, as Susana Draper has argued, have surreal afterlives; the Punta Carretas Prison in Uruguay, a detention center for political prisoners during the Uruguayan Dictatorship, was transformed into a shopping center that opened in 1994 after the dictatorship fell.[67]

India's postcolonial prison system's mimetic relationship to colonial discipline and punishment is impossible deny. As architectural byproducts of the age of Enlightenment and the rise of liberalism, the continued use of prisons was supposed to lend legitimacy to the independent Indian nation-state. However, the postcolonial prison system leaves an ambiguous narrative that clouds efforts to uncover clear distinctions between colonial and postcolonial spaces, which ultimately casts a larger shadow over the history of decolonization in the subcontinent. Perhaps as long as these inherited colonial buildings remain, this irreconcilable dichotomy between past and present will be unavoidable.

ACKNOWLEDGEMENTS

I wish to thank Daniel E. Coslett for organizing the Society of Architectural Historians (US) conference (2018) panel that led to this chapter, as well as my fellow panelists for inspiring my approach. I am also grateful to the staff at the British Library, the Orion Publishing Group, and Penguin Books Ltd. for their assistance with image rights and reproductions. Special thanks go to Mary Tyler for her generosity in allowing me to reprint her illustrations.

NOTES

1   Jawaharlal Nehru, "Great Speeches of the Twentieth Century: A Tryst with Destiny," *The Guardian*, April 30, 2007, https://www.theguardian.com/theguardian/2007/may/01/greatspeeches; Yasmin Khan, "The Ending of an Empire: From Imagined Communities to Nation States in Indian and Pakistan," *The Round Table* 97, no. 398 (2008): 696.

2   The colonial and postcolonial archives do not distinguish between prison and jail. The terms are used interchangeably here.

3   Phillip L. Reichel, *Comparative Criminal Justice Systems: A Topical Approach,* 5th ed. (Upper Saddle River, NJ: Pearson, 2008), 330.

4   Michel Foucault, "Governmentality (a lecture at the Collège de France given on February 1, 1978)," *Security, Territory, Population: Lectures at the Collège de France, 1977–78* (London: Palgrave MacMillan, 2007), 46–7.

5   See Mrinalini Rajagopalan and Madhuri Desai, "Introduction: Architectural Modernities of Imperial Pasts and Nationalist Presents," in *Colonial Frames, Nationalist Histories: Imperial Legacies, Architecture, and Modernity*, eds. Mrinalini Rajagopalan and Madhuri Desai (Burlington, VT: Ashgate, 2012), 1–23 for more on the "taming" of colonial architectural symbols in India.

6   See Ramachandra Guha's *India After Gandhi: The History of the World's Largest Democracy* (New York: Harper Perennial, 2008) for a general history on the end of the Raj and the rise of Indian democracy.

7   John Darwin, *The Empire Project: The Rise and Fall of the British World-System, 1830–1970* (Cambridge: Cambridge University, 2009), 537.

8   Ibid. See Yasmin Khan, *The Great Partition: The Making of India and Pakistan* (New Haven, CT: Yale University, 2008) for a history of the partition.

9   Letter from Listowel to Mountbatten, August 9, 1947, William Francis Hare papers, IOR Mss Eur C357, ff10-25. (IOR hereafter refers to the India Office Records and Private Papers held in the British Library Asia Pacific & Africa Collections, formerly Oriental and India Office Collections, London.)

10 Ujjwal Kumar Singh, *Political Prisoners in India* (New Delhi: Oxford University, 1998), 206.

11 Khan, "The Ending of an Empire," 697.

12 Partha Chatterjee, *The Nation and Its Fragments: Colonial and Postcolonial Histories* (Princeton, NJ: Princeton University, 1993), 204–05 and 218.

13 Jail Department (India), *Amendments to the Central Provinces and Berar Jail Manual*, revised edition correction slips to vol. 1, 1948–52 (Nagpur: Government Printing, November 4, 1949), 233, IOR, IOR/V/27/171/57.

14 Singh, *Political Prisoners*, 218.

15 Jail Department (India), *Amendments to the Central Provinces and Berar Jail Manual*, revised edition correction slips to vol. 1, 1948–52 (Nagpur: Government Printing, May 11, 1950), 63, IOR, IOR/V/27/171/57.

16 Ibid.

17 Bureau of Police Research Development, Ministry of Home Affairs (India), *National Policy on Prison Reforms and Correctional Administration* (New Delhi: Government of India, 2007).

18 Walter C. Reckless, *Jail Administration in India* (New York: United Nations Technical Assistance Programme, 1953).

19 Ibid., 15.

20 Ibid., 9.

21 Ibid., 35.

22 Nitai Roy Chowdhury, *Indian Prison Laws and Correction of Prisoners* (New Delhi: Deep & Deep, 2002), 40–41.

23 In 2000 an All India Model Prison Manual Committee met to prepare a *Model Prison Manual,* to be circulated to all Indian states in 2004. In 2005 the Bureau of Police Research & Development was tasked with drafting a national policy paper on prison reforms and correctional administration; the final version was published in 2007.

24 See Bureau of Police Research & Development (India), *National Policy on Prison Reforms and Correctional Administration* (New Delhi: Ministry of Home Affairs, Government of India, 2007), 13.

25 Mark Brown, "Postcolonial Penality: Liberty and Repression in the Shadow of Independence, India c. 1947," *Theoretical Criminology* 21, no. 2 (2017): 199.

26 Chatterjee, *The Nation*, 15.

27 For more on the constitutional connections between Britain and India see Upendra Baxi, "Postcolonial legality" in *A Companion to Postcolonial Studies*, ed. Henry

Schwartz and Sangeeta Ray (Malden, MA: Blackwell, 2005), 540–55; Mithi Mukherjee, *India in the Shadows of Empire: A Legal and Political History, 1774–1950* (New Delhi: Oxford University, 2010); Eleanor Newbigin, "Personal Law and Citizenship in India's Transition to Independence," *From Subjects to Citizens: Society and the Everyday State in India and Pakistan, 1947–1970*, eds. Taylor C. Sherman, William Gould, and Sarah Ansari (Cambridge: Cambridge University, 2014), 10–37.

28 Baxi, "Postcolonial legality," 544.

29 Ibid., 543.

30 Brown, "Postcolonial Penality," 187.

31 Central jails house long-term prisoners from surrounding districts (the administrative subdivisions of Indian states). District jails were smaller and designed to serve individual districts. Sub-jails, or lock-ups as they were known under the British, were jails for smaller regions of a district, which often hold prisoners under trial. Sub-jails make up sixty percent of all the prisons in India.

32 Lydia Polgreen, "Rehabilitation Comes to a Prison and to Its Inmates," *The New York Times*, July 18, 2011, https://www.nytimes.com/2011/07/19/world/asia/19delhi.html.

33 Ibid.

34 Ranvir Kumar, *The Metamorphosis* 18 (2013): 6–7, http://wbcorrectionalservices.gov.in/pdf/issue_18.pdf.

35 Ibid., 7.

36 Ibid.

37 John Mulvany, "Bengal Jails in Early Days," *Calcutta Review* 6, no. 292 (1918): 293–316.

38 See Mira Rai Waits, "Imperial Vision, Colonial Prisons: British Jails in Bengal, 1823–1873," *Journal of the Society of Architectural Historians* 77, no. 2 (2018): 146–67.

39 J.W. Heeley (India), *Annual Report on the Administration of Jails of the Bengal Presidency, 1871* (Calcutta: Alipore Jail Press), 109, IOR, IOR/V/24/2071.

40 F.J. Mouat (India), *Annual Report on the Administration of Jails of the Bengal Presidency, 1864–65* (Calcutta: Alipore Jail Press, 1865), ccli, IOR/V/24/2066.

41 See Indian Jails Committee, *Report of the Indian Jails Committee, 1919–20* (London: HM Stationery Office, 1921), 265, along with the model plan published in Appendix XIII, which affirms the preference for the radial plan, IOR/L/PARL/2/407.

42 Peter Scriver and Amit Srivastava, *India: Modern Architectures in History* (London: Reaktion, 2015), 137 and 139.

43 Ibid., 138.

44 See Waits "Imperial Vision," 153–8 for more on the colonial history of the Presidency Jail.

45 See Aurobindo Ghose, *Tales of Prison Life* (Pondicherry: Sri Aurobindo Ashram, 1997) for a discussion of inhumane conditions.

46 Amnesty International, *Short Report on Detention Conditions in West Bengal Jails* (report) (London: Amnesty International, 1974): 4.

47 Bar fetters "consist of an iron ring round the ankle, each of which is attached to an iron bar some 20 inches long, the bar being connected to another iron ring round the waist." Amnesty International, "Political Imprisonment and Torture in India," *Economic and Political Weekly* 14, no. 4 (January 27, 1979): 147

48 Amnesty International, *Short Report*, 5

49 Prisoners have recitation workshops, concerts, women's day celebrations, and anti-smoking celebrations. Yoga, Pranayama, and mediation classes are regularly held. Prisoners also have access to a library and can take part in athletic competitions.

50 Mary Tyler, *My Years in an Indian Prison* (London: Victor Gollancz/Orion Publishing Group, 1977).

51 Ibid., 31.

52 See Bureau of Police Research & Development (India), *National Policy on Prison Reforms and Correctional Administration* (New Delhi: Ministry of Home Affairs (India), 2007).

53 In West Bengal there are four open correctional homes in Lalgola, Durgapur, Raiganj, and Midnapore; several others can be found across India. An "open institution," according to the First UN Congress, is characterized "by the absence of material and physical precautions against escape (such as walls, locks, bars, armed or other special security guards) and by a system based on self-discipline and the inmate's sense of responsibility towards the group in which he lives." "Open institutions" reflect a global interest in less restrictive prisons explored at the First UN Congress on the Prevention of Crime and the Treatment of Offenders held in Geneva in 1955. See Manuel Lopez-Ray, *The First United Nations Congress on the Prevention of Crime and the Treatment of Offenders*, Journal of Criminal Law and Criminology 47, no. 5 (1957): 533.

54 West Bengal Correctional Services, "Open Air Correctional Home," accessed March 6, 2018, http://wbcorrectionalservices.gov.in/correctionalhome.html.

55 Ibid.

56 See Mira Rai Waits, "Carceral Capital: The Prison-Industrial Complex in Colonial India," in *Across Time and Space: Architecture and the Politics of Modernity*, ed. Patrick Haughey (New Brunswick, NJ: Transaction, 2017), 19–45.

57 Arun Kumar Gupta, *The Metamorphosis* 24 (2018): 6–7, http://wbcorrectionalservices.gov.in/pdf/issue_24.pdf.

58 Arun Kumar Gupta, *The Metamorphosis* 19 (2017): 4, http://wbcorrectionalservices.gov.in/pdf/issue_19.pdf.

59 Partha Chatterjee, "The Colonial City in the Postcolonial Era," *Inter-Asia Cultural Studies* 15, no. 1 (2014): 39.

60 Ibid.

61 J.G. Hercle, Registrar High Court (India), *Bengal Proceedings* (Calcutta: Government Press, July 9, 1913), 13, IOR, IOR/P/9146.

62 The buildings that comprise today's Presidency Correctional Home were known prior to 1913 as the Alipore Jail. When the new Alipore Jail was opened in 1913 the colonial government re-named the existing Alipore Jail the Presidency Jail to replace the buildings demolished to accommodate the memorial. The current Presidency Correctional Home has held that name ever since.

63 Dhananjoy Chatterjee's execution in 2004, in particular, drew national attention, and the execution was recently represented in *Dhananjoy*, a 2017 Bengali film about the prisoner's life.

64 Anon., "Bengal govt. to relocate 3 correctional homes," *The Hindu*, February 27, 2018, http://www.thehindu.com/news/cities/kolkata/bengal-govt-to-relocate-3-correctional-homes/article22863456.ece.

65 Russell Burge, "The Prison and the Postcolony: Contested Memory and the Museumification of Sŏdaemun Hyŏngmuso," *Journal of Korean Studies* 22, no. 1 (2017): 33–67.

66 Poloko Tau, "52 steps to death," *News 24*, August 13, 2017, https://www.news24.com/SouthAfrica/News/52-steps-to-death-20170812.

67 Susana Draper, *Afterlives of Confinement: Spatial Transitions in Postdictatorship Latin America* (Pittsburgh, PA: University of Pittsburgh, 2012).

Part IV

Globalization and heritage in contemporary postcolonies

10

Heritage, tourism, and the challenges of postcolonial globalization at Tunis' Bardo Museum

Daniel E. Coslett

Located with in the formerly walled royal outpost of Bardo, less than three miles to the west of Tunis' historic medina, the Bardo National Museum is Tunisia's premier antiquities museum. Housing a vast collection of Punic, Roman, Byzantine, and medieval Islamic artifacts, the renowned museum remains an obligatory stop on the itinerary of most tourists visiting the country, and has been since its 1888 inauguration by French colonial officials within disused portions of the Tunisian *bey*'s Bardo palace.[1] First celebrated by the French administration as a demonstration of Tunisia's long history, its connections to Europe (via the ancient Roman Empire), its exoticism (as an Orientalist fantasy), and as a justification for colonial occupation, after independence in 1956 the Bardo became a bulwark of national identity and a symbol of Tunisian cosmopolitanism and postcolonial sovereignty.[2] Throughout its storied existence, the building — which may be viewed metaphorically as a reflection of Tunisia's changing political status, identity, and manner of engagement with the world — has been repeatedly expanded to both accommodate its ever-growing collection, and to reflect changing socio-political and museological standards.

The most recent renovation of the museum, completed in 2012, was by far the most dramatic in its history. Produced by a collaboration among Tunisian, French, and global actors whose participation resulted from attempts by the Tunisian state and tourism professionals to see the country's tourism portfolio become more diverse, globally competitive, and economically productive, it engages Tunisia with broader trends in globalization, identity formation, and heritage tourism. By inviting visitors to witness the long history of Tunisia in a new space designed to be welcoming, contemporary, and recognizable in its appearance, the museum building aims to represent the nation and the state in accordance with officially sanctioned heritage discourse agendas. Indeed, the enlarged structure — funded by a substantial World Bank-backed investment — deploys stark modernist façades and expansive whitewashed halls that mask the building's pre-colonial core, as well as its Protectorate-era expansions, symbolically materializing the complexities of postcolonial hybridity and reappropriation. A deadly

terrorist attack at the museum in 2015 foregrounds the site's contested manifestation of identities, agendas, and approaches to foreign audiences. Although
such issues have been debated in Tunisia since the colonial era (and indeed well
before that), they have arguably become increasingly relevant since independence
from France and the 2011 "Arab Spring" revolution that uprooted the country's
longstanding authoritarian regime.

In studying the Bardo Museum building and institution, it becomes clear
that during the Protectorate era (1881–1956) the museum reflected the dominant socio-political and rhetorical messaging of the colonizer. By prioritizing
Punic, Roman, and early Christian artifacts within a Tunisian palace retrofitted by
French authorities, it validated Tunisia's pre-Arab past while arguably implying the
inferiority of its fetishized Arab history.[3] The museum thus reinforced colonialism
by presenting the colonizer as master of knowledge and authoritative savior of
material heritage, and also facilitated capital-driven tourism, all of which invited
involvement with, and intrusions from, the West. More recently, globalization
has extended and amplified these things, thus rendering the iconic museum an
enticing target for terrorists. Notwithstanding the changing dynamics, the Bardo
retains much of its physical structure (within its new additions) and contents, just
as it retains its essential function and effect — the preservation and presentation
of antiquities and the representation of Tunisia and Tunisians according to the
dominant beliefs held by the country's elites. A focused study of the Bardo therefore sheds light on conflicting postcolonial identities, potentially neocolonialist
relationships, violence, and resilience. Indeed, the Bardo's history and recent struggles illuminate questions regarding the very identity of the nation and the stability
of the postcolonial/post-revolutionary state. In exploring these issues, certainly
relevant beyond Tunisia, the chapter that follows addresses the sustained significance of Tunisia's pre-Arab past for heritage tourism professionals and politicians.
It introduces the museum's foundation, its expansion during the colonial period
and afterwards — paying particular attention to its most recent redevelopment —
as well as its position in the wake of the 2011 democratic revolution.

THE BARDO'S ESTABLISHMENT AND EXPANDING FORM

North Africa's pre-Arab pasts were extremely important to French colonial and
Catholic Church officials, many of whom viewed themselves to be modern inheritors of ancient civilizing authority in the region. References to such strategic fab-
rications appeared in speeches, architectural projects, regulations, and literature
throughout the colonial period.[4] "Here, in North Africa, we find everywhere the
traces of Rome beneath our feet, which proves that we belong here, in the front
lines of civilization," declared Morocco's French Governor Hubert Lyautey in 1924,
echoing this long-cultivated sentiment.[5] Intellectually, French and Italian colonialist historiographic processes championed outsiders in antiquity, "portraying
the Africans either as passive recipients of superior culture or as nomadic and
lawless people incapable of self-government."[6] This "double process of cultural

annexation and alienation" elevated colonizers as masters of knowledge — hence power — based on their promoted affiliation with ancient Romans and early Christians, as well as their scholarly expertise.[7] Museums, such as the Bardo, were essential components of these colonialist mythologies and power dynamics.

Though established after the major Catholic Church-run antiquities museum at nearby Carthage,[8] the Bardo quickly became preeminent. It remains the country's top tourist destination, having long since eclipsed its predecessor in size, significance, and popularity. Originally called the Alaoui Museum in honor of the titular sovereign, or *bey*, at its foundation (Ali Bey), its establishment by decree on November 7, 1882 — just a year after the French colonial Protectorate of Tunisia was established — indicates that it was a relatively high priority for the new regime.[9] When the intended building within the Tunis medina became unavailable, the Bardo site was chosen ostensibly because it cost less than building a new structure would have, and it retained some valuable degree of prestige.[10] As Myriam Bacha points out, French officials would have also been aware of — and likely drawn to — the Bardo's significance as the seat of Tunisia's government since the seventeenth century, as well its reputation among European tourists who often wrote of the palace after visiting Tunis. Further contributing to its celebrity, French people would have also known of the building because it served as a model for the Tunisian pavilion at the 1867 Universal Exposition in Paris, and its name would have been recognizable since the 1881 Bardo Treaty establishing the French protectorate was signed there, and hence bore its name. With the *bey*'s approval, an 1885 decree codified the museum's collection scope and its setting within derelict nineteenth-century portions of the Bardo Palace.[11] The site — to be extensively consolidated and restored by the colonizing power — was thus seen as an appropriately dignified and renowned setting for such a significant installation.[12]

With renovations still underway, in May 1888 the museum was inaugurated by the Antiquities Service in the presence of the *bey*, the French Resident General, members of the Institut de France, and other French dignitaries. At its opening the museum included just a ground-floor vestibule, a large covered patio, a grand ballroom, a small adjacent room, and the palace's former harem quarters [Figure 10.1].[13] Quickly overwhelmed by the growing collection's size, the facility was expanded into adjacent palace rooms in the spring of 1896.[14] Work for yet another expansion was underway again in 1899.[15] Although during its first decades existing spaces were refurbished for museum use, administrators would later see to it that new galleries were added to the building in order to accommodate its collection, which from the beginning was drawn almost exclusively from Tunisian soil and thus directly represented the country's rich cultural heritage.[16]

The original space dedicated to the nascent Bardo Museum had been built as the harem portion of the beylical palace during the 1850s, but was completed later under the reign of Mohammad es Sadok (r.1813–82).[17] Said to have been designed by Tunisian architects and decorated by Tunisian craftsmen (whose identities

remain elusive), the square planned-space incorporates a cruciform chamber with connected corner rooms. White marble columns hold aloft ornately carved plaster vaulting above walls clad in colorfully glazed tiles typical of the region. Adjacent to this space is a vast hall ringed in white Carrera marble "neo-Corinthian" columns [Figure 10.2].[18] Its arcade supports an open gallery enclosed by a cast iron balustrade, over which arched windows — some of which have been closed and covered over — facilitate the space's illumination. Intricately carved pendants are dressed in colorful pilasters, medallions and moldings, betraying Italian influence in an era of significant trans-Mediterranean linkages and Ottoman openness to Western aesthetics and plans.[19] Given over to the museum by 1896, an adjacent shallow-domed concert hall includes two balconies — one that gave women direct access to the harem and another for an orchestra — with Italianate bronze balustrades. Across the patio is another addition to the museum, a former dining room dressed in still more Italian-influenced woodwork and Baroque floral paintings. Both rooms also incorporate North African colored tilework and carved wood decorations. At the far end of the patio one finds a large reception hall, known as the *Salle des Fêtes* (ballroom). The last of these early incorporations into the growing museum, the room hosts a soaring carved wooden ceiling. Again reflecting a degree of Italian influence,[20] here sixteen gilt panels rise into a glittering cupola, resolving into a dramatic central stalactite-like pendant [Figure 10.3].[21] Each of these repurposed rooms within the restored palace quarters was eventually filled

Figure 10.1
The Bardo Museum's original primary façade and entrance. Photogra... 1914. Source: Agence de presse Meurisse, "Le... grandes manoeuvres navales: les escales, Tun... Le Bardo" (Paris, 1914) [Bibliothèque nationale ... France].

213 TUNIS. — Le Bardo. — Le Patio. — LL.   Lib. Yvorra et Barlier — Tunis

with artifacts; their walls and floors were clad in intricate Roman mosaics, their niches and arcades sheltered statuary recovered from across Tunisia.

By 1896, just fourteen years after its establishment, it was said that the Bardo's collection represented all eras of Tunisia's antiquity and included artifacts from all its regions.[22] The collection's initial materials came from a variety of sources, including amateur archaeologists, French military officials, railroad companies (who moved a considerable amount of earth in their work), and prominent Tunisian holders of excavated materials.[23] The Bardo collection was quickly enriched by excavations undertaken by archaeologists working for the Antiquities Service, including Dr. Louis Carton at Bulla-Reggia and Dougga, as well as others at

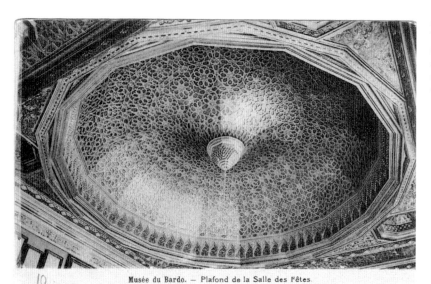

Musée du Bardo. — Plafond de la Salle des Fêtes

Musée du Bardo — La Grande Salle de la Mosaïque.

Edit. P. Louit, 22 rue d'Italie à Tunis.

Figure 10.3
The Bardo Museum *Sa*
des Fêtes interior and
ceiling, c.1920. Postca
c.1920. Source: Autho
collection.

Sousse, Lamta, Makthar, and elsewhere.[24] A full catalogue would not be published until 1897, but Paul Gauckler's 1896 guidebook included very brief descriptions of objects in all four of the museum's functioning rooms and adjacent halls/vestibules at that time.[25] Colonists continued to demonstrate fidelity to France by donating found objects in considerable numbers. They, with excavators, helped the collection continue to grow very quickly.[26] The 1951 edition of the official guidebook reveals that substantial growth and the collection's redistribution throughout the crowded space.[27] By this time rooms had been named for the most part by the origin of their most notable pieces. The Patio thus became the "Roman Carthage room," having previously been dedicated to epigraphic and architectural artifacts, rather than objects recovered from a specific location. Similarly, the *Salle des Fêtes* became the "Sousse Room." The cruciform harem room became the "Virgil Room," owing to its incomparable mosaic portrait of the author and muses.[28]

The Bardo Museum has been a popular destination since it opened, featuring prominently in travel literature since that time. Thanks to the "zeal and activity of its young conservator, Mr. Paul Gauckler[,]" who operated with "a beautiful and patriotic ambition," the Bardo Museum was becoming "one of the most important museums in Europe," said Louis Bertrand in 1905.[29] Bertrand (1855–1941), a vociferous advocate for French colonization of North Africa and champion of the region's Latin past, was quite impressed by the Bardo's collection of ancient Roman mosaics ("… admirable — so suggestive of ancient mores!" he said).[30] In general, however, he confessed to being somewhat overwhelmed. "One is crushed by the abundance of objects, and the eye is lost in the flickering of colors," Bertrand admitted.[31] Others reported similar impressions. Douglas Sladen claimed to have enjoyed his visit to the "valuable and perfectly delightful museum" in 1906,[32] and Emma Burbank Ayer noted that "The whole place bristled with mosaics of more or less fanciful designs, and more or less fine in finish."[33] The Bardo maintained the celebrity first cultivated at this time throughout the colonial period and well into the twenty-first century.

As noted above, the building has grown and changed during its many decades of existence. Both Sladen and Ayer[34] mention visiting chambers dedicated to Punic materials on the floor beneath the main level (viz. on the ground floor), indicating that by 1906 the museum had expanded from its first set of rooms on the second floor into additional chambers below. By 1951 the museum had come to occupy many smaller rooms on the building's ground floor, in addition to rooms on the second floor adjacent to the original spaces.[35] Structural additions had been made to the complex during the 1930s and 1950s,[36] and additional rooms were in use by 1970 on all three levels.[37] The museum's simple exterior was given an arcaded entrance portico that opened on to a vestibule and galleries located within the palace's old storage magazines in 1968.[38] By 1970 the museum filled forty rooms within the retrofitted portions of the palace and its purpose-built extensions on three levels;[39] most of the latter were boxy, whitewashed rooms lit by skylights, the aesthetic of which reflected broader modernist trends popular at that time in Tunisia. Most walls were clad in vast tapestries of ancient mosaic panels. The floors in many rooms were also paved in them, as they would have been in antiquity [Figure 10.4]. The most substantial expansion of the Bardo, however, would open in 2012. Although this expansion changed the museum's appearance dramatically in many ways, the original palace portion of the museum remains largely intact. The complex continues to manifest officially sanctioned interpretations of Tunisia's cultural heritage.

TUNISIA'S ANTIQUITY SINCE INDEPENDENCE

While French, British, and Italian colonizers aligned themselves with their ancient Roman predecessors in North Africa for strategic purposes, Arab Muslim societies

Figure 10.4
A modernist gallery at the Bardo Museum, constructed c.1950–70. Photograph 2016. Sourc[e] Daniel E. Coslett.

there and elsewhere have had different and diverse relationships with these the pre-Arab pasts. According to Stephennie Mulder "Muslims imagined Islamic and pre-Islamic antiquity and its localities in myriad ways: as sites of memory, spaces of healing or places imbued with didactic, historical and moral power."[40] Muslims have at times destroyed antiquities, and at other times simply dwelt among them, she adds. They have also exploited them for modern socio-economic and political purposes, in some ways not unlike the European colonialists who did so by basing identity claims on the preservation and presentation of antiquities to both local and foreign audiences. Mulder's assessments are in part borne out by Tunisia's experience with its own long history.

Tunisian independence in 1956 necessitated a renegotiation of identities, as well as affiliations with power and the past. Educated in France and an admirer of Western conceptions of modernity, Habib Bourguiba (1903–2000), as Tunisia's *pater patriae*, guided the country through independence and the immediate post-independence period with particular dexterity. He directed the state's attention towards the future, definitively away from Tunisia's past and cultural traditions. He aimed to propel his country along the path of modernity established by France and the West in order to guarantee state power and national sovereignty as had other countries in the region, such as Turkey, which also served as an influential model.[41] A free Tunisia — a secular, democratic republic — would maintain open windows on the West, he believed, and he ensured that ties to France and its culture were not severed entirely. His forward-looking approach notwithstanding, Bourguiba's vision of Tunisian future was in important ways anchored to the past.[42] While he at times disparaged Tunisian cultural heritage and traditions with vigor — deeming them tainted and backwards — he selectively chose to emphasize elements of the country's history that served his own personal views and ambitions. His appreciation of French culture notwithstanding, however, he did not perpetuate earlier French preoccupations with Rome and Roman North Africa. Instead, he is said to have likened himself to Jugurtha, the Berber king who opposed Roman domination of North Africa. Substituting France for Rome, Bourguiba proudly made it known that whereas Jugurtha had suffered an ignominious end at the hands of his Roman captors, he — Bourguiba — had won.[43] Bourguiba further opposed France-as-Rome through his adoration of Hannibal, ancient Carthage's iconic general whose elephants had famously terrorized Rome (viz. Europe, the West). In this way he manifested a certain ambivalence regarding the pre-Arab past, but recognized its significance as both symbol and cultural asset appreciated by Western powers and tourists who at that time visited Tunisia primarily for its beaches.[44]

When Zine al Abidine Ben Ali (1936–) ascended to the presidency by means of palace coup in 1987, he continued Bourguiba's veneration of Tunisia's Punic or Carthaginian past in opposition to the Roman history so admired by French colonialists, but he substantially advanced the process by more overtly deploying a resurrected and recast Hannibal, while also investing further in heritage management.[45] Tunisia was to represent a crossroads in the Mediterranean and a synthesis of its historic cultures, and Hannibal was deployed as its mascot.[46] Sadok Chaabane, political advisor and Minister of Justice under the autocratic Ben Ali, articulated the essence of the regime's historicist perspective in 1997:

> Tunisia's mission today concurs with Tunisia's project in Hannibal's time … . It is an undertaking that will make the Mediterranean play its former part, one in which Tunisia is an active participant, not with warfare and conflict but with free competition, not with an exploitative and hegemonic mentality but with the spirit of fair partnership for mutual development.[47]

Hannibal was thus restored to Tunisian political discourse and the nation's "thought structure … to build … [its] future and define its cultural mission … mapping out … horizons that befit the grandeur of his triumphs, more than two thousand years ago," Chaabane continued.[48] Ben Ali, not unlike Bourguiba before him, thus cultivated a cosmopolitan, sophisticated image of Tunisia. Among Tunisians he aimed, according to Kathryn Lafrenz Samuels, to inspire what she calls "heritage citizens'" through active excavation, preservation, and management of archaeological sites, seeking to shape "individuals into tolerant citizens of the world" for what were ultimately economic and political purposes.[49] Indeed, this process was part of a larger one intended by the Ben Ali regime to foster national pride and patriotism among the Tunisian people.[50] Carthage, a UNESCO listed site since 1979, became a symbol of the desired prestige and tolerance,[51] and its management aimed to integrate Tunisia, and Tunisians, into the globalizing world of inclusive, competitive heritage tourism.[52] Tunisia would thus engage the rest of the world, while maintaining its sovereignty (and the governing regime's dominance), for the purposes of economic development. Hannibal's revival was therefore ultimately a part of the government's broad attempt to construct a national identity that would help stem any potential Islam-based challenge by inculcating a tolerant, pluralistic (and docile) society. Heritage tourism became a means for showcasing the stability of Ben Ali's "façade democracy" both internally and abroad to audiences largely willing to overlook the oppressive acts of a dictatorial regime.[53]

Hannibal's rebirth was not just for internal audiences, however. Leslie Plommer noted in 1997 that the figure, "one of antiquity's boldest tacticians," had been "dusted off and deployed in a new battle — to win the favor of tourists."[54] Political scientist Waleed Hazbun describes Hannibal's reformed function as a "distinctive, territorially rooted identification for the nation's external image" presented in what amounted to a strategic "dovetailing of tourism development and image making with national identity formation and mythmaking."[55] To these ends, cultural "Hannibal Clubs" charged with resuscitating the figure's celebrity and representing an open, tolerant, welcoming Tunisia were established in the US and Japan during the late 1990s, there extending the regime's Janus-like mission around the globe.[56] In 1995 he was featured on a postage stamp designed by the prolific Tunisian artist Hatem El Mekki, further mobilizing his image. Museums — repositories of proof that might legitimize such ideological claims — were upgraded and the broader heritage sector was strengthened.

The Bardo, as the museological epicenter of Tunisia's pre-Arab cultural patrimony,[57] certainly owes its preeminence among the country's antiquities assets to the richness of its collection, but also to antiquity's sustained appeal to Western audiences, and to the Tunisian government's active validation of its contents and the history it has come to represent. By the end of the twentieth century the museum had been fully integrated into dominant heritage narratives that stressed Tunisia's place as a physical and symbolic regional crossroads. Demonstrating this, a 1993 guidebook to the museum boasts of the country's "privileged geographic location" and grand history, despite its small size.[58] "The Bardo Museum remains a beautiful history book for Tunisia, the Maghreb and the Mediterranean," writes M'hamed Fantar elsewhere, stressing the facility's universal significance and echoing a common refrain regarding the prestigious institution.[59]

The 2011 Tunisian revolution — the first of the so-called "Arab Spring" revolutions — saw the ouster of president Ben Ali, but the perceived value of antiquity appears to have escaped relatively unscathed. Indeed, the representation of Tunisia's pre-Arab past, long endorsed by the government as a part of what Laurajane Smith calls "authorized heritage discourse," remains very present in tourism literature and nationalist discourse.[60] It would thus appear that the widespread opposition to Ben Ali and his cult of personality did not transfer directly to Hannibal, antiquity, or the Bardo.[61] Long-lauded figures from the country's pre-Arab past, including Jugurtha, Hannibal, the Romans, early Christians, and others, remain important characters in the depiction of Tunisia's identity that still stresses its long duration, its regional significance, tolerance, modernity, and its cosmopolitan nature. The Bardo Museum has remained the crown jewel of the country's heritage assets in terms of visitation, publicity, and investment.

RENEWING THE BARDO

As competition for seasonal beach tourism has stiffened and become less lucrative in the changing global marketplace, Tunisian tourism officials have since the 1980s diversified the country's offerings through the augmentation of its heritage tourism options. Tunisia's distant past clearly remains a major component of its erstwhile "sun, surf, and sand"-centric portfolio,[62] as is made clear by the fact that in 2005 seventy-three percent of paying tourists visited the country's top four heritage centers, which include Carthage, the Bardo Museum, El Djem's Roman amphitheatre and museum, and the Islamic holy city of Kairouan.[63] Visitor statistics for the Bardo have been particularly impressive; almost 570,000 visitors came in 2000, and over 656,000 came in 2005.[64] The need for an upgrade to the crowded and immensely popular museum had been known for a long time and was acknowledged by the World Bank through its substantial financial support of the project.[65] The 2012 World Bank-backed US$12.7 million[66] expansion of the Bardo reflects the sustained importance of antiquities-driven touristic activities in recent years while also inducting Tunisia into current museology trends that celebrate grand projects and standout contemporary architecture (the so-called "Bilbao effect").[67] In this case the "transnational capitalist class" one might expect to see active — including members of the Ben Ali regime who set development and heritage agendas, influential NGOs, tourism professionals, and design firms — did indeed play large roles in the Bardo project and its "iconic architecture."[68]

Planning for the Bardo Museum renewal had begun in the early 2000s and construction began in 2009. In 2001 the World Bank, as part of its broader US$27 million loan for cultural heritage management and tourism development in Tunisia,[69] had allocated considerable resources to its Bardo component. Included elements were a full study of the existing museum facility, the renovation and redistribution of existing exhibition spaces and their contents, the development of visitors' orientation facilities, and the construction of necessary expansions.[70] An initial plan for more modest interior improvements was adjusted in 2003, as the Tunisian government — with the support of the World Bank — chose to pursue a much more ambitious development plan intended to aggressively "transform the Bardo into a high-standard museum focusing primarily on the display of Tunisia's unique collection of Roman mosaics … ."[71] French and Tunisian firms were awarded contracts following an international competition, and designs for the improvement of existing facilities and the construction of new ones were approved in 2007.[72] Interventions within the greatly expanded space were designed by SCPA Codou-Hindley (France) and Amira Nouira (Tunisia) who ultimately added 9,000 square meters to the museum's existing 11,000[73] [Figure 10.5]. The so-called "Arab Spring" revolution — which saw Bardo attendance drop by nearly half between 2010 and 2012[74] — caused delays, but the fully renovated museum debuted in May 2012.[75]

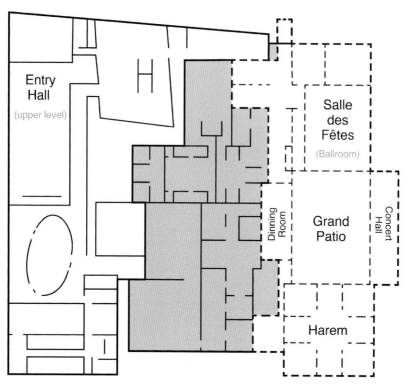

Figure 10.5
The Bardo Museum's evolving plan (main lev[
1888–2012. Plan 2018
Source: Daniel E. Cosle[
(Data sources: R. de la Blanchère, Collections Musée Alaoui: Première série (Paris: Firmin–Dide[1890), 14; Denis Lesag["2012: Métamorphose[muséale en Tunisie," Archibat 26 (2012): 77 The original museum (in 1888) on this level consisted of the ex-har[*Grand Patio*, *Salle des Fêtes*, and one of the small adjacent rooms. The museum's expande[quarters in 1896 are outlined in dashed lines[Additions prior to 2011 are shaded in grey. The 2012 addition is outline[in solid black lines.

Figure 10.6
The Bardo Museum's ne[primary façades, part of the 2012 Codou-Hindley/Nouira extensio[Photograph 2013. Sour[Daniel E. Coslett.

"Fairly neutral and resolutely contemporary" are the terms used by critic Denis Lesage of the addition in describing its general effect.[76] Others have seen in its monumental façade an abandonment of the human scale in favor of the vertical, and a reference to city gate in its main portal's appearance.[77] Its façades, which thankfully conceal those of their unsightly twentieth-century predecessors, Lesage says, are pierced by a patchwork of rectangular windows intended to reference an ancient Roman pavement technique called *opus Romanum* (Roman work) in which irregularly sized stone slabs were fit together [Figure 10.6].[78] Whitewashed planes and geometric masses define the museum's new interiors, as is made apparent in the entry hall. Whereas before one entered via a rather unceremonious and dark passage leading to cramped exhibition spaces on the old palace's ground floor, one now enters into a vast, open space, the ceiling of which soars eleven meters overhead [Figure 10.7]. There the triumphant Neptune

re 10.7
Bardo Museum's new
iors by Codou-Hindley
Nouira. Top: Entry
Bottom: Gallery
e. Photographs 2013
) and 2016 (bottom).
rce: Daniel E. Coslett.

mosaic from Sousse (13 × 10 m.) — for over a century displayed on the floor of the *Salle des Fêtes* — has been given pride of place, clearly stating the significance of the museum's dominant Roman collection.[79] A nearby glass-enclosed garden patio (reminiscent of a Roman atrium) enlivens the space and opens sightlines into adjacent galleries. The experience here sets the tone for rest of the museum addition, which includes a gift shop and cafeteria,[80] conference and classroom spaces, a temporary exhibition hall, and a media collection.

The addition's appearance and spatial experience can be seen as manifestations of the contemporary "Bilbao effect," though the architects describe their work in different terms. Speaking of her Bardo interventions, Nouira focused on spatial connections and light. "The streets — horizontal and vertical — as diagonals distribute the volumes of the structure and facilitate the penetration of light within," she says. For her here, a didactic modernity means "fluidity, simultaneity, [and] speed." She suggests that:

> [the] simultaneity of gaze on the geography of the past, this architecture, all these forms of art, all these ages presented in this sumpuous and magnificent setting, allow the visitor to propel himself from the past … to better project himself into the future.[81]

Indeed, clear circulation and consistent luminosity are hallmark characteristics of the expansive addition; they set it far apart from the many darker, labyrinthine rooms of the reprogramed palace [see Figure 10.7]. Codou confirms that his intent with the building was not to make a show of its form, but rather to "hide the surprises that are inside" in an architectural envelope.[82]

Moving through the renewed Bardo today — amidst a compelling mix of old and new architecture — one encounters the long history of Tunisia in rooms grouped by civilization (though gallery nomenclature generally retains the old city-name format), rather than by strictly chronological arrangement. Likely owing to the building's complicated construction history and the many challenges associated with relocating large, fragile mosaics within the expanded space, many of the mosaic displays remain in their pre-2012 configuration. Enhanced lighting, new gallery texts (written in Arabic, French, and now English as well), and new cases and pedestals fill rooms dedicated to Punic, Greek, Numidian, Roman, Christian, and Islamic civilizations.[83] The pathway through the museum necessitated in large part by the structure's layout, however, can obscure the chronology; the recommended circuit begins with Islamic galleries, then proceeds through Christian and Roman ones (in some publications grouped together as "Late Antique") on the ground floor, before leading up to Roman, Numidian, and Punic sections (in that achronological order) on the main level.[84]

CONFLICTING FORCES OF NEOCOLONIALISM AND GLOBALIZATION

Having already destroyed antiquities and archaeological sites elsewhere in the Middle East,[85] partisans of the so-called Islamic State (ISIS) assaulted the Bardo on March 18, 2015. The devastating terrorist attack resulted in the death of twenty-two people from ten European countries, Japan, Colombia, and Tunisia.[86] Great damage was done to artifacts and the museum's interior during the invasion and resulting three-hour siege launched by Tunisian special forces. In solidarity after the event, Tunisians, with many vocal supporters abroad, quickly rallied behind the motto *"Je suis Bardo"* (I am Bardo).[87] Recovery, however, has not been easy. Indeed, the museum, like the entire county, has struggled to re-establish its tourism industry since the stunning attack, which was the second deadly assault on tourism sites in Tunisia that year.[88] Negative publicity has rendered both the country and museum unattractive to many, and the scarred museum has gained unfortunate notoriety as a site of tragedy for those interested in "dark tourism."[89] Empty rooms — some still unfinished, others emptied after the attack — and bullet-ridden vitrines contribute to an air of incompletion or instability, reminding visitors of recent gruesome events. What had once been a crowded, cramped museum now feels sparse and largely desolate because of its new structural openness and dearth of patrons. Visitation numbers were abysmally low in 2016, totaling less than 15,000 visitors per month (or 180,000 per year), a distressing decline from the 600,000 per year average accommodated before the 2011 revolution.[90]

Attack victims have been memorialized through mosaic portraits created by artisans in El Djem, a town most known for its Roman amphitheatre, displayed outside the museum's main entrance [Figure 10.8].[91] Another prominent memorial panel inside the main hall — also rendered in mosaics — lists the names and nationalities of those killed and ensures remembrance. The somber cenotaph stands out in today's quiet, brightly lit, and whitewashed entry. The identities of those lost, as well as the tragic event itself, have thus been

Figure 10.8
Mosaic panel commemorating the victims of the 2015 Bardo Museum terrorist attack. Photograph 2016. Source: Daniel E. Coslett. At the center is a reproduction of the museum's iconic Ulysseus scene. Doves and the popular solidarity statement "Je suis Bardo" (I am Bardo) appear elsewhere in both French and Arabic.

integrated into the physical material of the museum. Indeed, they are unavoidably present.

The relationship between globalization and terrorism remains controversial. Some suggest that terrorism has proliferated because some people find themselves left out of globalization or suffer from its effects, while others conclude that transnational links facilitate the extension of terrorist networks that proliferate within the weakened state system.[92] Despite the differing assessments, it is clear that tourism can attract, but is also hindered by even the threat of, terrorism.[93] Indeed, with financial support from the World Bank the Bardo has intentionally facilitated tourism, which has invited involvement with, and what to some are intrusions from, the West. Some of this has clearly angered proponents of a more conservative and/or independent Tunisia.[94] The museum therefore manifests the conflictual nature of contemporary globalization and neocolonialism; it seeks to welcome as an agent of tolerance and multiculturalism, but also invites opposition and violence aimed at the Tunisian state and more liberal contingents of its population and visitors.

CONCLUSION

The Bardo Museum complex today may be seen as a metaphor for the greater colonial and postcolonial eras of Tunisian history. Originally a pre-colonial palace noteworthy for its cosmopolitanism (both in terms of the Beylical court's membership and in the eclectic building's design and decoration),[95] it was partially abandoned by the beylical regime that nonetheless retained it as its official seat. Partially razed and restored by the French administration, it was then filled with antiquities largely for the colonizers' own benefit and became an essential element of heritage tourism in the country. The building's newest addition is abstract and thoroughly distinct from the original structure of the old palace, as if to theoretically distance itself from that past and appeal to tourists and Western audiences weary of regional instability and terrorism, yet attracted to flashy architecture. It fails to obscure completely the original edifice, however. Instead, the structural envelope contributes yet another complicated layer to the palimpsestuous site. Ultimately the Bardo may be seen to embody the contemporary Tunisian identity, which by some has been described as suffering a postcolonial schizophrenia.[96] Others may see it as a manifestation of *Tunisianité*, or a distinctive Tunisian identity based on a mix of historical socio-cultural influences discernable in the country's contemporary built environments.[97]

Close study of the Bardo's recent history reveals that it remains very much entangled in the complicated networks of postcolonial identity-making, neocolonial challenges to national sovereignty, and globalization-driven tourism practices. The single site manifests Tunisia's engagement with its past — ancient, colonial, and postcolonial — as well as France, UNESCO, the World Bank, and tourists from places near and far.[98] The museum is entangled in the ongoing debates about Tunisian heritage, which has been radicalized by some since the 2011 revolution who disparage the region's pre-Arab past.[99] At the same time, the building's new image demonstrates a degree of participation in the generation of "starchitecture" projects for major museums in the Middle East designed to enhance competition among urban centers through cultural strategies and iconic landmarks.[100]

Objections to "authorized heritage discourse" and to globalized liberalism thus intersect at the Bardo, a site of repeated reinventions of the past. Indeed, French colonialists fabricated an image of Rome there to suit, and justify, their presence while essentially denigrating or obfuscating the country's Arabo-Muslim history, which has remained secondary at the museum. Post-independence regimes drew on its contents to symbolize their own authority and renovated the museum to facilitate heritage tourism. As they have done elsewhere, in their 2015 attack on the Bardo, terrorists aimed to sequester Tunisia from the West and destroy its pre-Arab past, yet another outcome of what Mulder calls "the logic inherent in globalized, cosmopolitan heritage ideals."[101] More than just a challenge to certain identity conceptions, the attack exposed weaknesses in the post-revolution government's stability and ability to thwart violence. It reflects uncertainty regarding the ultimate outcome of Tunisia's revolution,[102] and made a strong statement about the importance and vulnerability of the tourism sector there.

Travel and tourism accounted for a 6.6 percent direct contribution to Tunisia's GDP in 2016.[103] It is arguably an economic necessity in an era during which persistent unemployment remains a problem. Recent events and related security concerns are significant challenges, but it appears that the decline in tourism may be stabilizing and a slow growth in the industry may occur over the next decade.[104] Tunisia's external image, though far from unscathed, has demonstrated resilience. The resonance of Tunisia's pre-Arab past internally appears to have survived the recent revolution, despite its heavy-handed propagandistic exploitation by the ousted regime. According to the Bardo Museum's director, Tunisians appear to be embracing their cultural heritage even more since the crippling ISIS attack, and the number of Tunisian visitors at the museum has been increasing since 2015.[105] The globalized Bardo, as it were, is now a symbol of the new Tunisia according to some (particularly those in the heritage field) who see it as a demonstration of the nation's storied, diverse past, and its ability to unite Tunisians against terrorism.[106] It now represents democracy and republicanism, but not necessarily domestic pluralism and sovereignty, say others.[107] Indeed, according to Virginie Rey, perhaps the biggest challenge for the broader heritage sector — and indeed the whole country — is "creating an inclusive and dynamic space for all communities," including those marginalized in the past by Tunisia's rulers, such as Islamicists, Jews, Berbers, or others.[108] Whether or not the Bardo, so anchored in the country's ancient and colonial pasts, and neocolonial and post-revolutionary present, can accommodate such an inclusive identity remains to be seen.

ACKNOWLEDGEMENTS

The author sincerely thanks Dr. Zeynep Çelik for her insightful comments and suggestions on an early draft of this chapter, and Dr. Jessica Gerschultz for her kind assistance in acquiring several helpful documents used it its drafting.

NOTES

1 Naim Ghali, "Tourism culturel en Tunisie: État des lieux et perspectives," in *Le Tourisme dans l'empire français*, ed. Colette Zytnicki and Habib Kazdaghli (Paris: Société française d'histoire d'outre-mer, 2009), 406. The *bey* was the hereditary ruler of Tunisia, who after 1574 ruled under the aegis of the Ottoman Sultan with increasing autonomy. The *bey* remained the titular ruler of Tunisia throughout the French protectorate period (1881–1956) until the monarchy was abolished in 1957 with the establishment of the Tunisian Republic. On the colonization and independence of Tunisia, see Kenneth Perkins, *A History of Modern Tunisia* (New York: Cambridge University, 2014); Christopher Alexander, *Tunisia: From Stability to Revolution in the Maghreb* (New York: Routledge, 2016).

2 On the occasion of the museum's 1988 centennial, Mounira Harbi-Riahi (then director of the National Institute of Archaeology and Art or INAA) said that the museum and its history invites reflection on the "foundations of our national culture," and its work will demonstrate broadly that a "new Tunisia resolutely takes care of its heritage." Mounira Harbi-Riahi, "Avant-propos," in *Le Musée du Bardo: Hier et aujourd'hui 1888–1988,* ed. Mounira Harbi-Riahi (Tunis: Institut national d'archéologie et d'art, 1988), 1.

3 An "Arab Museum" was opened in 1899 in the "Small Palace" adjacent to the harem. It was enlarged substantially in 1912/1913, under the direction of a B. Pradère, and still exists as a department within the Bardo. See A. Merlin and L. Poinssot, *Guide du Musée du Bardo (Musée Alaoui)* (Tunis: Gouvernement tunisien: Protectorat français, 1951), 69–76. A 1912 article on the Bardo describes the Arab galleries and states that they were opened to ensure that the museum remained a popular destination, given that newcomers to the country were "very enticed (*très séduits*) by the Moorish or oriental style" and thus found the Arab art collection to be a "great attraction." See Dr. Lemanski, "Au Musée du Bardo (suite), *La Tunisie illustrée* 3, no. 37 (January 5, 1912): 6.

4 Patricia Lorcin, "Rome and France in Africa: Recovering Colonial Algeria's Latin Past," *French Historical Studies* 25, no. 2 (2002): 295–329; Zeynep Çelik, *Empire, Architecture, and the City* (Seattle, WA: University of Washington, 2008), 132–46; Caroline Ford, "The Inheritance of Empire and the Ruins of Rome in French Colonial Algeria," *Past & Present* 226 suppl. 10 (2015): 55–77; Daniel E. Coslett, "Re-presenting Antiquity as Distinction: Pre-Arab Pasts in Tunis' Colonial, Postcolonial and Contemporary Built Environments" (Ph.D. diss., University of Washington, 2017). See also Daniel E. Coslett, "(Re)creating a Christian Image Abroad: The Catholic Cathedrals of Protectorate-era Tunis," in *Sacred Precincts: The Religious Architecture of Non-Muslim Communities across the Islamic World,* ed. Mohammad Gharipour (Boston, MA: Brill, 2015), 353–75.

5 Hubert Lyautey in Prosper Ricard, *Les merveilles de l'autre France* (Paris: Hachette, 1924), 2.

6 David Mattingly and R. Bruce Hitchner, "Roman Africa: An Archaeological Review," *Journal of Roman Studies* 85 (1995): 169. See also Corisande Fenwick, "North

Africa," in *Oxford Companion to Archaeology* (Oxford: Oxford University, 2012), 512–15.

7   David Mattingly, "From One Colonialism to Another: Imperialism and the Maghreb," in *Roman Imperialism: Post-colonial Perspectives*, ed. Jane Webster and Nicholas Cooper (Leicester: School of Archaeological Studies, 1996), 52.

8   The Carthage Museum (until independence known as the Lavigerie Museum) had been founded in 1875 by Catholic excavator-priests from the *Société des Missionaires d'Afrique*. See Pierre Gandolphe, "Origines et débuts du Musée Lavigerie," *Cahiers de Byrsa* 2 (1952): 151–78; Coslett, "Re-presenting Antiquity as Distinction," 340–422. In the 1850s Tunisian officials had gathered a collection of architectural fragments and Latin inscriptions within the La Manouba Palace's garden. Perhaps in an effort to counter political and cultural provocation from ambitious Europeans in the years leading up to colonization, Khereddine Pacha (chief minister in the Tunisian government from 1873 to 1877) opened a public archaeological museum in Tunis in 1876 as a part of his broader modernization program. Bonnie Effros, *Incidental Archaeologists: French Officers and the Rediscovery of Roman North Africa* (Ithaca, NY: Cornell University, 2018), 256.

9   The museum was renamed the Bardo National Museum after independence. Such museum establishments were not unusual within the colonized Mediterranean region. See, for example, Bonnie Effros, "Museum-building in Nineteenth-century Algeria," *Journal of the History of Collections* 28, no. 2 (2016): 243–59; Robert Stuart Merrillees, "Towards a Fuller History of the Cyprus Museum," *Cahiers du Centre d'Etudes Chypriotes* 35, no. 1 (2005): 191–214.

10 Myriam Bacha, *Patrimoine et monuments en Tunisie* (Rennes: Presses Universitaires de Rennes, 2013), 104.

11 The walled Bardo compound had included not only the residence of the *bey,* but also a mosque, madrasa, bath complex, market, bakery, and a caserne. Eventually it housed a military school and mint as well. The palace had come into disrepair during the late nineteenth century when Tunisian budgets were constrained and a succession of *beys* opted to spend most of their time in palaces elsewhere. Mohamed El Aziz Ben Achour, "Le Bardo: Aperçu Historique," in Harbi-Riahi, *Le Musée du Bardo*, 3–5. In 1865 — during a period of greater usage — the full complex was home to 1,500–2,000 individuals in the service of the royal family. Bacha, *Patrimoine et monuments*, 105. In 1852 Aimé Rochas, a French writer, referred to the complex as the "Tunisian Versailles." Aimé Rochas, "Tunis," *L'Illustration* 20, no. 509 (November 27, 1852): 350.

12 Under the guidance of the director of the Antiquities Service, René de la Blanchère, structures in ruinous states were razed, and those portions to be used for the museum (primarily the nineteenth-century palace elements) were heavily restored. Many walls, which had been built of *pisé* (rammed earth), were replaced with masonry at that time. Bacha, *Patrimoine et monuments*, 106–07.

13 Ibid., 109.

14 Paul Gauckler, "Guide du visiteur au Musée du Bardo," *Revue tunisienne* 3, no. 10 (1896): 309.

15 Paul Gauckler, "Note" from *Direction des antiquités et des arts,* April 5, 1889, in the Centre des Archives diplomatiques de Nantes (CADN) 1TU/1/V/14235.

16 Selma Zaiane, "Le Musée national du Bardo en métamorphose," *Téoros* 27, no. 3 (2008): 18.

17 Gauckler says it was begun under Mohammed Bey in about 1855 and finished by Mohammad es Sadok (*r.*1859–82). See Gauckler, "Guide," 309. Binous, however, says the harem was initiated under the reign of Husayn Ibn Mahmoud (*r.*1824–35).

See Jamila Binous, "The Summer Palaces," in *Ifriqiya: Thirteen Centuries of Art and Architecture in Tunisia,* ed. Jamila Binous et al. (Vienna: Electa, 2002), 110. Essays published by the INAA say that much of the museum came to occupy the palace spaces (which were not specifically identified) built by Mohammed Bey (r.1855–59). It remains unclear exactly which rooms belonged to which phase of the palace's pre-colonial construction. Ben Achour, "Le Bardo," 4.

18 Jacques Revault, *Palais et résidences d'été de la région de Tunis* (Paris: Centre nationale de la recherche scientifique, 1974), 331. For additional details on the Bardo and its primary rooms in particular, see ibid., 303–36.

19 Gauckler said that the Italian-style "glitter" found on the "bizarrely" executed elements was typical of modern Tunisian palaces. Gauckler, "Guide," 310. See also Alia Nakhli, "Les palais beylicaux, miroirs des temps modernes (1837–1881)," in *L'Éveil d'une nation*, ed. Ridha Moumni (Milan: Officina Libraria, 2016), 95–111. On early modern interactions across the Mediterranean, see Julia Clancy-Smith, *Mediterraneans: North Africa and Europe in an Age of Migration, c. 1800–1900* (Berkeley, CA: University of California, 2011). Ottoman pleasure palaces erected during the eighteenth and nineteenth centuries reflected influences from the West and often incorporated grand halls and performance spaces. These buildings often exhibited Neoclassical, Baroque, and Rococo styles. See Shirine Hamadeh, "Ottoman Expressions of Early Modernity and the 'Inevitable' Question of Westernization," *Journal of the Society of Architectural Historians* 63, no. 1 (2004): 32–51; Tülay Artan, "The Politics of Ottoman Imperial Palaces: Waqfs and Architecture from the 16th to the 18th Centuries," in *The Emperor's House*, ed. Michael Featherstone et al. (Boston, MA: De Gruyter, 2015), 365–408; Zeynep Çelik, *The Remaking of Istanbul* (Los Angeles, CA: University of California, 1993). On the many beylical palaces in the capital region, see Revault, *Palais et résidences d'été*.

20 Ibid., 110.

21 Gauckler, "Guide," 309–11; M'hamed Fantar, *Le Bardo: Un palais, un musée* (Tunis: Alif, 1990), 8–27.

22 Gauckler, "Guide," 311.

23 Ibid.; Bacha, *Patrimoine et monuments*, 109–10. On the broader history of archaeology in Tunisia, see Clémentine Gutron, *L'Archéologie en Tunisie (XIXe–XXe siècles)* (Paris/Tunis: Karthala/IRMC, 2010). On similar circumstances in neighboring Algeria, see Effros, *Incidental Archaeologists*. See also Richard Hingley, *Roman Officers and English Gentlemen: The Imperial Origins of Roman Archaeology* (New York: Routledge, 2000).

24 Gauckler, "Guide," 311.

25 Ibid., 311–26. Guides appear to have been published exclusively in French at this point and no indication is given in this document that Tunisians are considered as potential patrons. Archived in a carton dated to 1895–1916, however, a paper template for exterior signage at the Bardo includes crudely scrawled (nonsensical) Arabic-like writing, indicating perhaps that there may have been a sign intended for Tunisian audiences, which could suggest that to some degree Tunisians were welcomed and/or accommodated as visitors. See CADN 1TU/171/601.

26 Testament to the collection's rapid growth, a supplement published in 1910 indicated that in 1897 there had been 168 mosaics and 920 sculpture fragments on display. By 1907 there were 332 mosaics and 1,173 sculptures held at the Bardo. P. Gauckler and L. Poinssot, *Catalogue des musées et collections archéologiques de l'Algérie et de la Tunisie: Musée Alaoui* (Paris: Leroux, 1910), v. R. Cagnat, in the same volume, describes the museum as unquestionably "the most important museum in Africa." Ibid., vi.

27 Merlin and Poinssot, *Guide du Musée.*
28 Mohamed Yacoub, *Le Musée du Bardo* (Tunis: Ministère des affaires culturelles, 1970), 73–74. The mosaic is said to be the only extant portrait done in Virgil's lifetime. Ibid., 74. Rooms were reclassified based on objects' origins under the tenure of Merlin in about 1910. See Taher Ghalia, "La collection de négatifs en plaques de verre du Musée national du Bardo," *Comptes rendus des séances de l'Académie des inscriptions et belles-lettres* 151, no. 1 (2007): 100.
29 Louis Bertrand, *Le Jardin de la mort* (Paris: P. Ollendorff, 1905), 296.
30 Bertrand, *Le Jardin,* 296.
31 Ibid.
32 Douglas Sladen, *Carthage and Tunis: The Old and New Gates of the Orient*, vol. II (London: Hutchinson, 1906), 510.
33 Emma Burbank Ayer, *A Motor Flight Through Algeria and Tunisia* (Chicago, IL: A.C. McClurg, 1911), 348–49.
34 Sladen, *Carthage and Tunis*, vol. II, 512; Ayer, *Motor Flight,* 347–48.
35 Merlin and Poinssot, *Guide du Musée*, 4.
36 Denis Lesage, "2012: Métamorphose muséale en Tunisie," *Archibat* 26 (2012): 75.
37 Yacoub, *Le Musée*, 9, 43, and 109.
38 Ibid., 5.
39 Zaiane, "Le Musée," 18.
40 Stephennie Mulder, "Imagining Localities of Antiquity in Islamic Societies," *International Journal of Islamic Architecture* 6, no. 2 (2017): 240.
41 Western perspectives came to Tunisia through Bourguiba via Kemalist Turkey as well, which served as a model and inspiration for post-independence pursuits of modernization, laicism, and openness. See Sylvie Thénault, "The End of Empire in the Maghreb: The Common Heritage and Distinct Destinies of Morocco, Algeria, and Tunisia," in *The Oxford Handbook of the Ends of Empire,* ed. Martin Thomas and Andrew Thompson (Oxford: Oxford University, 2017), http://www.oxfordhandbooks.com/view/10.1093/oxfordhb/9780198713197.001.0001/oxfordhb-9780198713197,
42 Driss Abbassi, *Entre Bourguiba et Hannibal* (Paris: Karthala, 2005), 25.
43 Anon., "Chadli Klibi rend hommage à Bourguiba ce 'Jugurtha qui a réussi,'" *Espace Manager*, April 6, 2016, accessed January 24, 2019, http://www.espacemanager.com/chadli-klibi-rend-hommage-bourguiba-ce-jugurtha-qui-reussi.html.
44 Bourguiba's government prioritized lucrative beach-based mass tourism. Despite the president's rhetorical affiliation with antiquity, the government was slow to accommodate and facilitate heritage-based tourism, relegating cultural patrimony initially to more academic circles and relegating elements of the country's cultural heritage to exotic backdrop status. Bourguiba's regime was, at least initially, uninterested in separating the country's cultural heritage from its history of colonization. Habib Saidi, "When the Past Poses Beside the Present: Aestheticizing Politics and Nationalising Modernity in a Postcolonial Time," *Journal of Tourism and Cultural Change* 6, no. 2 (2008): 103–06. See also Robert A. Poirier, "Tourism and Development in Tunisia," *Annals of Tourism Research* 22, no. 1 (1995): 157–71.
45 Perhaps reflecting this interest, a specific gallery dedicated on the occasion of the Bardo centennial in 1988 was predominantly filled with Punic artifacts, many of gold. Roman- and Vandal-era materials were also included. Existing Libyo-Punic galleries were "completely renovated," and temporary galleries exhibiting traditional popular arts were opened for the centennial as well. Anon., "Le Musée du Bardo est désormais centenaire," in Harbi-Riahi, *Le Musée du Bardo*, 2.
46 This idea is not without historic precedent. The ancient Roman author Livy noted Hannibal's strategic transculturalism and ability to unite people and mercenaries of

different origins. See Phillip C. Naylor, *North Africa: A History from Antiquity to the Present* (Austin, TX: University of Texas, 2009), 39.

47 Sadok Chaabane, *Hannibal Redux: The Revival of Modern Tunisia (Le retour d'Hannibal),* trans. Mounir Khelifa (Tunis: Maison Arabe du Livre, 2004), 78–79. See also Gutron, *L'Archéologie.* 230–31; Driss Abbassi, "De la colonie à l'état independent: Le tourisme en Tunisie entre propagande et pédagogie," in Zytnicki and Kazdaghli, *Le Tourisme*, 397.

48 Chaabane, *Hannibal Redux*, 78.

49 Kathryn Lafrenz Samuels, "Roman Archaeology and the Making of Heritage Citizens in Tunisia," in *Making Roman Places: Past and Present*, ed. Darian Marie Totten and Kathryn Lafrenz Samuels (Portsmouth, RI: Journal of Roman Archaeology, 2012), 159.

50 Saidi, "When the Past Poses," 103.

51 Gutron, *L'Archéologie*, 185. This equation of tolerance with Carthage — a site with a long and diverse history and broad appeal today — is further exemplified by the drafting of the "Carthage Charter on Tolerance in the Mediterranean" in 1995. This document, the product of a conference held in Carthage that year, "call[s] on intellectuals, politicians and communications authorities to do their best to contribute to the promotion of education for tolerance and to the consolidation of the values of freedom and respect for human rights, by propagating a culture of human fellowship." UNESCO, "Carthage Charter of Tolerance in the Mediterranean," *Report 146EX/INF.6* (Paris: UNESCO, May 22, 1995), 4. http://unesdoc.unesco.org/images/0010/001004/100440Eo.pdf.

52 Lafrenz Samuels, "Roman Archaeology," 165. See also Dallen J. Timothy, "Contemporary Cultural Heritage and Tourism: Development Issues and Emerging Trends," *Public Archaeology* 13, nos. 1–3 (2014): 37–39.

53 Larbi Sadiki, "Political Liberalization in Bin Ali's Tunisia: Façade Democracy," *Democratization* 9, no. 4 (2002): 122–41. Mulder's observation, that contemporary heritage discourse can often be seen "promoting hegemonic nationalistic agendas" that are selective and "often mitigate against the application of genuinely cosmopolitan heritage ideals," would thus seem to be relevant here. Mulder, "Imagining Localities," 239.

54 Leslie Plommer, "Hannibal Revived as Tunisia's New Mascot," *The Guardian,* April 11, 1997, 10. Plommer attributes his having been neglected in Tunisian historiography to "Islamic political correctness" that marginalized pre-Arab-conquest epochs, as well, perhaps, as a disinterest in "lionising a loser." Ibid.

55 Waleed Hazbun, *Beaches, Ruins, Resorts: The Politics of Tourism in the Arab World* (Minneapolis, MN: University of Minnesota, 2008), 71. See also Saidi, "When the Past Poses."

56 Tahar Ayachi, "Le Club Hannibal dépoussière l'histoire," *La Presse de Tunisie*, October 17, 2000, 13. Clubs in France, Italy, and Spain were said in 2000 to be forthcoming. Ibid.

57 Many of the country's archaeological sites have small museums showcasing finds nearby, and of course the Carthage Museum — part of the Carthage UNESCO site — is very important given that site's significance. The most significant finds from Tunisian sites, however, are generally sent to the Bardo, thereby ensuring its preeminence as the uncontested national museum.

58 Aïcha Ben Abed Ben Khader, *Le Musée du Bardo* (Tunis: Cères, 1993), cited in Abbassi, "De la colonie," 396.

59 Fantar, *Le Bardo*, 27.

60 Laurajane Smith, *The Uses of Heritage* (New York: Routledge, 2006), 11–43.

61 On the propagandistic efforts of Ben Ali's government to create "regime-compliant citizens" and their dismantling, see Laryssa Chomiak, "Spectacles of Power: Locating Resistance in Ben Ali's Tunisia," *Portal 9* (2013): 70–83.

62 Traditional beach tourism has remained the primary draw for tourists, however. Reflecting the considerable work to be done, in a 2001 survey conducted by the National Office of Tunisian Tourism (ONTT) revealed that 82.1 percent of visitors had come for the "beach and sun," while just 5.2 percent reported "culture" as their reason. A further 3.6 percent cited "culture and natural beauty," while 9.1 said just "natural beauty." 2001 ONTT statistics cited in Ghali, "Tourism culturel," 400.

63 Ibid., 408. On postcolonial tourism during the 1960s through the 1980s, see Hazbun, *Beaches,* 1–35.

64 It took several years to rebound from the decrease stemming from the 9/11 terrorist attacks of 2001. ONTT statistics cited in ibid., 406. The Bardo was by far the most popular museum in 2005. In 2010, while the museum's extension was under construction and the global economic downturn was still an issue, the Bardo welcomed over 279,000. In 2011 the total dropped to just over 79,000, indicating that the revolution (which had occurred in January 2011) had severely affected tourism. Ministère du tourisme (République tunisienne), *Le Tourisme tunisien en chiffres: 2012* (Tunis: 2012), 84.

65 On the occasion of the 1988 centennial administrators voiced aspirations for a restored and expanded museum facility that would be "a grand museum of civilizations truly worthy of our diverse collections renowned the world over." Anon., "Le Musée du Bardo est désormais centenaire," 2

66 The relatively inexpensive nature of construction in Tunisia made the project particularly appealing, according to the World Bank. "The cost of the renovation/extension of the Bardo museum is substantially lower than European comparators for a result of similar quality: about US$900 per square meter at the Bardo vs. US$9,000 to US$10,500 per square meter at the Prado museum and the Louvre Lens. The cost of the new Islamic Department of the Louvre … is in excess of US$35,000 per sq. meter." World Bank, "Implementation Completion and Results Report IBRD 7059-TUN (Report No: ICR2295)," (Washington, DC: World Bank, 2012), 17.

67 Rowan Moore, "The Bilbao Effect: How Frank Gehry's Guggenheim Started a Global Craze," *The Guardian,* October 1, 2017, https://www.theguardian.com/artanddesign/2017/oct/01/bilbao-effect-frank-gehry-guggenheim-global-craze. On "starchitecture," globalization, and museums, see Leslie Sklair, "Iconic Architecture and the Culture-ideology of Consumerism," *Theory, Culture, & Society* 27, no. 5 (2010): 135–59.

68 Ibid., 138.

69 The "Tunisia Cultural Heritage Project," of which the Bardo renovation was just one of six components, was a US$27 million program. See Kathryn Lafrenz Samuels, "Trajectories of Development: International Heritage Management of Archaeology in the Middle East and North Africa," *Archaeologies* 5, no. 1 (2009): 77–80. See also Kathryn Lafrenz Samuels, "Transnational Turns for Archaeological Heritage: From Conservation to Development, Governments to Governance," *Journal of Field Archaeology* 41, no. 3 (2016): 355–67.

70 World Bank, "Tunisia—Cultural Heritage Management and Development Project (Report No. PID6985)," (Washington, DC: 2001), 5.

71 World Bank, "Implementation Completion," 9.

72 Information regarding the competition, including its terms and submissions, remains elusive.

73 Lesage, "2012," 77. The goal was to produce a museum capable of hosting up to a million visitors annually.

74 David Robert, "Five Questions for the Director of the Bardo Museum," *Art Newspaper* 25, no. 275 (2016): 22. Museum attendance from 2010 to 2011 declined by 71.68 percent, though it rebounded slightly in 2012. Calculations based on Ministère du tourisme (République tunisienne), *Chiffres: 2012*, 84. In 2014 (thus before the 2015 attack) figures had remained low. The total visitors for that year was just over 106,000, or less than a quarter of what they had been in 2009. Ministère du tourisme (République tunisienne), *Le Tourisme tunisien en chiffres: 2014* (Tunis: 2014), 85.

75 Anon., "Bardo Museum Reopens in Tunis After Facelift," *Al Arabiya,* May 18, 2012. Much of the museum had remained open during construction.

76 Lesage, "2012," 76.

77 Soumaya Gharsallah-Hizem, "Le projet de renovation et d'extension du palais-musée national du Bardo à Tunis," in *Architectures au Maghreb (XIXe–XXe siècles): Réinvention du patrimoine*, ed. Myriam Bacha (Tours: Presses Universitaires François-Rabelais, 2011), 218.

78 Lesage, "2012," 76. One might fairly ask if today's tourists recognize such an abstracted and specific reference. Noting the flexibility of the abstract formal reference, Gharsallah-Hizem points out that these voids may also be seen as a nod to traditional *mashrabiya* patterning. See Gharsallah-Hizem, "Le projet," 217.

79 Transported to the Bardo in 1887, the Neptune mosaic was said in 1893 to be the largest one displayed in any museum. Gauckler, "Guide," 314. See also R. de la Blanchère, *Collections du Musée Alaoui: Première série* (Paris: Firmin-Didot, 1890), 17–32.

80 As of September 2016 the cafeteria space had been stripped of its furnishings and equipment and sat completely empty.

81 Amira Nouira, "Extension et réhabilitation du Musée du Bardo," *Arch/AN,* accessed January 24, 2019, http://www.nouira-architecture.com/index.php/culture/bardo.

82 Pierre-François Codou quoted in Gharsallah-Hizem, "Le projet," 216.

83 A relatively small room is dedicated to Tunisian pre-history.

84 Samir Aounallah, *L'abrégé du Musée national du Bardo* (Sousse: Contraste, 2018). The same guide, which bears the imprimatur of the Agency for the Development of National Heritage and Cultural Promotion (AMVPPC), does not include the one room dedicated to Tunisian pre-history on its route.

85 Mulder, "Imagining Localities."

86 Chris Stephen, Kareem Shaheen, and Mark Tran, "Tunis Museum Attack: 20 People Killed After Hostage Drama at Tourist Site," *The Guardian,* March 18, 2015, https://www.theguardian.com/world/2015/mar/18/eight-people-killed-in-attack-on-tunisia-bardo-museum. It has been said that the primary target may have actually been the adjacent parliament complex in which counter-terrorism laws were being debated at the time.

87 Supporters were repurposing the *"Je suis Charlie"* (I am Charlie) motto coined following the terrorist attack on the Paris headquarters of the satirical publication *Charlie Hebdo* on January 7, 2015. The *"Je suis X"* format has since then been redeployed after several attacks elsewhere, rendering it a globalized solidarity slogan.

88 Thirty-eight people had been killed on a crowded beach in Sousse on June 26, 2015.

89 Tom Westcott, "Why Tunisia's Bardo has Become a Museum of the Macabre," *The National*, March 22, 2016, http://www.thenational.ae/arts-life/the-review/why-tunisias-bardo-has-become-a-museum-of-the-macabre.

90 Robert, "Five Questions," 22.

91 Anon., "Tunisia Commemorates Victims of Bardo Museum Attack with Mosaic Memorial," *Tunisia-TN*, March 18, 2016.

92   Alam Khan and Mario Arturo Ruiz Estrada, "Globalization and Terrorism: An Overview," *Quality & Quantity* 51, no. 4 (2017): 1811–19; Sertif Demir and Ali Bilgin Varlık, "Globalization, Terrorism, and the State," *Alternatives: Turkish Journal of International Relations* 14, no. 3 (2015): 36–53.

93   Yilmaz Bayar and Marius Dan Gavriletea, "Peace, Terrorism and Economic Growth in Middle East and North African Countries," *Quality & Quantity* 52, no. 5 (2018): 2373–92.

94   Conflict between tourism and conservative Tunisians has been a significant issue since at least the 1970s. See Hazbun, *Beaches,* 37–50.

95   Nakhli, "Les palais," 95 and 99–105.

96   Walid Hedidar, "Postcolonialism: A Road To Schizophrenia," *Tunisialive,* March 30, 2017.

97   Leïla Ammar, *Histoire de l'Architecture en Tunisie* (Tunis: Agence MIM, 2005), 252.

98   China has announced plans to finance major Tunisian infrastructure projects, as it has done elsewhere in Africa. It acknowledges that tourism remains an area with great potential for growth in Tunisia, citing growing interest among Chinese tourists. Yassine Bellamine, "Ce qu'il faut savoir de la participation tunisienne au 3ème Forum sur la Coopération Sino-Africaine," *Huffpost Maghreb*, September 3, 2018, https://www.huffpostmaghreb.com/entry/ce-quil-faut-savoir-de-la-participation-tunisienne-au-3eme-forum-sur-la-cooperation-sino-africaine_mg_5b8cede4e4b0cf7b0037bd07.

99   Virginie Rey, "The Radicalization of Heritage in Tunisia," *International Journal of Islamic Architecture* 7, no. 1 (2018): 65–82. ISIS members described the museum as a "den of infidels and vice in Muslim Tunisia." Quoted in ibid., 67.

100 Sklair, "Iconic Architecture"; Sharon Zukin, "Competitive Globalization and Urban Change," in *Rethinking Global Urbanism* (New York: Routledge, 2012), 17–34.

101 Mulder, "Imagining Localities," 229. Mulder's assessment of ISIS-lead destruction of Palmyra describes a situation not unlike the work undertaken to create, and then recreate, the Bardo. She says the lost site of Palmyra "was a European reanimation of a continent-crossing, cosmopolitan imagined classical past. Instead of a caliphate, the French created a Roman-era site from a Christian and a living Islamic one. … This process is — when we consider what it preserves and destroys selectively of that past — not so very different from ISIS's ostensible desire to revive and enforce a return to an imagined time of purified monotheism. At Palmyra, we have two imaginings of the past: that of the French and that of ISIS. But we also have two belief systems: contemporary heritage values and the values of a contemporary revivalist Salafi movement." Ibid., 237.

102 On Tunisia's post-revolution progress towards full democracy and the damaging influence of terrorism, see Robert Anderson and Robert Brym, "How Terrorism Affects Attitudes Toward Democracy: Tunisia in 2015," *Canadian Review of Sociology* 54, no. 4 (2017): 519–29.

103 This is down from nearly 10 percent prior to the 2011 revolution. See World Travel & Tourism Council, *Travel & Tourism Economic Impact 2017: Tunisia* (London: World Travel and & Tourism Council, 2017), 1 and 3.

104 The World Travel & Tourism Council estimates a 2.3 percent growth in tourism's total GDP contribution by 2026. Ibid., 11.

105 Robert, "Five Questions," 22. See also Anon., "Tunisie: La Nouvelle vie du musée du Bardo," *Jeune Afrique,* March 21, 2018, http://www.jeuneafrique.com/419469/culture/tunisie-nouvelle-vie-musee-bardo.

106 Ibid. An exhibition on the Tunisian Revolution, called "Before the Fourteenth: A Tunisian Moment" (Ben Ali's ouster occurred on January 14, 2011), opened in January

2019. Featuring artifacts related to the suppression of free speech since independence, the month leading up to the revolution's climax, and the subsequent transition to democracy, the event further inscribes a non-antiquities based nationalist element to the Bardo Museum's contemporary identity. Frédéric Bobin, "A Tunis, une exposition ravive la mémoire sensorielle de la révolution de 2011," *Le Monde*, January 21, 2019, https://www.lemonde.fr/afrique/article/2019/01/21/a-tunis-une-exposition-ravive-la-memoire-sensorielle-de-la-revolution-de-2011_5412424_3212.html.

107 Rey, "Radicalization." See also Mulder, "Imagining Localities," 239.

108 Rey, "Radicalization," 68.

11

The riad's resurgence

Questioning the historical legacy and neocolonial currency of the Moroccan courtyard house

Nancy Demerdash-Fatemi

Like clockwork, recurring nearly every year from January to April — during the bleakest months of winter in the northern hemisphere — travel sections of Western newspapers and magazines feature articles showcasing exotic adventures to be had in the warmer climes of North Africa, specifically Morocco and to a lesser extent Tunisia. Riads (riad, singular), or multi-level courtyard houses, often replete with small gardens, are photographed in these Orientalist spreads in a manner not dissimilar to the drama of a stage set — darkened rooms framed by lavish drapery and potted date palms, candlelight reflected in the courtyard's pristine turquoise pool, bold multicolored hues of *zellij* tiles enveloping the viewer, and so forth. Though native to nearly all medinas of the Maghreb, in recent years rehabilitation and preservation institutions in Morocco have sought to renovate dilapidated riads throughout the country's cities, specifically with the Kingdom's developmental priorities and touristic ventures in mind. Undoubtedly, these projects to refurbish riads, though executed in the name of development, further entangle these countries in various forms of neoliberal, urbanistic inequity, and contribute to patterns of neocolonial economic dependency.

These architectural and urban renovations have a fraught past in the history of the colonial and post-independent Maghreb. Inasmuch as this housing typology has come to embody these exoticizing fantasies for Western indulgence (and Eastern, indulgence, considering the flock from the Arab Gulf to Morocco), for the respective French colonial administrations of Algeria, Tunisia, and Morocco and their colonial settlers in the late nineteenth and early twentieth centuries the riad represented a fantastically Orientalist model to emulate and replicate in particular contexts. Although the world's fairs of the same period would propagate myths of cultures in need of being civilized,[1] in architectural practice within the French colonial Maghreb, the imported functionalist, modernist building principles prevailed, foregrounding the infamous binarization of French colonial urbanism exported to the Maghreb, highlighted by Frantz Fanon, in the segregation of the Haussmann-inspired, orthogonally divided streets of the *villes nouvelles* from the medieval medinas.[2]

Nevertheless, the riad remained an object of fascination for colonial technocrats, geographers, and ethnographers, and its importance for Maghrebi urbanists in the postcolonial era did not dissipate. As an architectural form designed explicitly to enable privacy and familial intimacy, the courtyard plan of the riad or *dar* (house); small windows and protected portals are constructed so as to see the city and alleys beyond without being seen from within. Perhaps a leftover from colonial imaginaries, these homes embody the exotic and still serve as symbolic vessels of an Orientalist lifestyle coveted by tourists spawned from the marketing machinery of the Moroccan cultural heritage industry.[3] Postcards dating to the Protectorate period (1912–56) showcasing the spacious, sun-drenched horseshoe-arched courtyards of *dar* houses in Tangier [Figure 11.1], Fez [Figure 11.2], or riads in the southern city of Taroudant [Figure 11.3], circulated exoticizing myths of "1001 Nights"-inspired idyll. In the same era, an entire colonial tourism infrastructure, dominated most prominently by the shipping line Compagnie Générale Transatlantique, built hotels as oriental pastiches specifically for elite, European tourists.[4] The present-day media plays a prominent role in generating a kind of neocolonial foreign incursion, what Justin McGuinness has dubbed the "settler-restorer," or foreigners who live in and revive such houses in Moroccan medinas.[5]

This chapter explores the fraught geopolitical dynamics at the heart of the riad's reception, revitalization, and resurgence today, and it examines the potential neocolonial implications of preservation and rehabilitation practices of Moroccan riads, as well as the colonial imaginaries that these structures evoke, in order to

Figure 11.1
The Dar du Grand Chef
Tanger. Postcard c.1920
Source: Author's collect

72. TANGER – Dar du Grand Chef

e 11.2
Cour de Dar Glaoui,
Postcard c.1920.
ce: Author's collection.

ire 11.3
Taroudant Hôtel, a
, Taroudant. Postcard
920. Source: Author's
ection.

understand the riad's position within this problematic symbolic landscape. Of
course, there are all manner of narratives that play into the much politicized and
contested constructions of urban Moroccan life.[6] This chapter is divided into two
parts: the first historicizes the riad in the context of colonial-era documents on the
subject, and the second situates the riad within current preservationist discourses
to illuminate the riad's valorization so as to cater to touristic demand and advance
neoliberal development agendas. In connecting these two narrative threads,
this analysis questions the riad's resurgence in light of its historical legacies and
neocolonial currencies.

PROTECTORATE-ERA ASSOCIATIONISM AND
COLONIAL TYPOLOGIES OF THE RIAD

Much of what is known of Moroccan architecture derives from the innumerable colonial studies conducted under the order of French Resident General Hubert Lyautey during his tenure in Morocco (1912–25).[7] A vocal advocate for indigenous arts and handicrafts, he sought to understand the local culture so as to govern, subordinate, and control it. In the words of Gwendolyn Wright, administrators and architects alike "explored the political potential or liabilities of European versus indigenous styles, the destruction or preservation of key symbolic monuments or established neighborhoods, the strengths and weaknesses of Haussmannesque boulevards or vernacular housing types."[8]

Yet perhaps the most famous publication that delves into the structural history of the riad, as well as the decorative schemes of such buildings, is *Le jardin et la maison arabes au Maroc* (1926), featuring the combined contributions of Jean Gallotti (1881–1972), with 160 drawn renderings from the designer Albert Laprade (1883–1978), and Lucien Vogel (1886–1954). Albert Laprade, a graduate of Paris' École nationale supérieure des beaux-arts, served as general inspector of fine arts from 1932 to 1951, and is most often associated with his design and construction of the Moroccan pavilion at the 1931 International Colonial Exposition in Paris, and also for his collaboration with Emile Bazin and Léon Jaussely, the architects of the permanent Colonial Museum from the same Exposition. Laprade additionally worked, beginning in 1915, as the deputy under Henri Prost, the chief architect and planner brought by Lyautey in 1914 to redesign the urban landscapes of Moroccan cities.[9] Urban juxtapositions justified segregationist principles enforced by the French in Morocco, in the guise of "preserving" the cities and cultures of the indigenous population, what Janet Abu-Lughod has referred to as a system of apartheid.[10] Prost created a formulaic model for zoning and applied it to all of the *villes nouvelles* in Rabat, Casablanca, Fez, Meknes, and Marrakesh. Lucien Vogel, the founder of the magazine *Jardin des modes* (from the 1920s),[11] added his photographs of numerous sites throughout Morocco to this publication. Gallotti published the work with the intent of "guarding the purity"[12] of Moroccan architectural heritage, in light of the onslaught of French colonization. Although the architectural emphasis focuses on the courtyard home with interior garden features, aspects of craft, pattern, and ornament enter as key areas of inquiry. Descriptions of masonry in portals, tilework on walls, or woodwork and wrought iron components in windows and doors are juxtaposed with Laprade's crisply linear and perspectival drawings. That the cleanliness of these renderings mirrors the desire for a uniform aesthetic is quite purposeful.

From the summer of 1916, Lyautey implemented a special section dedicated to the amplification of an indigenous arts program, attached to the Service of Fine Arts, and Jean Gallotti headed it in Rabat until 1920.[13] Prosper Ricard (1874–1952), the director of the Service of Indigenous Arts in Morocco from 1920–35, rigorously advocated for a rejuvenation in indigenous craftsmanship for economic gain in foreign markets,[14] which ultimately served the associationist program[15] of Lyautey. In addition to his numerous writings on Moroccan handicraft traditions, Ricard contributed to the dissemination of romantic musings on the built environments of the country's medinas, as if picturesquely frozen in the Middle Ages.[16] Taken together the programs' main preservationist objectives targeted deteriorations in buildings, demolitions, and abandonments that would impact the overall heritage of the country.[17] Rather than a militaristic policy of assimilationism that brutally asserts the territorial claims to the colonial urban landscape, Lyautey's associationist efforts[18] sought to preserve indigenous sites and historic buildings in an attempt to pacify native peoples and thwart the potential for anti-colonial resistance.[19] But oftentimes, both riads and dars became sites of French occupation, functioning as military outposts from which pacifying operations would be carried out [Figure 11.4].

In his other writings too, Gallotti stressed the necessity to adopt the building strategies underlying indigenous architectural forms, for function and pleasure. In a short piece on "the modern villa of Moroccan inspiration," Gallotti laments that "among the innumerable Moorish style villas that were built in Morocco for the use of Europeans, almost none have been designed in accordance with the plan so characteristic of dars or riads."[20] Apart from the economic benefits resulting from the revitalization of riads, the potency of the building type laid, for the French colonial administration, in its capacity as a vehicle for pleasure. A review of Gallotti's text published by the Society of the History of French Colonies (Société

gure 11.4
rior view of the Casbah
Dar Chafaï, Dar Chafaï,
rocco. Postcard c.1920.
rce: Author's collection.

E. Limanton, Casablanca.

AU MAROC. — Casbah de Dar-Chafai. - Une Vue intérieure

des l'histoire des colonies françaises) goes so far as to liken the riad to the Garden of Eden:

> The Moroccan house is a *dar* or a *riad*. The *dar* is a house without a garden, the most common. … The charm that one seeks there is entirely made of the decoration: ceilings, walls, and courtyards, mosaics of earthenware (the *zellij*) — honeycombs of stone, and wood or plaster, which is never molded here but chiseled with love, grilles and ironwork, and painting, the traditional painting with stylized bouquets and bright colors, everything is intended to achieve the pleasure of the eyes and to make this oubliette that could have become the house without windows into an Eden for daydreams.[21]

The imagined paradisiacal quality of the riad — replete with trickling fountains, cool pools of water, lush trees and fragrant flowers, enveloped by the ceramic bouquets of *zellij* tilework — permeates both contemporary literature and official political discourse on the subject.[22] Andalusia is an oft-invoked locale in the colonial theorizations of the riad. For Albert Laprade and Robert Fournez, the designers of the Moroccan pavilion at the 1931 Paris International Colonial Exposition, the visual (and historical) continuities between Andalusia and Morocco lay at the heart of their pastiche pavilion: a monumental portal and a central garden surrounded by *sūqs* (markets) on both sides that terminated in a hexagonal, cupola-topped kiosk, which was modeled after the Dar El-Beida reception building in Marrakesh. The Alhambra in particular stood as an influential landmark to emulate, and indeed, Gallotti praised the architects' achievements in capturing "… the eminent dignity of the Hispano-Moorish art of Fez …"[23] Just as the pleasure palace imaginaries of dars and riads enhanced the desirability of the protectorate, their representations as derelict justified French architectural interventionism.

This seemingly contradictory combination of formal descriptions of the dar or riad as both timeworn and wondrous is mirrored in the colonial rhetoric of Lyautey, who often spoke in architectural metaphors, of building an empire out of "the crumbling vestiges of an admirable civilization, of a great past."[24] Lyautey, whenever traveling in the surrounds of Marrakesh, stationed himself in the Palais de la Bahïa (frequently referred to as La Bahïa), a grand riad with a resplendent garden that previously served as the residence of "Ba Ahmed," the vizier Moulaye Abdelaziz.[25] In a speech delivered on December 10, 1926, entitled, "How to Save the Art of a Country," Lyautey detailed his first impressions of La Bahïa as being "abandoned, cracked, [and] crumbling, giving the impression of a very old thing, a refined and disappearing art."[26] These observations are echoed by Edmond Doutté who details La Bahïa in terms of its frailty and "sad charm," reflexively criticizing the damage wreaked on the faience mosaics from the filth of European shoes.[27] Even the noted Orientalist traveler Pierre Loti said of Moroccan homes that "one should not worry about the outside of houses, as the entrances which are most miserable sometimes lead to palaces of fairies" [Figure 11.5].[28]

In parallel, the hyperbolic, fantastical association to both degradation and hedonism grafted onto the essentialist typology of the riad cannot be understated, and French architects and urban planners even deemed the riad's architectural form worthy of replication in other contexts.[29] Because of its chief formal characteristics that divide and uphold a barrier between the public realm and private space in societies across the Islamic world, the riad or dar in North Africa principally functioned as an "interiorized domestic architecture," in the words of Zeynep Çelik, where women's affairs would be protected and partitioned off from the street dealings of men.[30] French ethnographers and architects seized on the opportunities presented by these zonings and the implicit, cultural subtexts and gendered connotations of the riad to almost objectify the typology on its own terms. Even in the spatial regulation of prostitution in the colonial era, French architects looked specifically to the riad as an archetypal model for facilitating indulgence and repose. Félicien Durand, an architect writing in a 1933 article for the monthly periodical *Chantiers*, notes how the riad can be successfully repurposed to create a "reserved quarter" in the city of Meknès, citing the design of one architect by the name of Vernouillet.[31] The guiding principles in constructing this reserved quarter for prostitution comprised the following:

> (1) the creation of a resting center (garden, riad, etc.), (2) the voluntary concealment of prostitution, and (3) hygiene and security. The resting center for repose is the dominant motif of the plan, it is treated in an Arab riad with three large levels enlivened by gardens and fountains.[32]

According to Durand, in order to camouflage or conceal evidence of prostitution on site, shops and a café featuring belly dancing would put a lost tourist at ease. Fabricating this multifaceted space rich in amenities necessitated the discriminatory displacement of thirty-two indigenous households and only two European households in Meknès.[33] That the riad served as the spatial model to both facilitate and contain prostitution is curious, yet this projection of sensuality and intrigue onto the typology only reinforced these fraught symbolic meanings of the riad.

With the steady encroachments of the French and their erosion of Moroccan institutions such as the *hubus*,[34] which managed domainal lands deeded and under the direct fiscal control of the Sultan, blatant seizures and expropriations prevailed.[35] Following independence in 1956, affluent Moroccans fled the medinas of the imperial capitals (Fez, Marrakesh, Meknès, and Rabat) for the cities of Casablanca or elsewhere, and quickly took over the abandoned homes in the *ville nouvelle*, vacated by the French.[36] In spite of these evacuations, the French still frequented North Africa as vacationers, and Ellen Furlough notes that in the 1950s, the tone and vocabulary of French touristic literature (e.g. brochures, advertisements, packages, etc.) shifted toward an accentuated exoticism, with a more pronounced intermingling of sensuality and consumerism.[37] However, it would be years before the trend of "going native" would take hold, in terms of touristic interest and investment in medina courtyard homes.

For Morocco's medinas, these patterns of exodus and middle-class flight from riads and dars prevailed in the wake of decolonization, and as a consequence, these structures and their social compositions underwent tumultuous changes in the intervening years. Vacant dars and riads of the imperial medinas were quickly overpopulated with rural migrants. With the influx of rural populations to these riads and dars, some have called this phenomenon the *foundoukisation des médinas*,[38] or the over-occupation and subdivision of and squatting in buildings, deterioration of living spaces, and poor maintenance of public spaces.

As a consequence, the mid-1960s witnessed the growth of preservationist organizations in North Africa, with the birth of the Association for the Protection of the Medina of Tunis (Association de Sauvegarde de Medina de Tunis) in 1967, and in parallel, the first holistic analysis of the Casbah of Algiers in 1972, as well as the 1975 UNESCO project to develop the first master plan of Fez.[39] In spite of these efforts, Moroccan elites have come to link the idea of the medina — in an orientalizing manner not dissimilar to their French colonial forbearers/predecessors — to social devaluation, insalubrity, and ruin.[40] According to one study, about 3,700 of the 12,000 houses of the medina are in a state of dangerous precarity, and about three collapse each year, on average.[41] Marcello Balbo generalizes that this is a reflection of the Moroccan middle class's growing apathy and denial of medinas as legitimate containers of Moroccan cultural identity.[42]

NEOCOLONIAL IMPLICATIONS OF RIAD RENOVATIONS
AND REINVENTIONS

It would be fallacious to view 1956 — the year in which Moroccan independence was declared — as a clean rupture from colonial power relations. Despite the departure of European architects and their clients, urban policies maintained many of the practices accrued under French protectorate rule.[43] Many colonial-era institutions across also have remained intact.[44] Just as Frantz Fanon outlined in *The Wretched of the Earth* (1961), the national bourgeoisie took over the management of tourism infrastructure, inherited from colonization, rendering holiday resorts and casinos in former colonies the basis for the national industry of tourism.[45] In thirty-six years, from 1920–56, Morocco saw the development of a sizeable touristic infrastructure, and after independence, from 1956 to 1964, though still a prominent industry, the government began to view tourism as exclusively within the interests of the private sector.[46] Paradoxically, independence established a relationship of reliance upon the former colonial metropole and other European Union (EU) countries by virtue of certain economic policies, rendering Morocco more vulnerable to European protectionism[47] and more recently, the global recession.[48] The rhetoric through which Morocco is frequently positioned — as a so-called "darling" of the World Bank (in the early 1990s, the World Bank gave more than US$6 billion towards Moroccan development, a sum larger than any other presented to a country in the Middle East or Africa[49]) or a *bon élève* ("good student") by the EU — implies the questionable relations that this country has with its European neighbors.[50]

These colonial-era representations still resonate and live on in the spatial and cultural imaginaries of foreign purchasers of riads. In other realms of material heritage as well, colonial discourse on indigenous Moroccan crafts continues to inform textile and carpet-making industries in the country.[51] What perpetuates from this period is the presumed "authentic" value of objects, handicrafts or sites, and problematically, what tourists and foreign investors alike seek through the typology and mythologies of the riad is authenticity. Visitors often perceive this authenticity affectively through the richness of a riad's sensorial overload (e.g. the colorful bursts of zellij, the textured carpentry, the aural calm of the interior courtyard contrasting with the bustling medina alleys outside the home, the smells of aromatic blossoms, etc.).[52] Dean MacCannell and John Urry spearheaded sociological studies that analyzed the role of visual consumerism in the tourism industry.[53] Urry suggests that the tourist is driven by his or her "touristic gaze," fueled by a desire to authenticate and seek truths that are different from one's everyday encounters.[54] Yet as Geoffrey Porter claims, the more manicured and tailored a site is to attract tourists, the less appealing or worthy of consumption it will be. Tourists are after what they perceive to be unadulterated, uncorrupted qualities that somehow vouch for the preserved, timeless state of a medina forever trapped in a picturesquely medieval condition. Porter explains that this constitutes the primary paradox of Fez's medina (one could extend this notion to other Moroccan medinas), that signs of urban change or transformation disrupt the site's presumed authenticity for foreigners and that "… the maintenance of the illusion that the site exists the way it does not only in spite of tourists, but regardless of them."[55] Either way, governmental discourse deems tourism to be critical to the medinas' survival, and sustaining the riad's residential function — even if only for short-term touristic purposes — plays directly into that end goal.[56]

Today, such illusions lie at the crux of urban regeneration projects within the formerly marginalized spaces of the medina, and with renewed vitality, riads have become coveted by a largely European audience, encouraged by the official, state-authorized Moroccan patrimonial and tourist rhetoric.[57] The landscapes of those medinas of Marrakesh, Essaouira, and Rabat have been changing at a faster rate than those of Fez and Tangier, with new water and sewage systems, public lighting, and enhanced commercial spaces being installed in the last twenty years or so.[58] Predominantly European-led refurbishment of riads in these Moroccan medinas transforms these modest courtyard complexes into lavish boutique hotels. Since the late 1990s, French, British, American, Spanish, Italian, Dutch, and German investors have bought old residences across the country,[59] "flipping" these structures to varying degrees, without standardization.[60]

Manon Istasse argues that the ideal means of preserving the patrimony of Moroccan residential architecture is by investing in and inhabiting these structures.[61] Working with a host of actors in the medina of Fez, including public authorities, real estate and tourist agencies, and a number of boutique hotel or hostel proprietors, Istasse questions the actions taken by such settler-restorers on their new homes. As preservation is so often the means to money-making ends, Istasse cautions that, based on her interviews with various renovators, patrimonial motivations are secondary to financial interests.

Some scholars attribute these North-South migratory forms to "lifestyle migration," offering a kind of familiar exoticism that enables escapism and "elsewhereness"; for European retirees, Morocco incentivizes investment with a host of economic advantages and tax breaks, so it is important to bear in mind the different motivators underlying the refurbishments.[62] As Justin McGuinness and Zoubeïr Mouhli point out, acts of restoration create second homes for their buyers, or they can be profit-driven in nature (e.g. transforming the riads into boutiques for tourist consumption, or for post-restoration re-sale).[63] Yet it is not only foreigners who are actively purchasing and conserving these medina riads; in Fez, for instance, Moroccan residents who might live in the *ville nouvelle*, or another major city, purchase riads to rent and maintain them as alternative income sources.[64] In 2007, Fez's regional council of tourism sponsored a program called *Ziyarates Fès* (Fez Visitations) whereby Fassi families living within medina riads who agreed to upgrade their homes under official monitoring would open their doors and rent out rooms to tourists, promoting intercultural dialogue and encouraging local residents to actively engage in the preservation of their material and immaterial patrimony.[65] These residents were incentivized with interest-free loans to begin such refurbishment projects.[66] Without such enticements, typical residents might be reluctant to repair structural cracking, leaking, or degrading foundations.

The physical transformation of these buildings resulting from this inhabitation is another matter entirely. According to Jaâfar Kansoussi, the former official to the Ministry of Islamic Affairs in Morocco and current president of the Al Muniya Association (which works to preserve Marrakeshi heritage), the riad renovation projects are subject to little or no regulations by state authorities, save for building height limitations. Work permits are generally not required so long as individual projects are small in scope. McGuinness and Zouhli note that much of this information transference among client, architect, contractor, and craftsmen leaves no paper trail behind, as most of the discourse is communicated verbally, in a creole concoction of French, Moroccan Arabic, Amazigh, English, and even Italian languages.[67] Quality control is often gauged based on hearsay and the reputation of the maâlemine (master craftsmen) among the various trade communities, adding further to the informal nature of many projects.

Overall, the aesthetic tendencies and formal choices made in the rehabilitation process veer towards historicist decorative schemes that honor centuries of local craftsmanship — including mosaic zellij tilework, vegetal plasterwork, wood beams painted and mounted in the ceilings, iron grille work, etc. [Figure 11.6]. Summer Sutton identifies six degrees of intervention, depending on the current state of a building: maintenance (superficial repairs, with no new additions to the structure); refurbishment (updating the building without load-bearing changes or alterations to the floor plan); repair (replacement of dilapidated components such as piping, surfaces, utilities, etc.); restoration (using original materials to give structural integrity); extensions/additions (e.g. adding a livable space on the rooftop); conversion (alterations made to load-bearing markers).[68] Despite the efforts of some to maintain the integrity of historical materials and aesthetics, many riads undergo such stark cosmetic surgery that they are oftentimes rendered unrecognizable from their previous form. Many adopt contemporary interior designs or even culturally decontextualized styles, with some owners implementing South Asian aesthetics or motifs.[69] Some residents even discussed their homes' restoration as a process of "metamorphosis" to indicate the dramatic differences.[70] In these instances of tremendous change, the spolia of elaborately carved and painted ceilings, geometrically carved doors, portal fragments, and ornate windows are excised, scattered and sold, without any record. The ideals and expectations of the temporary, itinerant touristic customer are anticipated in these instances. One riad owner and resident expatriate, Alain Grunberg, suggested that the guidelines for rehabilitation have evolved very little since the protectorate era.[71] Though he strove to maintain the integrity of his Riad Mounia's original structure, Grunberg noted that plumbing and other features had to be radically altered so as to satisfy his international clientele.[72]

Figure 11.6
The courtyard of
a refurbished riad,
Marrakesh. Photograp.
2013. Source: Ruth W.

To fully map out the neocolonial implications of these spatial negotiations, it is critical to understand the complex matrix of stakeholders in Morocco's medinas, including private actors (e.g. patrons, investors, and real estate moguls), public entities (e.g. state and local authorities) and international organizations (e.g. UNESCO and the World Bank). The classification of the medinas of Fez, Marrakesh, and more recently, Essaouira, among UNESCO's World Heritage Sites

(Fez gained the title in 1981, Marrakesh in 1986, and Essaouira in 2001), coupled with persistent state-sponsored tourism initiatives and mostly European-led property investment (e.g. vacation homes for pensioners and expatriates) has amplified rehabilitation projects. UNESCO or International Council on Monuments and Sites (ICOMOS) consultants report in Morocco on an as-needed basis, when their services are requested by the Moroccan Ministry of Culture to oversee a project. Working independently of UNESCO to safeguard sites are the Moroccan Agency of Development and Rehabilitation (Agence de Développement et de Réhabilitation, or ADER), a semi-public institution created in 1989, and the Inspection of Historical Monuments, monitored by the Ministry of Culture. Among Moroccan medina-dwellers, Manon Istasse remarks that UNESCO and ADER specialists are often conflated, with much of the public confused about the institutions' respective state and non-state roles.[73] With national budget priorities concentrated in the realms of education, healthcare, employment, social housing and so forth, real estate investors — even if foreign — appear as attractive actors in the developmental management of the state's political economy.[74] The Moroccan government's "Vision 2010" program promoted the introduction of luxury hotels in order to finance architectural heritage preservation through foreign investment.[75] It is crucial to point out the dialectical and dependent relationship between heritage tourism and this property boom, often referred to as "riad fever."

By radically gentrifying these urban landscapes, these riad rehabilitations — rarely guided by any state-instituted conservation policy[76] — have effectively rendered much of the medina, particularly in Marrakesh and Fez, exclusive to foreign clienteles' tastes and consumption.[77] With Morocco's strongly neoliberal state policies,[78] urban regeneration projects financed by outside investors have spurred spatial restructuring and displaced local, low-income residents. Geographer Joomi Lee posits that these processes of urban renewal are indicative of a new urban colonialism,[79] in which local communities are pushed and priced out of medinas, to make way for upscale, redesigned riads for foreign consumption. As a means to integrate low-income residents in the conservation process, Summer Sutton advocates for greater involvement of non-profit organizations in attending to the needs of disenfranchised residents, while facilitating a collaborative approach to renovation that serves as an antidote to the impeded, inconsistent, unstandardized, and bureaucratically impractical regulations behind most architectural preservation projects in Moroccan medinas.[80]

CONCLUSION

Tourism development is inextricably connected to the rise in riad property investment in Morocco. Deeply connected to the destination branding at the heart of the government's tourism development strategies is the housing typology of the riad itself. By subsuming, rather than resisting, Orientalist mythologies of exoticism, the Moroccan Ministry of Tourism and the broader tourism industry have "generally adopted the strategy of performing the stereotypes and profiting off the performance" in a manner quite reminiscent of French colonialist predecessors.[81] In touristic advertising campaigns that one might encounter on the subway platforms of Paris, London, or Madrid, one can see how the government clings to the colonial, exoticizing constructs of old, and the myths of residential medina architecture are reinforced through these recycled representational tropes, promising hedonistic pleasures. Just as many of today's Moroccan handicrafts, like ceramics, carpentry, and carpet-production, are rooted in taxonomic frameworks of French colonial ethnographic studies,[82] much of the current representations and symbolic imaginings of the riad draw from colonial-era valorizations. The tourism industrial machine is an all-encompassing apparatus that engenders a neocolonial paradigm of geopolitical and economic dependency. While the motivations behind the redesigns and renovation projects of riads in Moroccan medinas are multiple, the colonial constructs and imaginaries remain as vivid sources of inspiration. Yet, as illustrated earlier in the chapter, government-sponsored initiatives like *Ziyarates Fès* centered on ideas of cross-cultural exchange seem to resist those very constructs of wanton consumption associated with the riad. In that vein, it is vital to recognize the agency that countries like Morocco exercise in making deliberate choices for the betterment of their political economy.[83] Although the riad's renovations and regenerations increasingly become conduits for a neoliberal, and arguably neocolonial, spatio-cultural presence in Morocco, these transformations are not without contestation. In sustaining an abiding loyalty to the myths that sustain touristic demand, it remains yet to be seen how these myths — and hope for their demystification — will transform the residential architecture of Morocco's medinas.

NOTES

1   See Zeynep Çelik, *Displaying the Orient: Architecture of Islam at Nineteenth-Century World's Fairs* (Berkeley; CA: University of California, 1992); Patricia Morton, *Hybrid Modernities: Architecture and Representation at the 1931 Colonial Exposition, Paris* (Cambridge, MA: MIT, 2000).

2   "The colonial world is a compartmentalized world. It is obviously as superfluous to recall the existence of 'native' towns and European towns. … The colonized world is a world divided in two. The dividing line, the border, is represented by the barracks and the police stations," he says. Frantz Fanon, *The Wretched of the Earth* (New York: Grove, 1961), 3.

3   Manon Istasse, "Dynamique de requalification des médinas et préservation du patrimoine: étude en acte dans la médina de Fès," in *Médinas immuables?*, ed. Elsa Coslado, Justin McGuinness, and Catherine Miller (Rabat: Centre Jacques-Berque, 2013): 259–83.

4   Ellen Furlough, "Une leçon des choses: Tourism, Empire, and the Nation in Interwar France," *French Historical Studies* 25, no. 3 (2002): 451. See also Serge Santelli, "Les hôtels de la Transatlantique," *Monuments historiques* 130 (1984): 67–70.

5   Justin McGuinness, "Errances vers un Orient imaginaire: nomadisme cosmopolite et la Médina de Fès, 2000–2005," *Revue de l'Institut de belles lettres arabes* 198 (2007): 3–33.

6   Geoffrey D. Porter, "The City's Many Uses: Cultural Tourism, the Sacred Monarchy and the Preservation of Fez's Medina," *Journal of North African Studies* 5, no. 2 (2000): 60.

7   Gwendolyn Wright, *The Politics of Design in French Colonial Urbanism* (Chicago, IL: University of Chicago, 1991), 75–76. Lyautey served in Indochina from 1892–97, then traveled to Madagascar where he stayed from 1897–1902. Morocco was his last outpost, where he led and managed the protectorate from 1912 to 1925.

8   Wright, *The Politics of Design*, 8.

9   Jean-Pierre Frey, "Préface," in Jean Gallotti, *Le jardin et la maison arabes au Maroc* (Paris: Éditions Albert Lévy, 1926, repr. Rabat: Actes Sud/Centre Jacques-Berque, 2008), 10.

10 Janet Abu-Lughod, *Rabat: Urban Apartheid in Morocco* (Princeton, NJ: Princeton University, 1980).

11 Frey, "Préface," 11.

12 Jean Gallotti, "Avant-Propos," in *Le jardin et la maison arabes au Maroc*, 39–40.

13 Frey, "Préface," 16.

14 Prosper Ricard, *L'Artisanat indigène en Afrique du Nord, rapport déposé par M. Prosper Ricard, chef du Service des Arts indigènes au Maroc, Conférence économique impériale, Paris, mars 1935* (Rabat: École du Livre, 1935). See also Hamid Irbouh, *Art in the Service of Colonialism: French Art Education in Morocco, 1912–1956* (New York: I.B. Tauris, 2005).

15 Raymond Betts, *Assimilation and Association in French Colonial Theory, 1890–1914* (New York: Columbia University, 1960, repr. Lincoln, NE: University of Nebraska, 2005), 106. Associationism was a new tactic for rule that stressed regional, religious and ethnic specificities of communities and it was thought that this would minimize social disruption and maximize the submission to colonial governance.

16 Porter, "The City's Many Uses," 67. On the allegedly "medieval" nature of the Fez medina, see Prosper Ricard, *Les merveilles de l'autre France* (Paris: Hachette, 1924).

17 Frey, "Préface," 17.

18 Lyautey's "Makhzen policy" — a *politique des grands caïds* (politics of the great chiefs or leaders) — was his application of associationist principles. By indirect rule, with Sultan Moulay Youssef recognized by the French, the Makhzen was bereft of its governing power. With the signing of the Treaty of Fez in 1912, the sovereignty and authority of the Sultan was not to be undermined, but French interventions effectively reconfigured how the Makhzen and governmental administration worked. See William Hoisington, *Lyautey and the French Conquest of Morocco* (New York: St. Martin's, 1995), 46–47. See also Anon., *Morocco Under the Protectorate: Forty Years of French Administration* (Washington, DC: Istiqlal Party of Morocco, Moroccan Office of Information and Documentation, 1953), 7.

19 Wright, *The Politics of Design*, 73–74.

20 Jean Gallotti, "Un projet de villa moderne d'inspiration marocaine," *Chantiers: Revue mensuelle illustrée de la construction en Afrique du nord* 10, no. 6 (1937): 318.

21 Review of Jean Gallotti, *Le jardin et la maison arabes au Maroc* (Paris: Éditions Albert Lévy, 1926), in *Revue de l'histoire des colonies françaises* 19, no. 2 (1931): 201.

22 Frey, "Préface," 32–33.

23 Morton, *Hybrid Modernities*, 231. Originally cited in Jean Gallotti, "Traité de géographie de l'Exposition coloniale d'après les plus récentes découvertes," *VU* 168 (1931): 779–80.

24 Lyautey made these remarks while addressing scholars at the Congrés des Hautes Etudes Marocaines in 1921: "We have found here the crumbling vestiges of an admirable civilization, of a great past. You are restoring the foundation, renewing construction work, and on the foundation which you rebuild in good cement you are undeniably aiding us to build the marvelous future that we wish to make spring from this past." Quoted in Wright, *The Politics of Design*, 77.

25 Edmond Doutté, "Le Palais de la Bahïa," *France-Maroc: revue mensuelle illustrée* 10 (1920): 203.

26 Frey, "Préface," 15. Originally cited in Hubert Lyautey, *Paroles d'action, Madagascar, Sud-Oranais, Oran, Maroc (1900–1926)* (Paris: Librairie Armand Colin, 1927), 448–49.

27 Edmond Doutté, "Le Palais de la Bahïa," *France-Maroc: Revue mensuelle illustrée* 10 (1920): 204.

28 Pierre Loti, *Au Maroc* (Paris: Calmann-Lévy, 1929), 143. Cited in Istasse, "Dynamique de requalification," 259–83.

29 Istasse, "Dynamique de requalification," 259–83.

30 Zeynep Çelik, *Urban Forms and Colonial Confrontations: Algiers Under French Rule* (Berkeley, CA: University of California, 1997). See Çelik's discussion of the "interiorized domestic" architectural design of the courtyard houses of Algiers, as in chap. 1, Figure 1.6. See also Zeynep Çelik, "A Lingering Obsession: The Houses of Algiers in French Colonial Discourse," in *Walls of Algiers: Narratives of the City Through Text and Image*, ed. Zeynep Çelik, Julia Clancy-Smith, and Frances Terpak (Seattle, WA: University of Washington, 2009), 134–60.

31 Félicien Durand, "Le 'quartier réservé' de Meknès," *Chantiers: Revue mensuelle illustrée de la construction en Afrique du nord* 6 (1933): 180.

32 Durand, "Le 'quartier réservé' de Meknès," 178.

33 Ibid., 180.

34 Susan Gilson Miller, "Finding Order in the Moroccan City: The *Hubus* of the Great Mosque of Tangier as an Agent of Urban Change," *Muqarnas* 22 (2005): 265–83. As Miller has identified in her case study of Tangier, the disintegration of the *hubus* there resulted from French accusations that the institution was "corrupt, mismanaged, badly in need of reform, and a *'caisse noire'* (slush fund) used by 'enemies of the state' to undermine authority." Ibid., 278.

35 Janet Abu-Lughod, *Rabat: Urban Apartheid in Morocco* (Princeton, NJ: Princeton University, 1980), 166. Abu-Lughod cites the work of Henri de la Casinière, *Les municipalités marocaines. Leur développement. Leur législation* (Casablanca: Imprimerie de la Vigie Marocaine,1924), who noted that "'the task of the protectorate,' namely, to obtain the land on which to build the European cities, 'had been facilitated in Meknes, Fez, and Marrakech by the fact that almost all of the suburban land was the property of the free domain of the state [domainal makhzan land] or of pious foundations controlled by the state [hubus land].'" For more on the reception of Casinière's study, see Eugène Werier, "Etwas über die kommunale Tätigkeit Frankreichs in seinen Kolonien: Die Marokkanischen Gemeinwesen," in *L'Echo des Communes et l'ancienne Revue communale d'Alsace et de Lorraine* 10, no. 4 (February 15, 1930), 37–38.

36 Istasse, "Dynamique de requalification," 259–83.

37 Furlough, "*Une leçon des choses*," 470.

38 Anne-Claire Kurzac, "Ces Riads qui vendent du rêve: Patrimonialisation et ségrégation en médina," in *Habiter le patrimoine: enjeux, approches, vécu*, ed. Maria Gravari-Barbas (Rennes: Presses universitaires de Rennes, 2005), 467–78.

39 Marcello Balbo, ed., *The Medina: The Restoration and Conservation of Historic Islamic Cities* (New York: I.B. Tauris, 2012), 4.

40 Kurzac, "Ces Riads qui vendent du rêve," 467–78.

41 Manon Istasse, "Affects and Senses in a World Heritage Site: People-House Relations in the Medina of Fez," in *World Heritage on the Ground: Ethnographic Perspectives,* ed. Christoph Brumann and David Berliner (New York: Berghahn, 2016), 41.

42 Balbo, *The Medina*, 5; see also 9. "The historic city may still represent a symbolic reference for a part of the population. Nevertheless, there are fewer and fewer households prepared to consider it a promising place to live and difficult working conditions are driving out economic activities. The exceptions are, at one extreme, the poor and, at the other, some national and international investors attracted by the exotic character of the place but, more often, by the expectation of promising financial profits linked to real estate operations." Ibid.

43 Jean-Louis Cohen and Monique Eleb, *Casablanca: Colonial Myths and Architectural Ventures* (New York: Monacelli, 2002), 15–16.

44 Mahmood Mamdani, *Citizen and Subject: Contemporary Africa and the Legacy of Late Colonialism* (Princeton, NJ: Princeton University, 1996), 4.

45 Fanon, *The Wretched of the Earth*, 100–01.

46 Mimoun Hillali, *La politique du tourisme au Maroc: Diagnostic, bilan et critique* (Paris: L'Harmattan, 2007), 37.

47 Gregory White, *A Comparative Political Economy of Tunisia and Morocco: On the Outside of Europe Looking In* (Albany, NY: State University of New York, 2001), xi; 16–17. Mimoun Hillali, a professor and researcher of the International Institute of Tourism in Tangier (l'Institut supérieur international du tourisme à Tanger), states that there is no choice with regards to tourism in Morocco, and its presence dares not be denounced or questioned publically, as it is dubbed the "motor of development" and "the grand generator of employment."

48 "IMF Survey: Africa Conference Debates Way Forward Amid Crisis," March 13, 2009, accessed October 5, 2018, http://www.imf.org/external/pubs/ft/survey/so/2009/car031309a.htm.

49 Joyce Chang et al., *Morocco: An Oasis of Investment Opportunity* (New York: Salomon Brothers' Emerging Markets Research, 1992).

50 White, *A Comparative Political Economy of Tunisia and Morocco,* 25.

51 Claire Nicholas, "Of Texts and Textiles …: Colonial Ethnography and Contemporary Moroccan Material Heritage," *Journal of North African Studies* 19, no. 3 (2014): 390–412.

52 Istasse, "Affects and Senses in a World Heritage Site," 54.

53 Dean MacCannell, *The Tourist: A New Theory of the Leisure Class* (New York: Schocken, 1976). See also John Urry, *The Tourist Gaze: Leisure and Travel in Contemporary Societies* (London: Newbury Park, 1990).

54 Nezar Alsayyad, ed. *Consuming Tradition, Manufacturing Heritage: Global Norms and Urban Forms in the Age of Tourism* (New York: Routledge, 2001), 3–4.

55 Porter, "The City's Many Uses," 60.

56 Lucien Godin and Gérard Le Bihan, "Moroccan Medinas: Meknes and Azemmour," in Balbo, *The Medina*, 141.

57 Ministère de la Culture (Moroccan Ministry of Culture), "Élements pour un vision patrimoine 2020" (2014), 18. "More generally, the medina has become a place of marginalization and exclusion due to increasing impoverishment of its occupants in recent decades: abandoned by the great clans, who judge these to be dilapidated and archaic; the progressive degradation of the buildings; deterioration of urban spaces and public infrastructure; and a loss of knowledge in maintaining these spaces as a result of the changing demographics. Since the late 1990s, some medinas have

experienced a certain revival of interest reinforced by the restoration of riads, transformed into guest houses or restaurants, but rarely cultural spaces." Ibid.

58 Kurzac, "Ces Riads qui vendent du rêve," 467–78.

59 Mohamed Berriane, Mohammed Aderghal, Mhamed Idrissi Janati, and Johara Berriane, "New Mobilities Around Morocco: A Case Study of the City of Fes," in *Final Report for the MacArthur-Funded Project on 'African Perspectives on Human Mobility'* (2010), 74.

60 In Tunisia by contrast, a country that has traditionally relied heavily on its seaside resort tourism, the riad renovation craze has been far slower to take hold, though in recent years luxury riad hotels have been developed as well.

61 Istasse, "Dynamique de requalification," 259–83.

62 Catherine Therrien and Chloé Pellegrini, "French Migrants in Morocco: From a Desire for *Elsewhereness* to an Ambivalent Reality," *Journal of North African Studies* 20, no. 4 (2015): 613 and 619.

63 Justin McGuinness and Zoubeïr Mouhli, "Restoration Dramas: Home Refurbishment in Historic Fès (Morocco), 2000–2009," *Journal of North African Studies* 17, no. 4 (2012): 701.

64 Istasse, "Dynamique de requalification," 259–83.

65 Ibid.

66 McGuinness and Mouhli, "Restoration Dramas," 699.

67 Ibid.

68 Summer Sutton, "Implications of 'Neo-Orientalist' Conservation in Fez, Morocco: Need for an Innovative Non-Profit Alternative," (MS in Architecture Studies thesis, Massachusetts Institute of Technology, 2012), 78.

69 Tarek Bouraque and Benjamin Bousquet, "Le patrimoine culturel de Marrakech en danger," *Telquel.ma*, March 11, 2016, http://telquel.ma/2016/03/11/marrakech-patrimoine-en-danger_1486966.

70 McGuinness and Mouhli, "Restoration Dramas," 703.

71 Bouraque and Bousquet, "Le patrimoine culturel de Marrakech en danger."

72 Ibid.

73 Istasse, "Affects and Senses," 43. "They mistake ADER technicians for UNESCO experts, and they associate UNESCO with the positive image of a saviour giving money to preserve the medina, in the view of most inhabitants and members of tourism institutions, the concrete benefit of World Heritage listing is financial: tourists are coming. Some inhabitants nonetheless have a critical or oppositional discourse vis-à-vis UNESCO, accusing it of not taking care of the medina and accusing UNESCO members and Moroccan politicians of stealing money. More than UNESCO as a myth in discourses, the medina as a cultural heritage doesn't seem to resonate with inhabitants' interests. Houses are first and foremost places to live and are at best — and hardly — considered as a familial heritage or an economic heritage when the house has been turned into a tourist accommodation." Ibid.

74 Joomi Lee, "Riad Fever: Heritage Tourism, Urban Renewal and the Médina Property Boom in Old Cities of Morocco," *E-Review of Tourism Research* 6, no. 4 (2008): 67.

75 Sutton, "Implications of 'Neo-Orientalist' Conservation," 33.

76 Kurzac, "Ces Riads qui vendent du rêve," 467–78.

77 Lee, "Riad Fever," 68.

78 Ibid., 70. Neoliberal urban regeneration schemes are motivated by the elite's concerns and are, by definition, less democratic.

79 Ibid., 71. Lee cites the work of R. Atkinson and G. Bridge, ed., *Gentrification in the Global Context: the New Urban Colonialism* (London: Routledge, 2005).

80 Sutton, "Implications of 'Neo-Orientalist' Conservation," 93.

81   B.T. Edward, *Morocco Bound: Disorienting America's Maghreb, from Casablanca to the Marrakech Express* (Durham, NC: Duke University, 2005), 25.

82   Nicholas, "Of Texts and Textiles," 407. "This discussion of key colonial texts on handicrafts highlights the persistent significance of colonial-era representations in the ongoing post-colonial struggle to define collective identities and their associated 'traditions' in Morocco, on a regional and national scale." Ibid.

83   Shelley Baranowski, Christopher Endy, Waleed Hazbun, Stephanie Malia Hom, Gordon Pirie, Trevor Simmons, and Eric Zuelow, "Tourism and Empire," *Journal of Tourism History* 7, no. 1–2 (2015): 6.

12

Cultivating (post)colonialism

Architecture, landscape, and the politics of the Taiwan Sugar Corporation

Justin Kollar

Contemporary political discourse in Taiwan has in many ways been shaped by the architecture of past colonial orders. Throughout the twentieth century Taiwan has undergone a rapid process of modernization under various authoritarian organizational regimes. First colonized by the Chinese, mostly during the 1800s, it was ceded to the budding Japanese Empire through the treaty of Shimonseki in 1895. During this time the Japanese radically reshaped the island through intimate restructuring of social and economic life. The Japanese colonial administration transformed the sub-tropical landscape into a valuable agricultural engine within the Japanese Empire. During the colonial period sugarcane was the largest cash crop, with production and export weaving commercial networks between the Japanese mainland and Taiwan tightly together.[1] In 1945, Taiwan was retroceded to China, which was then officially governed by the Chinese Nationalist Party or Kuomintang (KMT). After retreating from the mainland in 1949 during the civil war with the communists, the nationalist administration consolidated its rule on the island throughout the 1950s, marking the start of a geopolitical dispute over the island's sovereignty between the mainland Communist Party government and the governing party in Taiwan. The remaking of the island at this time would begin with a violent erasure of the Japanese past, a task that has proven to be rather impossible, with social and political consequences that reverberate to this day.

Sugar production remained the major export in the early days of KMT rule, but with the fall of sugar prices in the 1970s land use was diversified to support industry under import substitution policies.[2] This led to general pollution and degradation of the environment. By the 1980s there was a strong push for democracy alongside the environmentalist movement in response.[3] The success of these movements reprogrammed many of the institutions that had once been the backbone of the previous authoritarian regimes of the Japanese and early KMT. With democratization, the land that was once used for sugar production has become a major asset within competitive party politics, as each party utilizes it for their own nation-building agenda: building large-scale infrastructural projects, industrial estates, museums, parks, that respond to local political discourse, and attempts to inscribe a particular image of the Taiwanese landscape into the minds of its citizens.

This chapter is divided into sections along a linear historical narrative of the unfolding of colonial and postcolonial policies and interventions on the built environment that have attempted to construct a political narrative and subjectivity of Taiwan's residents. Rather than attempting to elaborate on all the complexities that exist within this discourse, it will focus on the role colonial-era institutions and infrastructures have played in framing the production of space to suit political narratives. Within an environment of gradual democratization in the 1980s and 1990s, Taiwanese politics has continued to be driven by debates over geopolitics, the global economic context, narratives of local culture and historicity, as well as the environmentalist movement.[4] These themes are contested within two contrasting positions formulated in the early days of democratization: an eventual unification with mainland China promoted by the KMT, and Taiwanese nationalism and a declared independence from China promoted by the Democratic Progressive Party (DPP). This chapter points out the ways in which historical colonial institutions, and the modern democratic reprogramming of these institutions, have shaped the environment and political discourse of postcolonialism in Taiwan. In doing so, it allows for the contemplation of ways in which colonial structures in other parts of the postcolonial world may be changed to support a more inclusive and democratic (re)creation of the built environment [Figure 12.1].

ıre 12.1
anese colonial-era
mitories that have been
verted to guest lodges
he Sugar Factory and
seum in Hualian.
tograph 2016. Source:
in Kollar.

THE POLITICS OF LAND AND LOCALITY

While institutions were being democratized in the 1990s, community-building activities wrestled with the particularities of Taiwanese history. This was characterized by opposing narratives of historical emphasis between the transformation and modernization of the island during Japanese colonization against the *longue durée* of Sinocentrism[5] previously enforced under KMT one-party rule. Much of this debate has also been influenced by a broader decolonization discourse that has driven Taiwanese nationalism.[6] Community-building platforms have allowed localized democratic processes to construct new spaces as part of a larger nation-building effort in the cultivation of the image of the nation through a process of collective imagining.[7] Considering the work of Benedict Anderson and his "imagined communities,"[8] one may understand both the KMT Sinocentrism and Taiwanese Nationalism as competing narratives vying for legitimacy in the formulation of the national community. This emphasis on the local has unfolded through a process of "recovering" elements of the past that had been suppressed by the Sinocentric narrative of one-party rule. The perceived "loss" of this past has only emboldened its recovery through educational campaigns, tourism, and historic preservation[9] — just as ecological conservation and revitalization attempts to recover an environment lost to industrialization. Many of these localized activities are integrated into mainstream politics through grassroots political networks, but this narrative conflict also rests on the geopolitics of contemporary Chinese economic power vis-à-vis the precarious position in which many Taiwanese have found themselves amidst the pressures of global competition[10] — pressures within the cultivation of neocolonial processes that further aggravate the political divide.[11]

While driven by debates on globalization, localism, nationalism, and environmentalism, much of this discourse is still grounded in institutions and infrastructures built up through a history of colonial processes. Within competitive party politics of Taiwan, the 60,000 hectares of land and assets of the Taiwan Sugar Corporation (TSC) have played a key role in the nation-building platform of each party.[12] The national (Taiwanese) government owns a ninety-seven percent stake in the TSC and manages it through the Ministry of Economic Affairs, thus rendering it an essentially state-owned enterprise.[13] Given this arrangement, the elected government of Taiwan is able to exercise significant power over company operations through the president's and party's selection of appointees to the Ministry of Economic Affairs as well as the president's nomination of the Chairman of the board (an appointment approved by the Ministry). This gives whichever party is in power direct control over the development of projects according to a list of "major constructions" promoted by each successive administration since the 1980s. Even though the TSC acts as an appendage of the national government, it also serves as a direct interface with the locals — empowering, redirecting, and resisting the will of local community institutions.

To recognize the ways in which the political use of TSC's land lies within a larger architecture of Taiwan's (post)colonial order, the following sections describe the order's construction through successive administrations, highlighting changes over time. Further exploration includes a comparison of the tenures of the KMT and DPP in the national government as well as the projects built which illustrate the competing narrative structures pursued by each in their utilization of TSC land. Ultimately the chapter reveals that, while many former colonies have been subject to the effects of neocolonial spatial processes which have restructured the environment in drastic ways due to loan-funded projects and policies of austerity, the case of Taiwan is one among those tied strongly to the persistence and adaptation of colonial-era institutions into more democratic forms.[14] Taiwan, with its own historical contingencies, offers a case from which larger questions stem: How can centralized colonial-era institutions be reprogrammed to promote democratization in the production of space? How are postcolonial spaces to be constituted in support of such a democracy?[15]

COLONIZATION AND THE RECOLONIZED PAST

Taiwan's pre-colonial history was complex and characterized by persistent conflict between local indigenous tribes and attempts at colonization by the Japanese, Chinese, and Western trade powers. For much of the seventeenth century, mainland farmers from the nearby Fujian province established small settlements on the island over many years, often pushing aboriginal groups inland away from the fertile plains. Chinese emigration increased with the establishment of a Dutch presence on the island, which had supplanted the Spanish by 1638. It was at this time that sugar production was established as a major export crop within international trade networks. In 1661, a Ming-loyalist, merchant-pirate nicknamed Koxinga (Zheng Chenggong) fought to expel the Dutch from Taiwan to set up his own base of operations against the newly established Qing dynasty on the mainland. This saw a moderate increase in Chinese settlement and further development of the sugar industry through the establishment of small-scale sugar mills known as *tangbu*.[16] The regime was short-lived, however, ending with an invasion of Qing forces in 1683.

The Qing ruled with a light touch, keeping Taiwan from falling into the hands of foreign powers while attempting to prevent a drain on state resources. The Qing government attempted to limit the conflict between Chinese settlers and aboriginals to prevent unnecessary expenditures, but by the mid-eighteenth century the Chinese administration's exploitative policies toward aborigines led to an uprising in 1731 that hastened the expulsion of aboriginal tribes into the mountains. By the end of the eighteenth century, they had succeeded, and the Chinese settled nearly the entire Western plains region.[17] Hoping to bolster the island against growing foreign pressures in the region, Taiwan was upgraded from a territorial dependency of Fujian to an official province of the Qing Empire after the short-lived Franco-Chinese War in 1885. Taiwan saw moderate investment in roads and telegraph lines while the sugar industry continued to develop using much the same traditional small-scale methods. Meanwhile, the Meiji restoration

in Japan heightened regional tensions and Japan's military successes increased. The First Sino-Japanese War of 1894–95 ended with the relinquishing of Taiwan to the budding Japanese Empire, thereby advancing a long history of colonization that would last until 1945.

BECOMING IMPERIAL SUBJECTS WITHIN THE ARCHITECTURE OF JAPANESE COLONIZATION, 1895–1945

Shortly after the acquisition of Taiwan in 1895, Japanese colonial administrators implemented a social system of control called the *hoko* throughout the island to manage ongoing resistance from the local population.[18] A mixture of Prussian-inspired administrative systems adopted by the Meiji government and traditional Japanese household tithing systems active on the mainland, its name derives from the *baojia*, an antiquated tithing system once employed in mainland China. The organization entailed the spatial ordering of people into hierarchical groupings where ten households formed a *ho*, and ten *ho*, or one hundred households, formed a *ko*, and again up to 1,000 households at larger scales of governance. Villages and communities of people within the *hoko* system were organized around the figure of the colonial police who were tasked to keep order and implement policies directly through centralized administrative channels.

The architect of this system, Goto Shinpei (1857–1929), was a doctor who had been appointed to the head of civilian affairs for the colonial Government-General of Taiwan. Within the *hoko* system, he employed his study of Prussian social systems, particularly related to public health and planning, such as a system of medical police.[19] The ideas expounded by Goto were echoed in the urban planning principles derived from the influential Prussian hygienist Max von Pettenkofer (1818–1901), under whom Goto studied in Germany while writing a dissertation on medical police administration.[20] As this system evolved, each *hoko* formed a basic unit of civic work, where alleged volunteers would build and maintain infrastructural systems that included irrigation, roads, and rail networks, in the modernization of Taiwan. The people were tied to the land through their labor, where new customs were introduced, controlled, and cultivated through the *hoko* hierarchy.

To fully exploit the capacity of Taiwan and build a self-sufficient revenue structure for the Japanese colonial administration, authorities strove to attract investment from large capitalists on mainland Japan. The government enabled Japanese private enterprise to take root by guaranteeing a minimum rate of return[21] through a risk-sharing mechanism called the *shokusan kogyo* allowing large *zaibatsu* (large industrial and financial conglomerates essential to the Japan's imperial economy) to lead the development of the sugar industry.[22] Under the aegis of the Japanese colonial state, Taiwan built much of its modern infrastructure and wealth on the sugar industry. The *hoko* system was at the foundation of labor administration in the sugar industry. Much of the land that produced sugarcane was managed by a large population of tenant-owners[23] within larger sugar districts where smaller-scale family farms were effectively required to sell to the district's local factory,[24] a practice facilitated by the centralized network of railway infrastructure built around supplying local factories within each company's district. Surrounding the sugar factories were smaller village clusters of farmers who relied on the factory system's fixed prices to sell sugarcane. The *hoko* system also ensured that each village was part of the Japanese administration's economic and social agenda in support of the sugar industry. The factory campuses were constructed as Japanese company towns with rows of houses and dormitories built for Japanese management and staff. Collective facilities such as dining halls, schools, and activity centers were also organized to support a microcosm of Japanese society [Figures 12.2 and 12.3].[25]

The Japanese established a durable colonial structure in urban form while leaving behind a legacy of modernization and an extensive architectural mark on the island. By the 1920s, the sugar industry had matured, extending across the entire island. The *hoko* system, too, had in effect become an institutionalized part of everyday life and the foundation of the colonial administration. Further policies of assimilation were pursued in the inter-war period with effective results.[26] The physical environment that was produced also reflected this broad reaching integration of society and colonial economy. The *hoko* system also reinforced the organization of neighborhoods around key community spaces, infrastructures and industrial landmarks built by the Japanese that in subsequent decades would play a significant role in shaping local perceptions of the environment.

ıre 12.2
ɔtou Sugar Factory in
ɔhsiung. Photograph
6. Source: Justin Kollar.
ʾas in operation from
ɔ2 to 1999.

(RE)BECOMING CHINESE UNDER NATIONALIST CONSOLIDATION, 1945–1980

With the loss of World War II, Taiwan was retroceded to China in 1945, at the time governed by the KMT on the verge of civil war with the communists. With echoes of the turbulence on the mainland, the five decades of divergent histories of the Taiwanese and mainland Chinese foreshadowed trouble as the KMT government began to consolidate its power over Taiwan. The Taiwanese had experienced a vastly different nation-building model under the Japanese, seeing the entire island developed to a higher degree than mainland China. Different cultural values and worldviews that were cultivated under the Japanese, not to mention the chasm in language, led to conflict and confrontation between the incoming KMT and Taiwanese elites. Rather than being treated as a liberated population, the Taiwanese were treated as enemy collaborators. Property was looted and the

Figure 12.3
The Qiaotou Sugar Facto in Kaohsiung. Photograp 1945. Source: Departme of Defense, U.S. Strategi Bombing Survey: Pacific Survey, Intelligence Bran Library and Target Data Section, 1945–1946 [National Archives at College Park, College Par MD]. The sugar factory village is located in the center of the image. To the West is the nearby village for Taiwanese. The southern area contains

incoming Chinese military assumed command of many government posts. Given the discontent raised by this, an island-wide uprising in 1947 led to a harsh military crackdown with many Taiwanese disappeared or purged, marking beginning of forty years of martial law.

As the KMT government quickly established its administration within the infrastructure left by the outgoing Japanese, another general frustration was caused with the reestablishment of the *hoko* system.[27] Renamed the *lilin* system by the reorganized KMT in the wake of its retreat from mainland China in 1949, it was subject to change and sustained party influence.[28] This infiltration was complemented by a thorough Sinicization campaign throughout the 1950s and 1960s. Schools were instructed to implement "nation-building" curricula[29] and adopted Mandarin-only policies that enforced the use of spoken Mandarin in all schools. In 1967 the Chinese Cultural Renaissance Movement Promotion

re 12.4
sugar industry in
van, 1980. Plan 2018.
rce: Justin Kollar
a sources: Taiwan
vernment Village Data;
. Database; National
d Survey and Mapping
iter Database; Taiwan
idred Years History
o System).

Sugar Districts

ormitories and houses
r Japanese staff. The
entral part of the factory
lage is composed of
ommunity facilities. The
orthern area contains the
perational buildings such
s the factory, warehouses
id storage.

△ Closed Sugar Factory
▲ Operational Sugar Factory
Railway
TSC-owned Plantation
Sugar-producing Farmland

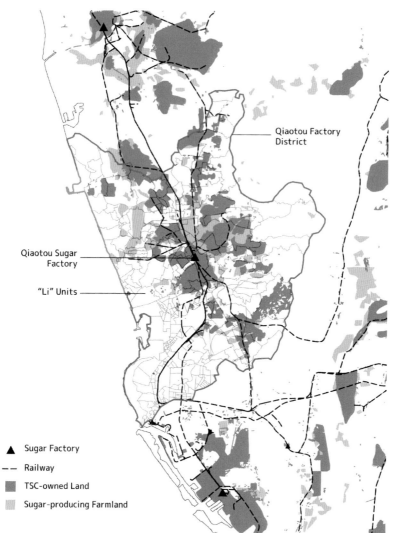

Figure 12.5
The Qiaotou Sugar
District, 1980. Plan 20
Source: Justin Kollar
(Data sources: Taiwan
Government Village Da
TSC Database; Nationa
Land Survey and Mapp
Center Database; Taiw
Hundred Years History
Map System).

Qiaotou Factory
District

Qiaotou Sugar
Factory

"Li" Units

▲ Sugar Factory

− − Railway

▓ TSC-owned Land

▒ Sugar-producing Farmland

Committee was established, ostensibly to promote traditional Chinese culture against the backdrop of the Cultural Revolution on the mainland. County-level cultural centers were created to promote cultural activities at the local level.[30] The efforts to remove the historical legacy of the Japanese and establish Taiwan as the authentic stronghold of Chinese culture was the state's only plea for legitimacy in the face of martial law, one-party rule, and the looming threat of Communist invasion from the mainland kept at bay by American pressure in the region with the start of the Korean War.

The new administration also managed to implement major reforms in land management. In 1947, nearly 120,000 hectares of land from the four major Japanese sugar corporations were expropriated and consolidated under the ownership of the TSC. This land became a valuable tool for centralized economic

244 ☐

development, but significant areas of agricultural land were also relinquished to single-household tenants. This quelled protest from local farmers on the monopolization of land by corporations like the TSC while also providing significant unemployment relief.[31] It also provided the KMT with an effective network through which to install loyal supporters at the local level within the *lilin* system and by staffing its members within local irrigation and farmers associations.[32] The consolidation of land within the sugar industry under the TSC became the backbone for large-scale economic development and land reform with over half of its land allocated to homestead support programs while rebuilding the sugar industry as a major economic support for a government-in-exile still keen on retaking the mainland. With little American support for an invasion and the fall of sugar prices in the 1970s, however, the government was forced to fast-track industrialization programs rather than pursue greater territorial objectives. By 1989 over 11,000 hectares of land were converted to industrial estates with over half of the industrial estates built on TSC land [Figures 12.4 and 12.5].[33]

These land policies of the Nationalist era largely reflected the centralized, corporate planning of the Japanese colonial administration. Coupled with the Sinicization campaigns, in the eyes of many Taiwanese nationalists, this was viewed as a secondary colonization that left a sharper emotional trauma than even the Japanese colonial regime.[34] However, the redistribution of TSC land benefited a large part of the population, and the land reform policies also allowed for a greater number of people to invest in the landscape. This paternalistic social and economic agenda in many ways extended the social systems established by the Japanese throughout Taiwanese society. These centralizing, authoritarian policies also cultivated a distaste that would sit, not only with the outspoken Taiwanese nationalists, but with a large part of the population. The contradictions that arose would ultimately lead to the breakdown of one-party authority, and a series of reactionary policies in response to the decades of Sinocentrism.

CULTIVATION OF THE DEMOCRATIC LANDSCAPE: CONTESTED (POST)COLONIAL NARRATIVES OF DEMOCRATIC LOCALISM, 1980–2000

During the 1980s, industrial policies pursued by the government led to environmental degradation. The growing politicization of grassroots environmentalism mixed with democratic activism, eventually coalescing into the mainstream of party politics. One of the major steps marking the beginning of democratization was the creation of the DPP in 1986 followed by the Civic Organization Law in 1989, which retroactively legalized the founding of opposition parties such as the DPP. The environmentalist movement gradually found favor within the newly formed political organization that embraced open advocacy for Taiwanese nationalism and independence[35] — views that were once severely punished. This yearning for a "homeland" based on the local community brought the environmental movement directly into politics in opposition to the KMT developmentalist state.[36]

Martial law was lifted the following year, and in 1988 Lee Tung-hui ascended to the presidency after the death of Chiang Ching-kuo. During his tenure, he openly advocated policies that shifted national consciousness toward a form of Taiwanese nationalism, a stark reversal that set him apart from many of his compatriots within the KMT.

One of the major programs initiated under Lee Tung-hui was the Community Construction (*shequ yingzao*) program. Promoted by the Council for Cultural Affairs throughout the 1990s, it saw the establishment of hundreds of community organizations tasked with building a stronger connection between the people, culture, and the environment of the community in response to the experiences of dislocation of the decades prior. Many of these organizations overlap with the administrative units of the *lilin* system, but are organized from the bottom up. The program takes notes from the *machizukuri* (community-making) experiences of the Japanese, which saw locals take initiative to develop their own communities.[37] Given the legacy of the *hoko* system from the colonial period, and the persistence of urban the institutions from that time, similarities among the local urban and administrative systems within current Japanese and Taiwanese systems have made these types of activities from Japan attractive still. However, this was not the only idealization made of Japan in the unfolding of the community-building process. The extensiveness of Japanese colonial infrastructure and buildings that remained after fifty years has allowed for a nostalgic recovery of many of these architectural objects. Both cultural and environmental displacement, produced by the Sinicization and industrialization policies of the KMT administration, respectively, were major drivers in the call for greater democracy as well as the recovery of a lost identity as demonstrated by the nostalgia[38] of the historic preservation projects at the center of the community-building movement. This nostalgia would later find its way into national politics through the extension of the community-building program to the TSC, by far the largest manager of Japanese colonial assets. As sugar production declined with the drop in global sugar prices, the TSC diversified into many lines of business, including real estate through selling territorial assets to maintain revenue. Also in response to these economic conditions, in 1986 the Ministry of Economic Affairs instructed the TSC to "choose appropriate land segments for development of tourism and tourism projects"[39] in coordination with local planning authorities. As with the land reform of the 1950s, the TSC dutifully complied. This, however, marked an important turn toward a particular form of subjectivity embedded within landscape through its cultivation as an historical asset. Complementing these plans was the fact that the land that the TSC owned was gaining in value — given that it was at the periphery of expanding cities or because of its utilization for infrastructure projects. This gave the organization, and the national government by extension, more leverage over the transformation of the land, allowing the TSC to develop along the national government's parameters.

Throughout the 1990s, many of the sites selected for the development of tourism comprised parks and hotels situated in scenic areas [Figure 12.6]. Initially,

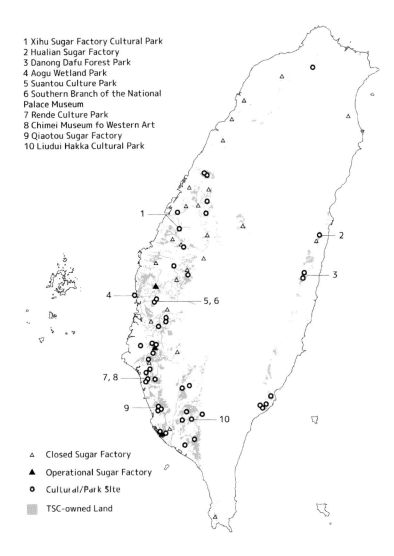

e 12.6
ure and tourism sites
SC land built from
)–16. Plan 2018.
ce: Justin Kollar (Data
ce: TSC Database).

1 Xihu Sugar Factory Cultural Park
2 Hualian Sugar Factory
3 Danong Dafu Forest Park
4 Aogu Wetland Park
5 Suantou Culture Park
6 Southern Branch of the National
Palace Museum
7 Rende Culture Park
8 Chimei Museum fo Western Art
9 Qiaotou Sugar Factory
10 Liudui Hakka Cultural Park

△ Closed Sugar Factory

▲ Operational Sugar Factory

○ Cultural/Park Site

▦ TSC-owned Land

very little had to do with the wealth of historic assets owned by the TSC, but by
the end of the 1990s, the TSC began to face the growing force of the officially
endorsed community-building program. A major shift in the management of the
TSC followed the election in 2000 prompted by the resignation of President Lee
Tung-hui, a champion of Taiwanese community-building, from office and from the
KMT altogether, leaving many of the hardliners behind. A split in the vote between
two pro-unification candidates allowed the DPP candidate, Chen Shui-bian, to
take the presidency, making him the first non-KMT president in Taiwan's history.

SHIFTS IN THE NATION-BUILDING ARCHITECTURE, 2000–2016

Since the 1980s, each successive administration has run on a platform that has
included a list of "major constructions" with plans for the implementation of major

nation-building projects such as the high-speed rail system,[40] national museums, universities, parks, and other major politically charged projects — most of which were to be built on TSC land. Many of the projects promoted by the DPP have included the preservation and reconstruction of Japanese colonial-era structures. These projects in particular build on the nostalgia that has permeated popular culture in Taiwan since the lifting of martial law in 1987.[41] This nostalgic recollection also offers a cultural counterbalance to politics of the KMT characterized by disadvantageous trade policies and mainland political influence.[42] Ironically, the preservation of Japanese colonial-era sites and the popularity of Japanese culture have helped to produce a cultural narrative that undermines the KMT's more Sinocentric rationale to draw closer political and economic ties with mainland China. This has much to do with the more recent experiences of martial law and imposed Sinicization policies of the 1940s–1980s, rather than the harsh colonization of Taiwan by Japan in the early 1900s. Time may certainly heal all wounds, but perhaps some faster than others — particularly when new ones make it more difficult to feel the old.

With oppositional politics in full gear, the TSC would be transformed to manage much of its antiquated colonial infrastructure as economic and community development tools. As the DPP rose to power in 2000, national projects were even more explicitly oriented toward the cultivation of a multifaceted historic narrative with special emphasis on the Japanese colonial era. A major catalyst in the cultural redevelopment of these sites began in Kaohsiung, in southern Taiwan. In 1999 the Qiaotou Sugar Factory closed its production operations. Established in 1902, it had been the first mechanized/modern sugar factory built in Taiwan and was in operation for almost 100 years. A lengthy battle ensued between the local community and the TSC over its future. The local community established the Sugar Community Art Village in 2001 in an attempt to save it, focusing mostly on turning it into a local venue for art. In 2002 it was declared an historic site by the Kaohsiung municipality. Plans were then drafted to transform it into a cultural park and museum, both of which opened in 2006. Anticipating additional projects of this kind, the TSC opened a special leisure department to manage its cultural and tourism operations. By 2010 the "Ten Drum Culture Park" was established as an extension of the Ten Drum Art Percussion Group's operations in the nearby Rende Sugar Factory. With a performance stage and classrooms, visitors and the local community can enjoy performances and learn to play the Japanese *taiko* drum. Within the museum, narratives of the lives of the factory's workers are told from the early days through the Japanese administration, and into the present. The depiction of life during the Japanese era is filled with photos and videos of people in Japanese dress, performing athletics, and participating in other communal activities. Special sessions are also held for people to learn about life on the sugar factory during the Japanese era through storytelling.

This nostalgic depiction of the Japanese colonial era presents a stark contrast with KMT-promoted narratives of the nation. Its reverence to the Japanese colonial era and culture more broadly is woven into the cultivation of the arts within the local community, providing the foundation for an interesting form of democratic politics.

An oppositional strand is also found in other projects completed at this time. Along with the development of the Qiaotou Sugar Museum and Cultural Park, a host of other sites were transformed into similar cultural parks and museums to be anchors of community-building projects and local economic development. The National Museum of Taiwan History, established on TSC land in Tainan, was the first official national museum to present comprehensive material on the Japanese colonial past — depicting the economy, social life and politics with increased depth. This history, however, would have been difficult to access only years earlier and includes some of the most daring exhibitions of the early authoritarianism under KMT one-party rule from the 1950s to the 1980s. The Suantou (sugar factory) Cultural Park in Chiayi (2002) anchors a larger development vision around the high-speed rail, and the Hualian Tourist Sugar Factory (2002) revitalized its Japanese colonial-era dormitories as hotels for guests [Figure 12.7]. The Japanese architecture is thus revitalized to support hospitality functions or to house historical collections for visitors. Xihu Sugar Factory Cultural Park in Changhua (2004) and the Rende Sugar (factory) Culture Park in Tainan (2007) are among other such culture parks that incorporate colonial-era heritage sites with an emphasis on local history incorporating the Japanese era in a relatively positive light. Clearly a privileged approach, nearly all of the existing factories that had ceased production were transformed into cultural parks and museums between 2001 and 2007.

re 12.7
v overlooking a large
-park on TSC land in
ayi. Photograph 2016.
rce: Justin Kollar. The
thern Branch of the
onal Palace Museum
be seen on the right.
he left, the Suantou
ar Factory and Culture
k can also be seen.

Under the DPP, the cultivation of an alternative history was explicit. But its political utility within the community-building movement lent much credence to the DPP as it gave a sense of cultural and historical restoration to many communities that felt like they had lost a part of the past under what may have felt like several decades of industrialization and cultural erasure.

After a corruption scandal involving Chen leading up to the 2008 elections,[43] the KMT won the majority of the vote and the KMT candidate, Ma Ying-jeou, became president. The policies of cultural development under the DPP were swiftly recalibrated. An illustrative example of this switch occurred with the delayed construction of the Southern Branch of the National Palace Museum in Chiayi. Planned by the DPP administration in 2004 and built on TSC land, it was part of a larger strategy of economic development with emphasis on Asian art and culture with the touristic development of the nearby sugar factory intended to balance the cultural weight of the National Palace Museum in Taipei which houses the treasures taken by the Nationalist government from mainland China. However, by 2008 the construction had run late and over budget. The incoming KMT administration abruptly changed the theme to the "Floral Heritage Museum" in an attempt to neutralize the cultural politics of the project, only to be rebuffed by the DPP-led county government and local residents.[44]

Under the KMT, the agenda of cultural and historical preservation was exchanged for a carefully calibrated emphasis on ecology and environmentalism, representing a major departure from the party's past. While much ground had already been lost, the strategic shift was designed to reposition the narrative from the cultural and historical particularity of Taiwan to the larger ecological context in which the island of Taiwan is placed, emphasizing Taiwan as a *province* — not a nation. This shift coincided with stronger economic ties with mainland China. In reinventing itself as a party that embraced both environmentalism and a strong economy, a string of "eco-parks" were constructed on TSC land in many counties. These took the form of large-scale wetland revitalization and afforestation projects combined with tourism and economic development strategies. The eco-park agenda also capitalized on partnerships, such as in the development of a museum project with Chimei, a major plastics corporation, in Tianan [Figure 12.8]. Planning for the museum was integrated into an ongoing project for Tainan Metropolitan Park, which had been transformed into the eco-park model built around the museum housed in a cliché of Western architectural style.

There were a few major parks established at this time. On the western coast of Taiwan, Chiayi County, a major wetland construction project was implemented on an old sugarcane plantation owned by the TSC. From 2008 to 2012 the Aogu Wetland Park was created on an immense site incorporating an environmental education center and facilities for the cultivation of the local handicraft industry. Other parks took on various forms, but all integrated an ecological narrative: the Liudui Hakka Cultural Park in Pingtung (2011), and the 1,250-hectare Danong Dafu Forest Park in Hualian (developed since 2008) that promotes local industries through environmental education, are among many other sites.

re 12.8
Chimei Museum
Vestern Art and the
an Metropolitan
, Tainan, Taiwan.
tograph 2016. Source:
in Kollar. The chimney
he Rende Sugar Factory
Culture Park can be
n to the left.

Much of this shift in development strategy between 2008 and 2016 served as the background to KMT policies that cultivated closer political and economic ties with mainland China in a process that may raise compelling questions regarding potential (neo)colonialism through economic integration intended to achieve a form of political leverage. Tourism has been driven by images of the landscape of Taiwan and its *Chinese* historic sites. The peak of Taiwan's tourism boom in 2013 had generated over US$12.3 billion[45] with the vast majority of incoming tourists from mainland China. The closer relations have angered many, with some particularly unpopular trade policies enacted in undemocratic fashion that eventually led to the "Sunflower Movement" of 2014,[46] marking the beginning of a renewed politics within the youth searching for both identity and economic security.

The 2016 elections were won by the DPP candidate, Tsai Ying-wen, and the majority of the legislature supported the DPP. Since then the new administration's agenda has focused on infrastructure development along with the continued promotion of community-building and economic development at the local levels.[47] Much of this, once again, has centered on TSC land and assets as a development instrument tied to the party's platform. Many new projects within the southern cities have a renewed focus on developing the old sugar industry infrastructure of the TSC into community-use programs.[48] While the TSC continues to play a major role in the political projects of the national government, the success remains unclear at the time of writing.

CONCLUSIONS AND UNCERTAIN FUTURES

In recent history, the TSC has served as an asset manager and developer of spaces that have played a major role in national political discourse through the preservation and cultivation of local Japanese colonial-era historical sites. While the legacy of the Japanese in the construction of the Taiwanese landscape is not synonymous with the politics of unification with China and more independent-minded Taiwanese nationalism, it has played a major underlying role in terms of the social, cultural, and economic factors driving much of the country's politics.[49] It should also be pointed out that the Taiwanese experience of Japanese colonialism was vastly different from that of mainland China and Korea, where the Japanese colonial administrators enacted harsher colonization policies and thus the living memory of colonialism there is different. The possession of Taiwan during WWII also meant that the Taiwanese were not exposed to the brutalities of the Japanese army as seen on the mainland and across Southeast Asia.

Although, with the recent election of the DPP there has been increased interest in utilizing TSC sites for economic development, larger questions remain as the proximity and policies of mainland China continue to weigh on the minds of its youth. While many of the recent generation have grown up with an identity cultivated in the discourses of Taiwanese nationalism, the economic prospects offered by, and political fears of, China hold sway for an educated generation facing a poor economic outlook in Taiwan.[50] Distrust in the DPP also grows among many of the young Taiwanese.[51] A new party has also emerged from the Sunflower Movement: the New Power Party has elected five of its leaders to the Taiwanese legislature on a left-leaning platform that speaks to the anxious youth and advocates declared independence from China.

Taiwan's political landscape is thus changing, but there remains much uncertainty regarding the island's future. The evolution of its institutions is also an interesting case in this respect: from authoritarian and colonial administrations, these institutions have developed to support democracy and inclusivity in the production of the built environment. Although the economic hardships Taiwan faces certainly reflect the influences of globalization, Taiwan's exclusion from many of the harshest effects of neocolonialism evident in many other postcolonies remains compelling. It certainly complicates developing discourses on postcolonialism. The KMT's role in Taiwan's recent development preserved the strength of state institutions in influencing the economy.[52] Its privileged position in American geopolitics may have also played a role in keeping at bay the Washington Consensus structural adjustment and privatization policies that provide the foundation for neocolonialism elsewhere. Taiwan's state-driven economic development and its other historical contingencies aside, the role played by localized democratization of space in preventing neocolonial processes from being established is a noteworthy contribution.

The localism of Taiwan's community-building movement reconfigured the histories of colonial space to suit contemporary political agendas, while top-down nation-building platforms as embodied in the cultural projects on TSC land have responded by cultivating a "national" space through this connection to the local. Instead of rejecting its Japanese colonial-era roots — as would be expected, given the Sinocentric formula — could the spatial emphasis of Japanese colonialism in Taiwan be a form of liberation from such proscription? Perhaps these spaces of nostalgia present themselves as *symptoms* of the cultural and environmental dislocation brought about by KMT policies. In speaking of space and democracy, Margaret Kohn leads one to imagine that the preservation and reconstruction of these spaces represent a "liberatory" attempt to construct new identities in response to "a particular form of domination."[53] Such domination may be embodied in the legacy of KMT one-party hegemony that has included oppressive control over cultural narratives and sometimes damaging economic policies, leading to the cultivation of a Taiwanese consciousness through local community-building in order to amend the dislocation. Such localized spatial operations involving preservation and community-driven investment are at the heart of democratic politics.

It is an interesting historical note that these local institutions developed by the Japanese in Taiwan were carried to other parts of Asia during Japan's imperialist WWII campaign. Similar versions of the *hoko* system were also established in Vietnam, Indonesia, and the Philippines, each of which continues to deal with the legacies of colonial state-building.[54] Perhaps this link between the physical environment and localized forms of democracy can inform a broader conversation on the transformation of postcolonial space. Indeed, as Anthony Giddens contends, "space is not an empty dimension along which social groupings become structured, but has to be considered in terms of its involvement in the constitution of systems of interaction."[55] Democracy, most of all, requires the construction of social, cultural, political, and physical spaces that can support it. In order to understand today's Taiwan, one must endeavor to understand the historical contingencies inherent in the constitution of space and thus the latent possibilities for a postcolonial democratic politics.

NOTES

1 Alice Amsden, "Taiwan's Economic History: A Case of Etatisme and a Challenge to Dependency Theory," *Modern China* 5, no. 3 (1979): 344; Taiwan Sugar Corporation, *Taitang wu shi nian nianjian* 台糖五十年年鑑 [Taiwan Sugar Corporation Fifty Year Yearbook] (Tainan: Taiwan Sugar Corporation, 1997).

2 Chih-Ming Shih and Szu-Yin Yen, "The Transformation of the Sugar Industry and Land Use Policy in Taiwan," *Journal of Asian Architecture and Building Engineering* 48 (2009): 45–7.

3 Jui-hua Chen, "Building a New Society on the Base of Locality: Transformation of Social Forces in Taiwan During the 1990s," *Inter-Asia Cultural Studies* 15, no. 2 (2014): 291–305.

4 Ibid., 295–96.

5 Sinocentrism refers to the emphasis on a singular, overarching identity of "China" as a territory or the "Chinese" as a trans-territorial identity. This nationalistic view often ignores or subordinates the extensive cultural and historical diversity.

6 Wolfgang Gerhard Thiele, "Decolonization and the Question of Exclusion in Taiwanese Nationalism since 1945," *Global Histories* 3, no. 1 (2017): 62–84.

7 Daniel C. Lynch, "Taiwan's Self-conscious Nation-building Project," *Asian Survey* 44, no. 4 (2004): 514.

8 Benedict Anderson, *Imagined Communities: Reflections on the Origin and Spread of Nationalism* (London: Verso, 1983).

9 Marylin Ivy, *The Discourses of the Vanishing: Modernity, Phantasm, Japan* (Chicago, IL: University of Chicago, 1995); Hsin-yi Lu, "The Politics of Locality: Making a Nation of Communities in Taiwan," (Ph.D. diss., University of Washington, 2001).

10 Mei-ling Wang, *The Dust That Never Settles: The Taiwan Independence Campaign and U.S.-China Relations* (Lanham, MD: University Press of America, 1999), 325–82.

11 Kuan-Hsing Chen, "The Imperialist Eye: The Cultural Imaginary of a Subempire and Nation-state," *Positions: East Asia Cultures Critique* 8, no. 1 (2000): 9–76.

12 Yang Songling 楊松齡, *Guoyou tudi liyong fangxiang yanjiu* 國有土地利用方向研究 [*Research on the Direction of State-owned Land Utilization*] (Taipei: China Association of Land Economics, 2003).

13 Taiwan Sugar Corporation, *Taitang qi shi nian nianjian* 台糖七十年年鑑 [Taiwan Sugar Corporation Seventy Year Yearbook] (Tainan: Taiwan Sugar Corporation, 2016).

14 There is evidence to suggest the institutional legacy of postcolonies has played a role in the success of the state-building. See Rollin F. Tusalem, "The Colonial Foundations of State Fragility and Failure," *Polity* 48, no. 4 (2016): 445–95.

15 For a broader exploration on space and democratic society see Anthony Giddens, *The Constitution of Society: Outline of the Theory of Structuration* (Cambridge, MA: Polity, 1984); Margaret Kohn, *Radical Space: Building the House of the People* (Ithaca, NY: Cornell University, 2003).

16 Liu Wanlai 劉萬來, *Jindai riben tangye shi* 近代日本糖業史 [*Modern History of Japan's Sugar Industry*] (Tainan: Republic of China Sugar Technology Society, 2007), 269–92.

17 Denny Roy, *Taiwan: A Political History* (Ithaca, NY: Cornell University, 2003), 25–28.

18 Hui-yu Caroline Tsai, "One Kind of Control: The 'Hoko' System in Taiwan Under Japanese Rule, 1895–1945" (Ph.D. diss., Columbia University, 1990).

19 Christos Lynteris, "From Prussia to China: Japanese Colonial Medicine and Goto Shinpei's Combination of Medical Police and Local Self-Administration," *Medical History* 55 (2011): 343–47; Tsai, "One Kind."

20 Jong-Chan Lee, "Hygienic Governance and Military Hygiene in the Making of Imperial Japan, 1868–1912," *Historia Scientiarum* 18 (2008): 7; Goto Shinpei 後藤新平, *Eisei seido ron* 衛生制度論 [Hygiene System Theory] (Tokyo: Goto Shinpei, 1890), National Diet Library, Tokyo.

21 Christopher Howe, *The Origins of Japanese Trade Supremacy* (Chicago, IL: University of Chicago, 1996), 309.

22 Cheng Tun-Jen, "Transforming Taiwan's Economic Structure in the 20th Century," *The China Quarterly* 165 (2001): 21; Wen-Huan Lee 李文環, "Chanye yimin cun zhi xian-daihua yu zhimin: Xing rizhi shiqi Taiwan zhitang zhushu huishe qiao zi tou zhitang suo zhi ge'an yanjiu" 產業移民村之現代化與殖民性：日治時期台灣製糖株式會社橋仔頭製糖所之個案研究 [The Modernization and Colonialism of Industrial Immigrants Village — A Case Study on Kio-A-Thau Sugar Refinery of Taiwan Sugar Refinery Company during Japanese Rule in Taiwan], *Gaoxiong shi da xuebao* 26 (2009): 1–25.

23 Cheng, "Transforming," 22.

24 Samuel Ho, *Economic Development of Taiwan, 1860–1970* (New Haven, CT: Yale University, 1978).

25 Yu Chen Wu 吳育臻, *Suantou tangchang zhi zhu xing juluo de shenghuo fang-shi* (1910–2001) 蒜頭糖廠職住型聚落的生活方式 (1910–2001) [*The Way of Life in Working and Living Settlement of Suantou Sugar Factory* (1910–2001)] (Ph.D. Diss., National Kaohsiung Normal University, 2008), 39–57.

26 Leo T. Ching, *Becoming "Japanese": Colonial Taiwan and the Politics of Identity Formation* (Berkeley, CA: University of California, 2001), 89–132.

27 Chih-ming Ka, *Japanese Colonialism in Taiwan: Land Tenure, Development, and Dependency, 1895–1945* (Boulder, CO: Westview, 1995).

28 Yun-han Chu and Jih-wen Lin, "Political Development in 20th Century Taiwan: State-building, Regime Transformation and the Construction of National Identity," in *Taiwan in the 20th Century: A Retrospective View*, ed. Richard Louis Edmons and Steven M. Goldstein (New York: Cambridge University, 2001), 113–14; Civil Affairs Department of the Taiwan Provincial Government, *Taiwan sheng cunli zuzhi gong-neng* 台灣省村里組織功能 [Taiwan Province Village Organizational Function] (Nantou: Taiwan Provincial Government, September 1998).

29 Zhong Mengxue 鍾孟學, *Taiwan de gushi: shehui pian* 臺灣的故事：社會篇 [*The Story of Taiwan: Society*] (Taipei: Government Information Office, Republic of China, 1999).

30 Allen Chun, "From Nationalism to Nationalizing: Cultural Imagination and State Formation in Postwar Taiwan," *Australian Journal of Chinese Affairs* 31 (1994): 65–67.

31 Yang, *Research on the Direction*, 3–16.

32 Lam Wai Fung "Irrigation Foundations of a Robust Social-ecological System: Irrigation Institutions in Taiwan," *Journal of Institutional Economics* 2, no. 2 (2006): 209.

33 Ministry of Economic Affairs, *A Brief Introduction to the Industrial Estates in Taiwan, Republic of China* (Taipei: Industrial Development and Investment Center, 1989).

34 Thiele, "Decolonization," 62–84. On the independence movement in relationship to the "223 Incident," see Wang, *The Dust,* 75–126.

35 Ho Ming-sho, "Environmental Movement in Democratizing Taiwan (1980–2004): A Political Opportunity Structure Perspective," in *East Asian Social Movements: Power, Protest, and Change in a Dynamic Region,* ed. Jeffrey Broadbent and Vicky Brockman (New York: Springer, 2011), 283–314.

36 Chen, "Building a New Society," 295–96.

37 For more on the difference between *machizukuri* and urban planning, see Carola Hein, "Toshikeikaku and Machizukuri in Japanese Urban Planning," *Japanstudien* 13, no. 1 (2002): 221–52.

38 For a general discussion of nostalgia in relation to "shared spatial experience" see Melinda J. Milligan, "Displacement and Identity Discontinuity: The Role of Nostalgia in Establishing New Identity Categories," *Symbolic Interaction* 26, no. 3 (2003): 381–403. In relationship to postcolonial nostalgia as produced by physical and cultural displacement see Dennis Walder, *Postcolonial Nostalgias: Writing, Representation, and Memory* (New York: Routledge, 2012).

39 Ministry of Economic Affairs, *Letter 9637 in State Council's Letter No. 2097 007 to the Executive Yuan* (May 9, 1986), quoted in Taiwan Sugar Corporation, *Taitang wu shi nian nianjian* 台糖五十年年鑑 [Taiwan Sugar Corporation Fifty Year Yearbook] (Tainan: Taiwan Sugar Corporation, 1997), 213.

40 Much of the planned rail route takes advantage of the TSC-owned land. Many new stations have also been established as anchors for urban development elsewhere.

41 For instance, movies have provided an alternative, if not positive, lens through which to view life in the colonial era. See Han Chen, "Hou zhimin xiangchou: Dangdai Taiwan dianying de riben xiangxiang" 韓琛, 后殖民乡愁：当代台湾电影的日本想象 [Postcolonial nostalgia: Imagined Japan in contemporary Taiwan Films], *Orient Forum* 1 (2012): 51–57.

42 This is illustrated by the political uproar that has followed sometimes-secretive trade deals with mainland China under the KMT administration. Much of the controversy is driven by economic factors but is also linked to Taiwanese nationalism

43 Jim Yardley, "Corruption Scandal at Top Tests Taiwan's Democracy," *New York Times,* November 25, 2006, https://www.nytimes.com/2006/11/25/world/asia/25taiwan.html.

44 Shao Bingru 邵冰如, "Gugong nan yuan ding diao zhuanxing wei hua boguan" 故宮南院定調轉型為花博館 [The Southern Branch of the National Palace Museum Changes into the Flower Culture Museum], *United Evening News* (Taipei, Taiwan), March 19, 2009.

45 Joy Lee, "Tourism Income Reaches Record High in 2013," *The China Post* (Taipei, Taiwan), July 10, 2014, https://chinapost.nownews.com/20140710-61709.

46 Austin Ramzy, "As Numbers Swell, Students Pledge to Continue Occupying Taiwan's Legislature," *New York Times*, March 22, 2014, https://sinosphere.blogs.nytimes.

com/2014/03/22/as-numbers-swell-students-pledge-to-continue-occupying-taiwans-legislature.

47 National policies and programs from the Executive Yuan can be found on the National Development Council's website. See National Development Council (Taiwan), "Overview," accessed July 3, 2018, https://www.ndc.gov.tw.

48 For an example, see the development of Sinying District and the "Taiwan Sugar Green Bikeway" project that tours through historic sites in Tainan: Bureau of Urban Development Tainan City Government, *Tainan shi dushi fazhan nianbao* 台南市都市發展年報 [Tainan City Development Annual Report] (Tainan: Bureau of Urban Development, 2015), 6–8 and 33–34.

49 Even under the recent KMT administration, while a Taiwanese consciousness was strong, there is variation in the expression of Taiwanese nationalism. Liao Da-chi, Liu Cheng-shan and Chen Bo-yu, "Taiwanese nationalism in the age of cross-Strait integration," in *Assessing the Presidency of Ma Ying-jiu in Taiwan,* ed. André Beckershoff and Gunter Schubert (New York: Routledge, 2018), 59–89.

50 Par Hugo Tierny, "Taiwan Youth: The Rise of a Generation," *Asia Focus* 22 (2017): 1–13.

51 Ibid., 12.

52 Amsden, "Taiwan's Economic History."

53 Kohn, *Radical Space*, 90.

54 An overview of these types of organizations within various Southeast Asian countries can be found in Benjamin L. Read and Robert Pekkanen, *Local Organizations and Urban Governance in East and Southeast Asia: Straddling State and Society* (New York: Routledge, 2009).

55 Giddens, *The Constitution,* 368.

Epilogue

13

Working through the neocolonialist habit

Vikramāditya Prakāsh

In the final scene of the 1981 Bollywood film *36 Chowringhee Lane,* directed by Aparna Sen, the protagonist Mrs. Stoneham, an elderly Anglo-Indian English school teacher who loves teaching Shakespeare and who stayed behind after India's Independence in 1947, stands outside with a cake in hand looking through the window of a house into a Christmas party, to which she has not been invited. The party is in the home of young newly married "modern" Indian couple, both former students of Mrs. Stoneham, who, in their days of romance had persuaded the gentle schoolteacher to let them use her house — a typical colonial-era bungalow — for their illicit romantic rendezvous. Once married, the couple moves on, not inviting Mrs. Stoneham to their party thinking she will be a "fish out of water" among their modern postcolonial Indian guests. Mrs. Stoneham bakes them a cake for Christmas and comes to drop it off, setting up the final scene.

Exploited via a loophole in the social, Mrs. Stoneham's old colonial bungalow — temporary refuge for the yet-unwed couple — stands in for the plight of the colonial caught up in the entanglements of desire and disdain of the postcolonial world [Figure 13.1].[1] The bungalow might well ask: is it ok to use and discard the erstwhile venerable institutions of the colonial for postcolonial purposes, modernist or otherwise? Put in terms of architectural thinking: how can one outline and recognize a critical postcolonial design (or heritage management) agency? Or, more expansively, how does one differentiate a critical and self-critical reimagining of one's colonial inheritance from one that is simply a symptomatic repetition of the old colonial relations? In other words, if one critiques a particular appropriation of a colonial-era building for, say, tourism purposes as being neocolonialist — arguably because the result reproduces and capitalizes on the colonial affect of the superiority of the Western idiom and institutions in the colonies — that begs the question of how one is to actually construct or reconstruct a postcolonial architecture, in a form that is decidedly non-neocolonial, without denying or repressing the persistence of colonial entanglements between the postcolonies and the metropoles.

Figure 13.1
The colonial-era Indian bungalow (Hamilton's Bungalow, Gosaba, Ind Photograph 2013. Sou Lockenrc [Wikimedia Commons].

Neocolonial architectural and cultural objects and narratives proliferate in the postcolonies not only because both modernism and globalization continue to recirculate the economies of desire and capital of the colonial world, but also because individual postcolonial subjectivities seem to continue to be impelled by the pushes and pulls of the master-servant, dominant-submissive relationships of their colonial past. Whether it is nostalgia that surrounds a tattered old colonial bungalow in a Bollywood film (as in *36 Chowringhee Lane*), or a freshly minted gated community optimistically marketed as *"The Colonial,"* or even if it is one more state-sponsored museum of culture and anthropology remade or repurposed in colonial idiom for tourist purposes because that somehow sells and signifies authority and authenticity, the neocolonial in the postcolonial testifies to the abiding strength and persuasion of the Enlightenment authorized colonial world order that set up the metropolitan West as center of the new modern world of the nineteenth century with the rest as its vassal colonies in waiting.

Neocolonialism in this sense is an old habit, a habit both in the sense of way of dressing and inhabiting and as a settled and comfortable way of being. It is just as much historical and economic as it is cathectic and haptic.

The neocolonialist habit is widespread and obvious in the postcolonies. But, as the chapters in Part I of this volume reveal, the neocolonial habit infects postcolonial metropoles as well. The hierarchic us-versus-them binary structures identity not just of the postcolonies (taking on the master's signs as one's own) but also that of metropolitan centers (taking on the identity of the "universalist" as one's autonomous identity). One can think of this as, for instance, the problem of architecture's identity. In the West, that is to say in the metropoles, architecture is constructed as the discourse of architecture as such, while in the postcolonies it is always constructed as being necessarily entangled with the identitarian problem of being of the non-West. The normative discourse of architecture as just-architecture is in fact a discourse of Eurocentrism constructed as the non-non-West, precisely at the moment when it is presented as being free of any identitarian concerns.[2]

The point here being that if the postcolonial adoption of Western habits is a symptom of the neocolonialist problem, the metropole's steadfast differentiation of itself from those of the non-West, in its quest for universalist-autonomy, is also a neocolonialist symptom of their entangled colonial histories. Thus, if the dilemma in the postcolonies concerns what to do with their colonial/Western architecture with all its attendant asymmetries, that intractable problem is symmetrical with, and entangled with, the more unrecognized problem of what to do in the former metropoles with their continuing inability to engage with architectures that are anything other than Western/colonial. That in Dubai today we continue to see the proliferation of the steel and glass skyscraper and just outside Bangalore in India we watch with horror the proliferation of another round of "Colonial Villa" residential gated colonies for the elite, is a symptom, I would argue, just as much of the persistence of the neocolonialist frame of mind as it is a symmetrical con-sequence of the *lack* of the proliferation something like "neo-Hindu" communes in California and Arizona, or of a neo-zen transformation of central London parks.

In this way we can begin to see how the neocolonialist problem is truly a global problem. It is global not only in the sense that it entangles the whole world in its tentacles, but also in the sense that the construction of any particular instance of a neocolonialist situation — such as say the unexamined continuing adoption of Lutyens' imperial buildings as the sites and symbols of the independ-ent Indian nation-state — can only be understood when situated in the global field that includes, for example, Washington, DC's unproblematized proselytiza-tion of neoclassicism as its official state architecture and Norman Foster's uncritical reconstruction of the Reichstag in unapologetic neo-modernist vetements.

A key neocolonialist problem, as seen from a globalist perspective, is thus the persistence of modern architecture in the world today as if it were free of neo-colonial entanglement. Even as the classical orders of architecture have decidedly been stripped of their claim to being the "universal style," modern architecture still continues to uncritically ply its wares worldwide as a universalist architectural idiom. The difference is — and it is this difference that constitutes the continuing circuit of neocolonialism in the world today — the postcolonies struggle with and are expected to "shake off" the neocolonial/modernist habit, while the metropo-les labor under no such expectation. The colonial/modernist habit is considered to be the legitimate and proper heritage of the metropoles, but not that of the post-colonies. Thus, if the neocolonial problem lies in its continued reproduction of the hierarchic opposition between the West and non-West, metropole and periphery, this problem cannot be solved by resorting to a universalist modernism.[3]

In this way, shaking off the neocolonialist habit requires not just a more equi-table political and economic reimagining of the contemporary world, but also a rigorous critique of the kinds of architectural agencies, particularly modernist, that quickly and easily claim to be standing outside its purview. By way of critique of such architectural agencies, I offer the following readings from my autobiography as an example in wayfinding, rather than a rigorous template for thinking.

I host a podcast called "ArchitectureTalk," in which I curate conversations with invited contemporary thinkers from diverse disciplines on how to "advance the frontier of architectural thinking." In a recent episode, my friend and collaborator Mark Jarzombek and I discussed the constraints of trying to "exit" the "modernist problem."[4] In that episode I argued for the necessity of working our way *through* the formidable, if fallible, contentions of modernism. Mark, on the other hand it seemed to me, advocated for the possibility, and even the necessity, of re-activating the non-modern and the pre-modern, as something like an alt-modernist/Western epistemology. Mark was deeply suspicious of modernism's collusion with the hegemonies of the nation-state and also with its doctrines of practiced violence against all of its Others, such as indigenous first-societies peoples. However, I insisted that even the critique of modernism's hegemonic practices was a critique framed by the modernist worldview, which made critique of the project as the work of somehow working through the contradictions of the modernist project, rather than one that could be originated outside of it.

Readers of this essay will have to decide for themselves if we settled on a middle ground by listening to the full podcast. One of our major takeaways from that conversation, however, was that in spite of our card-carrying commitment to the rigors of objectivity in critique, our respective biographies as postcolonial (mine) and post-Holocaustian (his) individuals were in fact constitutively inscribed into our arguments. How we saw the world, and the world we wished to see and critique was not isolated from, and indeed was entangled with, the world derived from our respective biographies. This should not have been a surprise, but it was. The lesson we learned was that since personal autobiography is ineluctably inscribed into historiography and critique, critical thinking must include — and perhaps begin with — accounting for personal inscription in a constructive manner.

The impetus for my articulation of the argument in that podcast discussion comes from my training in postcolonial theory during the 1980s and 1990s, with its roots in poststructuralism and Derridean critiques. My attraction to these theories in turn stemmed — in ways that are still not entirely clear to me — from my autobiography as one cultivated into the postcolonial condition via the accident of my birth in Nehruvian India, in Chandigarh. Educated entirely in English, with a deep investment in the forms and contentions of modern architecture as the expression of a benevolent semi-socialist nation-state, my autobiography could even be described as being straightforwardly neocolonial in the context of this essay. Postcolonial theory, even as it was evangelized in the high-culture institutions of the West where I went to graduate school in the 1980s, seemed to offer both a mirror of my own life experience and also a glimmer of a possible means (as yet unknown) to work my way into another way of being in the world freed from my past.

From amongst the poststructuralist and postcolonial registers, it was psychoanalytic theory — as conveyed in the writings of my professor Dominick LaCapra — that stayed with me the most.[5] Although conceived as an individualized clinical practice (and quite controversial in terms of its applicability today), psychoanalytic concepts, LaCapra argued, can usefully be applied to a wide register of disciplines — in particular the humanities — because of their engagement with the human psyche. What stayed with me in particular was the key distinction in psychoanalytic theory between "acting out" and "working through." The former, as I understood it, describes the tendency, even a compulsion, to repeat as an adult deep pathological patterns from one's childhood. The latter, as the "talking cure," requires a re-presentation of the past in a distancing and self-critical manner. Working through, in this sense, seemed to be the key self-critical practice that was necessary to work my way into another way of being in the world.

Importantly, I also learned that "working through" does not assume that there is a truly autonomous way of liberating oneself from the pathologies of one's past, as a modernist subject position might contend, nor does it promise a mythical return to one's prepathological past, that a postmodernist stance offered. Rather, "working through" requires persistent critique, a determined accounting of one's deep unconscious habits that requires breaking from the fallacy that one singularly speaks and acts from an autonomous Ego-reinforcing subjectivity. Psychoanalytic process hopes to work by activating one's unconscious and subconscious historically layered selves and bring them into constructive, contestatory and at times playful, dialogue with the Ego via processes such as free association, dreamwork, and carnivalization.

The task of psychotherapy in this sense is not to produce a "normal" subjection, but something like a self-reflective but not narcissistic subject who can function in an equally "disfunctioning" (though supposedly normalizing) world in an adequately self-empowered way. As Mark and I discovered in our podcast discussion, and as psychoanalytic thinking insists, working through cannot be done in the abstract; one cannot simply sit outside in the supposedly objective chair of the analyst/critic and critique the pathological neocolonial work. Rather, the work of critique has to be done as part of the process of working through one's own complex autobiography as entangled with the larger, already entangled processes of history.

Neocolonialism, I would argue, can be thought of as a psychoanalytic problem because of its deeply embedded entanglement with the desires and repression of our recent past and because of our continuing personal and political entanglement with its forcefields of desire and disdain. The colonialist relationship, with a dominating and caretaking metropolitan center with the colonies as its charge, was after all structured along a classic parent-child paradigm. Critique as working through, in this psychoanalytic recasting, can be described as the work of situating and activating the deeply internalized normatives of the colonial and bringing them into the contestatory dialogue with the supposedly transparent imperatives of the neocolonial and modernist present, with a view towards generating functioning critiques that are adequate to the present but by no means absolute or unimpeachable. These hopefully open up a path for the imagination that leads towards alternate, more diverse, as yet unknown, world-opening futures. The graphing of one's own biography must be a constitutive part of this process.

In more specific terms, working through the problematic of the neocolonialist present requires a rethinking of history, historiography, and the role of architectural history in professional practice. After a brief flirtation with post-modernist pedagogies, architectural history (save perhaps Modern architectural history) is being pushed off the table of architectural curricula,[6] discarded as obsolete knowledge — the continued legacy of the protracted conflict with the ideology of modernist presentism. Because of the dire imperatives of climate change and also because of the continuing investment in the putative universality of the modernist idiom, history is in danger of being remarginalized as peripheral to the core problems of architecture, or useful only to those with identitarian agendas as in the form of "heritage." We are in danger of returning to a technologically driven, neo-modernist architectural discourse whose only interest in history is as a reference for specialist practices such as historic preservation. Working through the neocolonial/modernist problem requires a globalist approach to history and historiography.

For the past few years, my colleague Mark Jarzombek and I have been part of a teaching collective dedicated to preparing materials that can enable faculty in schools of architecture and allied disciplines to teach globally. While there is significant thrust in ensuring that globally diverse teaching materials and syllabi are made readily available, the goals of the Global Architectural History Teaching Collaborative (GAHTC) are not just to diversify the teaching of architectural history, but to open up an epistemic space where the unexamined contentions of modernist and neo-modernist ways of architectural thinking can be brought into dialogue with other architectural epistemologies that may be radically different, and that, though in the margins, may contain kernels of innovative ideas that can help one reconsider our present and future in unexpected and potentially transformative ways.[7] It is our hope that bringing global historical architectural epistemologies into play within architectural studios and critiques, a future generation of architects and architectural thinkers will not only be better prepared for a diverse and globally inter-connected world, but will also continue along a path that could, perhaps even serendipitously, open up to post neocolonialist ways of doing and thinking architecture.

Our modus operandi is suggestion and annotation. Every time a faculty member searches for a term or concept that s/he is hoping to teach, such as say Petra, our search engine generates not only slides and lectures that speak to the sought material directly, but also all the other lectures and modules that discuss Petra incidentally or peripherally. The interface is designed to easily enable users to download individual lectures, or full lecture sets (or modules) and wrap them up into "bundles" of lecturing materials. When faculty open their "bundles" on their own desktops, we are hoping that in those they find not only materials that they can rapidly deploy in the classroom to make their presentation more diverse and globally inclusive, but will also find unexpected associated ideas and case studies that will lead them at least a little farther towards engaging concepts and knowledges that might otherwise have remained opaque and conveniently "othered." GAHTC membership, in early 2019, includes almost 600 registered contributors, users, and observers. We have 230 curated lectures available for free on our teacher-to-teacher web platform (as of January 2019), through which lectures have been downloaded over 1,000 times. This demonstrates both the vast interest in this organization's approach and the potential breadth of its impact. While there is much room to grow, and this remains very much an evolving work in progress, there is reason to appreciate and anticipate ongoing change.

GAHTC is focused on the development of teaching and lecture materials because within the frame of a lecture there is inherent flexibility. The lecture for-mat includes an openness to dialogue and the tentatively exploration of materials that would otherwise never even be considered for inclusion in published research, given the expectations and limitations of the peer-review process. We think of this as a world-opening way to learning, knowing, and teaching — a way that is not predicated on the assurance of mastery but on the vulnerabilities of venturing into the unknown and the underrepresented. If, on the one hand, new digital institu-tions such as Khan Academy offer easily digestible capsules of useful knowledge via YouTube, our hope is that digital searches on our platform will offer faculty the opportunity to not only quickly and easily familiarize themselves with the obvious, but also to be led astray by the unexpected, the uncertain, and the intriguing. This is what we mean by "world-opening," an analog to "working through," which is say to open an ear or a peripheral glance at other epistemologies of the world — synchronic, diachronic, disciplinary — not just with a view to including them pla-tonically in the global parliament of representation, but also with the desire to potentially fall in love with them and make them one's own.

I would like to conclude with a short exergue into "globalist" thinking.

In the 18th century, Qing China functioned as an efficient pre-modern Empire and quickly became the cynosure of European intellectuals. Colonial ships carried missionaries to China, who settled there and subsequently produced detailed accounts of life and order during the Qing dynasty. These illustrated accounts made their way to Europe where they were avidly read and citied by Enlightenment thinkers, particularly those who were keen to demonstrate non-Church based moral and political orders. In this way, European stroll gardens — such as Stourhead and Stowe in England — that were trying to establish the new human subject who was comfortable in nature rather than differentiated from it, can be seen as a reading of Chinese garden precedents [Figure 13.2]. Today they are all over the United States as well, in various parks of the Olmsteadian era and its descendants. Along the way, the Chinese garden as origin, with its own long and complex history, was forgotten in the rush to frame the picturesque garden as English and the Enlightenment as decidedly European.

The deconstruction of Eurocentrism, thus, is not about undoing Europe or the Enlightenment, and pretending that a self-interested and narrow world

Figure 13.2
The "English" stroll ga
(Stourhead, near Mere
England). Photograph
2013. Source: xlibber
[Wikimedia Commons]

view will *eo ipso* "solve the problem" and disrupt neocolonialist processes. The question of history's astonishing breadth and all its entanglements remains, no matter what. In the same way, the deconstruction of neocolonialism and modernism, as a future activity of architectural practice, is not so much about building more guaranteed representational politics into it, I would argue, as it is about opening it up to engaging with other-to-modernist architectural epistemologies of the world, like "speaking trees," "listening earths," and "multiple consciousnesses."

NOTES

1   On the British colonial bungalow in India, see Madhavi Desai, Miki Desai, and Jon Lang, *The Bungalow in Twentieth-Century India* (Burlington, VT: Ashgate, 2012); Anthony D. King, *The Bungalow: The Production of a Global Culture* (New York: Oxford University, 1995).

2   At a more haptic and emotional level, this neocolonial-postcolonial problem can also be parsed as that of clothing. Why is it that the peoples of the postcolonies happily and easily slip into western clothing conventions, at home and in the West, while for the peoples of the former metropoles all interest in non-Western clothing remains anthropological and/or cultural?

3   It should be clear here that nor can it be solved by resorting to an uncritical ideal of multiculturalism, as if all identities could a.) be uncritically constructed and represented and b.) able to be present in a global parliament in a non-hierarchical manner. The much sought-after release from the colonial vicious circle is thus also a global problem. The focus of my critique here is not on modernism's transparently neocolonialist ability to insinuate itself into the postcolonial theatres of the world, as for instance in the world stage of Beijing's Olympics, but in its continued uncritical proselytization in schools of architecture and in the practicing communities of the metropoles as the discourse of "just" architecture, rather than a neocolonialist and Eurocentric habit that is difficult to shake off for the same reasons as in the postcolonies. This also applies, I would argue, to post-universalist metropolitan quests, such as the post-modern and the post-structuralist.

4   Vikramāditya Prakāsh and Mark Jarzombek, "How to Think the Global with Mark Jarzombek" (Episode 35), *Architecture Talk*, January 16, 2019, https://www.architecturetalk.org/home/2019/1/22/35-how-to-think-the-global-with-mark-jarzombek.

5   The first text by LaCapra that I read, and that has stayed with me the longest is Dominick LaCapra, *Rethinking Intellectual History: Texts, Contexts, Language* (Ithaca, NY: Cornell University, 1983).

6   The Society of Architectural Historians (US) has recently undertaken a large study intended to determine precisely the extent and nature of this ongoing process of architectural history's marginalization.

7   The GAHTC began its work in 2013 and has received generous funding from the Andrew W. Mellon Foundation. See "GAHTC," Global Architectural History Teaching Collaborative, accessed January 30, 2019, http://gahtc.org.

Index

Page numbers in *italic* indicate illustrations.